A Guide to Sources of Educational Information

by MARDA WOODBURY

INFORMATION RESOURCES PRESS

WASHINGTON, D.C.   1976

Available from
Information Resources Press
2100 M Street, N.W.
Washington, D.C. 20037

Library of Congress Catalog Card Number 75-37116

ISBN 0-87815-015-3

"Knowledge is of two kinds: we know of a subject ourselves, or we know where we can find information about it."

—SAMUEL JOHNSON

Figures

Preface

Everyone is interested in education—teachers, parents, legislators, educational researchers, administrators, policymakers,
and, sometimes, even students. Approximately 51 million young
people between the ages of 5 and 17 are currently attending
elementary and secondary schools, supported by educators, administrators, legislators, school board members, teachers-in-
training, allied professionals, paraprofessionals, concerned parents, and taxpayers, who pay almost $100 billion a year for educa-
tion. Education, in fact, is the principal occupation of 30 percent
of the nation.

While young people are required legally to go to school, adults,
for the most part, go to school voluntarily, for self-development
or job training. According to a fairly recent study, by 1976, 149
million adults will be enrolled in some type of educational
program—67 million within and 82 million outside the traditional
school system.[1]

As education expands upward in the age scale, it is simultaneously reaching down beyond three-year-olds to infants. With
mothers of 8.6 million preprimary children working outside the
home, increasing numbers of young children and babies are being
placed in formative institutions: educational institutions, in es-
sence, which often fail to acknowledge or fulfill their educational
functions.

With all of our education, education policymaking, and educational research, there is surprisingly little printed guidance available to assist individuals involved in education to locate materials

[1] Educational Policy Research Center. *The Learning Force.* Syracuse, N.Y., 1970.

relevant to education. This is partially due to the nature of the subject: education is a topic both vast and nebulous, intimately involved with such disparate fields as child psychology, methods of teaching, research methods, statistical methods, tests and measurements, the legislative process, finance, architecture, administration, organization theory, values, goals, and ethics.

Education is a vast topic in another sense: just as almost everyone can be taught or is involved in education, almost anything can be taught—from agriculture to transcendental meditation. Name a topic and you have an area of education. All academic, practical, and vocational areas also are teaching areas, with their own controversies and their own experts.

The library—that objective, eclectic, and selective institution which traditionally organizes information and transmits resources—has not produced the broad but brief guides that are needed in education. In Great Britain—a smaller, more homogeneous country—education librarians, who constitute a recognized specialty, have provided satisfactory guides and guidance. Here, however, education libraries are scattered among public libraries, special libraries, the academic world, and various levels of school systems (where they are almost invariably severely underfinanced). They owe their primary allegiance to fragmented institutions and serve only portions of the education public, for whom they have provided some limited guides.

While much federal and foundation funding has been appropriated for setting up systems intended to bring educational research information into practice, very little of these funds have been apportioned to the library profession or to education libraries, which are the principal resources of teachers who need information. None has been channeled to the creation of widely distributed, comprehensive guides to existing tools and sources.

There is, however, a tremendous need for a current, comprehensive, yet selective, guide. While I do not hope to meet the needs of every individual seeking educational information, I hope this book—a guide to sources and a directory of directories—may prove helpful to those many individuals researching the problems of the schools, preparing for careers within the schools, setting policy for the schools, and facing the day-to-day problems within the schools.

My coverage is largely current and almost exclusively American, although I have included a few tools that lead to past or foreign sources.

This book deals with only four of all potential sources of information. First, the majority, are printed (occasionally non-printed) materials which consolidate information, keep information current, or lead to further sources of information; second are the education libraries or quasi-libraries (information centers), especially those having unique collections of materials or those offering useful or unheralded services; third are the organizations and government agencies, active or knowledgeable in education-related fields, which can provide answers to specific queries in their fields of interest; and fourth are the special search or bibliographic services (mostly commercial) which provide efficient access to some types of education-related information.

I have selected the tools that I felt were most useful, although I frequently checked my judgment with other education librarians, education researchers, and teachers. Since this guide is brief, I have omitted some of the more widely known tools that can be found in most public libraries and some that are popular with educational researchers, and have substituted other, perhaps lesser known, ones.

In my descriptive annotations, I have tried to convey the scopes, uses, strengths, and weaknesses of these selections for educators, policy-setters, parents, researchers, and librarians.

I have probably omitted some education information sources which should have been included. Many of those included, however, have not been listed previously and do provide worthwhile services.

While every effort has been made to ensure that the sources cited in this book are up-to-date, a significant number will undoubtedly be obsolete by the time of publication. For this, I can only apologize.

For much practical assistance in the preparation of this guide, I would like to thank my many colleagues among the Bay Area Education Librarians, especially Lois Heller of ACCESS Information System, Dulcie Blume of the Alameda County Curriculum Library, Louise Harsch of San Francisco State University, Julie Rousseau of *Learning Magazine*, Anne Protopoppoff of the California Teachers Association Library, and Roberta Steiner of American Institutes for Research.

Thanks, also, to Wayne Rosenoff of the Far West Laboratory of Educational Research and Development for encouraging me to write a previous guide; to Margaret Kendrick, my former assistant at the Far West Library, whose exertions always went beyond the call of duty; and to Sharon Entwistle, Kathy Devaney, and others of Far West for their moral support when it was needed.

Acknowledgements

ACKNOWLEDGEMENTS

Figures 2 and 3 are from the *Thesaurus of Psychological Index Terms,* copyright 1974 by the American Psychological Association; reprinted by permission. Figure 7 is from Williams, F. E., *Classroom Ideas for Encouraging Thinking and Feeling,* and is reprinted by kind permission of the publishers, D. O. K. Publishers, Inc., Buffalo, N.Y. 14214. Figure 8 is from *Appraisal,* 8(5):39, and is reprinted by kind permission of the publisher. Figure 9 is reprinted by kind permission of the Day Care and Child Development Council of America. Figure 16 is reprinted by kind permission of the Center for the Study of Evaluation. Figure 17 is from *EPIEgram,* 4(3):3, November 1, 1975, and is reprinted by kind permission of The Educational Products Information Exchange Institute. Figure 18 is a reprint of a DIALOG search in *Psychological Abstracts,* copyright 1973 by the American Psychological Association, reprinted by permission; and by kind permission of Lockheed Information Systems. Figure 20 is reprinted by kind permission of Wisconsin Information Retrieval for Education of the Wisconsin Department of Public Instruction.

Acronyms and Abbreviations

The acronyms and abbreviations listed below occasionally may be used in this book without nearby references. Other acronyms and abbreviations, when used, will be preceded by the original terms.

AFT	American Federation of Teachers
AIM/ARM	*Abstracts of Instructional and Research Materials in Vocational and Technical Education*
ASCA	Automatic Subject Citation Alert
ASCD	Association for Supervision and Curriculum Development
CIJE	*Current Index to Journals in Education*
ECRC	Early Childhood Resource Center
EDNET	Educational Network
EFLA	Educational Film Library Association
EIN	Educational Information Network
ERIC	Educational Resources Information Center
ERIE	Eastern Regional Institute for Education
ESEA	Elementary and Secondary Education Amendments
(D)HEW	U.S. Department of Health, Education, and Welfare
NDEA	National Defense Education Act
NEA	National Education Association
NERAC	New England Research Applications Center
NIE	National Institute of Education
OE	U.S. Office of Education
PADAT	Psychological Abstracts Direct Access Terminal
P.A.I.S.	Public Affairs Information Service
PASAR	Psychological Abstracts Search and Retrieval Service
PATELL	Psychological Abstracts Tape Edition Lease or Licensing

PPBS	Program, Planning, and Budgeting Systems
PROBE	A batch search method for searching ERIC, developed by Indiana University
QUERY	A batch search method for searching ERIC, developed by Computer Resources Corporation
R&D	Research and Development
RCU	Research Coordinating Units
RIC	Resource Information Center, University of North Dakota
RIE	*Resources in Education* (formerly *Research in Education*)
SDI	Selective Dissemination of Information

PART I
Effective Research

1 | *The Research Process*

Effective research, in education and elsewhere, can be divided into three parts: defining the question, locating materials, and (sometimes) preparing a report. This chapter deals largely with the first two aspects.

While this book essentially is an introduction to some major features and sources of educational information, this chapter suggests approaches to using the materials listed and annotated throughout the book. Two approaches are included. The first, THE RESEARCH PROCESS, presents an outline for using the sources discussed; the second, the CHECKLIST FOR RESEARCH QUESTIONS, is intended to help clarify questions in a manner that will lead to effective research.

Chapters 2 to 7 discuss categories of reference books (directories, bibliographies, etc.)—arranged in a research order; that is, the order in which one would most likely consult materials for research projects.

Ideally, the research process starts with these compilations and reference books, which sometimes successfully organize large quantities of information for easy consultation and often lead to other sources of information as well. Reference books are especially important in education, since information in this field tends to be partial, scattered, and difficult to find. Some of the more useful information sources are categorized briefly below. In all cases, there is a constant interaction between the sources of information and the printed products.

3

FOR	INFORMATION SOURCES
Vocabulary and Concepts, Single Subjects, and Summaries	**Dictionaries, Encyclopedias, Thesauri** (Chapter 2): Provide information in context and relate it to other fields or areas that might furnish additional information. While expensive encyclopedias and dictionaries are produced by large institutions, others are produced by individuals who compiled information they could not locate elsewhere. Some are designed as operating tools for working groups that need common vocabularies.
People and Institutions (Who, What, Where)	**Directories** (Chapter 3): These are sometimes compiled by professional directory makers; also by groups or individuals who need to locate and contact specific types of individuals or institutions (such as libraries, state officials, music teachers, research centers, and administration specialists). As information sources, these directories tend to compile information on other information sources.

Directory and Institutional Information Sources (Chapter 14): These agencies, as well as the associations and individuals listed in directories, can provide information on individuals or institutions working in their areas of interest. |
Special Subjects and Summaries	**Monographs** (short, one-subject booklets or bulletins) (Chapter 4): An increasingly important source of information in education, emerging from a need for timely information; usually produced or commissioned by institutions or individuals who are information sources in their own right. Books, libraries, associations, periodical articles, and some information sources are additional sources for information on specific subjects.
Yearly Summaries	**Yearbooks** (Chapter 4): Although declining as a source of educational information (the need may be for more current, but more brief, fill-ins), yearbooks provide continuity and serve as an updating mechanism; possibly better at recording slow progress than a series of crises. More yearbooks have been produced by organizations than by commercial firms.
Hot News	**Newsletters** (Chapter 4): Like monographs, newsletters are a by-product of the need for timely information. They are created and distributed by organizations who have something to tell. Commercially, they provide an information interface between a need for information and a bureaucracy that fails to provide it in usable form.

FOR   INFORMATION SOURCES

Books, Articles, and
Printed Materials

Bibliographies and Review Sources (Chapter 5): While general lists are usually compiled by large bibliographic agencies, special-subject lists, like directories, are often compiled by institutions or individuals who gather information to perform ongoing tasks. Annotated or subject-arranged bibliographies, published at intervals, are extremely useful for keeping current with significant works.

Library Card Catalog: Provides subject, author, and title access to published materials.

Statistics (How many,
What is, What was,
Trends, Projections)

Statistical Sources (Chapter 6): Statistics and statistical compilations often are collected by organizations as part of a bureaucratic responsibility, in which case they may not be disseminated quickly (or at all), even though they are available at some headquarters office and can be obtained through a determined effort. Statistics gathered or located by interest groups are apt to be printed much sooner.

Periodicals and Periodi-
cal Articles

Abstracting, Indexing, and Current Awareness Services: Indexing and abstracting services are discussed in Chapter 7. *Education Index* is the best single index for most purposes.

Periodicals (Chapter 4): Often produced by institutions, associations, and interest groups. A good way to keep current with information in limited areas of education is to select one or two good publications and read them faithfully. The periodical directories and guides listed in this chapter can be helpful in making these selections.

Government Documents

Abstracting, Indexing, and Current Awareness Services (Chapter 7): Some good choices are:

> *Resources in Education (RIE)* for documents filtered through or produced by ERIC Clearinghouses.
> *Monthly Catalog of United States Government Publications, P.A.I.S.* (Public Affairs Information Service) *Bulletin,* and *Education Index* for materials produced and distributed by the U.S. Government Printing Office.
> *P.A.I.S. Bulletin, Education Index*, and *State Education Journal Index* for local documents.
> *Weekly Government Abstracts* for materials available from the National Technical Information Service.

Educational Dissertations

Abstracting, Indexing, and Current Awareness Services (Chapter 7): Some of the best are: *Disserta-*

tion Abstracts International, American Doctoral Dissertations, Psychological Abstracts, P.A.I.S. Bulletin, Research Relating to Children, and DATRIX (Direct Access to Reference Information; a Xerox Service)—see Chapter 7 and P2.

Educational Finance and Government

Printed Sources on Funding, Legislation, and Foundations (Chapter 8): Includes some special directories, compilations, and current awareness sources for law legislation, funds, foundations, and educational financing. Information sources in these fields are covered in Chapter 15.

Educational Curricular Materials

Educational Products and Curricular Resources (Chapters 9 to 13): Specially published bibliographies, directories, and selection tools are included in separate sections of this book: Selecting Instructional Materials (Chapter 9), Curriculum Materials and Activities (Chapter 10), Guides to Nonprint Instructional Materials (Chapter 11), Children's Books (Chapter 12), and Tests and Assessment Instruments (Chapter 13). Some associations and information sources in this field are listed in Chapter 16.

Compact Storage of Ephemeral or Permanent Materials

Microfiche Collections: This format (of increasing importance in the field of education) provides a space-saving means of publication and storage; if supported by an abstract journal or an indexing medium, it provides a built-in means of dissemination and access. This is the method that ERIC (M12) wisely chose to produce materials. Other significant microfiche collections in education are (or were) available from I/D/E/A Publications (C8); New York State Department of Education (Chapter 19); Association for Supervision and Curriculum Development (C2); U.S. Government Printing Office; U.S. Department of Commerce, Bureau of the Census (E3); National Technical Information Service; Human Relations Area Files (M24); Committee on Scientific and Technical Information (COSATI); American College Public Relations Association (M1); Entelek CAI/CMI Information Exchange (M11); Clearinghouse for Sociological Literature (M6); Curriculum Materials Clearinghouse (O10); and the College of Health, Physical Education, and Recreation at the University of Oregon, Eugene. According to *Microform Market Place,*[1] there were 375 micro-

---

[1] Veaner, Allen B. *Microform Market Place.* Weston, Conn., Microform Review, 1974.

publishers in 1974. This means of producing and distributing materials requires rigorous selection and a good index.

Microfilm Collections: The best-known source of microfilm collections is University Microfilms (Q2), which has films of both periodicals and dissertations. The New York Times is also an important source. Both are supported by competent indexing systems.

Unpublished Information

ERIC and Some Special Libraries and Information Centers (Chapters 14, 15, and 16): The primary medium of unpublished information in education is the so-called unpublished research report. The primary sources of unpublished research reports are ERIC and the National Technical Information Service (NTIS), although special libraries and information centers frequently collect and disseminate such reports, particularly those emanating from their parent organizations.

Ongoing Research

ERIC and Other Research Analysis and Coordinating Organizations: *Library and Information Services Today* (*LIST*) (D20), Smithsonian Science Information Exchange (P16), *Research Relating to Children* (F18), *CEDaR Catalog of Selected Educational Research and Development Programs and Products* (H4), *Research Annual on Intergroup Relations* (D24), and *Inventory of Current Research on Post-Secondary Education* (D42).

Computer Research

Computerized Retrieval Services (Chapter 17): Included are a group of service agencies, most of which process ERIC tapes. Check also State Library Services to Educators (Chapter 19) to see if your state provides such services.

Other computer data banks are available at education libraries and information centers, The Foundation Center (N10), Funding Sources Clearinghouse (N11), National Institute of Mental Health (M30), National Institute for Drug Abuse Information, and some ERIC clearinghouses (Chapters 14 and 16).

Education Libraries

State Library Services to Educators (Chapter 19), Gaining Access to Educational Information and Materials (Chapter 18), Directory and Institutional Information Sources (Chapter 14), Nonprint Sources of Government and Financial Information (Chapter 15), Institutional Sources of Product and Curricular Information (Chapter 16), and Directories (Chapter 3) all list some education libraries.

THE RESEARCH PROCESS (a composite outline of which follows) is a suggested format and outline of a step-by-step process for using the information sources discussed here. Depending upon knowledge, time, and availability, steps could be skipped or transposed.

The individual works listed are representative or significant reference works (plus some good substitutes from public libraries) which are frequently used in educational research. In any particular search, other or additional works might be more appropriate. The search order given is convenient for most extended research projects.

A shorter search form, which would be appropriate and simple for many brief searches, is:

> Encyclopedias, Yearbooks, Reference→Card Catalog→ Periodical Indexes→*Resources in Education.*

In other cases, an encyclopedia article (since educational encyclopedias are, fortunately, quite current), plus one or two periodical articles, would be adequate; or one step may be all that is needed.

THE RESEARCH PROCESS
COMPOSITE OUTLINE

  I. Define the question.
 II. Locate appropriate education library or other sources.

Search Background Information and Refine Question Through Reference Books.

A. General background and vocabulary.

DICTIONARIES, ENCYCLOPEDIAS, AND THESAURI

Acronyms in Education and the Behavioral Sciences
Dictionary of Education
†*Webster's Unabridged Dictionary*
Encyclopedia of Education
Encyclopedia of Educational Research
†*International Encyclopedia of the Social Sciences*
Thesaurus of ERIC Descriptors
†*Roget's Thesaurus*

(Do Not Skip Step A Unless You Can Write the Encyclopedia Article!)

B. If information on people or institutions is needed.

DIRECTORIES

Educator's World
Education Directory
†*Patterson's American Education*
†*Foundation Directory*
Annual Register of Grant Support
Special and Local Directories

REFERRAL AGENCIES

*National Referral Center
Library of Congress
Smithsonian Science Information
Exchange

C. If updating or statistical information is needed.

ALMANACS OR YEARBOOKS, MONOGRAPH SERIES

†*World Almanac*
†*Statistical Abstract of the United States*
*Macmillan's *Education Yearbook*

Use Information From Steps A and B for Relevant Names and Subject Search Terms to Locate Materials.

D. For obtaining books.

LIBRARY CARD CATALOG

Author-Title Catalog
Subject Catalog
Dictionary Catalog
Classed Catalog (shelf-list)

BIBLIOGRAPHIES

†*American Reference Books Annual*
Review of Educational Research

E. For periodicals and current documents.

PERIODICAL INDEXES

Education Index
*Current Index to Journals in
    Education*
†*Readers' Guide to Periodical
    Literature*

DOCUMENT INDEXES

Resources in Education
†*Monthly Catalog of United States Government
    Publications*
†*P.A.I.S.* (Public Affairs Information
    Service) *Bulletin*

F. For really current information.

Personal contacts
*Newsletters
†*CQ Weekly Report*

G. For unpublished data.

People and institutions located through the same process as "F" above.

*Vital working tools in education.
†Widely available in public libraries.

The information sources in this book and the outline of THE RESEARCH PROCESS provide the tools and approaches for locating information in education. The CHECKLIST FOR RESEARCH QUESTIONS which follows is included to help clarify any existing questions before beginning a search.

CHECKLIST FOR RESEARCH QUESTIONS
DEFINING THE QUESTION

I. BASIC QUESTIONS

  A. *What do I want to know; for what purpose?*
     Subjects; Synonyms; Related Concepts; Approaches

  B. *What do I know already?*

  C. *Who else might have performed similar research, and why?*
     Where is it apt to be?
     Individuals; Groups or Organizations; Structures; Hearings; Records;
     Other

  D. *What summarizing or descriptive literature is available?*
     Statistics; Directories; Reviews or Monographs; Encyclopedias; Other

II. TIME QUESTIONS

  A. *For which time spans do I need information? What kinds of information for*
     each?
     What is?   What was?   What will be?   What can be?

  B. *Would my collection of information be affected by recurrent or other temporal*
     events in education?
     School Terms; Budget Hearings or Recommendations; Conventions or
     Conferences; Training Programs; Legislative Sessions; Paperwork
     Deadlines; Policy Decisions; Administrative Changes or Procedures

III. LIMITATION AND RESTRICTION QUESTIONS

  A. *Do I have other restrictions or limitations?*
     Language; Age Group; Grade Level; Type of Student; Type of School;
     Type of District; Geographic; Curricular Area; Style of Teaching; Other

IV. ASPECT QUESTIONS

  A. *What aspects am I interested in?*
     Financial; Administrative; Teaching; Legislative; Theoretical; Research;
     Parental; Developmental; Practical; Overview; Other

V. SUBJECTIVE ASPECT QUESTIONS

   A. *What are my values, prejudices, biases, and areas of ignorance in these areas?*

   B. *Will I let these prejudice or limit my research in any manner?*

      Choice of Vocabulary and Indexing Terms; Choice of Research Tools; Selection of Data; Evaluation of Work of Individuals; Inclusion of Conflicting Theories; Note Taking; Reporting or Annotating Data; Arrangement of Data; Conclusions

Although logically the clarification process comes before the research process, it is included here after the discussion of information sources and approaches, because even a slight knowledge of research tools and resources can be helpful in framing answerable questions.

Since most questions will be different, this should be considered a flexible framework for analysis of questions, both before and during the research process, as the materials discovered along the way may alter the course of research.

The Research Information Request form used by the special library of the Far West Laboratory (Figure 1) demonstrates how the tools and the research process interrelate in practice.

A basic and final part of the research process involves the effective handling and organizing of relevant information discovered during the search. Some of the guides to reference books and research tools included in Chapter 3 can provide a great deal of assistance in this area, particularly: Hillway's *Handbook of Educational Research* (D5) and *Who-What-Where-When-How-Why Made Easy* by Mona McCormick (D13). Cheney's *Fundamental Reference Sources* (D2) and Burke's *Documentation in Education* (D1) also are helpful. Robert Collison's *30,000 Libraries: A Practical Guide* (Encino, Calif., Dickenson Publishing, 1973) provides clear and understandable guidance to note taking, research methods, and preparation of bibliographies. Other "classics" also are available in this area, notably, Kate Turabian's *Manual for Writers of Term Papers* (frequently revised by the University of Chicago Press).

The following comments are intended as tips for the sophisticated or relatively experienced researcher.

1. If you are planning to prepare *any* kind of report or

RESEARCH INFORMATION REQUEST   *Library, Far West Laboratory*

FOR REQUESTOR   **FOR LIBRARY STAFF**

Name: *Subject classification:*
Position: *Received by:* ( ) *Written*
Mail stop: *Phone ext.:*   ( ) *Phone*
Date requested: *Date needed:*   ( ) *In person*
Code: *Searched by:*
Maximum hours (your estimate):   *Date completed:*
    (Less than 30 minutes, free)   *Time:* ( ) *Librarian* ( ) *Clerical*

SEARCH REQUEST

Topic (Please be specific):

Type of search: ( ) *In-depth*   ( ) *Research oriented*   ( ) *Evaluations only*
                 ( ) *Overview*   ( ) *Program oriented*   ( ) _____
Particular aspects:

Omit any aspects?

Purpose of search:

Grade level:
Time span (How far back?):
Geographic restrictions:

SOURCES *(List or summarize those used so far.)*

Books:
Abstracts & indexes (Include issues & index terms):

Newsletters & periodicals (Include dates & headings searched):

Private files:
Human resources:
Other libraries (Include headings searched):
Other:

ACTION DESIRED *(Note: photocopies take time & money)* **ACTION TAKEN** *(For Library staff)*

ERIC search: ( ) *List of references* ( ) *Microfiche*
             ( ) *Resumes*   ( ) *Photocopies*
Library collection: ( ) *List of materials*
             ( ) *Selected materials*
Bibliography: ( ) *Existing bibliographies*
          ( ) *Compile bibliographies*
Encyclopedia: ( ) *Reference citations*
          ( ) *Photocopies*
Periodical articles: ( ) *Reference citations*
            ( ) *Photocopies*

Additional notes or instructions: *Comments:*

FIGURE 1   Sample of Research Information Request form used by Far West Laboratory.

evaluation from your research—even an oral report or a summary for your own use—it is almost essential, during the course of your research, to prepare citations of items you intend to use or that you think are interesting enough to look at later.

2. These citations should be in a standard bibliographic format. Two good, all-purpose formats are those illustrated in the University of Chicago's *Manual of Style* (Chicago, University of Chicago Press, 1969) and those used by the American Library Association for preparing library catalog cards. One simple form which can be adapted to other bibliographic formats is:

> **For Books:** Author (last name, first name or initials). *Title of Book*. Place of publication, publisher, date. Number of pages. Price. (From: [if obscure])
>
> **For Journal Articles:** Author (last name, first name or initials). "Title of Article," *Periodical Title, Volume Number* (Issue Number): Page Numbers, Date (Month, Day, and Year).

If you wish to adapt this form to other materials, be sure to include all additional information (for example, ERIC ED numbers) *after* the major information shown above.

3. With broad or multifaceted research topics, notes should be arranged in some flexible format: marginal punched cards or the newer, magnetic (Herax) punched cards, usually available at university book stores and stationery stores, are convenient for extended bibliographies or research projects. Half sheets of standard-size paper are cheaper and also convenient. These can be color-coded easily (for instance, blue for bibliographic entries, yellow for administration, green for teaching methods, etc.). Notebooks can be quite satisfactory for single-subject research.

4. Sort your notes as you go along and keep them in some kind of order, preferably a combination of subject and author; but author, subject, time, or relative importance all have their values.

5. To reduce research clutter to a minimum, do *not* keep original documents (books, articles, research reports). Prepare notes for those parts of the documents that are interesting to you or relevant to your purposes. These notes should include correctly styled citations, plus any comments you find meaningful or appropriate: direct quotations (cite the page), paraphrases, anno-

tations, outlines, commentaries, and cryptic or shorthand notes are satisfactory for various purposes.

6. For the sake of objectivity, separate your paraphrase or analysis of a work from your interpretation of it. See the work in context before committing your personal reactions to paper.

These procedures should help you to organize your research for use as you proceed and enable you to report and use the results of your research.

PART II

Printed Research Tools

Dictionaries, Encyclopedias, Thesauri
Directories
Yearbooks, Monograph Series, Periodicals, Newsletters
Bibliographies and Review Sources
Statistical Sources
Abstracting, Indexing, and Current Awareness Services

2 | Dictionaries, Encyclopedias, Thesauri

The standard basic reference tools listed in this chapter, selected on the basis of value and availability, are the first tools to consult in most extended research assignments. While their main functions are to provide definitions, background information, and supplementary vocabulary, and to place research searches in a larger educational context, some of these tools also provide directory information, bibliographic access, and means of organizing education materials. General unabridged dictionaries and standard thesauri also can be quite helpful in education.

DICTIONARIES

A1   **ACRONYMS IN EDUCATION AND THE BEHAVIORAL SCIENCES**   By Toyo S. Kawakami and Lois J. Inskeep. Chicago, American Library Assn., 1971. $5.75.
An invaluable dictionary and directory of nearly 3,000 acronyms (words formed from initial letters of major parts of compound terms), arranged in strict alphabetical order, including names and, usually, addresses and zip codes of the acronymal institutions. Also includes a reverse, full-name, alphabetical index of the institutions and a list of verification sources.

17

A2   **A CONSUMER'S GUIDE TO EDUCATIONAL INNOVA-**
      TIONS   By Mortimer Smith, Richard Peck, and George Weber.
      Washington, D.C., Council for Basic Education, 1972. $2.50.
This "guide through the thick underbrush of innovative proposals," like
other consumer guides, was intended to help educational consumers—
parents, teachers, school board members, and administrators—make
wise and rational choices. The readable, scholarly, and, sometimes,
opinionated definitions in this book are essentially miniature essays—
complete with well-chosen bibliographic references—on the educational
innovations of the 1960s and early 1970s. The publisher is a nonprofit
educational organization pledged to the encouragement of high
academic standards in American schools.

A3   **DICTIONARY OF EDUCATION**   Edited by Carter V. Good
      and Winifred R. Merkel. 3rd Edition. New York, McGraw-Hill
      Book Co., 1973. $17.50.
Financed by Phi Delta Kappa, this long-awaited third edition based its
vocabulary selection on a thorough word analysis of education indexes,
handbooks, thesauri, and subject literature. With the continuing expansion of educational terminology, this edition contains some 33,000
entries and cross-references, compared to 25,000 in 1959. Although an
unabridged dictionary is adequate for most social sciences, educational
usage is sometimes unique; the clear, precise definitions contained in the
Dictionary of Education are the product of the collaborative efforts of
a team of subject specialists and coordinators who incorporated relevant
terms from such allied fields as psychology, philosophy, sociology, and
statistics. Because of the increasing number of American terms, the old,
useful, separate section on foreign terminology is missing from this
edition. The foreign terms, fortunately, are covered in the *Encyclopedic
Dictionary and Directory of Education* (A5).

A4   **DICTIONARY OF TERMS AND CONCEPTS IN READING**
      By Delwyn G. Shubert. 2nd Edition. Springfield, Ill., Charles C.
      Thomas, 1969. $7.
This dictionary contains extended definitions of approximately 2,000
topics related to all aspects of reading: psychological and physiological,
as well as educational.

A5   **ENCYCLOPEDIC DICTIONARY AND DIRECTORY OF**
      EDUCATION   With special reference to India. By A. Biswas
      and J. C. Aggarwal. New Delhi, India, Academic Publishers, 1971.
      3 Parts. $10.

An unusual work by two Delhi educators, which combines the scope of an encyclopedia with the brevity and conciseness of a dictionary. It is a one-volume, three-part compendium of information slanted towards British, European, and Indian experience.

The first part is a well-researched dictionary containing thoughtful definitions, as well as a highly useful glossary of national terms (languages other than English) arranged by nations. The second part contains a comprehensive list of world educators and educational thinkers, from Abelard to Zwingly, including some of the great teachers of Ancient India, who are not apt to appear in standard biographical dictionaries or encyclopedias. This section is particularly good for Indian educators and European thinkers. The third part, "Educational Systems of the World," covers Afghanistan to Zambia, mostly with 1967 to 1969 statistics. For each country, it includes sections of the state constitutions relating to education, education's relationship to government, current educational levels, structures, and organizations—all briefly and readably covered.

A6   **GUIDE TO PEDAGUESE: A Handbook for Puzzled Parents** By James S. Le Sure. New York, Harper and Row, 1965. $3.95. (Out-of-Print)

A subjective effort by a school principal to overcome the linguistic barrier between teachers and parents by translating educational jargon into English. Contains clear, light, deft, humorous definitions of words and phrases, with good illustrations. Useful primarily for parents and noneducators involved in education.

A7   **STANDARD TERMINOLOGY FOR CURRICULUM AND INSTRUCTION IN LOCAL AND STATE SCHOOL SYSTEMS** Compiled and edited by John F. Putnam and W. Dale Chismore. State Educational Records and Report Series, Handbook VI. Washington, D.C., U.S. Government Printing Office, 1970. $3.

A classified guide to terms used in describing instructions and curricula in elementary, secondary, junior college, and adult education institutions in the United States, representing five years of collaboration with 70 national education organizations and the U.S. Office of Education. The classified section itself is an interesting example of a facet classification system for education which is adaptable to computer methods. Some terms are listed in a glossary; most are listed in the main section. All can be found through the index.

ENCYCLOPEDIAS

A8　**A CYCLOPEDIA OF EDUCATION**　Edited by Paul Monroe.
Detroit, Gale Research, 1968. 5 Vols. $165.
This is a reprint of a 1911 to 1913 encyclopedia, originally edited and
written by such men as John Dewey and Paul Monroe, who were part of
the intellectual ferment of their times. It is a scholarly, intelligent
encyclopedia whose equivalent is not likely to appear again. Many of the
articles are still valuable, especially those on the history and philosophy
of education. The prime value of others lies in their portrayal of their
times and the history of American education. It is interesting to see how
many current ideas on education are included in this 62-year-old work.
Alphabetically arranged, with long bibliographies and an analytic subject
index.

A9　**ENCYCLOPEDIA OF EDUCATION**　Edited by Edward
Blishen. New York, Philosophical Library, 1970. $20.
A one-volume encyclopedia with concise articles on a wide variety of
topics (including some biographical sketches), valuable mostly for its
articles on British terminology and British practices.

A10　**THE ENCYCLOPEDIA OF EDUCATION**　Edited by Lee C.
Deighton et al. New York, Macmillan and Free Press, 1971. 10
Vols. $199.
This recently published encyclopedia, edited by Lee Deighton with the
help of a 32-member advisory board, provides well-rounded, reasonably
well-balanced, competent articles on approximately 1,000 topics in
education, although they are not always located where one would expect
to look for them. The final index volume, however, is quite satisfactory.
By decision of the board, articles are primarily on educational topics—
very few are about individuals or institutions, since such information can
be found elsewhere. While it is a welcome and necessary addition to
education libraries, this encyclopedia, although generally well-balanced,
is sometimes spotty in coverage. It includes some excellent comprehensive articles and some that are simplistic. Seemingly accurate and
current, it is not sufficiently research-oriented to meet the needs of the
educational researcher nor sufficiently practical to provide more than
competent introductory articles for teachers and administrators. It is the
logical starting point for most searches, however, with bibliographies of
past research and a new *Education Yearbook* (C6) to keep it updated.

A11　**ENCYCLOPEDIA OF EDUCATIONAL RESEARCH**　Edited
by Robert L. Ebel. 4th Edition. New York, Macmillan, 1969.
$38.95.

A project of the American Educational Research Association, this encyclopedia does not cover individuals or institutions, but provides well-researched, commissioned articles on educational topics by subject specialists. Materials are sometimes hard to find, since the book is arranged by broad subject categories, and the subject index (on yellow stock in the middle of the book) uses broad concepts rather than specific subject terms. Bibliographies are long (generally current as of 1966 and 1967), but omit periodical months and other useful data. Since this work is almost completely rewritten every 10 years, older editions should be kept and consulted for educational research of their decades.

A12　**HUMAN BEHAVIOR: An Inventory of Scientific Findings**　By Bernard Berelson and Gary Steiner. New York, Harcourt, Brace, Jovanovich, 1964. $12.

Although this book is not current, it is a highly useful, simple, nontechnical, and well-organized inventory and summary of the state-of-knowledge of human behavior. It organizes research evidence from the fields of psychology, sociology, anthropology, and education into 1,045 numbered propositions (hypotheses or assertions) under such broad categories of behavior as development or learning and thinking. Although it does not include recent research, few of its propositions or hypotheses have been overturned. This is an easy starting place to review behavioral backgrounds. Complete with subject and bibliographic indexes.

Human Behavior Shorter Edition (a popular version) was issued by the same publisher in 1967. No new edition is planned at this time.

A13　**INTERNATIONAL ENCYCLOPEDIA OF THE SOCIAL SCI- ENCES**　Edited by David L. Sills. New York, Macmillan, 1968. 17 Vols. $495.

The encyclopedia of choice for recent authoritative articles in all social science fields; it can substitute for an education encyclopedia if no other is available. The index volume (number 17) is usually the place to locate most education articles, although the set itself begins with an article on academic freedom. Bibliographies are comprehensive and generally current as of 1967.

A14　**WORLD SURVEY OF EDUCATION Volume V: Educational Policy, Legislation and Administration**　Paris, UNESCO, 1971. $75. From: Unipub, P.O. Box 433, New York, N.Y. 10016.

This final volume of *World Survey of Education* provides statistical and descriptive data on the organization and administration of education in countries throughout the world. Covers aims and policies, legal bases, educational administration, and other considerations. The first four volumes of this set, dealing with school systems and levels (out-of-print in English editions), are available at most large education libraries.

THESAURI

A15 **INFORMATION RETRIEVAL THESAURUS OF EDUCA-TION TERMS** By Gordon C. Barhydt and Charles T. Schmidt. Cleveland, Case Western Reserve University Press, 1969. $5.50.

A logical thesaurus of education terms based on the facet system. Very suggestive for leading to further terms or other facets of a subject, as well as for designing a list of terms or an index. It could be used, in itself, as a basis for organizing some education collections. This thesaurus is consistent with both library practices and computer retrieval methods.

A16 **THESAURUS OF ERIC DESCRIPTORS** With a special chapter on the Role and Function of the Thesaurus in Education by Dr. Frederick Goodman. 6th Edition. New York, Macmillan Information, 1975. $7.95 (paperback).

A necessary tool when conducting a subject search using either *Resources in Education* (*RIE*) or *Current Index to Journals in Education* (*CIJE*). It provides a logical framework for organizing and locating approximately 7,000 index terms (descriptors) used in the ERIC system up to January 1974. The introductory chapter by Dr. Goodman examines the logic and the possibilities of the ERIC system.

A17 **THESAURUS OF PSYCHOLOGICAL INDEX TERMS** Edited by Robert G. Kinkade. Washington, D.C., American Psychological Assn., 1974. $12.

This thesaurus is a well-designed, 4,000-word vocabulary derived from the 800 indexing terms in *Psychological Abstracts* and a computer-produced inverted dictionary whose most frequently used terms were reviewed by editors and information specialists. It is a highly useful tool for those whose research is oriented towards the psychological aspects of education and learning theory. Relevant sections include Psychometrics and Statistics, Cognitive Processes and Motivation, and Educational Psychology. The classifications in its Hierarchical Section (see Figure 2) are quite productive in suggesting relationships between educational topics. Also includes an alphabetical list of terms and a Relationship Section (see Figure 3) to aid in choosing terms.

EDUCATIONAL PSYCHOLOGY

Initial Teaching Alphabet
Letters (Alphabet)
Antonyms
Ethnolinguistics
Etymology
Grammar
   Form Classes (Language)
      Adjectives
      Adverbs
      Nouns
      Pronouns
      Verbs
   Inflection
   Morphology (Language)
   Orthography
   Phonology
   Syntax
      Sentence Structure
   Transformational Generative Grammar
Homographs
Paragraphs
Phonetics
   Morphemes
   Phonemes
      Consonants
      Vowels
   Syllables
   Words (Phonetic Units)
Phrases
Psycholinguistics
Semantics
Sentences
Monolingualism
Multilingualism
   Bilingualism
Public Speaking
Sign Language
Vocabulary
   Anagrams
   Antonyms
   Homographs
   Homonyms
   Neologisms
   Sight Vocabulary
   Slang
   Synonyms
Written Language
   Alphabets
      Initial Teaching Alphabet
      Letters (Alphabet)
   Handwriting
      Cursive Writing
      Handwriting Legibility
      Printing (Handwriting)
   Literacy
   Numbers (Numerals)
   Paragraphs
Speech Characteristics
   Articulation (Speech)
   Pronunciation
   Speech Pauses
   Speech Pitch
   Speech Rate
   Speech Rhythm
Speech Processing (Mechanical)

   Clipped Speech (Mechanical)
   Compressed Speech
   Filtered Speech
   Synthetic Speech
   Verbal Fluency

School Administration And Educational Processes
Community Facilities
   Community Mental Health Centers
Educational Personnel
   School Administrators
      School Principals
      School Superintendents
   School Counselors
   School Nurses
   School Psychologists
   Teacher Aides
   Teachers
      College Teachers
      Elementary School Teachers
      High School Teachers
      Junior High School Teachers
      Resource Teachers
      Special Education Teachers
      Student Teachers
Paraprofessional Personnel
   Paramedical Personnel
      Attendants (Institutions)
      Medics
      Physical Therapists
      Psychiatric Aides
   Teacher Aides
Personnel Training
   Apprenticeship
   Inservice Teacher Education
   On The Job Training
Professional Consultation
   Mental Health Consultation
Teacher Education
   Inservice Teacher Education
   Student Teaching
Volunteer Personnel
   Volunteer Civilian Personnel

Curriculum Development And Teaching Methods
Behavior Modification
   Classroom Behavior Modification
   Contingency Management
      Token Economy Programs
Classical Conditioning
   Conditioned Responses
      Conditioned Emotional Responses
      Conditioned Suppression
   Conditioned Stimulus
   Unconditioned Responses
   Unconditioned Stimulus
Computer Applications
   Computer Assisted Diagnosis
   Computer Assisted Instruction
   Computer Simulation
Curriculum

FIGURE 2   The Hierarchical Section of the *Thesaurus of Psychological Index Terms* is arranged by concepts which are listed in descending order of broadness.

Education/ RELATIONSHIP SECTION Educational

Education/ — (Continued)
Related
    Religious Education
    School Adjustment
    School Enrollment
    School Facilities
    School Integration (Racial)
    School Learning
    School Readiness
    Schools
    Secondary Education
    Social Work Education
    Special Education
    Student Admission Criteria
    Student Attitudes
    Students
    Study Habits
    Teacher Attitudes
    Teacher Education
    Teacher Personality
    Teacher Student Interaction
    Teacher Tenure
    Teaching
    Theories of Education
    Vocational Education

Educational Administration
Used For School Administration
    School Organization
Related Education/

Educational Aspirations
Broader Aspirations
Related Education/

Educational Audiovisual Aids
Used For Audiovisual Aids (Educational)
Broader Audiovisual Communications
    Media
    Communications Media
    Instructional Media
    Teaching
Narrower Motion Pictures (Educational)
Related Audiovisual Instruction
    Educational Television
    Film Strips
    Televised Instruction
    Videotape Instruction

Educational Background
Narrower Parent Educational Background
Related Education/

Educational Background (Parents)
Use Parent Educational Background

Educational Counseling
Used For Educational Guidance
    Guidance (Educational)
Related Counseling/
    Education/
    Occupational Guidance

Educational Degrees
Used For College Degrees
    Degrees (Educational)
    Graduate Degrees
    High School Diplomas
    Undergraduate Degrees
Related Education/
    Higher Education

Educational Field Trips
Used For Field Trips (Educational)
Broader Teaching
    Teaching Methods

Educational Financial Assistance
Used For Educational Financial Need
    Financial Assistance (Education-
    al)
    Scholarships
    School Federal Aid
    School Financial Assistance
    Stipends
Related Education/

Educational Financial Need
Use Educational Financial Assistance

Educational Guidance
Use Educational Counseling

Educational Incentives
Broader Incentives
    Motivation
Related Education/

Educational Laboratories
Used For Laboratories (Educational)
Broader School Facilities
Narrower Language Laboratories

Educational Measurement
Narrower Entrance Examinations
    Grading (Educational)
Related Education/
    Measurement/

Educational Personnel
Used For Faculty
Narrower College Teachers
    Elementary School Teachers
    High School Teachers
    Junior High School Teachers
    Resource Teachers
    School Administrators
    School Counselors
    School Nurses
    School Principals
    School Psychologists
    School Superintendents
    Special Education Teachers
    Student Teachers
    Teacher Aides
    Teachers

FIGURE 3 The Relationship Section of the *Thesaurus of Psychological Index Terms* indicates alternate and related terms.

3 | *Directories*

This chapter lists educational directories that are relevant and basic to the needs of educators, administrators, and researchers: directories of people, directories of schools and educational facilities, and directories of resources. Many widely used directories have been omitted—especially directories of colleges and universities which are well-known, widely dispersed, and frequently listed—while some less-known tools which could be more widely used have been included. The useful directories which have been excluded, however, can be located through sources discussed elsewhere in this book. Klein's *Guide to American Educational Directories* (D3) lists more than 2,700 directories by subject categories. They can be updated annually by referring to the education section of *American Reference Books Annual* (D14), or weekly by checking "Directories—Education" in the *P.A.I.S.* (Public Affairs Information Service) *Bulletin* (F16). Others can be located through the descriptor "Directories" in *Resources in Education (RIE)*. With today's fast-changing pace, individual directories also may be updated by information gleaned from newsletters and newspapers.

Check the index in this book under "Directories" for additional directories which are listed in the sections on instructional materials, statistics, curriculum, and media materials. Information sources that offer referrals to sources of information, such as the National Referral Center (M31), function as ongoing directories and are listed in the index under "Referral Agencies." Bibliographies (which list sources) and institution indexes (like those in *RIE*) can function as directories in practice. Yearbooks also provide some directory information.

Of all the available directories, perhaps the most valuable is the relatively unknown *Educator's World* (B39). It is a multifaceted directory of reasonably current information on a variety of sources important to educators. The two *Directories of Information Resources in the United States* (B33 and B34) issued by the National Referral Center, also are excellent and highly current. All of the tools included can save searching time and, generally, do not duplicate each other.

DIRECTORIES OF PEOPLE

B1   **CONSULTANTS AND CONSULTING ORGANIZATIONS DIRECTORY**   A Reference Guide to Concerns and Individuals Engaged in Consultation for Business and Industry. Edited by Paul Wasserman and Janice McLean. 2nd Edition. Detroit, Gale Research, 1973. $58.

A directory of approximately 5,000 consultants and consulting firms. Although intended primarily for business, it includes a section on education consultants which lists from 2 to 100 educational consultants for each state. Entries are complete and helpful, and include name, address, telephone number, founding date, and principal officers for each firm, plus a summary of interest areas and competence for each listing.

B2   **LEADERS IN EDUCATION**   A Biographical Directory. Edited by Jacques Cattell Press. 5th Edition. New York, R. R. Bowker, 1974. $40.

A reliable reference work (based on a questionnaire) that provides 17,000 detailed biographical sketches of key persons in the field of American and Canadian education, with some emphasis on administrators. There are some unexplained gaps and lapses in coverage, which may be due to the nonreturn of questionnaires or the elusiveness of educators. This edition includes a specialty index (by educational interest fields such as bilingualism, early childhood education, etc.) and a geographic index.

B3   **NATIONAL ASSOCIATION STATE EDUCATION DEPARTMENT INFORMATION OFFICERS DIRECTORY 1974-75**   National Association State Education Department Information Officers, 1974. $3. From: Tom I. Davis, Special Assistant, Public Information, State Department of Public Instruction, 352 Education Bldg., Raleigh, N.C. 27611.

The information officer is one of the best sources of information on what is happening in education in any state. This directory, arranged by state, lists names, addresses, and telephone numbers of information officers, and names and addresses of state superintendents.

B4 **THE NATIONAL FACULTY DIRECTORY—1975** 5th Edition. Detroit, Gale Research, 1975. 2 Vols. $85.
This directory, a printout of a computer-maintained address bank, provides the institutional name, departmental designation, city, state, and zip code for approximately 450,000 faculty members of colleges, universities, and junior colleges in the United States and Canada.

B5 **STATE EDUCATION LEADERS DIRECTORY 1975-1976** By Education Commission of the States (ECS). 4th Edition. Denver, Colo., 1975. $3.
A concise, compact, and inexpensive biennial handbook of current, state-level educational leaders. For each state and territory, entries include the names and addresses of state educational personnel for public schools of all levels, and key political leaders concerned with educational matters. Contains listings for the governor, executive assistant, education aide, lieutenant governor, state budget officer, legislative council director, chief state school officer, chief higher education officer, state board of education, Vocational Advisory Council, president of state PTA, state School Boards Association, officials of the State Education Association and State Federation of Teachers, higher education coordinating board and facilities commissions, legislative education committees, education council, and ECS commissioners.
  The names of the states are shown in the margins of this attractive booklet, and there is an index inside the back cover.

DIRECTORIES OF SCHOOL PROGRAMS AND FACILITIES

B6 **ANNUAL GUIDES TO GRADUATE STUDY, 1975, Book 6 – Education and Nursing** Edited by Karen C. Hegener. 9th Edition. Princeton, N.J., Peterson's Guides, 1975. $5.
Book 6 contains a useful graphic summary which provides an overview of the range of graduate programs offered by graduate schools of education. Education schools are listed under classified subject sections. Full-page entries for some of the schools give excellent descriptions of programs offered and research facilities, including libraries, costs, communities in which colleges and universities are located, etc.

B7   **CONTINUING EDUCATION PROGRAMS AND SERVICES FOR WOMEN**   By Women's Bureau, U.S. Department of Labor. Washington, D.C., U.S. Government Printing Office, 1971. $0.70. Single copy free from Women's Bureau, Washington, D.C. 21210.
This guide reports on 450 programs for adult women who wish to return to school or to work. The appendixes list, by state, schools that offer special programs or services and related state services. The section on federal funds and the reading list are not current, but the latter includes many good titles.

B8   **THE DIRECTORY FOR EXCEPTIONAL CHILDREN**   Edited by D. R. Young. 7th Edition. Boston, Porter Sargent, 1972. $14.
The main section of this detailed directory describes more than 4,000 institutions for disturbed, maladjusted, and handicapped children— schools, clinics, and treatment centers, both public and private. Facilities are arranged by type of handicap, special needs, or age groups— psychiatric facilities, orthopedic and neurological handicaps, facilities for the autistic, schools for the deaf and blind, schools providing life care, schools accepting teenagers, etc.—and are subdivided by state under these categories. Entries describe facilities, staff, fees, and requirements for acceptance. A general alphabetical index is included.

Since this directory is specifically intended to describe sources of help for all exceptional children, not only those sources that are accessible to the wealthy, it also lists federal and state agencies, associations, societies, and foundations which may offer additional assistance and information. This is the first edition of the directory that includes a listing of Canadian resources.

B9   **DIRECTORY OF ALTERNATIVE SCHOOLS**   Compiled by New Schools Exchange. In issue No. 101 of *New Schools Exchange Newsletter,* Sept. 15, 1973. $3. (With subscription to *New Schools Exchange Newsletter,* 10 issues/year, $10.) From: New Schools Exchange, Pettigrew, Ark. 72752.
A continuing directory of alternative schools in the United States and Canada, issued irregularly (as finances permit) and updated and supplemented in individual issues of the *New Schools Exchange Newsletter* by compilers who are competent and adept at locating and describing alternative schools. Issue 101 is arranged alphabetically by state and school name, and includes information on approximately 900 schools providing alternative education for children between the ages of 5 and 15, as well as networks and clearinghouses. It provides the name, address, telephone number, number of students, age or grade levels, tuition, and other vital information for each school, in a descriptive format. The New Schools Exchange is discussed in (O38).

B10 **DIRECTORY OF EDUCATIONAL PROGRAMS FOR THE GIFTED** By Lavonne B. Axford. Metuchen, N.J., Scarecrow, 1971. $7.50.

This book was based on standard reference sources and a questionnaire distributed to state departments of education. The questionnaire, returned by 34 states with varying degrees of accuracy and completeness, is the major data base of this directory, which is a good starting place for anyone studying educational programs for the gifted.

B11 **DIRECTORY OF FACILITIES FOR THE LEARNING-DISABLED AND HANDICAPPED** By Careth Ellingson and James Cass. New York, Harper and Row, 1972. $20.

While this directory is not as well-indexed or as comprehensive as *The Directory for Exceptional Children* (B8) (750 entries as compared to 4,000), entries are well-arranged and well-presented. Its aim is to meet the needs of both parents and professionals, and it includes analytic descriptions and comparative data on diagnostic facilities in the United States and Canada serving more than half a million handicapped children and adults, and similar descriptions of remedial, therapeutic, and developmental programs serving 300,000 individuals described as handicapped. "Handicap," as used here, covers educational handicaps, speech and language handicaps, physical handicaps, emotional handicaps, and intellectual handicaps.

Entries include name, address, and a detailed description covering scope, case load, procedures, testing instruments, fees, faculty, and funding for each facility. U.S. institutions are arranged alphabetically by state, then alphabetically by city and institution. Canadian institutions are arranged alphabetically by province, then by city. A useful appendix indexes available services by major metropolitan areas. Less useful is a title index to facilities, which needs more cross-references. No subject index.

B12 **DIRECTORY OF POSTSECONDARY SCHOOLS WITH OC-CUPATIONAL PROGRAMS, 1971: Public and Private** By National Center for Educational Statistics. Washington, D.C., U.S. Government Printing Office, 1973. $3.95.

Provides information on 9,182 schools offering occupational programs as of 1971. It covers noncollegiate institutions as well as 2- and 4-year colleges offering certificates and degrees below the baccalaureate level. Brief entries, arranged alphabetically by state and then by city and institution, include vendor number, accreditation, telephone number, address, and programs. Contains both program and school indexes.

B13 **DIRECTORY OF PUBLIC, ELEMENTARY AND SECON-
DARY DAY SCHOOLS, 1968-69** By National Center for Edu-
cational Statistics. Washington, D.C., U.S. Government Printing
Office, 1972. 5 Vols. *Volume 1: North Atlantic Region*, $2; *Volume 2:
Great Lakes and Plains Region*, $2; *Volume 3: Southeast Region*, $2;
Volume 4: West and Southwest Regions, $2; *Volume 5: Nonpublic
Elementary and Secondary Day Schools*, $2.

This five-volume directory, much of which is dated, contains a comprehensive listing of every public and nonpublic elementary and secondary day school in the United States: a total of 114,000 schools, including
18,718 nonpublic schools. Data includes state and post office, zip code,
name of school, street address, grade span, number of pupils and
teachers, types of programs offered, and name of district.

B14 **DIRECTORY OF REPRESENTATIVE WORK EDUCATION
PROGRAMS, 1972-73** By U.S. Office of Education. Washington, D.C., U.S. Government Printing Office, 1973. $2.95.

One of a series on work education programs, this directory identifies
approximately 550 programs. It is arranged by state and includes
information on grade level, purpose, enrollment, name and address of
school, and director. Indexes are arranged by industrial setting and
primary purpose.

B15 **DIRECTORY OF SECONDARY SCHOOLS WITH OCCUPA-
TIONAL CURRICULUM: Public–Nonpublic, 1971** By Na-
tional Center for Educational Statistics. Washington, D.C., U.S.
Government Printing Office, 1973. $4.20.

This directory lists a total of 17,460 schools offering occupational
curricula, arranged alphabetically by location, with coded information
on career offerings; published in computer printout format.

B16 **EARLY CHILDHOOD EDUCATION DIRECTORY** A
Selected Guide to 2,000 Preschool Education Centers. Edited by
E. Robert LaCrosse, Jr. New York, R. R. Bowker, 1971. $20.25.

Arranged alphabetically by state and subdivided alphabetically by town,
this guide includes abstracts or summaries of relevant legal credential
requirements for each state. Although selection criteria and investiga-
tory procedures are vague, the information on schools included in the
directory is fairly extensive, and includes name, address, telephone
number, history, educational philosophy, calendar, curriculum, fees,
facilities, administration and admission policies, staff licenses, and
financing. There is an incomplete index by type of schools. Also includes
names and addresses of regional directors of the HEW Office of Child
Development and Head Start regional offices.

B17 **FINANCIAL AIDS FOR HIGHER EDUCATION: 74-75 Catalog** (Formerly *National Catalog of Aids for Students Entering College.*) By Oreon Keeslar. 6th Edition. Dubuque, Iowa, Wm. C. Brown Co., 1974. $13.95 (paperback).
The sixth edition of this recently updated book provides accurate, concise, and current information on approximately 2,500 sources of financial aids for students entering and attending college. Well indexed.

B18 **GUIDE TO SUMMER CAMPS AND SUMMER SCHOOLS, 1975-1976** Edited by Porter Sargent staff. 20th Edition. Boston, Porter Sargent, 1975. $5; paperback, $3.
Revised via a thorough national check, this standard guide covers work projects, wilderness camping, travel tours, academic programs, specialized sports programs, and opportunities for the handicapped and maladjusted, as well as standard recreational camps—a total of 1,100 programs in the United States and Canada. Descriptions include cost, business address, subject and skill orientations, and type of child for whom each program is intended. Arranged by type of program and interest area, with regional subgroupings, and a general alphabetical index.

B19 **HANDBOOK OF PRIVATE SCHOOLS** An Annual Descriptive Survey of Independent Education. Edited by Porter Sargent staff. 55th Edition. Boston, Porter Sargent, 1974. Annual. $16.
A leading directory of independent schools, with careful annual revisions (publication began in 1915). The 55th edition lists more than 2,000 schools, arranged by regions and states. Descriptions of individual schools include the name, address, administrative officer, costs, number of students, special programs, and physical facilities, with detailed information on the presence and scope of summer sessions, tutoring programs, religious affiliations, specialized sources, and recreational opportunities. Classified tables help locate schools by type. Although the bulk of the book is devoted to staff-prepared, objective descriptions and analyses, the last 400 pages consist of advertising representations by some 400 schools, a feature some users object to and others find helpful.

B20 **INNOVATIVE EDUCATION PRACTICES** By National Advisory Council on Supplementary Centers and Services. Washington, D.C., 1973–1975. Free. From: Suite 529, 425 13th St., N.W., Washington, D.C. 20004.
An annual, selected list of validated Elementary and Secondary Education Amendments (ESEA) Title III projects, arranged under broad categories (school administration, special education, guidance, staff development, early childhood education, environmental education,

etc.). Also included is a state-by-state listing of the regional and state personnel responsible for administering Title III projects. The headquarters office has project information—on cards—of approximately 2,400 Title III projects.

Volume 2 (1974) lists 84 projects, arranged alphabetically by project title, under broad categories. Brief but well-written descriptions include name, address, telephone number, and project director.

B21   **THE NEW YORK TIMES GUIDE TO CONTINUING EDUCA-TION IN AMERICA**   Prepared by the College Entrance Examination Board. Edited by Frances Coombs Thomson. New York, Quadrangle Books, 1973. $12.50; paperback, $4.95.

A survey of options—from high school equivalency tests to postgraduate university programs for professionals—available to adult men and women, based on a national canvas of all accredited postsecondary institutions and correspondence schools, covering 2,281 schools in 50 states teaching more than 50,000 courses. Despite its scope, it succeeds quite well in its aim of being a "mercifully simple guide." The basic arrangement is alphabetical, by state and by institution, with a separate listing of correspondence schools. Descriptions, which are clear and complete, include name, address, telephone number, and zip code, as well as a description of the school (in context) and its offerings. Also includes an annotated bibliography on adult education, an annotated listing of organizations active in continuing education, a list of 900 institutions that award credit on the basis of college board examinations, and a list of accrediting associations and agencies recognized by the U.S. Office of Education. This compilation is the first serious effort to assemble a comprehensive guide for adults seeking further education.

B22   **THE NEW YORK TIMES GUIDE TO STUDENT ADVEN-TURES AND STUDIES ABROAD, 1974**   By Beatrice and Howard Rowland. New York, Quadrangle Books, 1974. $4.95 (paperback).

The first section of this guide is addressed to young people from ages 16 to 25 and provides criteria for selecting summer programs in European schools, with helpful suggestions for travel. The second section provides information about special-interest activities—archaeological expeditions, hiking, sciences, language-learning, etc. The third section is organized by countries.

B23   **PATTERSON'S AMERICAN EDUCATION, 1975**   Edited by Norman F. Elliott et al. Mount Prospect, Ill., Educational Directories, 1904– . Annual. $27.50.

A comprehensive annual directory, arranged by state, whose major section, School Systems, attempts to arrange information about each state's public school districts, high schools, and junior high schools in comparable format. State information includes officials of state departments of education and names and addresses of county superintendents or their equivalents. The community listings include county and population, names of superintendents and principals of junior and senior high schools, and the names and grade levels of private and parochial schools and colleges. The second section lists classified schools, arranged alphabetically by categories—architecture, art, bible schools, etc.—and then by state, including only the names and addresses of schools and the name of the admissions officer. The latest volume contains a helpful classified listing of educational associations and societies.

B24 **SOMEWHERE ELSE: A Living-Learning Catalog** Edited by Center for Curriculum Design. Chicago, Swallow Press, 1973. $6.00; paperback, $3.95.

A project of the Center for Curriculum Design, a nonprofit educational foundation, *Somewhere Else* is a well-organized directory of approximately 400 of the many alternatives to school learning—for those "who can't bring themselves to go to college" and adults who wish to pursue learning without grades and credentials—divided into centers and networks. Centers—whether places, people, or things—provide direct instructions; networks provide sources to check for further information. Categories include alternative futures, artisan skills, media, new learning, outdoors, overseas programs, social and political changes, spiritual groups, and women's groups. Informative, annotated entries provide addresses, telephone numbers, costs, and persons to contact. It contains competent geographical and alphabetical indexes, as well as a brief bibliography. The second printing includes corrections to January 1974.

B25 **THIS WAY OUT** A Guide to Alternatives to Traditional College Education in the United States, Europe and the Third World. By John Coyne and Tom Herbert. New York, Dutton, 1972. $10.00; paperback, $4.95.

A three-section guide offering alternatives to traditional college education. The first section provides detailed advice and information on independent study, on community resources and services, on correspondence study, on external degree programs, and on the College Level Examination Program, which could be supplemented by *The New York Times Guide to Continuing Education in America* (B21). The second section is a comprehensive directory of approximately 100 experimental and innovative colleges in the United States, analyzed for philosophy, methods, faculty, students, cost, and locations, with suggested criteria for a "good" experimental college and advice on interpreting college catalogs. The third section is a study/travel handbook on foreign education: what to expect and how to survive, with emphasis on experimental programs.

B26 **UTILIZING RESOURCES IN THE HANDICAPPED SERVICES FIELD: A Directory for Head Start Personnel** Edited by Lynne Glassman. Reston, Va., Council for Exceptional Children, 1974. $4.80.

A guide to help early childhood specialists identify agencies and organizations that provide direct or indirect services for handicapped children. Three major sections cover federal agencies, associations, and directories; program descriptions of regional, state, and local resources; and state-by-state resource entries. A list of publications used in compiling the directory is included.

B27 **WORLD DIRECTORY OF ENVIRONMENTAL EDUCATION PROGRAMS: Post-Secondary Study and Training in 70 Countries** Edited by Philip W. Quigg. New York, R. R. Bowker, 1974. $14.95.

Sponsored by the International Institute for Environmental Affairs and the Institute for International Education, this book provides directory information on more than 1,000 instructional programs in environmental education, approximately 400 outside the United States. Materials are arranged alphabetically by country (subdivided by state in the United States); information includes name of institution, programs offered, director's name, eligibility requirements, tuition, fees, faculty, and scholarships. Programs listed include university courses, training and introductory courses, courses for technicians, and courses at research centers.

B28 **WORLD OF LEARNING, 1974-75** London, Europa Publications, 1974. 2 Vols. $50. From: Gale Research Co., Book Tower, Detroit, Mich. 48226.

This is the standard guide to international educational organizations and education in foreign countries. The major section, arranged alphabetically by country, includes current, reliable, and fairly comprehensive information on varied educational institutions and research organizations of these countries, including names and addresses of institutions and names of principal officials and college professors at major universities.

DIRECTORIES OF RESOURCES

B29 **CALENDAR OF MEETINGS OF NATIONAL AND REGIONAL EDUCATIONAL ASSOCIATIONS, 1974-75** Edited by Mary R. Laidig. Washington, D.C., National Catholic Educational Assn., 1974. $3. From: Suite 350, One Dupont Circle, Washington, D.C. 20036.

A continuing service made available each September to the educational community by NCEA, with a calendar corresponding to the school year, from September through August. The calendar checklist is arranged by date, with association names underneath. A full listing is given for September through August, with preliminary information on meetings planned for September through August of the following year. The primary list consists of an alphabetical listing of associations with full data on meetings, which includes the name of the association, place and date of the meeting, theme (if any), person to contact for further information, whether the meeting is open or closed to nonmembers, and whether exhibits are included.

B30 **DIRECTORY OF AFRO-AMERICAN RESOURCES** Compiled by Walter Schatz. New York, R. R. Bowker, 1970. $21.

This directory is the result of a project conducted by the Race Relations Information Center of Nashville, Tennessee to identify centers in the United States holding materials which document Black American history. Arranged alphabetically by state, city, and institution, each entry includes the name of the institution, organization, or library; address, telephone number, and person to contact; statement of purpose; and services, publications, and a description of the materials.

B31 **DIRECTORY OF DATA BASES IN THE SOCIAL AND BE-HAVIORAL SCIENCES** Edited by Vivian S. Sessions. New York, Science Associates/International, Inc., 1974. $35.

Identifies and describes 1,500 groups of data files from more than 650 organizations in the United States and throughout the world in an attempt to make these files accessible to individuals outside their immediate environment. Although not intended primarily for educators, it includes some substantive data files that can be used for educational research. Information on the individual files includes major subject fields; name, telephone number, address, and person to contact; source and scope of file; conditions of access; and documentation and data-processing information. Contains subject, geographic, and senior staff indexes. Although these files are primarily nonbibliographic, the book identifies a few specialized files referring to research reports and similar documents.

B32   **DIRECTORY OF ERIC MICROFICHE COLLECTIONS**   (Arranged by Geographic Locations.) Prepared by ERIC Processing and Reference Facility for National Institute of Education. Bethesda, Md., ERIC Processing and Reference Facility, 1974. Free. From: 4833 Rugby Ave., Bethesda, Md. 20014.

The lists of ERIC standing-order customers that are generally issued once a year serve as directories to ERIC microfiche collections. This particular list includes 572 names and addresses of regular subscribers; of these, 524 are in the United States, conveniently arranged by state, and 48 are foreign, mostly in Canada, arranged by country. Organizations are listed as they appear on subscription labels, sometimes resulting in inaccurate organization titles. Addresses include zip codes but not telephone numbers. Since not all of these organizations are open to the general public, it would be wise to inquire as to hours and availability before dropping in.

B33   **A DIRECTORY OF INFORMATION RESOURCES IN THE UNITED STATES: Federal Government**   With a Supplement of Government-Sponsored Information Analysis Centers. Compiled by the National Referral Center, Science and Technology Division, Library of Congress. 2nd Edition. Washington, D.C., U.S. Government Printing Office, 1973. $4.25 (paperback).

This guide, containing 1,242 entries, is a major source of information on Federal Government activities, including many relevant to education. Entries, arranged alphabetically by organization, provide current addresses, resources, and information services. ERIC clearinghouses are listed in a supplementary section on information analysis centers.

B34   **A DIRECTORY OF INFORMATION RESOURCES IN THE UNITED STATES: Social Sciences**   Compiled by the National Referral Center, Science and Technology Division, Library of Congress. Revised Edition. Washington, D.C., U.S. Government Printing Office, 1973. $6.90 (paperback).

Listed in the directory's 2,480 entries are the addresses, telephone numbers, areas of interest, holdings, publications, and information services of a wide variety of organizations capable of meeting specific information needs in the social sciences. These include libraries, information centers, museums, professional societies, associations, institutes, universities, foundations, citizens' groups, and federal, state, and local government offices. Entries are arranged alphabetically under organizations and indexed by subject. Depending on the comprehensiveness of one's definition of "education resources," perhaps as many as one-third of the entries might be considered relevant to education.

B35   **A DIRECTORY OF NATIONAL ORGANIZATIONS CON-CERNED WITH SCHOOL HEALTH 1974-75**   By American School Health Assn. Kent, Ohio, 1974. ASHA members, $3.00; nonmembers, $3.50.

A comprehensive listing of more than 130 organizations concerned with school health. Includes organization, name and title of chief adminis-trator, mailing address, telephone number, list of major meetings for 1974–1975 (with name, place, and date of meeting), publications, and committees, councils, sections, and subdivisions concerned with school health. Also includes a brief description of the purposes and objectives of each of these organizations, with additional comments as appropriate.

B36   **DIRECTORY OF ORGANIZATIONS AND PERSONNEL IN EDUCATIONAL MANAGEMENT**   By Philipp K. Piele and Stuart C. Smith. 4th Edition. Eugene, Ore., ERIC Clearinghouse on Educational Management, 1974. $3.50.

A useful analytic directory of 152 organizations and 535 individual researchers active in the field of educational management. It includes name, address, service area (national or local), subject areas, publication topics, and whether or not a catalog of publications is available. The information on individual researchers (mostly professors) includes name, address, subjects of research, agencies with which affiliated, and publications available from researchers. Both the institutions and the researchers are arranged in separate, numbered, alphabetical lists, with clear, detailed, separate subject indexes, plus a geographic index for organizations only.

B37   **A DIRECTORY OF THE EDUCATION DIVISION OF THE UNITED STATES DEPARTMENT OF HEALTH, EDUCA-TION AND WELFARE**   Edited by Judith MacKown and Steven G. Harris. Washington, D.C., Capitol Publications, 1975. $15.95 (paperback).

A much needed directory of HEW's Education Division, the U.S. Office of Education, and the National Institute of Education. Section A contains organization charts of HEW and all of its divisions, as well as the names, addresses, and telephone numbers of directors. Section B lists education-related, federal-domestic assistance programs administered by NIE and HEW and provides detailed information on authorization, administering agency, eligibility, objectives, uses and restrictions, contact persons, and related programs, with an appendix that can be used to update this section. Section C provides cross-references by programs, organizations, and personal names. Despite its high price, it is highly recommended for institutions and individuals communicating with the Education Division.

B38 **EDUCATION DIRECTORY** By National Center for Educational Statistics. Washington, D.C., U.S. Government Printing Office, 1912– . Four sections, issued separately. Published irregularly. Each section priced separately.

A basic source of educational data. The *Directory* is now largely computer-produced and is published in four separate sections, at intervals of one year or more; often a year or two out-of-date.

Part 1: State Governments, 1971-73 (1974, $1.25). Out-of-Print. Lists principal officials in state education and library extension agencies; accurate as of 1971.

Part 2: Public School Systems, 1973-74 (1974, $2.25). Provides a listing—by state, names, and other basic information (location, address, grade span, number of schools, and enrollment)—of the 1,700 elementary and secondary school systems in the United States, as well as five church organizations maintaining state, regional, or national school systems.

Part 3: Higher Education, 1974-75 (1975, $6.45). Lists accredited institutions, arranged by state, including two-year, college-level programs and occupational studies beyond grade 12.

Part 4: Educational Associations, 1974 (1974, $1.10). Includes national, college, regional, and international associations and foundations, plus a subject index.

B39 **EDUCATOR'S WORLD** The Standard Guide to American-Canadian Educational Associations, Conventions, Foundations, Publications, Research Centers, 1971 through 1974. 3rd Edition. Philadelphia, North American Publishing, 1972. $20.

Although the price for the third edition was increased, and it is not as current as was the second edition (issued by Fisher Publishing Company), this tool does contain much useful information. It includes current information on more than 2,400 educational associations—including membership, purpose, publications, and conventions—and a separate annotated listing of more than 2,000 educational journals, magazines, newsletters, and proceedings published either by the associations or independently. This edition is a reprint of the second edition—green sheets contain updated information. Materials on the 92 foundations listed appear not to be updated; materials on 170 research centers often are inaccurate; while convention information (700 items for four years) is rather sketchy and incomplete for 1973 and 1974.

The second edition is worth keeping or locating for its "Areas of Interest" section (missing from the third edition), which grouped associations, research centers, publications, foundations, meetings, and conventions into 67 useful interest categories.

B40 **ENCYCLOPEDIA OF INFORMATION SYSTEMS AND SERVICES** Edited by Anthony T. Kruzas. 2nd Edition. Ann Arbor, Mich., Anthony T. Kruzas Associates, 1974. $77.50. Distributed by Edwards Brothers.

This greatly expanded edition provides information on 1,750 (including 225 foreign) interesting and assorted information systems and services, which now include publishers, computer software and timesharing agencies, micrographic firms, libraries, information centers, government agencies, clearinghouses, research centers, professional associations, and consultants, but exclude traditional academic and special libraries. Many of these organizations are related in some way to education. Since the book is based largely on responses to questionnaires, there are still some significant gaps in coverage. Information on systems and services covered, however, is comprehensive and usable. The first section includes name, date established, department head, staff, description of services, subject coverage, input, holdings, publications, microforms, and sponsoring organizations—up to a full page of information for many items. The remainder of the book includes 13 supplementary indexes for a variety of approaches: geographic, interest area, individual and institutional names, etc.

B41 **LIBRARY AND REFERENCE FACILITIES IN THE AREA OF THE DISTRICT OF COLUMBIA** Edited by Mildred Benton and Legare H. B. Obear. 8th Edition. Washington, D.C., The Joint Venture, 1971. $5.95. From: 2001 S St., N.W., Washington, D.C. 20009.

A joint venture of one university and five library and information groups resulted in this guide to 426 well-described libraries in the Washington, D.C. area, with a handy subject index to numbered entries. If it is convenient to research in Washington, D.C., this is an excellent guide to the right libraries.

B42 **MENTAL HEALTH DIRECTORY, 1973** By National Institute of Mental Health. Washington, D.C., U.S. Government Printing Office, 1973. $3.75. Single copy free from National Institute of Mental Health, 5600 Fishers Lane, Rockville, Md. 20852.

The bulk of this directory contains a state-by-state listing of approximately 3,000 facilities. Items, arranged by city under state, include name, address, and telephone number of facility; geographic areas serviced; and services provided. Other sections deal with state and territorial authorities, mental health associations, and other sources of mental health information. This could be a useful tool for counselors and others concerned with childrens' mental health problems.

B43 **NEA HANDBOOK, 1974-75** National Education Assn. Washington, D.C., 1974. $3.
Published annually for use by members, officers, and staff of NEA, its state and local affiliates, and other leaders in the field of education. While it changes format from year-to-year, its basic purpose is to provide information about the association: its policy documents, governing bodies, goals and objectives, programs and administrative structure, and components. The *Handbook* includes the names, addresses, and telephone numbers of elected leaders, staff, and affiliates of NEA—nationally and by state, with a section showing membership statistics and another section listing basic documents.

B44 **RESEARCH CENTERS DIRECTORY** Edited by Archie M. Palmer. 5th Edition. Detroit, Gale Research, 1975. $68.
Approximately 300 items in this classified directory deal with education. Other relevant sections include government and public affairs, labor and industrial relations (including occupations), law (including legislation), regional and area studies, social sciences (including human development and linguistics), multidisciplinary programs, and research coordinating offices. Items are arranged alphabetically by parent institution. Each item includes name of institution, address, telephone number, director, date of founding, a brief description of the research center (information on its staffing, source of support, and principal fields of research), information on library facilities (name of librarian, etc.), and where to obtain results. The *Directory* is supplemented between editions by a periodical, *New Research Centers.*

B45 **THE SCIENTIFIC INSTITUTIONS OF LATIN AMERICA** With Special Reference to Their Organization and Information Facilities. By Ronald Hilton. Stanford, Calif., California Institute of International Studies, 1970. $12.
Prepared by the professor of Latin American studies at Stanford University. It covers the libraries and information centers of Latin America, as well as its scientific institutions; should be extremely helpful to anyone concerned with Latin American studies. Contains clear, brief descriptions and histories of the institutions in both current and historical contexts.

B46 **SUBJECT COLLECTIONS**   A Guide to Special Book Collections in Libraries. Compiled by Lee Ash. 4th Edition. New York, R. R. Bowker, 1975. $38.50.

This edition contains approximately 70,000 references to special collections in 15,000 libraries and 1,000 museums, arranged alphabetically by subjects (Library of Congress subject headings) and cross-referenced to related topics. Under each subject, libraries are arranged alphabetically by state, city, and then library. Includes information on library holdings and photocopying access. While it is less complete than some other directories, it is easy to use and can lead to an education library in your vicinity.

B47 **TEACHERS' ASSOCIATIONS**   2nd Edition. Paris, UNESCO, 1971. $5. From: Unipub, P.O. Box 433, New York, N.Y. 10016.

A compact little directory providing information on 801 national teachers' associations and 200 international and regional organizations. Section A lists international and regional associations; Section B lists associations by country and territory. Arrangement is in English alphabetical order, although the text is in French and Spanish as well. For associations listed, this directory provides name, address, officer to whom correspondence should be addressed, number of members, types of institutions with which affiliated, budget, sources of revenue, functions of the association, and a list of publications. Most of the information is presented in coded form. Section C is a subject index; Section D, a 1966 recommendation of the Special Intergovernmental Conference on the Status of Teachers, is printed in Russian as well as the other three languages.

B48 **UNITED STATES GOVERNMENT MANUAL, 1974-75** (Formerly *United States Government Organization Manual.*) Compiled by National Archives and Records Service. Washington, D.C., U.S. Government Printing Office, 1975. Annual. $5.75.

This standard guide to the programs and functions of U.S. Government agencies is revised annually in July. It includes descriptions of agencies and quasi-official agencies in a Guide to Government Information section, lists of officials, and organization charts.

B49 **WORLD INDEX OF SOCIAL SCIENCE INSTITUTIONS** Research, Advanced Training, Documentation, and Professional Bodies. Paris, UNESCO, 1970. $16.50. From: Unipub, P.O. Box 433, New York, N.Y. 10016.

A card index, in loose-leaf format, to all social science, research, advanced training, and documentation institutions and professional bodies about which information was available in the Social Science

Documentation Center in mid-1970. It is updated through the *International Science Journal,* which costs $7/year. The institutions are arranged alphabetically in the appropriate language (international institutions listed first), then they are filed alphabetically by the English-language name of the country. Information (in English on one side of the card and in French on the other) includes country; name and address of institution; date of establishment; present head of institution; areas of interest; broad, specific, and geographic area coverage; plus detailed coded information on size of staff, activities, research facilities, finance, and relationship to intergovernmental organizations. A good guide to current information on organizations in education and related fields.

B50 **YOUTH INFORMATION DIGEST–'74** A Guide and Directory to National Private Organizations in Areas of Concern to Today's Youth. 2nd Edition. Washington, D.C., Washington Workshops Press, 1974. $6.

A directory for and by youth (researched in Washington, D.C., by a group of high school and college students). For the most part, it includes Washington, D.C., offices of an interesting assortment of youth-related private organizations. Categories cover economy, media, and consumer affairs; employment; education; environment; family and population; foreign affairs; government organization and reform; legal rights and justice; narcotics, poverty, and welfare; minority group relations; science and the arts; and youth programs. Address, telephone number, names and acronyms, descriptions, and publications are given for organizations cited.

B51 **YOUTH RESOURCES MANUAL FOR COORDINATORS** By President's Council on Youth Opportunity. Washington, D.C., U.S. Government Printing Office, 1971. $1.75.

While this may be somewhat out-of-date, it is still a well-organized, well-written summary of information useful to groups or individuals working with disadvantaged youth. Includes background information, selected annotated reference materials, and directories in many related areas, including employment, occupational education, educational resources, recreation and arts, transportation, drugs, communications, foundations, and conference planning. Extensive appendixes lead to names of key people in many state, local, regional, and national organizations concerned with youth, employment, welfare, industry, education, and government. A great deal of information is tied together in a succinct and useful fashion.

4 | *Yearbooks,*
Monograph Series,
Periodicals, Newsletters

This chapter discusses four types of educational literature which can be helpful to individuals who want to keep current with trends and innovations in education: yearbooks, monographs, periodicals, and newsletters.

YEARBOOKS

Yearbooks, like other digest and summary publications, select significant materials from current information, then condense and publish these materials annually. In the last few years, however, educational yearbooks have had a tendency to interrupt publication, either intermittently or permanently, resulting in a break in continuity. (Recently discontinued yearbooks include the *International Yearbook of Education* [last issue was 1969] and assorted *Britannica Yearbooks*—which were very worthwhile publications during their existence. The *World Yearbook of Education*— published in Britain—has changed American distributors so often that it has become exceedingly difficult to locate or buy in the United States.) Since most of the remaining yearbook series are essentially monographs, they will be listed together in the next section.

MONOGRAPH SERIES

While the number of yearbooks being published has been decreasing, sets of educational monographs have been proliferating. The monographs listed in this chapter are not primarily technical; they are largely bulletins or small books that report on particular subjects, or research reports that deal with specific problems. Although the individual publications in the series listed may vary in quality, as a group they are recommended as an excellent (and underused) means of keeping current with important trends in education. The series listed here are worthwhile for teachers, laymen, and administrators, and also can serve as introductory summaries for research purposes.

Many ERIC clearinghouses and some educational laboratories and research and development centers issue series in their various areas of interest. Their individual publications generally are available through ERIC, while many of the monograph series listed here are not.

Other educational publishers also produce excellent monographs or monograph series, which can be located through the bibliographical channels discussed in Chapter 5. Highly valuable titles, for instance, are published by Teachers' College Press and Parker Press; Educational Technology Publications are considered valuable in the research-technology area. Many of the information sources listed in Chapters 14, 15, and 16 also issue occasional monographs.

Monograph series included in this chapter were selected from among other series as being particularly useful.

C1   **ASSOCIATION FOR CHILDHOOD EDUCATION INTER-NATIONAL (ACEI)**   3615 Wisconsin Ave., N.W., Washington, D.C. 20016. (202) 363-6963

This international membership organization, founded in 1892, is open to teachers, administrators, parents, librarians, community workers, and all individuals concerned with promoting desirable conditions in the schools and the environment, in the well-being and education of children from infancy to early adolescence, and in the professional development of educators and allied professionals. Although publishing is not its primary interest, following are some of the association's well-written, well-researched series that express its concerns.

Leaflet series, which include *Research: Children's Concepts* ($0.10), *Young Deprived Children* ($0.25), and *Guide to Children's Magazines* (0.25).

Position papers, which include *Play Is Valid* ($0.10), *We Reconsider Reading* ($0.10), and *Children and War* (0.35).

Bulletins, which are substantial, researched pamphlets often expressing a child development point of view. Titles include *Children's International Education* ($1.75), *Children and TV* ($1.25), *Migrant Children* ($2.00), *Nursery School Portfolio* ($1.50), *Parenting* ($2.50), *Children and Intercultural Education* ($2.95), *Nutrition and Intellectual Growth in Children* ($2.00), *Playgrounds for City Children* ($1.50), and *Young Deprived Children and Their Educational Needs* ($0.50).

Childhood Education, which is included in membership, is the association's periodical (six issues from October to May); often a quasimonograph that devotes perhaps five of its six yearly issues to specific themes. Individual copies are available for $2.50.

Sampler sets and portfolios of ACEI's materials are available at a discount, below the usual modest prices.

The association's Washington, D.C. headquarters houses the Childhood Education Center, which provides materials, equipment, displays, a meeting room, a professional library, and an information center which answers more than 6,000 queries each year.

C2   **ASSOCIATION FOR SUPERVISION AND CURRICULUM DEVELOPMENT**   Suite 1100, 1701 K St., N.W., Washington, D.C. 20036. (202) 467-6480

A membership organization, in existence since 1921, concerned largely with the improvement of curriculum and instruction. Its activities include the publication of yearbooks, books, booklets, and audiocassettes, which compatibly combine research and readability.

The association has issued more than 60 paperback books and booklets which are available at reasonable prices ($1 to $5). Some typical titles are: *Open Schools for Children, Educational Accountability, Beyond Behavioral Objectives, Supervision in Action,* and *On Early Learning.* Depending on type of membership, some or all of these publications are free to members.

Its yearbooks actually are topical series of important, in-depth, curricular-related subjects. The latest yearbook, *Education for an Open Society* (1974, $8.00), is extremely competent and interesting; other relevant titles are: *Education for Peace: Focus on Mankind* (1973, $7.50); *A New Look at Progressive Education* (1972, $8.00); *Freedom, Bureaucracy, and Schooling* (1971, $6.50); and the best-selling *Perceiving, Behaving, Becoming: A New Focus for Education* (1962, $5.00).

Audio-cassette series (mostly $6.00 each) are live recordings of addresses by educational leaders.

C3   **CEMREL, INC.**   3120 59th St., St. Louis, Mo. 63139. (314) 781-2900

CEMREL, a national education laboratory, is the originator of the "Five Sense Store," and is a major source of research, activity, and information in aesthetic education and early cognitive development, as well as in mathematics. Its competent and thorough monographs cover research, literature reviews, curriculum development and selection, reports on projects in the arts, teacher education in aesthetic education, parent education, and tests in the arts. Some typical titles and prices are *Defining Behavioral Objectives for Aesthetic Education* ($2.80), *All the Arts for Every Child* (free), and *The Artist as Teacher* ($0.50). Write for free announcements and news reports.

C4   **CITATION PRESS**   A division of Scholastic Magazines, Inc., 50 W. 44th St., New York, N.Y. 10036. (212) 867-7700

Publishes well-researched, teacher-oriented titles (paperback and hard cover) dealing with innovative teaching methods, classroom activities, and current issues in education and administration, as well as some reference books dealing with educational books, periodicals, and media materials. Also publishes works by professional organizations such as the National Council of Teachers of English, American Association of School Librarians, Designing Education for the Future Project, and National Commission on Resources for Youth. Several current titles include *Smiles, Nods, and Pauses: Activities to Enrich Children's Communication Skills* ($8.95) and *Let Them Be Themselves: Language Arts for Children in Elementary Schools,* 2nd Edition ($6.50; paperback, $3.25). *Half-Hour Notice: Fifty Mini-Lessons for High School Substitutes* and *Science Can Be Elementary: Discovery-Action Programs K-3* are reviewed elsewhere.

Citation Press is the sole American distributor of the working papers, examination and curriculum bulletins, and research reports stemming from Britain's Schools Council for Curriculum and Examinations. It is the U.S. publisher of the *Informal Schools in Britain Today* series, prepared under the aegis of the Schools Council with a Ford Foundation grant, and distributes a number of titles dealing with open education and early childhood education, which are published in the British Commonwealth by Evans Brothers Limited. Among the latest are a series of volumes by two noted English educators—Alice Yardley: *Learning to Adjust* ($2.65), *The Teacher of Young Children* ($3.25), *Young Children Thinking* ($2.65), *Structure in Early Learning* ($3.25), and others; and Joan Dean: *Room to Learn* (3 volumes, $1.45 each).

C5 **EDUCATION U.S.A. Special Reports** By National School Public Relations Assn. (NSPRA). Arlington, Va., 1970– . $4.75 each; quantity discount. From: 1801 N. Moore St., Arlington, Va. 22209. (703) 528-6771

Current, readable reports that probe single areas of education in depth, report on successful operational programs in school districts (often with case studies and profiles of effective projects), and serve as guides to further information. Recent reports cover such "hot issues" as vandalism and violence, informal education, dropouts, school lunch programs, and school volunteers.

Another high-quality NSPRA monograph series is *Current Trends* ($6.75 each). Typical titles are *Citizens Advisory Committees* (1973), *Grading and Reporting* (1972), and *Evaluating Teachers for Professional Growth* (1974). NSPRA also publishes a helpful series of handbooks on school-community communications ($2.00 to $8.00 each), and a series of pamphlets and filmstrips on school-parent communications. A complete list of publications is available upon written request.

C6 **EDUCATION YEARBOOK, 1974-1975** Edited by Bob Famighetti, Prudence Randall, and Jean Paradise. New York, Macmillan Co. and the Free Press, 1975. $49.50.

This five-section yearbook, issued each September since 1972 to update Macmillan's *Encyclopedia of Education* (A10), is a laudable attempt to create a well-rounded, comprehensive reference book. It includes articles on current issues in education—some by big names like Mario Fantini, a section of current statistics, a brief glossary, and biographical information on educational administrators and policymakers (legislators, chief state officers, etc.); also highlights—in topical and state articles—last year's major educational news. Contains three well-conceived, annotated review articles on new books, films, and tests which cover materials approximately one year old.

C7 **FASTBACKS** By Phi Delta Kappa Educational Foundation. Bloomington, Ind., 1971– . Six for $2.50.

A series of inexpensive, authoritative minibooks (usually 32 to 48 pages each) issued twice a year in sets of 6 or 12 titles. These books, written by competent authorities in nontechnical language, keep the reader informed on the "ideas being discussed and tried in schools across the country." Fifty titles were issued as of October 1974, some of which are *Selecting Children's Reading, Sex Differences in Learning to Read, Systematic Thinking About Education, How to Recognize a Good School, Alternative Schools in Action, Informal Learning, Learning Without a Teacher, Metrication: American Style,* and *Competency-Based Teacher Education.*

C8   **I/D/E/A PUBLICATIONS** Institute for the Development of
      Educational Activities, Inc., Information and Service Program,
      P.O. Box 446, Melbourne, Fla. 32901. (305) 723-0211
This educational affiliate of the Charles F. Kettering Foundation is
something of a "think tank" in educational innovation, evaluation, and
development, which prepares inexpensive, attractive, and readable
publications and films dealing with current issues and innovations for
teachers. *The Greening of the High School* ($2) is a typical title. Its catalog
lists films, filmstrips, monographs, occasional papers, resource materials,
and bibliographies. Current list available upon written request.

C9   **INTERNATIONAL READING ASSOCIATION (IRA)** 6 Tyre
      Ave., Newark, Del. 19711. (302) 731-1600
IRA's monograph series are limited to reading and related areas, with
thorough coverage. Its series, which offer discounts to members, include:

   Reading Aids: Practical suggestions for the classroom teacher, with
such titles as: *How to Read a Book, Guidance and the Teaching of Reading,*
and *Tests of Reading Readiness and Achievement.* $2.00 each.
   Perspectives in Reading: Papers expressing varied viewpoints on specific
topics, with such titles as *First Grade Reading Programs, Folklore and
Folktales Around the World,* and *Strategies for Adult Basic Education.* $3.50
each.
   Annotated Bibliographies: Include such titles as *Contingency Management
and Reading, Readability and Reading,* and *Reading in the Content Fields.*
$0.75 each.

   IRA also issues other series, some jointly with ERIC; all are highly
competent yet inexpensive papers dealing with all aspects of reading.

C10   **NATIONAL ASSOCIATION OF SECONDARY SCHOOL
      PRINCIPALS (NASSP)** 1904 Association Dr., Reston, Va.
      22091. (703) 860-0200
A 59-year-old membership and service organization for *all* secondary
school administrators, which has prepared approximately 200 excellent
small publications and films intended primarily for school administrators, yet simply written, comprehensive, and useful for other
educators and for the public at large. Some of NASSP's many series
include:

   Curriculum Reports: Current reports ($0.50 each) covering such topics
as *Alternatives to Conventional School, Notes on Some Very New National
Curriculum Development Projects,* and *Putting It All Together: Unified Science.*

Legal Memoranda: Twenty-five cents ($0.25) each, with quantity discounts. Titles include: *Search and Seizure: Right to Privacy, Student Marriage and Pregnancy,* and *Confidentiality of Pupil School Records,* among others.

Special Publications: Generally range from $0.50 to $3.00 each. Titles include: *Disruption in Urban Secondary Schools* and *Test Norms—Their Use and Interpretation.*

Student Activities Publications: Generally $1.00 or $2.00 each, they are concerned with student government.

Model Schools Project Publications, Films, and Filmstrips: Available at varied prices, they are concerned with changes and improvements in education.

NASSP's monthly journal, the *Bulletin* (included in membership), is something of a monograph itself. Recent single issues, available at $2.00 each, deal with alternative schools, career education, accountability, scientific literacy, and other current issues.

A complete list of publications is available on request. Payment should accompany all orders.

C11 **NATIONAL COUNCIL FOR THE SOCIAL STUDIES (NCSS)** 1201 16th St., N.W., Washington, D.C. 20036. (202) 833-4476

This affiliate of the National Education Association (NEA) is a professional organization of educators at all levels (elementary school to university) interested in teaching social sciences and social studies. Membership includes its periodical, *Social Education,* and yearbooks. NCSS also publishes bulletins, curriculum studies, *How-to-Do-It* series, position statements, and other helpful, inexpensive publications.

NCSS yearbooks are a carefully edited series combining topicality with thoroughness: valuable for reference, browsing, research, and classroom use. Some recent exemplary yearbooks are listed below (others are in press):

Teaching Ethnic Studies: Concepts and Strategies (43rd Yearbook, 1973; $6.00, paperback).

Teaching About Life in the City (42nd Yearbook, 1972; $5.50, paperback).

Values Education: Rationale, Strategies and Procedures (41st Yearbook, 1971; $5.00, paperback).

Focus on Geography: Key Concepts and Teaching Strategies (40th Yearbook, 1970; $5.50, paperback).

Social Studies Curriculum Development (39th Yearbook, 1969; $4.50, paperback).

International Dimensions in the Social Studies (38th Yearbook, 1968; $4.50, paperback).

C12　**NATIONAL SCIENCE TEACHERS ASSOCIATION** 1201 16th St., N.W., Washington, D.C. 20036. (202) 833-4283
A society of science teachers, with a growing publication program covering research, curriculum, teacher education, teaching procedures, science teaching facilities, and evaluation procedures, available at fairly low prices.

Its "how-to-do-it" series ($0.35 to $1.00) includes *How to Plan and Manage Minicourses* ($1.00), *How to Care for Living Things in the Classroom* ($0.50), *How to Record and Use Data in Elementary School Science* ($1.00), *How to Handle Radioisotopes Safely* ($1.00), and many more.

Teaching aids include a Drug Education Packet ($3.00), an Energy and Environment Packet ($2.00), a Measurement and Metric System Packet ($3.00), and other inexpensive materials dealing with career education, organization of science clubs, and convention reports.

Membership ($8 for elementary school teachers, $15 for secondary school teachers, and $12 for college science teachers) includes appropriate periodicals *(Science and Children* for elementary school teachers, *Science Teacher* for high school teachers, or the *Journal of College Science Teaching* for college teachers) with supplementary services. Publications can be purchased separately.

C13　**NATIONAL　　SOCIETY　FOR　　THE　　STUDY　　OF EDUCATION** 5835 Kimbard Ave., Chicago, Ill. 60637. (312) 753-3813
This group has published an impressive series of monograph-yearbooks since 1902, dealing with many significant topics. The two yearbooks published in 1974 are *Media and Symbols,* edited by David Olson ($10.00), and *Uses of the Sociology of Education,* edited by C. Wayne Gordon ($10.00). Other titles include: *Art Education* (1965, $7.50), *Early Childhood Education* (1972, $9.00), *Educational Evaluation* (1969, $8.00), *Elementary School in the United States* (1973, $9.50), *Linguistics in School Programs* (1970, $8.00), *Programmed Instruction* (1967, $7.50), and *Vocational Education* (1965, $7.50).

C14　**PHI DELTA KAPPA EDUCATIONAL FOUNDATION MONOGRAPHS** Compiled by Phi Delta Kappa Educational Foundation. Bloomington, Ind., 1971– . Various prices.
The Phi Delta Kappa Educational Foundation commissions authors to write about important topics comprehensively and authoritatively, without jargon; part of an ongoing publishing effort by the Foundation (see

also *Fastbacks,* C7). Some recent titles are *The Gallup Polls of Attitudes Toward Education, 1969-73,* $2.25; *The Teaching of Reading* by George Spache; *Building a Learning Environment* by Edgar Dale; and *The Educational Significance of the Future* by Harold Shane. Prices for the last three titles are $5.50 (clothbound) and $3.95 (paperback) each.

C15 **WHAT RESEARCH SAYS TO THE TEACHER** Assn. of Classroom Teachers, National Education Assn., Publications Order Dept., Academic Bldg., Saw Mill Rd., West Haven, Conn. 06516. (203) 934-2669

An extremely helpful series—in booklet, filmstrip, and multimedia packages—providing accurate, frequently updated summaries or overviews of educational research findings and their implications for teaching, with selected references for further reading at the end of each. Thirty-four frequently revised booklets (approximately 32 pages long, $0.35 to $0.65 each) relate to the practical and immediate problems of teachers: topics such as development of course content, problem-solving techniques, learning and motivation, and adapting instruction to individual needs.

Titles include: *Improving Classroom Testing, Controlling Classroom Misbehavior, Sensory Factors in the School Learning Environment,* $0.50 each; *Anxiety as Related to Thinking and Forgetting; Creativity; Juvenile Delinquency; Teaching High School Science; Class Organization for Instruction;* etc., from $0.35 to $0.65 each. The complete set is available for $11.75.

Current titles of filmstrips, which cost from $10.00 to $16.00 each, are: "Controlling Classroom Misbehavior," "Educational Media," "Guided Study and Homework," "Listening: From Sound to Meaning," "Nursery School and Kindergarten," "Teaching the Disadvantaged," "Understanding Intergroup Relations," "When Every High School Teacher is a Reading Teacher," and "Creativity: A Way of Learning."

Special-interest packets at reduced prices are available for elementary and high school teachers.

C16 **WORLD YEARBOOK OF EDUCATION** Produced in association with the University of London's Institute of Education. London, Evans Brothers Limited, 1965– . Various prices.

An international, monographic-type, English-language yearbook. Individual volumes consist of approximately 400 pages of comprehensive, commissioned articles on important international subjects by experts from many geographic areas and educational disciplines. The latest yearbook, *Education and Rural Development, 1973-74* ($20.00), can be obtained from International Publications Service, 114 East 32nd Street, New York, N.Y. 10016. *Universities Facing the Future, 1972-73* ($15.00), is available from Jossey-Bass, 615 Montgomery Street, San Francisco, California 94111. *Education Within Industry, 1968* ($16.50), *Education in Cities, 1970* ($16.50), and *Higher Education in a Changing World, 1971-72* ($16.50) also are distributed by International Publications. Back issues, including *Examinations, 1969,* can be obtained from the English publisher.

PERIODICALS

It is difficult to select 10, or even 50, of the best educational journals from the thousands published. All of them have some value, and the educational audience is so large that many different subject-oriented journals are produced. Some specific titles are mentioned in Chapters 8 through 13. Choosing journals intelligently requires matching journals with readers. To decide on an appropriate journal, it is necessary first to analyze one's interests (music teaching? alternative schools? parent involvement?) and then to locate a journal that reports or represents these interests and points of view.

In addition to *Educator's World* (B39), which contains a comprehensive listing, with descriptions, of approximately 2,000 educational journals, some other sources also are valuable. Library browsing, or asking around, can be very helpful; checking subject indexes, periodical lists, or contents pages of journals, or using *Education Index* and/or *CIJE* to find names of periodicals that cover areas of interest also is recommended. Articles themselves can be scanned for content and readability. The periodicals indexed in *Education Index* are a good place to start, since these originally were selected for value. *Education Index* and *CIJE* both include lists of educational publications, complete with current addresses and prices.

The Federal Government also publishes some inexpensive and worthwhile periodicals on education and child welfare, including *American Education* and *Children Today*. These are listed, complete with prices, in the February issue of the *Monthly Catalog of United States Government Publications* (F15).

Educator's World—although it does not index by subject— provides comprehensive information (depending, of course, on the cooperation of the publisher) that includes name, address, editor, contents, frequency of publication, cost, availability of back issues, circulation, and (sometimes) manuscript requirements and advertising information. If *Educator's World* is not available to the user, the following tools may help:

C17 **AMERICA'S EDUCATION PRESS**   By Educational Press Assn. of America. 32nd Edition. Syracuse, N.Y., 1974. $7.50.

This publication changes its format slightly in each edition, but does offer information on approximately 2,300 U.S. and Canadian educational publications, arranged by title, with access by region, state, and subject. Coded entries include such information as starting date, publisher, price, circulation, and size.

C18 **GUIDE TO PERIODICALS IN EDUCATION AND ITS ACADEMIC DISCIPLINES**   By William L. Camp. 2nd Edition. Metuchen, N.J., Scarecrow Press, 1975. $19.50.

Contains information obtained from the editors and publishers of approximately 600 nationally distributed education and education-related periodicals issued in the United States. It is intended to provide authors, educators, and researchers with detailed data necessary for the preparation of manuscripts to be submitted for publication; also a valuable reference tool for students, librarians, publishers, and others interested in education or education-related journals. Entries are arranged alphabetically within 57 general and subject categories, with a master list of subject headings to assist in locating subjects in the general classification system. Each entry contains subscription information, editorial address, a statement of editorial policy, information on manuscript preparation and disposition, copyright, and additional significant information. Includes subject and title indexes.

C19 **ULRICH'S INTERNATIONAL PERIODICALS DIRECTORY**   A Classified Guide to Current Periodicals, Foreign and Domestic. New York, R. R. Bowker, 1932– . 2 Vols. Biennial. $46.50/set.

Provides information on approximately 55,000 periodicals from all over the world, arranged alphabetically by title under subject categories. It contains approximately 800 abstracting and indexing services of possible interest to educators, plus thousands of periodicals. Information on each includes title, frequency of publication, price, name and address of publisher, circulation, languages used in text, first year published, type of materials covered, and availability of microfilms of periodicals. The fifteenth edition includes, for the first time, International Standard Book Numbers as well as Dewey Decimal Classification numbers. *Irregu-*

lar Serials and Annuals, also from Bowker ($43.50), provides biblio-
graphic and buying information on some educational publications which
come out irregularly.

NEWSLETTERS

Educational newsletters, like educational monographs, are increasing in number—probably for similar reasons: the need for
information, combined with a shortage of time and money. They
are simple to produce, and, at base-level, can be done by one
person with a typewriter and access to an offset press.

   A rather extensive commercial series of newsletters that reports
the Washington scene with thoroughness and accuracy is published by Education News Services of Capitol Publications (2400
Pennsylvania Avenue, N.W., Washington, D.C. 20037). Titles
include *Report on Education Research, Report on Preschool Education,
Report on Education of the Disadvantaged,* and *Education Daily.* Croft
Educational Services (100 Garfield Avenue, New London, Connecticut 06320) also issues an extensive and competent series of
newsletters for groups of teachers and various levels of administrators: of these, *Education Summary* is the most comprehensive
and popular. *Education Recaps,* published by Educational Testing
Service (O13) assembles, in one place, interesting bits and pieces
from other newsletters and current sources, and is far less costly
than most newsletters.

   Newsletters issued by the various ERIC clearinghouses have been
limited by the rise in paper prices and by governmental regulation. They vary in quality and are published irregularly—
sometimes as news bulletins—but can contain valuable information and can serve as free subject updates. Newsletters issued by
other information sources are mentioned in context.

   Most newsletters concerning education are included in
Educator's World (B39) if they existed in 1972. Another source for
selection is:

C20   **STANDARD DIRECTORY OF NEWSLETTERS**   1st Edition.
         New York, Oxbridge Publishing, 1972. $20.
This directory, published in a format similar to a newsletter, organizes
newsletters by 230 categories, lists related categories, and cross-indexes

by subjects. Information on newsletters includes title; address and names of editor, publisher, and advertising director; description of editorial content and scope; purpose; year founded; subscription rate; price per copy; qualifications for receiving publication; circulation; and advertising rates. It contains some interesting discussions on the history and current status of newsletters in the front of the directory, and an alphabetical title index at the end. While at current prices ordering newsletters on the basis of information given here is not recommended, information in the *Standard Directory of Newsletters* can be used to contact publishers for sample copies.

5 | Bibliographies and Review Sources

Most of the information sources discussed in this chapter are bibliographies on limited facets of education or on education over a limited period of time. Due to the nature of educational publishing, there is no simple method or combination of sources that can be used to obtain a comprehensive, exhaustive list of publications in this field. The first section of this chapter, Reference Books and Research Tools, should be helpful for users who require access to more specialized reference research tools, some of which have useful sections on research methods and how to use reference books. These can be supplemented with the sources listed under Directories of Resources (B29 to B51) in Chapter 3.

The section of this chapter on Continuing Bibliographies suggests some useful updating and selection tools. Others can be found under Yearbooks and Monograph Series in Chapter 4. Some extremely useful annual guides and compilations were discontinued during the last two years, but a few which can be valuable for retrospective searches have been included here.

A good way to keep current with bibliographies that appear in the ERIC system is by checking the descriptor "Annotated Bibliographies" in *Resources in Education,* to see whether relevant subject bibliographies exist.

Other selection tools can be found in the section of this chapter on Reviews and Bibliographic Sources. The heading "Book Reviews" in *Education Index* also is a good means of locating reviews of particular books, as is *Child Development Abstracts and Bibliographies.*

Reviews of children's books and media materials are covered in the discussion on selecting instructional materials (Chapter 9); test reviews are discussed in the chapter on measurement (Chapter 13).

A few selected bibliographies also have been included in this chapter. Usually, they are outstanding for organization, annotations, or coverage; sometimes they deal with educationally significant topics; generally, they go well beyond the standard ERIC sources of many recent bibliographies. All are time-savers.

Three book collections for school libraries, professional libraries, and education libraries (D44, D46, and D50) offer basic reading lists on a wide variety of educational topics and, as such, are good starting points for subject searches, as well as for comprehensive guides to educational literature. Other sources for subject bibliographies are the encyclopedias listed in Chapter 2, the information sources listed in Chapters 14, 15, and 16, and the organizations listed in *Educator's World*.

For anyone trying to keep current with all of the educational literature, the bibliographic tools discussed in *Fundamental Reference Sources* (D2) will be useful.

Fundamentally, trade books are covered in *Books in Print, Forthcoming Books in Print, Subject Guide to Books in Print, Cumulative Book Index,* and other bibliographical tools discussed in *Fundamental Reference Sources. Alternatives in Print* [1] lists approximately 20,000 publications by some 800 social-change publishers, some relevant to alternative and innovative education.

Resources in Education (F20) lists some ephemeral and research materials. These are fairly widely distributed in microfiche. Others are covered in the *Vertical File Index* and the *P.A.I.S. Bulletin* (F16).

Relevant Federal Government publications, other than those issued by ERIC, can be found in the *Monthly Catalog of United States Government Publications* (F15) or may be available from the National Technical Information Service.

State publications are more difficult to locate, although a certain proportion of them can be located through the *Checklist of State Publications* and others can be found through lists issued by state printers, state libraries, and state departments of education. Two recent articles in the *Library Journal* by Peter Hernon (especially "State Publications: A Bibliographic Guide for Reference Collec-

---

[1] Compiled by the Task Force on Alternatives in Print, Social Responsibilities Round Table, American Library Association. San Francisco, Glide Publications, 1973. $6.95.

tions," *99*:2810–2822, Nov. 1, 1974) provide a helpful guide to locating state publications.

Educational periodical articles are covered in a wide variety of indexing and abstracting journals (see Chapter 7). Of these, *Current Index to Journals in Education* is the most comprehensive, while *Education Index* is more current; both include lists of periodicals with current prices. Another source, *Educator's World,* provides a list of 2,000 American educational publications.

REFERENCE BOOKS AND RESEARCH TOOLS

D1   **DOCUMENTATION IN EDUCATION**   (Formerly *How to Locate Education Data.*) By Arvid J. and Mary A. Burke. 5th Edition. New York, Teachers' College Press, 1967. $9.95.

Although this publication is not current, it is extremely thorough and well-organized, and perhaps the best tool for anyone interested in retrospective or specialized research beyond the educational information sources listed in this *Guide.*

D2   **FUNDAMENTAL REFERENCE SOURCES**   By Frances Neel Cheney. Chicago, American Library Assn., 1971. $8.50.

A valuable, reasonably current guide to reference sources in the fields of biography, bibliography, statistics, linguistics, and geography, with an excellent section on guidelines for reviewing and selecting reference books. Although this book was intended as an introductory textbook for the beginning library school student, it should prove equally helpful to anyone who needs to locate reference sources in these fields. The sections on statistics, linguistics, and bibliography should be particularly helpful for teachers. The indexing is good; annotations are superb. The book can be updated by *American Reference Books Annual* (D14).

D3   **GUIDE TO AMERICAN EDUCATIONAL DIRECTORIES**   Edited by Barry T. Klein. 4th Edition. Rye, N.Y., Todd Publications, 1974. $22.50.

Lists approximately 2,700 directories in the field of education published by educational organizations, foundations, government agencies, private companies, and research firms. Descriptive entries are arranged alphabetically by title under 100 subject classifications and include directory name, bibliographic description, publisher, price, subject covered, and address of publisher or source.

D4 **A GUIDE TO INFORMATION SOURCES FOR READING**
Compiled by Bonnie M. Davis. Newark, Del., International
Reading Assn., 1972. $2.50 (paperback).
This guide, published jointly by the National Reading Center and the
International Reading Association, is devoted to an explication of the
reference books, directories, indexes, associations, journals, bibliographies, etc., that are useful for research in reading. Since reading is a
multidisciplinary field, information sources extend through education,
research methods, behavioral science, and medicine. Materials are
divided into reading information sources, general information sources,
and related information sources. Complete and helpful, with sections on
bibliographies, journals, and conference proceedings; comprehensive for
reading sources and intelligently selective in other fields, with extensive
overall coverage. Annotations are concise and salient. Information is
current as of 1972, although prices are not included.

D5 **HANDBOOK OF EDUCATIONAL RESEARCH** A Guide to
Methods and Materials. By Tyrus Hillway. Boston, Houghton
Mifflin, 1969. $4.95 (paperback).
An all-purpose guide, intended to "take the fear out of research," which
does a good job of combining materials and methods in one book. It
includes an introduction to research, a guide to methods, a manual of
style, and a form for preparation of research reports, as well as a checklist
of guides to library materials.

D6 **HOW TO FIND OUT** By G. Chandler. 4th Edition. London,
Pergamon, 1974. $8.50.
This concise British guide provides descriptive examples of sources of
information—books and nonbooks—on all topics, with subject summaries
on sources of information in various fields. Arranged by Dewey Decimal
Classification.

D7 **INFORMATION SERVICES FOR ACADEMIC ADMINIS-
TRATION** By J. B. Lon Hefferlin and Ellis L. Phillips, Jr. San
Francisco, Jossey–Bass, 1971. $7.50.
A thoroughly competent and practical survey of sources of information
in higher education. It discusses problems of obtaining information, reports the results of a survey on the information needs of college and
university administrators, and analyzes and describes six types of academic information services: internal campus communication, communication between institutions, institutes and workshops, publications,
consulting services, and information centers. The last chapter is a
directory, complete with addresses and telephone numbers, of ap-

proximately 90 agencies and organizations concerned with academic administration; but there also is much directory information throughout. The sections on publications, information centers, workshops, and consulting services in particular contain informative, evaluative annotations and clear referrals to other sources of information. An important, well-done book, suitable for both browsing and reference.

D8   INFORMATION SOURCES AND SERVICES IN EDUCATION
       By Lorraine Mathies. Bloomington, Ind., Phi Delta Kappa
       Educational Foundation, 1973. $0.50. (*Fastback* No. 16)
A concise and inexpensive little handbook, primarily intended for college students. It includes a useful guide to using ERIC manually and via computer, an introduction to ERIC clearinghouses and other national and regional information systems, and selected reference works.

D9   PUBLICATIONS OF THE UNITED NATIONS SYSTEM: A
       Reference Guide   Edited by Harry N. M. Winton. New York, R.R.
       Bowker, 1972. $11.45.
An annotated listing, arranged by subject, of hundreds of reference works and periodicals published by the United Nations and its related agencies. It is the most convenient and accessible tool for studying the United Nations or international education. Contains extensive subject indexes.

D10   THE SOURCE BOOK FOR HIGHER EDUCATION: A Critical
       Guide to Literature and Information on Access to Higher
       Education   By Warren W. Willingham, with Elsie P. Begle et al.
       New York, College Entrance Examination Board, 1973. $15.
A topical bibliography and directory with chapters on guidance, admissions, financing, curriculum, evaluation, manpower, utilizations, organization and administration, and structure. Contains 1,519 well-annotated items. Mr. Willingham, who headed the College Board's Access Research project, anticipates that this compilation should prove useful and relevant for 10 to 15 years. Its value extends beyond a narrowly conceived field of higher education. There are good references on guidance, decision making, economics of education, the talented student, and a fine guide to college guides, as well as a directory of institutions, agencies, associations, research centers, and special commissions relevant to higher education.

D11   SOURCES IN EDUCATIONAL RESEARCH   By Theodore
       Manheim et al. Detroit, Mich., Wayne State University Press, 1969.
       Vol. I. $11.95.
A bibliographic tool derived from a large education collection: a selected

and annotated bibliography devoted first to educational research as a discipline and then to separate fields. A good guide for research, as well as a good buying guide for an educational research center.

D12 **SOURCES OF INFORMATION IN THE SOCIAL SCIEN-CES** A Guide to the Literature. By Carl M. White et al. 2nd Edition, Revised. Chicago, American Library Assn., 1973. $25.

This basic, scholarly guide to printed sources in the social sciences has added a much needed section on geography and an improved subject index. Its education section lists 607 titles appropriate for an academic study of education, with annotations of some reference titles, including a substantial number of abstract journals, retrospective bibliographies, and directories of colleges.

D13 **WHO-WHAT-WHERE-WHEN-HOW-WHY MADE EASY: A Guide to the Practical Use of Reference Books** By Mona McCormick. Chicago, Quadrangle Press, 1971. $5.95.

A lively, well-written, and lavishly illustrated guide on where to locate and how to use reference tools competently and well. Written for students and the general reader, it is an excellent resource for teachers and students at any level. The illustrations (which include sample pages, with clear explanations) and the discussions enable the reader to see examples from the books described. Chapters on note-taking, report writing, and bibliographic form are brief, clear, and helpful. Reprinted in paperback as the *New York Times Guide to Reference Materials* (Popular Library, 1972, $1.50).

CONTINUING BIBLIOGRAPHIES

D14 **AMERICAN REFERENCE BOOKS ANNUAL (ARBA)** Edited by Bohdan S. Wynar. 6th Edition. Littleton, Colo., Libraries Unlimited, 1975. $23.

A well-annotated annual listing, with evaluative reviews by competent subject specialists: published each year in April, it aims to be a permanent record of reference books published in the United States during the previous year. It includes some works from the U.S. Government Printing Office, some from the United Nations and UNESCO, plus a few foreign titles.

The section on education provides an easy means of keeping current with new tools and sources in education, generally including 80 to 100 numbered and annotated reviews of bibliographies, dictionaries, encyclopedias, handbooks and yearbooks, directories, instructional materials, biographical tools, and works on reading and other special topics—all with accurate citations and prices.

The book is indexed, browsable, interesting, and easy to use. Approximately 1,800 reference books are reviewed in the sixth edition, many in education-related fields such as statistics, sociology, women's studies, and minority groups. A separate (author, title, subject) *Index to American Reference Books Annual, 1970-1974* is available from the same publisher.

D15   **ANNUAL EDUCATIONAL BIBLIOGRAPHY OF THE IN-TERNATIONAL BUREAU OF EDUCATION, 1969** By International Bureau of Education. Geneva, 1970. $4. From: Unipub, P.O. Box 433, New York, N.Y. 10016.

This is the last edition of the annual list of materials added to the International Educational Library, which serves as a classified multinational catalog and summary of significant education books of the year. Information formerly included in this publication is now incorporated into the International Bureau of Education's quarterly, *Educational Documentation and Information.*

D16   **CATALOG. U.S. DEPARTMENT OF HEALTH, EDUCATION, AND WELFARE PUBLICATIONS, July 1974** By U.S. Department of Health, Education, and Welfare. Washington, D.C., 1972– . Free. From: Office of Administration and Management, HEW, 330 Independence Ave., S.W., Washington, D.C. 20201.

This cumulative publication—originally a quarterly—is generally published annually. As of November 1975, 1974 was the latest edition, issued at the end of that fiscal year (1973-74). It lists the publications of all HEW agencies: child development, civil rights, health, etc. Part of a new computerized sysem, it includes well-organized and well-annotated citations, with adequate purchase information and subject and title indexes, but omits authors and page numbers. If the *Education Price List* is discontinued, this will be the only comprehensive list of federal education publications.

D17   **EDUCATIONAL DOCUMENTATION AND INFORMATION: Bulletin of the International Bureau of Education** By International Bureau of Education. Geneva, 1926– . Quarterly. $8/year. From: Unipub, P.O. Box 433, New York, N.Y. 10016.

The first part of this periodical, "Sources and Resources," consists of short descriptive articles on reference books and national and international institutions of educational documentation and research. The second part contains selected annotated bibliographies on specific themes, including adolescence, vocational education, innovation in secondary school curricula, and evaluation of achievements.

D18 **EDUCATION BOOK LIST, 1972-73** By Pi Lambda Theta. Bloomington, Ind., 1974. Annual. $2.95. From: 2000 E. 8th St., Bloomington, Ind. 47401.

Lists U.S. education books published in varied forms since 1926—under the supervision of Pi Lambda Theta since 1966. Currently, it is published each year, sometime between March and July. The latest edition lists approximately 1,000 education books published between July 1972 and July 1973 and is arranged in broad subject classes, based on Library of Congress classification. Information on each book includes author, title, publisher, date of publication, number of pages, price, and Library of Congress catalog card number. This book list is comprehensive, if out of date; it covers all areas of education, as well as such materials as study outlines, workbooks, manuals, and textbooks, but omits pamphlets under 50 pages. It contains an author index, subject cross-references, and a thoroughly annotated list of "Outstanding Books" of the year. This work, like others dependent on the cooperation of education publishers, does miss some education books published by education laboratories and other nonpublishers. Back issues are available for $1.50 each.

D19 **EDUCATION PRICE LIST 31** By U.S. Government Printing Office. 56th Edition. Washington, D.C. 1973. Free. From: U.S. Government Bookstores or the Superintentent of Documents, U.S. Government Printing Office, Washington, D.C. 20402.

A complete list of "in-print" government educational publications published by the Superintendent of Documents up to January 1973; available in paper form, arranged alphabetically by subject and then by title. It provides an extensive index of excellent materials, including directories and authoritative materials on topics such as federal aid to education, foreign education, etc. An order blank is included at the end, as well as a list of retail government bookstores. The U.S. Government Printing Office price lists, like this extremely valuable location tool, may be discontinued because of the difficulties in keeping prices current in a period of rapid price rises. A substitute, *Publications of the Office of Education,* issued in July 1974, lists publications from June 30, 1972 to July 1, 1974. To receive a free copy, write to the Information and Materials Branch, U.S. Office of Education, Washington, D.C. 20202.

D20 **LIBRARY AND INFORMATION SERVICES TODAY (LIST)** (Formerly *Library and Information Science Today.*) Edited by Paul Wasserman. 4th Edition. Detroit, Gale Research, 1974. $38.

A directory of more than 1,300 ongoing research efforts, projects, and books dealing with library and information science research, mostly in the United States and Britain, with several sections that might interest the educational researcher: reading research, use of media in education, media other than print, computer software, learning behavior, plus others of marginal interest. Information on projects includes names of investigators, project titles, funding agencies or sources, names and addresses of institutions, project dates, and full descriptions of the projects.

D21 **LITERATURE OF HIGHER EDUCATION, 1972** Edited by Lewis E. Mayhew. San Francisco, Jossey–Bass, 1971– . Annual. $8.75.

The latest published volume in an excellent, but short-lived, series which annually reviewed approximately 200 recently published books: intelligently selected and annotated; arranged by categories.

D22 **QUESTIONNAIRE STUDIES COMPLETED, 1972** (Bibliography No. 43.) By Educational Research Service. Washington, D.C., 1972. $1. From: Suite 1012, 1815 N. Fort Myer Dr., Arlington, Va. 22209.

The 43rd, and final, annual bibliography of completed questionnaires published by ERS. These bibliographies provide access to a wide variety of questionnaires on education; a research tool that has declined both quantitatively and qualitatively over the years (from more than 200 entries per year to 30 entries in 1972). The surveys, maintained in an ERS Clearinghouse of Questionnaire Studies, were collected through the reporting efforts of state and local school systems.

D23 **RECENT PUBLICATIONS IN THE SOCIAL AND BE-HAVIORAL SCIENCES: The ABS Supplement** 9th Supplement to *The ABS Guide to Recent Publications in the Social and Behavioral Sciences.* By American Behavioral Scientist. Beverly Hills, Calif., ABS, Div. of Sage Publications, Inc., 1966– . $15.00; $12.50, standing order.

An annual compilation, published around March, of approximately 1,000 numbered, annotated citations of books, articles, government reports, and a few pamphlets selected by social scientists as being significant contributions theoretically or methodologically; sometimes selected on the basis of the areas investigated. Essentially provides a well-rounded selection from the previous year or so of significant materials in the social sciences, with emphasis on interdisciplinary studies. Citations are arranged alphabetically by author. Brief annotations are clear and well-written. A logical, compact title and subject index makes the volumes easy to use. This is a handy tool for reviewing important contributions in education and social science fields allied to education.

The original guide, similar in arrangement to its supplements, listed and indexed 6,664 publications of the early 1960s. With the publication of the ninth supplement in March 1975, the entire set provides a comprehensive review of more than 16,000 selected works.

New Studies in the Social and Behavioral Sciences, published every two months as part of the journal *American Behavioral Scientist* (bimonthly, $18/year), provides a means of keeping current with significant publications in the social sciences.

The publishers are considering updating and publishing a new edition of the original and complete *Guide.*

D24 **RESEARCH ANNUAL ON INTERGROUP RELATIONS, 1972** Edited by Melvin M. Tumin and Barbara A. Anderson. New York, Quadrangle Books and Anti-Defamation League of B'nai B'rith, 1958– . $8.95; $4.95, paperback (available only from the Anti-Defamation League of B'nai B'rith).

Lack of funds has caused the discontinuance of this not-quite-annual publication, prepared under the auspices of B'nai B'rith. It is an international listing of studies dealing with relationships between ethnic, racial, religious, national, and linguistic groups—based on questionnaires which drew responses from 1,500 of 22,500 addressees. Includes 904 of these, mostly from the United States, where much of the work was concerned with human relations curricula and interracial reactions in the schools. Numbered entries are assigned to specific categories in an elaborate, but well-cross-referenced, system backed up by an author index that includes institutional authors. Bibliographic information is at the minimal acceptable level, but authors' addresses are generally listed. The brief descriptions provide categorization as to status—ongoing, proposed, completed, or published. Some of the relevant areas included in this work are general education, foreign education, school administration, curriculum, disadvantaged children, teacher preparation, bilingualism, and delinquency.

D25 **REVIEW OF EDUCATIONAL RESEARCH** By American Educational Research Assn. Washington, D.C., 1931– . 5 issues/year. $10.

Specializes in "critical integrative reviews of research literature bearing on education." Up to June 1970, each issue was devoted to a single topic; initially, 15 major topics in education were continuously updated on a revolving basis over a three-year period. Although its reviews are no longer continuous, they are still high-quality.

D26 **REVIEW OF RESEARCH IN EDUCATION** Edited by Fred N. Kerlinger. Itasca, Ill., F. E. Peacock, 1973– . 3 Vols. Vol. 1 – 1973, $12.50; Vol. 2 – 1974, $15.00; Vol. 3 – 1975, $13.50.

An ongoing review series, prepared by the American Educational Research Association, that attempts a "disciplined inquiry in education through critical and synthesizing essays" by covering the major substantive and methodological concerns of educational research over a period of years. The literature covered in the review articles emphasizes current research, but is not limited to materials appearing in any definite period of time.

Volume 1 consists of nine chapters dealing with various aspects of learning and instruction, school organization, effectiveness, and change; the history of education; and research methodology. Volume 2 covers the broad areas of child development and educational intervention, the economics of education, and organizational theory. Volume 3 contains a substantial section on comparative education.

REVIEWS AND BIBLIOGRAPHIC SOURCES

D27 **BIBLIOGRAPHIC INDEX** New York, H. W. Wilson, 1938– . 3 issues/year, with annual cumulation. Prices based on size of periodical holdings of subscribing libraries.

This bibliography of bibliographies includes bibliographies (with approximately 40 citations) appearing in books, pamphlets, and periodicals. It is not annotated; arrangement is by subject, with full bibliographic information, including source. Approximately 1,900 periodicals are regularly examined for bibliographies.

D28 **BOOK REVIEW DIGEST** New York, H. W. Wilson, 1905– . Monthly, with annual compilations. Sold on service basis, based on annual book budget.

A digest and index of book reviews from more than 70 periodicals and journals in all fields. Covers more than 6,000 books a year—popular rather than scholarly. Book review digests are arranged alphabetically by author, with price, publisher, descriptive notes, and citations for all reviews. An excellent reviewing tool for the books it covers. Title and subject indexes for efficient and fast reference are cumulated every five years. An author and title index to the books included in the *Book Review Digest* from 1905 through 1974 is scheduled for publication in the winter of 1975-1976.

D29 **BOOK REVIEW INDEX**   Detroit, Mich., Gale Research, 1965– .
Bimonthly and cumulative. $68/year.
A computer-produced index of approximately 70,000 reviews of 35,000
new books that appeared in 235 periodicals. Each entry cites author's
name, title of book, reviewing publication, date, and page on which review
appeared. Valuable for its comprehensiveness and currency.

D30 **BOOK REVIEW INDEX TO SOCIAL SCIENCE PERIODI-
CALS**   Edited by C. Edward Wall. Ann Arbor, Mich., Pierian
Press, 1970– . Annual. $25.
Indexes book reviews from approximately 450 journals in the fields of
sociology, education, history, political science, economics, anthropology,
and geography.

D31 **MENTAL HEALTH BOOK REVIEW INDEX: An Annual Bibliography of Books and Book Reviews in the Behavioral Sciences**   New York, Council on Research in Bibliography, 1956– .
Annual. $10/year; $132/complete set. From: Paul Klapper Library,
Queens College of the City of New York, Flushing, N.Y. 11367.
This annual review, unfortunately discontinued in 1972, was prepared by
a team of specialists and librarians who selected and collated reviews of
approximately 300 significant books and monographs in the fields of
mental health and behavioral sciences. This exercise in socio-bibliography
integrated book citations from a wide variety of journals in the behavioral
sciences, using authoritative cross-disciplinary evaluation as a means of
studying the problems of access to knowledge, and uncovered many good
books in education not widely reviewed.

D32 **READERS ADVISORY SERVICE: Selected Topical Booklists**
Edited by Leonard Cohan. New York, Science Associates/Inter-
national, 1973– . Annual (15 to 20 issues/quarter). $49.50/year.
A new reference tool that brings together approximately 75 useful
annotated bibliographies, reading lists, guides to the literature, and
booklists—which were compiled and written by bibliographical specialists
in libraries, information centers, scholarly societies, and professional
associations. Provided in loose-leaf format, accompanied by a fully
updated, comprehensive subject and title index and Dewey Decimal and
Library of Congress Classification numbers. Topics are current and
include many of potential interest to educators: Afro-Americans, aging,
American history, American Indians, biography, biology, Black studies,
book review sources, busing, computers, consumerism, environment,
education, educational research, mental retardation, Mexican-

Americans, narcotics, occupations, psychology, reading, recreation, term papers, urban education, and women.

SELECTED BIBLIOGRAPHIES

D33 **BEHAVIOR MODIFICATION IN CHILD AND SCHOOL MENTAL HEALTH: An Annotated Bibliography on Applications with Parents and Teachers** By Daniel G. Brown. Washington, D.C., U.S. Government Printing Office, 1971. $0.30.
This bibliography should be required background reading for any teacher, district, or school considering behavior modification. It presents 118 selected and annotated references to reports on (largely successful) applications of behavior modification by parents and teachers. Precise, informative annotations include accurate citations and complete descriptions of the works cited, plus the address of the author of each paper. Publisher, address, and price are included for books. A detailed subject index leads to references that deal with topics such as "disruptive classroom behavior," "ethical and moral issues," and "fears."

D34 **BIBLIOGRAPHY ON HUMAN INTELLIGENCE** By Logan Wright, for National Clearinghouse for Mental Health Information. Washington, D.C., U.S. Government Printing Office, 1970. $2.50. From: National Institute of Mental Health, 5600 Fishers Lane, Rockville, Md. 20852.
Contains 6,736 numbered entries of reference materials on the psychology of human intelligence, including books, articles, and dissertations. Categories include historical antecedents, related concepts, theoretical works, nature of intelligence, factors influencing intelligence, and group intelligence tests.

D35 **COMPUTERS AND EDUCATION: An International Bibliography on Computer Education** Edited by H. J. Van Der Aa. New York, Science Associates/International, 1970. $15 (paperback).
Provides abstracts of more than 1,800 articles of the 1960s—mostly in English, but also in French and German—dealing with education about computers and computers in education, plus related areas such as programmed instruction, learning theory, and television, with many abstracts on computers in elementary and secondary schools and training for automation professions. No subject index, but extensive cross-references.

D36 **DAY CARE: An Annotated Bibliography** By Alberta Wells. Minneapolis, Minn., Institute for Interdisciplinary Studies, 1971. 2 Vols. Vol. 1, $17.40 (ED 068 199); Vol. 2, $2.60 (paperback) (ED 068 200); microfiche, $0.75 each. From: ERIC Document Reproduction Service, P.O. Box 190, Arlington, Va. 22210.

An excellent comprehensive bibliography of 1,700 items examined by the Day Care Policy Studies Group of the Institute for Interdisciplinary Studies in preparing a 10-volume report of the study of day care policy and research needs. Materials are arranged by major categories: general issues, child development, specific programs, personnel, economic issues, licensing standards, legislation and regulation, special issues, evaluation, facilities and supplies, general resources, and public schools. These categories are further subdivided to form a useful series of bibliographies on all aspects of day care and early childhood education, including both popular and scholarly materials.

D37 **THE EDUCATION OF THE MINORITY CHILD: A Comprehensive Bibliography of 10,000 Selected Entries** Edited by Meyer Weinberg. Chicago, Integrated Education Assn., 1970. $10.95; $3.95, paperback.

This 10,000-item bibliography was financed by the U.S. Department of Health, Education, and Welfare and includes just about everything: books, articles, dissertations, and congressional hearings. Its broad subject index includes various ethnic groups and such topics as poor whites, school organization, teachers in the classroom, law, and government. Also includes a list of 500 periodicals and a bibliography of 250 bibliographies.

D38 **FOR THE READING TEACHER: An Annotated Index to** *Elementary English,* **1924-1970** Edited by Larry A. Harris and E. Marcia Kimmel. Urbana, Ill., National Council of Teachers of English, 1972. $3 (paperback). From: 1111 Kenyon Rd., Urbana, Ill. 61801.

A well-organized, annotated bibliography of nearly 50 years of articles from *Elementary English* related to various aspects of reading and teaching English. Thirty-six categories are set forth in the detailed table of contents, which also serves as a subject classification for all materials on reading. These are, in effect, a series of subject bibliographies on topics such as linguistics, readability, remedial reading, evaluation, readiness, and developmental reading. 715 items are included, with well-written, useful annotations, as well as an author index.

This project was sponsored by two ERIC clearinghouses which have now merged to form the ERIC Clearinghouse for Reading and Communication Skills.

D39 **INSTRUCTIONAL OBJECTIVES: A National Compendium** By G. Michael Kuhn and Lorraine R. Gay. Tallahassee, Fla., Florida State Dept. of Education—Div. of Elementary and Secondary Education, 1972. Microfiche, $0.65; hard copy, $6.58. ED 062 743. From: ERIC Document Reproduction Service, P.O. Box 190, Arlington, Va. 22210.

An annotated bibliography dealing with education objectives, course objectives, and behavioral objectives.

D40 **INTERNATIONAL EDUCATION RESOURCES: A Summary of OE-Funded Research Projects and Reports, 1956-71.** Compiled by Karen Bruner, Kent Weeks, and Pat Kern. Washington, D.C., U.S. Government Printing Office, 1972. $3.50.

A needed, comprehensive compilation which brings visibility for the first time to that large portion of OE-funded programs having international dimensions not sponsored by the Institute of International Studies under NDEA Title VI, Section 607. Lists 450 projects, complete with ERIC abstracts, arranged by traditional subjects and grade levels and cross-indexed by geographic areas. The major drawback is the computer printout format, which seriously impedes readability and browsability.

D41 **INTERNATIONAL GUIDE TO EDUCATIONAL DOCUMENTATION 1960-1965** 2nd Edition. Paris, UNESCO, 1972. $28 (paperback). From: Unipub, P.O. Box 433, New York, N.Y. 10016.

A three-language (English, French, Spanish) updating, as of 1965, of resources in educational documentation in 95 countries, presented in the form of annotated bibliographies covering national directories, major educational bibliographies, and publications. More are planned.

D42 **INVENTORY OF CURRENT RESEARCH ON POST-SECONDARY EDUCATION** By J. B. Lon Hefferlin et al. Berkeley, Calif., Center for Research and Development in Higher Education, University of California, 1972. $3.

Sponsored by the Ellis L. Phillips Foundation, this is a well-done inventory of 1,129 research projects—under way or recently completed—in the United States and Canada. Numbered and annotated entries are arranged alphabetically by major researcher and include the name, title, address, and telephone number of the researcher; the scope and methodology of the study; and the source of financial support for the study. Projects are indexed by subject and institution.

D43 **LITERATURE AND THE READER: Research in Response to Literature, Reading Interests, and the Teaching of Literature** By Alan C. Purves and Richard Beach. Urbana, Ill., National Council of Teachers of English (NCTE), 1972. $3.90. From: 1111 Kenyon Rd., Urbana, Ill. 61801.

A substantial literature review, in practical narrative form (followed by references), of research dealing with psychological, humanistic, and aesthetic interactions between literature and the reader, with a cutoff date around 1970, but with due value given to older research. Studies are divided into three nontaxonomic categories: response to literature, reading interests, and teaching of literature. Discussions are thorough, logically organized, analytic, and evaluative. The bibliographies included are substantial and well-selected. One of the many excellent research reviews of NCTE.

This project was carried out with the assistance of the National Endowment for the Humanities and the University of Illinois.

D44 **THE NEW YORK UNIVERSITY LIST OF BOOKS IN EDUCATION** Compiled by Barbara S. Marks. New York, Citation Press, 1968. $8 (paperback).

This list, comprised of books recommended by the New York University education faculty, contains approximately 2,900 titles, annotated and arranged under 178 subject headings. Although not all of them are still available for purchase, this is a competent guide for colleges and universities that want to build an education collection.

D45 **NON-FORMAL EDUCATION: An Annotated International Bibliography** Edited by Rolland G. Paulston. New York, Praeger, 1972. $17.50.

Nonformal education in this international bibliography refers to structured, systematic learning, of brief duration, outside formal school hierarchies and structures. In the United States, the majority of entries refer to adult education, continuing education, management training, remedial training, and some projects involving infants, children, and youth; in the newly developing countries, most entries deal with adult education, health education, and community development. Items, selected from the Hillman Library of the University of Pittsburgh, were chosen because they were conceptually relevant, illustrative, and relatively recent.

Non-Formal Education contains 7,308 entries arranged in a classified structure. Major categories are orientation and basic issues, area studies, organizations, target-learner populations, program content, instructional methods and materials, and reference works (including bibliographies).

Annotations, when given, cover content, point of view presented, and research results. Also included is a chart comparison of the characteristics of formal and nonformal education. This extensive work has no overall index, but does have separate indexes for geographic areas and authors.

An unusual bibliography, valuable for international education as well as for education outside traditional structures.

D46 **RECOMMENDED MATERIALS FOR A PROFESSIONAL LIBRARY IN THE SCHOOL** Compiled by Helen J. Healy. Revised Edition. Kalamazoo, Mich., Michigan Assn. of School Libraries, 1969. $4. Out-of-Print.

An annotated list of books for educators, arranged by broad curriculum areas, with a supplementary annotated list of periodicals and a directory of publishers. These books were carefully selected to meet the practical needs of teachers.

D47 **REVIEWS AND INDEXES TO RESEARCH IN EDUCA-TIONAL MEDIA** By Thomas J. Johnson. St. Louis, Mo., CEMREL, Inc., 1972. 2 Vols. Vol. 1, $3.80; Vol. 2, $12.00.

The format is odd, but the research is thorough, in this series of literature searches covering periodicals, books, and assorted documents from 1900 to 1968. This one includes approximately 2,500 references arranged by an arbitrarily assigned *rec*ord *id*entification number (RECID)', with resumés for some items and none for others. Bibliographic information is fairly complete (prices, book pagination, and journal month, however, are omitted). Stylized resumés include purpose, methods, and results of studies. Also included are an author index and a Keyword-in-Context (KWIC) index which provides some subject access. Because of the numerical arrangement, items on the same topic (for example, comparison of the effectiveness of various media) are scattered, but the total compilation is quite impressive.

Four other titles in this series are *Reviews and Indexes to Research in Creativity* (1970, $5.00), *Reviews and Indexes to Research in Dance* (1970, $5.60), *Reviews and Indexes to Research in Film* (1970, $3.30), and *Reviews and Indexes to Research in Literature* (1970, $7.40).

D48 **SELECTED BIBLIOGRAPHY OF SPECIAL EDUCATION** By I. Ignacy Goldberg. New York, Teachers College Press, 1967. $4.75.

An extensive bibliography comprised of approximately 2,000 items, published mostly between 1955 and 1967 (with key items from earlier periods retained), selected by Dr. Goldberg (President of the American Association on Mental Deficiency, 1955-1966) with the assistance of graduate students and faculty at Columbia University. Although summaries are not included, the materials are categorized by type: physically handicapped, mentally retarded, gifted, emotionally and socially handicapped, and multiply handicapped, with another 300 references on rehabilitation of the mentally retarded.

D49 **A SELECTED GUIDE TO CURRICULUM LITERATURE: An Annotated Bibliography** By Louise L. Tyler. Washington, D.C., National Education Assn., 1970. $2 (paperback).
This rigorously annotated, conceptually organized book is part of the action and publication program of NEA's Center for the Study of Instruction—an attempt to explore the major issues in curriculum. This guide, which is more than just an annotated bibliography, is a must for any educator interested in curriculum issues.

D50 **THE TEACHERS' LIBRARY: How to Organize It and What to Include** By NEA and American Assn. of School Librarians. Washington, D.C., National Education Assn., 1968. $1.75 (paperback).
A comprehensive, well-rounded collection of books, pamphlets, films, filmstrips, and periodicals in education selected for a teachers' professional library by a joint committee of the American Association of School Librarians and NEA. Arranged by Dewey Decimal Classification, with brief annotations, it is perhaps more research oriented than *Recommended Materials for a Professional Library in the School* (D46). A good checklist for anyone using or buying educational materials.

D51 **TELEVISION AND SOCIAL BEHAVIOR: An Annotated Bibliography of Research Focusing on Television's Impact on Children** Edited by Charles K. Atkin et al., National Institute of Mental Health. Washington, D.C., U.S. Government Printing Office, 1971. Free. Distributed by NIMH, 5600 Fishers Lane, Rockville, Md. 20852.
A well-researched, well-annotated review publication, based on a massive literature search under the guidance of the Surgeon General's Advisory Committee on Television and Social Behavior. Areas covered include television's content and programming, and their effect on the audience—especially children and youth. Two hundred eighty-five citations were selected for annotation, and an additional 250 items appear in a supplemental list.

6 | *Statistical Sources*

This chapter is devoted to statistical information sources; it also provides some tools that either contain valuable information or lead to other sources that do, and a few sources that suggest possibilities for statistical research in education. Abbott L. Ferriss' *Indicators of Trends in American Education* (New York, Russell Sage, 1969) provides in its introduction a discussion of the relationship between various statistical indicators and the need for more knowledge and measures of educational interactions and variables.

There are three major sources of nationwide U.S. education statistics: the National Education Association's Research Division, the Bureau of the Census (U.S. Department of Commerce), and the National Center for Educational Statistics (part of HEW's Office of Education, Education Division). UNESCO, which can be accessed through D9, D15, and D17, is the best international source, and A5 provides some international statistics. *Resources in Education* and the *P.A.I.S. Bulletin* are useful tools for keeping current with new documents and reports; the two terms (descriptors) "statistical surveys" and "statistical data" can locate most of the reports cited and abstracted in *Resources in Education*.

Two expensive but competent commercial sources which can provide access to educational statistics are the Curriculum Information Center, 1020 15th Street, Denver, Colorado 80202, (303) 573-7167, and the Congressional Information Service (see G6).

E1 **NATIONAL CENTER FOR EDUCATIONAL STATISTICS (NCES)** U.S. Office of Education, Rm. 3055, 400 Maryland Ave., S.W., Washington, D.C. 20202. (202) 245-8511

NCES bases its statistics on information furnished by school systems, institutions, and state and local agencies. Its statistics for schools per se generally are more comprehensive, although perhaps less accurate, than those collected by the Bureau of the Census. The current NCES catalog lists 61 available publications, most of which are more than two years behind the current calendar year. A list of publications, with ordering information and prices, will be furnished upon written request. Continuing publications include the *Digest of Educational Statistics* (annual), *Fall Statistics of Public Elementary and Secondary Day Schools* (annual), *Statistics of State School Systems* (biennial), *Opening Fall Enrollment in Higher Education* (annual), and *Financial Statistics of Institutions of Higher Education* (annual).

More recent statistics (which have been collected by NCES, but not published) are available from the Reference, Estimates, and Projections Branch at the headquarters office—the normal channel for queries on educational statistics. This office can be contacted for a free handy pocket folder, "Statistics of Trends in Education, 1962-63 to 1982-83"; other queries also will be answered, if possible.

NCES is now disseminating National Assessment of Educational Progress data in computer tape format. (See M26 for more details.)

In 1973, the Bureau of the Census, in cooperation with NCES, produced census statistics related to school districts (in addition to block statistics and large-area statistics). These are available from Dr. William Dorfman, Chief, Statistical Systems Branch, (202) 245-8760. If you are interested in obtaining demographic statistics for your school district or for school districts in your state, he is aware of what is available in print, tape, and microfiche.

Each state educational agency receives computer printouts of 103 items of information from the 1970 Census of Population and Housing from First Count Tape (a series) for state school districts (which provide a rather complete analysis of each district's housing and population), and computer printouts of geographic reference information for state school districts. If these cannot be located in your state department of education, contact Mr. Dorfman.

Two printed reports from school district tapes are planned for late 1975: *Social and Economic Characteristics of School Districts* and *School Resources and Community Characteristics*. Prices will be set by the U.S. Government Printing Office.

E2 **NATIONAL EDUCATION ASSOCIATION RESEARCH DI-
VISION** 1201 16th St., N.W., Washington, D.C. 20036. (202) 833-5462

This group issues its statistics much earlier than NCES issues its comparable statistical series; the figures generally are in agreement with those issued later by NCES. Its data are based on state estimates, preliminary data, and some direct reporting by teachers.

Rankings of the States ($2.00) comes out early every year and compares states on the basis of their programs and educational expenditures. *Estimates of School Statistics* ($1.50), published annually late in the calendar year (but early in the school year), provides statistics on current enrollment. Neither title is available for general distribution or sale. Other reports deal with the salaries and economic status of teachers and teacher supply and demand, although almost any topic may be covered.

E3   **U.S. DEPARTMENT OF COMMERCE, BUREAU OF THE CENSUS** Washington, D.C. 20233. (301) 763-7273
In the course of researching this chapter, it was found that users of census statistics express much admiration for their accuracy, authority, and thoroughness. Census reports are based on population surveys collected under carefully controlled procedures that link factors such as school enrollment with other personal characteristics on an individual basis.

The 1970 (19th) Census of Population used 120 million forms, 185 thousand workers, and tabulated 4 billion facts. Other less-known, ongoing Census Bureau surveys are based on continuing information from well-selected samples (often two percent or five percent of total population); while still other census series, all of which provide some statistics for education, deal with housing, governments (including school districts and state agencies), business (including education business and the media market), economics, and agriculture. Two significant reports are PC (2)-5B *Educational Attainment* ($3.75) and PC (2)-5C *Vocational Training* ($3.70).

Current Population Reports (based on a sample of 47,000 households interviewed eight times a year) issues information related to education in its P-20 and P-25 series, which deal with educational attainment, school enrollment, and projections of school enrollment to the year 2000. A complete list of the contents of these reports is available in the annual cumulations of the *Bureau of the Census Catalog*, obtainable on request. A suggested source for subject reports concerning education is Larry E. Suter, Chief, Educational and Social Stratification Branch, Population Division, Bureau of the Census, Washington, D.C. 20233, (301) 763-5050. Another helpful source for census users is the Users' Service Staff, Data User Services Bureau, Bureau of the Census, Washington, D.C. 20233, (301) 763-5238 and 763-7360. The *Census Users' Guide* is designed to assist individuals in using census materials effectively. Single copies of Bureau of the Census publications are available from the U.S. Department of Commerce field offices (see Figure 4).

For Information About Census Products and Services

Data Access and Use Laboratory, Data User Services Office, Bureau of the Census, Washington, D.C. 20233. Telephone: 301/763-7454 or 7455.

To Obtain or Order:

Computer Tape Products and Census Maps

(Summary Tapes, Test Tapes, MEDList, DAULists, Public Use Samples, Address Coding Guides, DIME Files, ADMATCH, etc.)

Users' Service Staff, Data User Services Office, Bureau of the Census, Washington, D.C. 20233. Telephone: 301/763-5266.

Microfiche of Final Printed Reports

National Technical Information Service, Springfield, Virginia 22151.

Microfilm of 1st and 3rd Count Tapes

Users' Service Staff (See Computer Tapes)

Special Tabulations

Users' Service Staff (See Computer Tapes)

To Obtain Order Forms for Reports:

(1970 Census Printed Reports and Microfiche, 1970 Census Users' Guide, Census Use Study Reports.)

Publications Distribution Section, Publications Services Division, Social and Economic Statistics Administration, Washington, D.C. 20233. Telephone: 301/763-5853.

Printed Reports

Superintendent of Documents, U.S. Government Printing Office, Washington, D.C. 20402, or any of the U.S. Department of Commerce Field Offices listed below.

Albuquerque, N. Mex., 87101, U.S. Courthouse
Anchorage, Alaska, 99501, Loussac-Sogn Bldg.
Atlanta, Ga., 30303, 75 Forsyth St., N.W.

Baltimore, Md., 21202, U.S. Customhouse
Birmingham, Ala., 35205, 908 S. 20th St.
Boston, Mass., 02203, John F. Kennedy Fed. Bldg.
Buffalo, N.Y., 14203, 117 Ellicott St.

Charleston, S.C., 29403, 334 Meeting St.
Charleston, W. Va., 25301, 500 Quarrier St.
Cheyenne, Wyo., 82001, 2120 Capitol Ave.
Chicago, Ill., 60604, 219 S. Dearborn St.
Cincinnati, Ohio, 45202, 550 Main St.
Cleveland, Ohio, 44114, 666 Euclid Ave.

Dallas, Tex., 75202, 1114 Commerce St.
Denver, Colo., 80202, Federal Building
Des Moines, Iowa, 50309, 210 Walnut St.
Detroit, Mich., 48226, Federal Bldg.

Greensboro, N.C., 27402, Federal Bldg.

Hartford, Conn., 06103, 450 Main St.
Honolulu, Hawaii, 96813, 1015 Bishop St.
Houston, Tex., 77002, 515 Rusk Ave.

Jacksonville, Fla., 32202, 400 West Bay St.

Kansas City, Mo., 64106, 911 Walnut St.

Los Angeles, Calif., 90015, 1031 S. Broadway

Memphis, Tenn., 38103, 147 Jefferson Ave.
Miami, Fla., 33130, 25 W. Flagler St.
Milwaukee, Wis., 53203, 238 W. Wisconsin Ave.
Minneapolis, Minn., 55401, 110 S. Fourth St.

New Orleans, La., 70130, 610 South St.
New York, N.Y., 10007, 26 Fed. Plaza, Foley Sq.

Philadelphia, Pa., 19107, 1015 Chestnut St.
Phoenix, Ariz., 85025, 230 N. First Ave.
Pittsburgh, Pa., 15222, 1000 Liberty Ave.
Portland, Oreg., 97204, 520 S.W. Morrison St.

Reno, Nev., 89502, 300 Booth St.
Richmond, Va., 23240, 400 North 8th St.

St. Louis, Mo., 63103, 1520 Market St.
Salt Lake City, Utah, 84111, 125 S. State St.
San Francisco, Calif., 94102, 450 Golden Gate Ave.
San Juan, P.R., 00902, Post Office Building
Savannah, Ga., 31402, 125-29 Bull St.
Seattle, Wash., 98104, 909 First Avenue

FIGURE 4   Sources of Bureau of the Census materials.

Materials listed below will provide some printed and taped sources of information.

E4   **CHARACTERISTICS OF AMERICAN YOUTH: 1972**   By U.S.
     Department of Commerce, Bureau of the Census. Washington,
     D.C., U.S. Government Printing Office, 1973. $1.25. *(Current
     Population Reports, Series P-23, No. 44.)*
This publication, updated irregularly, provides detailed information on
the 14- to 24-year-old segment of the U.S. population, including
educational attainment, school enrollment, income, family status, labor
force status, and voting patterns.

E5   **DATA USES IN SCHOOL ADMINISTRATION**   By U.S. De-
     partment of Commerce, Bureau of the Census. Washington, D.C.,
     1970. $0.25. *(Census Use Study: Report No. 10.)* From: Publications
     Distribution Section, U.S. Department of Commerce, Bureau of
     the Census, Washington, D.C. 20233, or from any U.S. Department
     of Commerce field office.
One of an 11-part *Census Use Study,* based on a pilot program in the New
Haven, Connecticut area: it analyzes local, state, and census data sources;
details uses of these data sources in school administration; and suggests
methods for improving local school records and for combining census
and local data. Appendixes include six illustrative case histories of data
use, plus an analysis of 1970 Census materials useful for school administrators.

E6   **DIGEST OF EDUCATIONAL STATISTICS, 1974**   By National
     Center for Educational Statistics. Washington, D.C., U.S. Govern-
     ment Printing Office, 1975. $2.50.
An annual abstract of statistical information that covers all levels of
education as well as federal programs with related statistics; tends to be
one year, or more, out-of-date. Source notes provide leads to more
detailed statistics.

E7   **DIRECTORY OF FEDERAL STATISTICS FOR LOCAL
     AREAS: A Guide to Sources, 1966**   By U.S. Department of
     Commerce, Bureau of the Census. Washington, D.C., U.S. Gov-
     ernment Printing Office, 1966. $1.
A good guide to, and analysis of, recurrent statistics of the Bureau of the
Census and 32 other federal agencies that issue local area reports
(metropolitan areas and smaller). Arranged in tabular form, it includes

subjects, titles, brief descriptive information, geographic areas covered, frequency of publication, source documentation, and explanatory notes for 182 publications.

E8 **DIRECTORY OF FEDERAL STATISTICS FOR STATES: A Guide to Sources, 1967** By U.S. Department of Commerce, Bureau of the Census. Washington, D.C., U.S. Government Printing Office, 1967. $2.25.

A guide to source references of state socioeconomic data contained in more than 750 federal agency publications. Pages 55 to 97 contain a detailed subject analysis of sources of educational statistics as of 1967, most of which are still current. Arranged in tabular form, information for each publication includes subject, title, frequency of publication, recent references, sources and notes, and inclusiveness (years, extent of information, etc.).

E9 **DIRECTORY OF NON-FEDERAL STATISTICS FOR STATES AND LOCAL AREAS: A Guide to Sources, 1969** By U.S. Department of Commerce, Bureau of the Census. Washington, D.C., U.S. Government Printing Office, 1970. $6.25.

The first issue of a recurring guide to nonfederal sources of statistics for the 50 states, the District of Columbia, Guam, Puerto Rico, the Virgin Islands, and some component local areas. Arranged alphabetically by states and then by field of information, it includes sources of statistics on education as well as 12 other areas sometimes relevant to education: welfare, labor, banking, finance, insurance, commerce, transportation, utilities, agriculture, conservation, government, and government finance.

Education, a subject area under each state, is subdivided into such headings as elementary schools, enrollment, apportionment of funds, finance, and graduates. Another section lists organizations and other nonfederal sources of education statistics. Indexes a total of 1,800 publications in 13 subject areas.

E10 **FACT BOOK ON HIGHER EDUCATION** By Judith Guthrie. Washington, D.C., American Council on Education, 1958– . Annual (4 issues/year). New subscription, $35; renewals, $20.

A series of four pamphlets, approximately 50 pages each, issued at regular intervals during the year. Compiles, in one convenient form, facts and figures on higher education in the United States: enrollment data is issued in March; population, business activity, and employment, in June; information on institutions, faculty, and staff, as well as characteristics and finances of students, in October; and earned degree data, in December.

E11 **PROJECTIONS OF EDUCATIONAL STATISTICS TO 1983-
84** By National Center for Educational Statistics. Washington,
D.C., U.S. Government Printing Office, 1975. Annual. $2.50.
Statistical projections include enrollments, graduates, teachers, and
expenditures for elementary, secondary, and higher education.

E12 **SCHOOL DISTRICT FOURTH COUNT TAPES** By U.S. Department of Commerce, Bureau of the Census. Washington, D.C.,
1973. Available, by state, at $77.25 per reel. Also available in
microfiche. From: Robert Heintze, NCES, 400 Maryland Ave., S.W.,
Washington, D.C. 20202.
These Fourth Count Tapes provide selected social and economic data
from the 1970 Census for school districts with enrollments of 300 or
more, which include individual and family income, educational attainment, school enrollment, ethnic background, nativity, migration, occupation, employment, and other variables. Data are tabulated separately for
the entire population, as well as for the Negro and Spanish-American
populations within each school district.

E13 **STATISTICAL ABSTRACT OF THE UNITED STATES:
1974** By U.S. Department of Commerce, Bureau of the Census.
95th Edition. Washington, D.C., U.S. Government Printing Office,
1879– . Annual. $10.20; paperback, $6.85.
The standard summary of statistics on social, political, and economic
organizations in the United States. The 95th edition contains more than
1,300 tables and charts, as well as an extensive guide to sources of
additional data. Also includes a fairly comprehensive selection from the
1970 Census of Housing and Population, with improved formatting.
Recent trends are well-covered. An inexpensive, exact reprinting of this
book is published commercially by Grosset and Dunlap for $3.95 under
the title *The American Almanac.*

E14 **STATISTICS OF PUBLIC, ELEMENTARY AND SECONDARY
DAY SCHOOLS, Fall 1972** By National Center for Educational
Statistics. Washington, D.C., U.S. Government Printing Office,
1974. $1.
A recurring descriptive study, well-designed and intended to provide
current state summaries on public schools, for use by legislators,
educators, and the general public; generally published about two years
after data is collected. Conveniently arranged, it includes information on
available classrooms, construction, expenditures per pupil, salaries of
teaching staff, enrollment, and organization.

E15 **SURVEY OF PUBLIC EDUCATION IN THE NATION'S BIG CITY SCHOOL DISTRICTS** By National School Boards Assn. Evanston, Ill., 1972. $6.

Provides an abundance of information on 51 school systems serving large cities, including personnel data with enrollment, ethnic distribution, instructional staff, and 1970 population; financial data, fiscal status, total and per pupil expenditures; and varied information on school board organization and members. A good tool for analyzing or comparing large urban systems.

7 | Abstracting, Indexing, and Current Awareness Services

This chapter deals with some of the major indexing, abstracting, and current awareness tools in education and related fields. Although these tools may appear to be a confusing assortment of overlapping services intended for a variety of purposes and audiences, with different indexing terms and principles of organization, they are treated in one chapter because, in practice, they share common functions and purposes as well as a common subject core. All of these tools are useful for keeping current with the literature; the indexing and abstracting journals are major retrospective searching tools as well.

Only titles which are basic for particular kinds of searching and current awareness are included. These cover the vast field of English-language educational literature as well as some significant foreign materials. Titles selected are annotated for content, scope, arrangement, ease of use, strengths, and weaknesses. Some indexes of lesser importance are included at the end of the chapter.

PERIODICAL INDEXES

Periodical indexes should be familiar to most library users: The *Readers' Guide to Periodical Literature* is a ready example. In these indexes, individual periodical articles are reduced to bibliographic entries which can be located through detailed, analytical subject indexing. *Education Index,* perhaps the first index to consider for most library research in education, is produced by the makers of *Readers' Guide* and is similar in format. *P.A.I.S.* (Public Affairs Information Service) *Bulletin* also is similar in design, although both the *P.A.I.S. Bulletin* and *Education Index* cover far more types of publications than the *Readers' Guide. British Education Index* and *State Education Journal Index* also follow the *Education Index* and *P.A.I.S.* format, as do most of the indexes shown in the supplementary list at the end of this chapter.

CURRENT AWARENESS SERVICES

Current awareness services may be less familiar. These provide announcements of recent publications: sometimes with full bibliographic entries, such as in the *Monthly Catalog of United States Government Publications;* sometimes with title announcements; and sometimes with reproduction of title pages, such as *Current Contents.* While announcement services may have some subject indexing or logical arrangement (for example, the *Monthly Catalog,* which tries to be a complete bibliographic record, rates high on both), they tend to emphasize current rather than retrospective information.

ABSTRACT JOURNALS

Abstract journals are important tools. They offer, in one package, bibliographic entries plus summaries of the essential contents of the original documents, arranged in a convenient order, with supplementary author and detailed subject indexes. Most of the publications in this chapter are abstract journals.

When there is a very broad choice, three factors (other than subject coverage) to consider in choosing and using abstract journals are the quality of their abstracts, the quality of their indexing, and the currency of their coverage.

FORMS OF MATERIALS PROCESSED

Another way to categorize the research tools discussed in this chapter is by the form of printed materials they process. Although **books** are not the prime materials covered by any of the services discussed here, some books, or parts of books, are indexed, announced, abstracted, or reviewed in *Child Development Abstracts, Current Contents, Education Abstracts, Education Index, Language and Language Behavior Abstracts, Language Teaching Abstracts, Poverty and Human Resources Abstracts, Psychological Abstracts, P.A.I.S. Bulletin,* and *Resources in Education.*

Dissertations are indexed or listed in *American Doctoral Dissertations, Dissertation Abstracts International, Psychological Abstracts, P.A.I.S. Bulletin,* and *Research Studies in Education.*

Government-generated documents are covered in *AIM/ARM, Exceptional Child Education Abstracts, Psychological Abstracts, Resources in Education, Education Index, P.A.I.S. Bulletin, Monthly Catalog of United States Government Publications,* and *Weekly Government Abstracts.*

Convention papers are covered (although not completely) in *Current Contents, Resources in Education, Sociological Abstracts,* and, occasionally, in *Psychological Abstracts.*

Some **pamphlets** are listed or indexed in *Psychological Abstracts, Resources in Education, Education Index,* and the *P.A.I.S. Bulletin.*

Periodical articles are covered in *Child Development Abstracts, Education Abstracts, Educational Administration Abstracts, Exceptional Child Education Abstracts, Language and Language Behavior Abstracts, Language Teaching Abstracts, Mental Retardation and Developmental Disabilities Abstracts, Poverty and Human Resources Abstracts, Psychological Abstracts, Sociological Abstracts, Current Index to Journals in Education, Education Index, P.A.I.S. Bulletin, Current Contents, British Education Index,* and *State Education Journal Index.*

Research projects are indexed in *AIM/ARM, Research Relating to Children, Research Studies in Education,* and *Weekly Government Abstracts.*

SELECTING THE RIGHT TOOL

Other tools can be selected largely on the basis of subject relevance and availability; however, choosing the best index or abstract journal is often a compromise with the realities of time and location.

If library resources are poor and no educational indexes are available, general indexes such as the *Readers' Guide* can help the user locate information on most educational topics. Since education is such a wide field, almost every indexing or abstracting tool covers some aspect of education.

To locate supplementary indexes and services, Arvid Burke's *Documentation in Education* (D1) provides a thorough and analytical discussion of many indexes (some of which are useful in curricular fields), and *Ulrich's International Periodicals Directory* (C19) lists 800 abstracting and indexing services. Since the titles tend to indicate the subjects covered, choosing supplementary indexes is largely a matter of common sense—that is, *Art Index* is logical for art education, *Women Studies Abstracts* for women studies, etc.

SEARCH PROCEDURES

Since neither the occasional researcher nor the experienced librarian can know the vagaries of every index or abstract journal, another approach is necessary. Intelligent use of the tools in this chapter is particularly dependent on careful clarification of the research question.

For an advance awareness of the synonyms, related concepts, and various approaches indexers might use:

1. Scan the CHECKLIST FOR RESEARCH QUESTIONS on pages 10 and 11. Consider alternative approaches and sources.

2. Consult educational dictionaries and thesauri for additional clarification and terminology.

3. Read background articles to obtain cited references, names, and approaches.

4. If planning a comprehensive search, or if materials on a topic are difficult to locate, it would be well to set up some method for recording the search terms that were used successfully and unsuccessfully in various indexes. Indexing terms used in each index can be listed either on cards (preferably 3" × 5"), for a really comprehensive search, or in a notebook in parallel format. These can double as search records and can include authors and notes as well as subject terms.

For a search involving *Resources in Education* or *Current Index to Journals in Education,* a good starting point is the *Thesaurus of ERIC Descriptors* (A16). Although ERIC's vocabulary of indexing terms is redundant,[1] it is well-organized through this *Thesaurus,* which is, in effect, a list of descriptors (indexing terms) and cross-references that refer the user to broad, narrow, or related terms, and terms *used for* other terms.

For most indexes, the user can start with the latest bound volume of a particular index (apt to include all the terms as well as recent vocabulary), turn to the most likely subject, and check the cross-references until the one or two terms that are peculiar to a high proportion of relevant articles are located. Work forward in time (the current year) and then backward, modifying terms if they have changed. Indexes usually place most articles dealing with a single topic under one or two terms, sometimes highly specific; therefore, it is worth taking the time to locate the best term or terms. Since the indexing terms and cross-references appear in the same volume as the items indexed, it is fairly easy to locate the most appropriate terms. For instance, an article on "Evaluating New Methods of Teaching Speech" would be indexed in *Education Index* under the single term "Speech Education – Teaching Methods – Evaluation." In the ERIC data-base *(Resources in Education* and *Current Index to Journals in Education),* it would be indexed under three separate descriptors: "Speech Education," "Teaching Methods," and "Evaluation." For a manual or standard library search of this topic, terms related to speech would still be the best starting point, since an extremely high proportion of unrelated materials are apt to be found under more general descriptors. A computer search of the ERIC data base could combine the separate terms, "Speech Education," "Teaching Methods," and "Evaluation" in one operation, and probably would include extraneous articles on "Speech Evaluation" or "Speech Therapy."

When computer searches are handy and inexpensive, they are the best method by which to search the ERIC data base for broad subjects or combinations of subjects. For topics with single specific descriptors, a standard library search is satisfactory. A helpful, detailed guide to techniques for searching the ERIC data base can be

[1] For a detailed analysis on the problems of inconsistent indexing and near synonyms in the ERIC data-base, see Schippleck, Suzanne, "Impossible Indexing, or Looking for ERIC," *In: RQ,* 11:352-355, Summer 1972.

found in Lorraine Mathies' *Information Sources and Services in Education* (D8). Two other tools useful for searching ERIC are: *Search Strategy Tutorial: Searcher's Kit* by Sharon Jewell and W. T. Brandhorst (Washington, D.C., National Institute of Education, 1973; ED 082 763; $4.20, $0.75 for microfiche), a rather comprehensive workshop manual developed for tutorial sessions on computer searches of the ERIC data base, which provides a step-by-step analysis and structuring of three typical searches, together with useful information on output formats, evaluation, and record-keeping; and "ERIC: What It Is, How to Use It" (a kit available from the Order Section of the National Audiovisual Center, Washington, D.C. 20409, for $35), which provides information and materials for groups or individuals who need guidance in searching ERIC.

Keyword-in-Context (KWIC) indexes, like those of *Sociological Abstracts,* actually are not subject indexes, but indexes to some words in article titles. If an indexed item has a rigorous title, such as those found in dissertations, the index works relatively well, although there is no way of verifying success in subject areas. For entries with cute or catchy titles, and those using new or unusual terminology, the system can be ineffective and frustrating. Since *Sociological Abstracts* is arranged by broad topics, it is best to begin by browsing, rather than attempting a subject search in the index. If browsing is not possible, the user should begin with the most significant terms and trust to luck, logic, and thoroughness.

Two minor problems encountered among the indexing and abstracting journals are varying and inconsistent practices in (1) alphabetizing and (2) indexing authors and/or institutions. While most indexes use a word-for-word alphabetical filing order, some computer-produced indexes, including those in the ERIC data base, use a letter-by-letter order. Since most indexes do not provide their alphabetical filing rules or philosophies, the user should first scan the indexes to locate appropriate terms filed in unexpected order. Acronyms also may be alphabetized in several ways.

A flexible approach and awareness of possibilities also is necessary when searching through indexes for authors and/or institutions. If the user is working with an unfamiliar index, it would be worthwhile to read the fine print or to scan the index to determine how many authors are indexed (one, two, or more), whether institutions such as research centers are filed under names of cities or universities, and how government organizations are handled. Awareness of particular approaches and alternate approaches can mean the difference between successful and unsuccessful searches.

F1 **ABSTRACTS OF INSTRUCTIONAL AND RESEARCH MATERIALS IN VOCATIONAL AND TECHNICAL EDUCATION (AIM/ARM)** Columbus, Ohio, Center for Vocational and Technical Education, 1967– . Bimonthly. $34/year.

AIM/ARM announces and abstracts instructional and research materials dealing with vocational and technical education. Except for typography, the format resembles that of *Resources in Education,* with subject and author indexes referring to numbered abstracts (which include bibliographic citations and information on availability) appearing in two separate sections—instructional and research.

Formerly two separate indexes, *AIM/ARM* covers a wide variety of fields, including agricultural education, business education, career education, health occupations, consumer and home economics, various aspects of trade and industrial education, and related fields such as occupational guidance and rehabilitation. A "Projects in Progress" section announces curriculum and research projects funded through the Office of Education's Bureau of Occupational and Adult Education. An annual cumulative index to *AIM/ARM,* beginning with 1967, provides author, institutional, subject, and identifier indexes. Each issue includes information on how to obtain *AIM/ARM* microfiche copies of materials abstracted and announced in that particular issue.

F2 **AMERICAN DOCTORAL DISSERTATIONS** Ann Arbor, Mich., University Microfilms, Inc., 1933– . Annual. $15/year.

Intended as an index to all doctoral dissertations accepted by universities in the United States and Canada. Listings are by field and institution. It is more complete in coverage, although less handy to use, than *Dissertation Abstracts International.* For a discussion and comparison of sources for doctoral dissertations, see Moore, Julie L., "Bibliographic Control of American Doctoral Dissertations: A History," *In: Special Libraries, 63:*227-230, May-June 1972; and part two of the same article, ". . . : An Analysis," *In: Special Libraries, 63:*285-291, July 1972.

F3 **CHILD DEVELOPMENT ABSTRACTS AND BIBLIOGRAPHIES** Chicago, Ill., Society for Research in Child Development, 1927– . 3 times/year; 2 sections each issue. $15/year.

Divided into two sections, this journal provides abstracts of articles and book reviews (plus a listing of books received but not reviewed). Areas covered include biology, medicine, health, psychology, personality, sociology, education, counseling, and psychiatry. The typography and format are good, citations are complete, and article summaries and abstracts are clear and concise. Approximately 1,000 items are covered each year. The final issue of each volume contains an author index and a well-done subject index, plus a list of the periodicals regularly searched. Literature coverage is augmented by exchange agreements with other journals. Book notices provide brief evaluative summary reviews that discuss the intent of the book and the reviewer's evaluation. A highly valuable buying or selection tool.

F4 **CURRENT CONTENTS: Social & Behavioral Sciences** Philadelphia, Institute for Scientific Information, 1969– . Weekly. $135/year; foreign, $165/year; group discounts available.

Reproduces table of contents pages of more than 1,100 journals in the social and behavioral sciences, defined here to include library science, business, and management, as well as education. Each issue is arranged in sections for easy and timesaving browsing, and includes both an alphabetical index of journals covered and an author index (first authors only) complete with address and zip code.

This section of *Current Contents* now includes a computer-produced "Weekly Subject Index" which lists, under significant words or phrases from article titles, the page numbers in *Current Contents* and the starting page number of the original journal article. A new "Current Book Contents" section announces significant new technical books, conference proceedings, and symposia, including full bibliographic information. Book titles and chapter titles also are indexed in the "Weekly Subject Index."

The periodicals whose contents are listed are rarely more than one month old and sometimes are prepublication issues. A list of periodicals, keyed to publishers' addresses, is printed quarterly, while changes in coverage are noted weekly.

The *Current Contents* group of services provides weekly contents-page coverage of six different disciplinary areas: *Life Sciences; Agriculture, Biology & Environmental Sciences; Social & Behavioral Sciences; Engineering, Technology & Applied Sciences; Physical & Chemical Sciences;* and *Clinical Practice. Agriculture, Biology & Environmental Sciences; Clinical Practice; Engineering, Technology & Applied Sciences;* and *Social & Behavioral Sciences* include "Weekly Subject Indexes" in their particular segments of literature at no extra cost. The entire series covers 4,500 journals.

An Original Article Tear Sheet Service (OATS) mails out, within 24 hours, reprints of any article covered in *Current Contents,* at a cost of $3 for each article up to 10 pages; $2 for each additional 10 pages or fraction thereof. Air mail delivery in the United States, Canada, and Mexico, and orders to foreign countries are charged an additional $0.50 per article.

F5   **CURRENT INDEX TO JOURNALS IN EDUCATION (CIJE)**
New York, Macmillan Information—a Division of Macmillan Publishing, 1969– . Monthly. $50/year. Semiannual cumulations, $40; monthly index plus semiannual cumulation, $90/year. Order from 216R Brown St., Riverside, N.J. 08075.

Currently indexes and abstracts more than 750 education and education-related journals (approximately 20,000 articles each year), including approximately 70 foreign journals and some articles in journals not primarily concerned with education.

The selection and abstracting of journals is performed at various ERIC clearinghouses and at Central ERIC, using the 7,200 descriptors of the *Thesaurus of ERIC Descriptors* as indexing terms, with apparent variations in meaning and usage between clearinghouses (for example, the term "environment" was used in five different senses in one list of 10 articles). Citations are arranged by EJ (educational journal) number under 52 broad subject headings, complete with descriptors and a (usually one or two sentence) resumé. This arrangement lends itself more readily to browsing, current awareness, and/or computer searching than to a library subject or author search, because, to locate the resumé, the user has to go back and forth from varied subject terms or author entries to EJ numbers scattered throughout the main entry section. Indexes include a separate subject index based on ERIC descriptors; a separate author index; an alphabetically arranged journal contents index; a source journals index listing the names and addresses of publishers of periodical titles and the cost of subscriptions (and of single issues, when obtainable); as well as an acronym identifying the clearinghouse that indexes a particular journal. Since some of the journals indexed in *CIJE* are obscure or difficult to obtain in libraries, the ordering information implicit in this feature improves the accessibility of the journals indexed. *CIJE's* abstracts and wide coverage are its major assets to libraries, especially those that subscribe to many, or very few, periodicals.

Despite the "current" in its title, it is the least current of the major education indexes. Its April 1975 issue, arriving in June, primarily indexed articles from October, November, and December 1974; most articles indexed were 5 to 12 months old.

Compared to *Education Index,* this is a ponderous tool for a specific current, noncomputerized library search, and the individual issues are slower to search. Since its cumulations are published only twice a year and usually arrive late, searching *CIJE* late in the year (which can involve searching a large number of issues) can be very time-consuming.

F6   **DISSERTATION ABSTRACTS INTERNATIONAL** (Formerly *Dissertation Abstracts.*) **A – The Humanities and Social Sciences; B – The Sciences and Engineering.** Ann Arbor, Mich., University Microfilms, Inc., 1938– . Monthly. Section A, $60/year; Section B, $60/year; Sections A and B, $115/year.

A monthly compilation that abstracts doctoral dissertations submitted to University Microfilms, Inc., by approximately 250 cooperating institutions. Arranged in broad academic disciplines (rather than subject categories), with combined annual subject and author indexes. European titles were added in 1968. *Dissertation Abstracts International Retrospective Index* (9 volumes, $225), published in 1970, is a single source for searching this data base from inception to 1970. The set is arranged by keywords under academic subjects. Volume 7 deals with Education; Volume 4, with Psychology, Sociology, and Political Science; and Volume 5, with Social Sciences. The last volume provides an author index, plus information for ordering copies of dissertations from the publisher. The *Comprehensive Dissertation Index, 1861-1972* (Ann Arbor, Mich., University Microfilms, 1973) represents further expansion.

A computerized data base, DATRIX II, which uses the same information, is discussed in Chapter 17. See *American Doctoral Dissertations* (F2) for comparative comments.

F7   **EDUCATION ABSTRACTS** Washington, D.C., American College Public Relations Assn., 1963– . Monthly. $12/year.

More a news digest than an abstract journal; summarizes articles and book notices on higher education topics from newspapers, periodicals, and education journals.

F8   **EDUCATION INDEX** Bronx, N.Y., H. W. Wilson, 1932– . 10 issues/year, including cumulations and annual volume. Various pricing, depending on number of educational volumes in subscriber's periodical collection; from $34 to approximately $350/year.

This basic index to periodical literature is issued monthly except July and August, with frequent cumulations. Indexes approximately 250 of the more valuable and accessible English-language education periodicals, which are selected by subscriber and user vote on criteria of subject balance and reference value. In addition to periodicals, it also indexes proceedings, yearbooks, monographs, bulletins, and some U.S. Government publications. Subjects include education and curriculum in all subjects (for preschool to adult), plus school administration and finance, counseling, and guidance. One extremely useful feature is the "Book Review" section, which contains reviews of individual authors and titles, as well as continuing review sections and special articles or sections on books about education.

From 1929 to 1961, *Education Index* provided author and subject indexes; from 1961 through 1969, subject indexes only. Authors and subject categories are now combined in one alphabetical index. Its indexing and selection policies are intelligently geared to library use; an American Library Association liaison committee advises the publisher about indexing and editorial policy on the basis of in-depth contents studies conducted every few years. Its indexing terms are fewer and more logical than those of *CIJE:* they are subdivided rather than scattered, and cross-referenced within the volume itself rather than in a separate thesaurus.

For ease of subject and author searching, *Education Index* is the most convenient, although not the most comprehensive index. It is well-designed to provide one-stop searching of relatively accessible periodicals, yearbooks, monographs, and government documents. Because of its frequent cumulations, most single issues can be discarded, enabling the user to perform a search using relatively few volumes. For a really thorough search, both *Education Index* and *CIJE* must be used, since their coverage does not completely overlap. A library or user who wants to research additional periodicals can rely on *Current Contents* and/or supplementary subject indexes listed in this section.

Education Index is fairly current and frequently indexes articles within one month of their original publication. Addresses, prices, and ordering information for periodicals indexed are included in the front of each issue.

F9   **EDUCATIONAL ADMINISTRATION ABSTRACTS**   Columbus, Ohio, University Council for Educational Administration, 1966– . 3 issues/year. $10/year; foreign, $11/year.

Each issue contains approximately 300 abstracts of journal articles on educational administration (from approximately 80 journals), arranged by subject, with journal and author indexes. Educational administration is broadly defined. The journal includes a section on societal factors (such as values, economic development, and population change) that influence education programs and policies, and a section on planning and futurology.

F10   **EXCEPTIONAL CHILD EDUCATION ABSTRACTS (ECEA)**   Reston, Va., The Council for Exceptional Children, 1969– . Quarterly. Institutions, $50/year; supplementary subscriptions, $25/year; members, $25/year; individuals, $35/year.

ECEA is designed to provide comprehensive abstract coverage of important publications in all aspects of the field of special education. It is an indispensable tool for persons working or studying in any field involving the education of the handicapped or gifted—librarians, teachers, curriculum supervisors, administrators, students—and those engaged in publishing, research, and writing of surveys. Coverage includes research reports, journal articles, curriculum guides, teachers' activity manuals, administrative surveys and guidelines, texts for both professionals and beginning students, plus current nonprint media (tape cassettes). Also includes abstracts of ERIC documents on the handicapped and gifted.

All literature is thoroughly scanned to provide continuing and up-to-date information. There is some occasional abstracting of significant material from older publications. Many of the publications abstracted in *ECEA* are available in microfiche or hard copy from the ERIC Document Reproduction Service. The ED number needed for ordering, and the number of pages needed to compute cost, are included for each item available in this form.

Indexes by author, subject, and title are computer-generated and are cumulated annually. Back volumes are available.

F11 **HUMAN RESOURCES ABSTRACTS** (Formerly *Poverty and Human Resources Abstracts*.) Beverly Hills, Calif., Sage Foundation, 1966– . Quarterly. Institutions, $50/year; foreign, $51/year.
An abstract journal (published through the cooperation of the Institute of Labor and Industrial Relations, University of Michigan/Wayne State University) consisting primarily of books and periodical articles in the areas of poverty, manpower, and human development, including sections on education and vocational education. Approximately 1,000 well-selected, well-written abstracts each year are classified, arranged by number, and cross-indexed; perhaps one-tenth to one-eighth deal with education.

F12 **LANGUAGE AND LANGUAGE BEHAVIOR ABSTRACTS** Ann Arbor, Mich., University of Michigan, 1967– . Quarterly. Institutions, $80/year; individuals, $40/year.
A scholarly reference work that screens almost 1,000 publications in more than 30 languages. While much of it is beyond the scope of the educator, sections dealing with special education, speech and language, language acquisition, verbal learning, etc., often are relevant. Easy to use, with well-written, current abstracts listed in a number and classification order. Also includes author and subject indexes, book reviews, and source publications.

F13   **LANGUAGE TEACHING ABSTRACTS**   London, Cambridge
University Press, 1968– . Quarterly. $13.50/year.
The aim of this British publication, edited jointly by the English-Teaching
Information Centre and the Centre for Information on Language
Teaching and Research, is to provide current research information on
teaching modern languages, including English as a second language. It
presents objective English-language summaries of articles from 400
foreign-language journals, covering psychology, linguistics, educational
technology, and teaching methods, as well as brief notes about new books
dealing with languages. Indexed by country as well as subject.

F14   **MENTAL RETARDATION AND DEVELOPMENTAL DIS-
ABILITIES ABSTRACTS**   (Formerly *Mental Retardation Ab-
stracts.*) By U.S. Department of Health, Education, and Welfare,
Office of Human Development, Developmental Disabilities Office.
Washington, D.C., U.S. Government Printing Office, 1964– .Quar-
terly. Price to be set.
Numbered, classified abstracts—mostly from medical journals (including
many foreign publications)—covering all aspects of mental retardation.
The abstracts on developmental aspects and on treatment and training
are perhaps the most valuable available for educators concerned with the
mental retardate. Materials on planning and legislative aspects might be
valuable for administrators and legislators. Type and format are good.
Author and subject indexes are excellent.

F15   **MONTHLY CATALOG OF UNITED STATES GOVERNMENT
PUBLICATIONS**   Washington, D.C., U.S. Government Printing
Office, 1895– . Monthly. $27/year, including index.
This monthly catalog is the basic tool for keeping current with the
previous month's government publications (other than ERIC microfiche
and NTIS publications). The range is enormous: books, pamphlets, maps,
and periodicals of all types—approximately 20,000 items each year.
Congressional, departmental, and bureau publications are arranged
alphabetically by department and bureau, with monthly and cumulative
author, title, and subject indexes. These indexes had been compiled
manually, but as of July 1973 have been computer-produced. Complete
bibliographic information includes price as well as Library of Congress
and Superintendent of Documents classification numbers. The February
issue contains the *Directory of United States Government Periodicals and
Subscriptions,* a complete yearly listing of government periodicals with
revised prices; the September issue lists government depository libraries.
Addresses of retail government bookstores (which sell the documents

listed and indexed in the *Monthly Catalog)* are inside the back cover. Recent issues have been as much as six months late.

F16   P.A.I.S. (Public Affairs Information Service) BULLETIN   New York, Public Affairs Information Service, 1915– . Weekly, plus cumulations. $150/year.

An excellent research tool widely available in public libraries, but seriously underused in educational research; however, a first choice in areas where public affairs and economics intersect with education. It is a current, cumulative subject index to a wide variety of library materials (with full bibliographic citations, sources, and prices), which generally were published the same or previous month; that is, the April cumulative issue, usually arriving in May, will index materials published in March and April. It is cumulated five times a year, so weekly issues can be discarded. The fifth cumulation, a bound volume, supersedes the other cumulations in a particular year, so those, too, can be discarded. The indexing is well-done, compact and logical, compatible with current terminology and library usage, and is adequately cross-referenced. New subject headings are listed separately.

The *P.A.I.S. Bulletin* provides access not only to periodicals (it indexes selected articles from more than 1,000 English-language periodicals a year), but also to current pamphlets, books, speeches, government documents, and other relevant materials, concentrating on factual and statistical materials to meet the needs of its member municipal, legislative, special, public, research, and academic libraries. It is particularly valuable both for subject searches and current awareness in such areas as school finance and business, the public areas of school administration, politics and education, legislation and legal decisions in education, training of public officials (such as accountants, sheriffs, and public health workers), teaching subjects related to public administration (such as sociology, forestry, and population), and to such broad areas as drug abuse, prison education, and vocational education. It also is excellent as a directory, and is a prime source for locating state or municipal documents, listing specialized dissertations of interest to educators.

In addition to its main subject indexes, the *P.A.I.S. Bulletin* includes a variety of lists designed to make the entries accessible: a key to periodical references, an address directory of publishers and organizations, lists of publications analyzed, and lists of U.S. Government agencies whose publications were included. Addresses of some small publishers are included with the entries so that sources and prices are given for every item cited. If materials listed become out-of-print, a backup service is provided by the New York Public Library's Photographic Services Department, which can generally provide microcopies at cost.

Since this tool dates back to 1915, it is convenient and useful for historic research. An author index to some of the volumes is available from the Pierian Press in Ann Arbor, Michigan.

F17 **PSYCHOLOGICAL ABSTRACTS (PA)** Washington, D.C., American Psychological Assn., 1927– . Monthly. Institutions, $220/year; individuals, $95/year.

A necessary tool for researchers concerned with the psychological aspects of learning and education. It provides nonevaluative summaries and citations of relevant dissertations, (approximately 1,200) books and documents, and articles from more than 850 journals covering psychology and related areas. Approximately one-fourth of the materials were originally in another language. *PA* is arranged alphabetically by author under subject categories, and indexed by subject and author. Six-month cumulative indexes are computer-produced; machine-readable tapes are simultaneously produced. The tapes can be leased by an information center or searched through Psychological Abstracts Information Services (see Chapter 17 for more details). The categories most relevant to education are Cognitive Processes and Motivation, Developmental Psychology, and Educational Psychology. The Psychometrics and Statistics category is good for tests and measurements. APA's *Thesaurus of Psychological Index Terms* (A17) provides search terms for educational researchers and psychologically oriented teachers.

F18 **RESEARCH RELATING TO CHILDREN** By ERIC Clearinghouse on Early Childhood Education. Washington, D.C., U.S. Government Printing Office, 1954– . Occasional; approximately one-year intervals. $2.00 for latest issue; $1.50 for others.

An abstract journal that reports research in progress and/or recently completed research dealing with children. Materials, arranged by subject, include long-term research, growth and development, special groups of children, the child in the family, socioeconomic and cultural factors, educational factors and services, social services, and health services. Information on the projects reported includes investigators, purpose, subjects, methods, findings, directions, cooperating groups, and publications. Indexes are arranged by institution, investigator, and subject. Except for a few long-term research projects, annual issues have not repeated research reported in previous bulletins, but included only the reports received during the previous year. Dependence on voluntary reporting and a small budget are its major weaknesses. Early bulletins (Numbers 1 to 26) were prepared by the Children's Bureau; recent issues are under the supervision of the ERIC Clearinghouse on Early Childhood Education. The Children's Bureau, now part of the Office of Child

Development (see N23), has completed other valuable bibliographies of research on particular groups of children: for example, the battered child, emotionally disturbed children, etc.

F19 **RESEARCH STUDIES IN EDUCATION** A Subject Index to Doctoral Dissertations. Bloomington, Ind., Phi Delta Kappa, 1953– . Annual. $7/year.
The latest edition of this now annual guide was published in 1970. It is a convenient index to doctoral dissertations, as well as to ongoing and completed research studies from 100 universities in the United States and Canada, arranged by author, title, and institution. Since it deals only with education, it is more convenient to use than the publications of University Microfilms, which are divided into 60 categories.

F20 **RESOURCES IN EDUCATION (RIE)** (Formerly *Research in Education.*) Washington, D.C., U.S. Department of Health, Education, and Welfare, National Institute of Education, Educational Resources Information Center (ERIC), 1966– . Monthly. $42.70/year, not including semiannual and annual indexes (variously priced). From: Superintendent of Documents, U.S. Government Printing Office, Washington, D.C. 20402.
RIE is the monthly documents abstracting service of ERIC. It includes resumés of hard-to-find or limited-distribution documents selected by ERIC clearinghouses located throughout the country, technical and research reports, conference papers, documents from school districts, etc. Reports are arranged by clearinghouse and then assigned ED (educational document) numbers in the ERIC system (so the output of any clearinghouse can be read each month); they are indexed by author and institution, and by subject descriptors selected from the *Thesaurus of ERIC Descriptors.* Although an increasing number of copyrighted documents are entered into the ERIC system for informational purposes, most documents abstracted are available in microfiche or hard copy from the ERIC Document Reproduction Service in Arlington, Virginia. Approximately 14,000 items are entered each year. Recent issues include a helpful list of new *Thesaurus* terms, as well as explanations about the format of the abstracts.

F21 **SOCIAL SCIENCES CITATION INDEX** Philadelphia, Institute for Scientific Information, 1973– . Monthly. $1,250/year; includes *Citation Index, Permuterm Subject Index,* and *Source Index.*
A complete indexing system to approximately 1,000 journals in the social sciences, in all languages, with occasional articles from some 2,200 additional journals in scientific fields. A one-year subscription includes

two triannual indexes and an annual cumulation incorporating the data from the last four months of the year. These citation tools, which can be completely machine-produced, allow users to search for cited-author references, organizations, permuted keywords, and authors. Topics relevant to education include psychology and educational research.

F22   **SOCIOLOGICAL ABSTRACTS**   Brooklyn, N.Y., Sociological Abstracts, Inc., 1954– . 6 issues/year (April, May, July, August, October, December). $120/year; cumulative index, $36; special supplementary issues on sociological conferences, $3 each.

Provides complete coverage of every aspect of sociology, in all languages. Arranged by classification, the abstracts are well-done, readable, interesting, and lengthy; selection is good. A computerized subject index (KWIC) is difficult to read and to use. *Sociological Abstracts* is worth consulting for studies that deal with the sociological aspects of education. There are only approximately 50 significant items per issue, however, that are concerned with education; therefore, an organization with limited funds or whose primary education interests concern aspects other than sociology would not be apt to give it priority consideration. A computerized cumulative index is issued every year within nine months of the final issue.

F23   **STATE EDUCATION JOURNAL INDEX**   An Annotated Index of State Education Journals. Westminster, Colo., 1964– . Semiannual. $30/year. From: Dr. L. Stanley Ratliff, P.O. Box 244. Westminster, Colo. 80030.

A lithographed publication, published semiannually, the February issue indexes state education journals from September to December of the previous year, while the July issue indexes January to June issues of the current year. It has a subject index arrangement modeled after *Education Index,* and is the only comprehensive source for indexing journals of state education associations.

F24   **WEEKLY GOVERNMENT ABSTRACTS**   Springfield, Va., National Technical Information Service, 1973– . Weekly. Various prices.

There are 12 of these weekly professional abstract services covering fields of interest to business and technology. Probably more valuable for the educational researcher than for the practitioner.

_____**Behavior**   Weekly. $35/year.

Covers federally sponsored research and analysis on attitudes, motivation, social concerns, education, job training, man's reaction to his environment, and employment. Provides approximately 1,100 abstracts in 52 weekly issues, with concise but complete abstracts of 25 documents a week; appealingly formatted and easy to read.

_____**Library and Information Sciences**   Weekly. $20/year.
Covers information systems, marketing, operations, planning, personnel, and reference services in 1,100 abstracts each year.

OTHER TOOLS

While almost any indexing or abstracting service will unearth some materials on education, the indexing and abstracting journals listed below include the more widely useful secondary and backup services.

F25   **BRITISH EDUCATION INDEX**   London, British National Bibliography, 1961– . 3 issues/year. $20/6 issues.
Covers approximately 50 publications; with separate author and subject indexes. Cumulated every two years. Good source for comparative education.

F26   **BUSINESS PERIODICALS INDEX**   Bronx, N.Y., H.W. Wilson, 1958– . Monthly (except August). Service basis.
Cumulative subject index to English-language business periodicals dealing with communications, economics, marketing, finance, and labor. Covers topics such as educational broadcasting, university investments, education in newly developing countries, and technical and industrial education.

F27   **COLLEGE STUDENT PERSONNEL ABSTRACTS**   Claremont, Calif., College Student Personnel Institute, 1965– . Quarterly. Individuals, $22/year; institutions, $27/year.
Each issue is topically arranged and includes approximately 225 items dealing with student characteristics and behavior, academic achievement, and vocational elements in higher education. Primarily for college counselors and student personnel.

F28   **dsh ABSTRACTS**   Washington, D.C., Deafness, Speech and Hearing Publications, 1960– .Quarterly. $18/year; foreign, $20/year.
A nonprofit, joint venture of Gallaudet College and the American Speech

and Hearing Association. Includes brief noncritical summaries of literature on deafness, speech, and hearing, published in all major languages.
Topically arranged, with separate author index.

F29   **INDEX MEDICUS**   Bethesda, Md., National Library of Medicine,
      1960– . Monthly. $63.00/year; foreign, $73.75/year. From: Super-
      intendent of Documents, U.S. Government Printing Office,
      Washington, D.C. 20402.
A computer-produced, comprehensive index to the world's medical
literature.

F30   **INDEX TO LEGAL PERIODICALS**   An Author and Subject
      Index. Bronx, N.Y., H. W. Wilson, 1908– . Annual, plus 3-year
      cumulation. Service basis.
Includes yearbooks, institutes, and annual reviews; also, a table of cases
and a separate book review section.

F31   **LIBRARY LITERATURE**   An Author and Subject Index.
      Bronx, N.Y., H.W. Wilson, 1933– . Bimonthly; annual cumulation.
      Service basis.
Good for reviews, media materials, and information on school libraries
and media centers.

F32   **NEW YORK TIMES INDEX**   New York, New York Times,
      1913– . Bimonthly; annual cumulation. $182/year for both.
Indexes *New York Times* only, but good for dates, Washington reporting,
and national picture of education.

F33   **READERS' GUIDE TO PERIODICAL LITERATURE**   Bronx,
      N.Y., H. W. Wilson, 1900– . Semimonthly; monthly in July and
      August; quarterly and annual cumulations. $35/year.
Often as valuable as any education index; particularly useful for topical
materials, as well as early years of the twentieth century.

F34   **REHABILITATION LITERATURE**   For Use by Professional
      Personnel and Students in All Disciplines Concerned with Rehabili-
      tation of the Handicapped. Chicago, National Easter Seal Society
      for Crippled Children and Adults, 1940– . Monthly. $10/year.
      From: 2023 W. Ogden Ave., Chicago, Ill. 61612.
Recommended by special education people; includes abstract bibliographies of all types of materials and an index to book reviews. Microform
copy available.

F35   **SOCIAL SCIENCES INDEX**   Bronx, N.Y., H.W. Wilson, 1974– .
      Quarterly. Service Basis.
This new publication is one of two indexes replacing the *Social Sciences &*
Humanities Index (1916-1974). Includes author and title entries to 263
indexed periodicals in the fields of anthropology, area studies, economics,
environmental sciences, geography, law and criminology, medical sciences, psychology, public administration, sociology, and related subjects.
Most useful for sociological and psychological aspects of education.

   The *Humanities Index*, which also replaces part of the *Social Sciences &*
Humanities Index, indexes 260 periodicals in archeology, history, and
classic studies, folklore, criticism, philosophy, religion, performing arts,
and related fields.

F36   **SOCIOLOGY OF EDUCATION ABSTRACTS (British)**   Liver-
      pool, England, Information for Education, Ltd., 1965– . Quarterly.
      $23/year.
Each issue of this British quarterly is a miniature bibliography of
approximately 200 well-cited, well-written abstracts of English-language
books, articles, and sections of monographs and yearbooks dealing with
sociological areas in education. Items are arranged alphabetically by
author, with a topical index. Areas covered include curriculum, educational research as an activity, etc. The last issue each year includes a
cumulated author index and a list of sources.

PART III

Special Subjects

8 | *Printed Sources on Funding, Legislation, and Foundations*

Although vital indeed to education, and fundamentally affecting its practices, educational funding and the laws that control education often are not well-covered in traditional educational information sources. This chapter lists a few special tools which select or compile legal and legislative materials relevant to education, as well as some information sources on funding and foundations which might be useful to educators and administrators. Some monograph series and newsletters, discussed in Chapter 4, also are relevant, as are the sources discussed in Chapter 15.

This chapter is divided into three sections: law and legislation, federal funds, and foundations. Although they overlap, each is treated separately.

LAW AND LEGISLATION

The listings included in this section are generally intended for laymen. Legal compilations, which have their own logic and organization, but which are sometimes difficult to use by those who lack expertise in legal documents, have been avoided. A good general legal bibliography is the *Index to Legal Periodicals* (F30).

Three indexes listed in Chapter 7 also can be very helpful in locating materials pertaining to law and legislation: *Resources in Education, Monthly Catalog of United States Government Publications,* and *P.A.I.S. Bulletin.* While ERIC (and hence *RIE*) does not cover law with any thoroughness or consistency, there are many documents relating to law and legislation which usually can be found by searching the overlapping descriptors "Laws," "Legislation," and "State Laws."

The *P.A.I.S. Bulletin* is a prime index for materials dealing with public administration and law, and specific areas of interest can be searched at the state or governmental level; U.S. education laws are listed under "Education—United States—Legislation." The *State Education Journal Index* also is a source of state information. The *Monthly Catalog* and *Education Index,* both of which index government publications, laws, hearings, etc., are worth checking.

The *Congressional Record,* issued daily while Congress is in session, includes proceedings, lists of bills introduced, and texts of some important bills—as well as extraneous and sometimes important supplementary materials inserted by members of Congress. A "Daily Digest" at the back of each issue summarizes proceedings for that day.

The *Weekly Compilation of Presidential Documents* ($15/year), issued every Monday, provides access to the public speeches, news conferences, messages to Congress, and other materials released by the White House the previous week.

Single copies of Senate and House documents and bills cited in the above sources can be obtained by writing the House and/or Senate Document Room, Washington, D.C. 20015, and enclosing self-addressed mailing labels. The Bill Status System, discussed in Chapter 15, can provide speedy information on the status of specific bills.

State laws generally can be obtained as "slip laws" from the legislative reference bureaus of the various states. In the event they do not mail them out themselves, they usually can direct the inquirer to another source. These legislative reference bureaus are listed in *Book of the States* (G2) and in other productions of the Council of State Governments, and appear as an appendix to the various legislative summaries of the Education Commission of the States (G23, for instance). To obtain slip laws, send written requests giving exact citations (including source) and enclose self-addressed mailing labels, with postage attached.

Anyone seriously interested in following the legal aspects of education should peruse, at a minimum, all NEA and ECS publications listed here, as well as Congressional Quarterly publications and the Congressional Information Service (G6).

G1 **AMERICAN EDUCATION** By U.S. Department of Health, Education, and Welfare. Washington, D.C., U.S. Government Printing Office, 1965– . Monthly (10/issues year). $13.50/year; $3.40 additional for foreign mailing.

Reports highlights of the National Institute of Education and U.S. Office of Education programs, new legislation, and statistical data on federal funds for education—especially for elementary and secondary schools. Includes ongoing "Statistics of the Month" and "Research and Development" news, as well as a brief review section listing most of the recent books on education that are available from the U.S. Government Printing Office. A "Guide to OE-Administered Programs" usually is part of the November issue.

G2 **BOOK OF THE STATES** By Council of State Governments. Lexington, Ky., 1935– . $13.50; with two supplements, $19.50.

This book, published biennially in even-numbered years, is the authoritative source of information on structures, working methods, financing, and functional activities of state governments. Each volume includes a convenient review of state legislation and legislative sessions in the immediately preceding odd-numbered year. For example, the 1974-1975 volume covers state legislation through late 1973: reviews of individual states and overall trends in state legislation, and reviews of the judiciary, interstate relations, and federal-state relations. The *Supplements,* issued in odd-numbered years, provide comprehensive listings of elected state officials and legislators. Typically, the section on major state services includes a substantial chapter on education trends.

G3 **CLEARINGHOUSE REVIEW** By National Clearinghouse for Legal Services. Chicago, 1967– . Monthly. Free to Legal Services attorneys; $25/year to others. From: Suite 2220, 500 N. Michigan Ave., Chicago, Ill. 60611.

A monthly publication of the National Clearinghouse for Legal Services, Inc., funded by the Community Services Administration (CSA), to provide current information on poverty law to attorneys and active project participants. Although education is not the only concern of this publication, it does provide good coverage of those aspects of educational legislation and litigation that touch on poverty law. The bulk of each issue is devoted to a "Poverty Law Developments" section which consists of brief, well-written, well-indexed synopses of litigation, memoranda, briefs, and judicial decisions; "Education" is one of the headings. This subject also is covered in the monthly *Poverty Law Bibliography,* which lists materials acquired by the Clearinghouse Library (a library that supports the *Clearinghouse Review* by providing copies of its documents free to CSA projects and at a nominal cost to others).

A Casetable identifies all documents reported in each issue; a cumulative topical index appears annually. Limited back issues are available at $2 each.

G4   **COMPILATION OF FEDERAL EDUCATION LAWS** (as amended through December 31, 1974) By U.S. House of Representatives, Committee on Education and Labor. Washington, D.C., 1975. Free. From: Committee on Education and Labor, U.S. House of Representatives, Washington, D.C. 20515.

A helpful compilation, updated at intervals, and available without cost while supply lasts. It includes an alphabetical table of statutes, which serves as an index to a well-organized edition of education laws. Separate sections are devoted to the education division; elementary and secondary school programs; higher education programs; educational research, experimentation, and priorities; educational personnel training programs; vocational education programs; adult education programs; programs for the handicapped; and selected statutes related to education, such as the National School Lunch Act.

The House Committee on Education and Labor also makes available, at no cost, a *Legislative Calendar* which includes lists of hearings by the Subcommittee on Education; subject, title, and author indexes; a list of Committee Prints and Subcommittee Reports; and summaries of legislative action for recent congressional sessions.

G5   **CONGRESS AND THE NATION**   Edited by Nelson and Henrietta Poynter. Washington, D.C., Congressional Quarterly, 1965– . 3 Vols. Volume 1, 1945-64 – $27.50; Volume 2, 1965-68 – $35.00; Volume 3, 1969-73 – $35.00.

An award-winning series of reference books that provide in-depth, perspective, and complete coverage of Congress and the basic issues of the times. The latest volume is (and future volumes will be) a record of government for one presidential term.

G6   **CONGRESSIONAL INFORMATION SERVICE (CIS)**   600 Montgomery Bldg., Washington, D.C. 20014.

This private publisher offers abstracts and microfiche copies of master indexes to U.S. Government documents through a series of expensive and competent reference books and services. Its congressional publications are abstracted and made available in microfiche format on a subscription service basis. Files of publications by 300 congressional agencies include committee hearings, committee prints, House and Senate reports, documents, special publications, executive reports, and executive documents.

CIS' main printed index, *CIS Index,* provides access through subjects of documents and hearings; subjects discussed by individual witnesses or authors; names and affiliations of witnesses and authors; subcommittee names; and official and popular names of laws, reports, bills, etc. Other indexes provide access by official titles, numbers (of bills, reports, documents), and names of chairmen. Its yearly *CIS/Annual*, 1970– , includes more than 14,000 abstracts and 80,000 indexing references. Annual sets of indexes and abstracts cost $220. Complete microfiche sets of publications cost approximately $3,000 per year; complete sets of hearings, approximately $2,200 per year. Its *American Statistics Index* provides a comparable series of abstracts, indexes, and microfiche copies of Federal Government statistical sources.

G7   **CQ ALMANAC**   By Congressional Quarterly. Washington, D.C., 1945– . Annual. $47.50.

Compendium of legislation enacted during one session of Congress— published every spring—with excellent summaries and quotes of committee actions, floor actions, conference reports, requests, and results. The major section, "Congressional Action," is subdivided into subject categories. An excellent index covers legislation by title. Other valuable features include summaries and occasional quotations from important committee hearings, plus a section on presidential messages and statements; also includes roll calls and vote charts from both houses of Congress. An excellent publication, designed to provide a complete, concise, and unbiased "link between the local newspapers and Capitol Hill."

G8   **CQ WEEKLY REPORT**   By Congressional Quarterly. Washington, D.C., 1945– . Weekly. $151; includes 52 *Weekly Reports*, 4 *Quarterly Indexes*, and the *CQ Almanac.*

Mailed every Saturday, this is a weekly up-date and analysis of major issues and happenings in Congress: major reports, speeches, messages, presidential press conferences, actions on public bills, debates, votes, committee hearings, and conference reports. A well-researched survey of public issues, sold only with the *CQ Almanac* (G7) and quarterly indexes. Each *Weekly Report* systematically updates previous coverage and, through cross-references and citations, provides a system of weekly indexing.

G9   **DAY CARE FACTS**   By U.S. Department of Health, Education,
       and Welfare, Office of Child Development. Washington, D.C., U.S.
       Government Printing Office, 1973. $0.40. Single copy free from
       P.O. Box 1182, Washington, D.C. 20013.
A compact pamphlet providing current information on day care services
in federal and private sectors. Includes information on federal legislation,
centers operated by federal agencies and private business, and ongoing
commitments to day care needs.

G10   **DIGEST OF STATE AND FEDERAL LAWS: Education of
       Handicapped Children**   Edited by Elaine Trudeau. 2nd Edition.
       Reston, Va., Council for Exceptional Children, 1972. $8.25.
A digest of laws relating to education of handicapped children; covers all
states and the District of Columbia as of 1972.

G11   **EDUCATION COMMISSION OF THE STATES BULLETIN**
       Denver, Colo., Education Commission of the States, 1968– .
       Bimonthly. Free.
Four-page newsletter; a good source for news on ECS (publications,
activities, etc.) and educational activities originating in or related to state
governments.

G12   **EDUCATION COMMISSION OF THE STATES LEGISLA-
       TIVE REVIEW**   Denver, Colo., Education Commission of the
       States, 1971– . Weekly or biweekly when most state legislatures are
       in session (approximately January to April); monthly during re-
       mainder of year. Free.
The best single source of information on state legislation; usually about
four pages long. Topically arranged, covering such broad areas as
educational finance, teacher tenure, handicapped children, busing, early
childhood education, minorities, and school discipline. Provides highlights of state legislation (selected by ECS from a wide variety of sources),
including state departments of education, state legislative reference
bureaus, state offices of educational associations, boards of education,
and administrators associations. Background information covers relevant
testimony, hearings and summaries, actions of Boards of Regents, leading
court decisions, and a Governor's Corner. Includes bill numbers so bills
can be obtained from state offices. While back issues of the *Review* are not
available, complete sets are on file in many state libraries, state departments of education, and legislative reference libraries.

G13   **THE EDUCATION COURT DIGEST**   New York, Juridical Di-
       gests Institute, 1957– . Monthly. $15/year. From: 1860 Broadway,
       New York, N.Y. 10023.

One of a series of court digests, in newsletter format (approximately six pages), published by this firm. Provides monthly summaries of reported state and federal court decisions on "public, parochial, and private school administration on all levels, higher education, school and teacher accreditation, libraries, and judicial decisions on education legislation." Subscriptions are available only to government, educational, and non-profit institutions and to professional persons, including students. Subject index only.

The *Court Digest* series also includes: *The Administrative Court Digest, The Conservation Court Digest, The Civil Rights Court Digest, The Ecclesiastical Court Digest, The Mental Health Court Digest, The Public Health Court Digest, The Sex Problems Court Digest, The Social Welfare Court Digest,* and *The Corrections Court Digest.*

G14 **EDUCATION FOR A NATION** Compiled by Congressional Quarterly. Washington, D.C., 1972. $4.

A competent and inexpensive publication providing background and relatively current information on major political and financial aspects of education. It includes a history of federal aid to education and chronologies of education legislation from 1945 to 1972, with information on the 1972 Education Bill, President Nixon's record on education, the current federal role, current problems in legislation and school financing, the school lobby, busing, college financing, career education, the school prayer controversy, and education projections to 1980.

G15 **FEDERAL REGISTER** By National Archives and Records Service. Washington, D.C., U.S. Government Printing Office, 1936– . Daily. $45/year; $0.75/issue.

The *Federal Register* is published Monday through Friday and contains full texts of federal regulations, executive orders, presidential proclamations, guidelines, proposed and adopted rules, and assorted notices "having general applicability and legal effect" which appear no place else. (See Figure 5 for a sample page from the *Federal Register* describing its services to the public.)

With improved format and typography in recent issues, it is somewhat less difficult to follow than it used to be. "Highlights" on the front cover, a table of contents arranged alphabetically by agency, a "reminders" list covering rules which take effect each day, and a weekly listing of public laws are useful features.

Some examples of the significance of the *Register* are the February 6, 1973 issue (Volume 38, Number 4), which contained 21 pages of detailed rules and regulations dealing with emergency school aid, and the April 24, 1973 issue (Volume 38, Number 7), which contained 14 pages revising the regulations of February 6th.

PART 3—SERVICES TO THE PUBLIC

Sec.
3.1 Information services.
3.2 Public inspection of documents.
3.3 Reproductions and certified copies of acts and documents.
3.4 Availability of Federal Register publications.

AUTHORITY: 44 U.S.C. 1506; sec. 6, E.O. 10530, 19 F.R. 2709; 3 CFR 1954-1958 Comp. p. 189.

§ 3.1 Information services.

Except in cases where the time required would be excessive, information concerning the publications described in § 2.5 of this chapter and the original acts and documents filed with the Office of the Federal Register is provided by the staff of that Office. However, the staff may not summarize or interpret substantive text of any act or document.

§ 3.2 Public inspection of documents.

(a) Current documents filed with the Office of the Federal Register pursuant to law are available for public inspection in Room 405, 633 Indiana Avenue NW., Washington, D.C., during the Office of the Federal Register office hours. There are no formal inspection procedures or requirements.

(b) The Director of the Federal Register shall cause each document received by the office to be filed for public inspection not later than the working day preceding the publication day for that document.

(c) The Director shall cause to be placed on the original and certified copies of each document a notation of the day and hour when it was filed and made available for public inspection.

(d) Manual, typewritten, or other copies of documents or excerpts may be made at the inspection desk.

§ 3.3 Reproductions and certified copies of acts and documents.

The regulations for the public use of records in the National Archives (41 CFR Part 105-61) govern the furnishing of reproductions of acts and documents and certificates of authentication for them. Section 105-61.108 of those regulations provides for the advance payment of appropriate fees for reproduction services and for certifying reproductions.

§ 3.4 Availability of Federal Register publications.

(a) The publications described in § 2.5 of this chapter are published by the Government Printing Office and are sold by the Superintendent of Documents, Government Printing Office, Washington, D.C. 20402. They are not available for free distribution to the public.

(b) Federal Register publications are available through subscription, as follows:

(1) Slip laws. In accordance with section 709 of title 44, United States Code, printed slip form copies of public and private laws are available from the Superintendent of Documents, individually or by subscription service on a yearly basis.

(2) U.S. Statutes at Large. In accordance with section 728 of title 44, United States Code, copies of the United States Statutes at Large are available from the Superintendent of Documents.

(3) Federal Register. Daily issues are furnished to subscribers on a monthly or yearly basis, at a price determined by the Administrative Committee and paid in advance to the Superintendent of Documents. Limited quantities of current or recent copies may be obtained from the Superintendent of Documents at a price determined by him.

(4) Code of Federal Regulations. Subscription services on a yearly basis to the volumes comprising the Code, and individual copies thereof, are sold by the Superintendent of Documents at prices determined by him, under the general direction of the Administrative Committee.

(5) U.S. Government Organization Manual. Placed on sale by the Superintendent of Documents at a price determined by him, under the general direction of the Administrative Committee.

(6) Public Papers of the Presidents of the United States. Annual volumes are placed on sale by the Superintendent of Documents at a price determined by him, under the general direction of the Administrative Committee.

(7) Weekly Compilation of Presidential Documents. Placed on sale by the Superintendent of Documents at a price determined by him, under the general direction of the Administrative Committee.

FIGURE 5   Sample page from the *Federal Register* describing its services to the public.

This document is a daily supplement to the *Code of Federal Regulations,* revised each January 1st, with supplements available in July. (Parts 100 to 199 of Title 45 of the *Code* pertain to education and are available from the Superintendent of Documents, U.S. Government Printing Office, Washington, D.C. 20402, for $5.30.)

G16 **FOOD FOR ALL** By League of Women Voters of the United
States. Washington, D.C., 1972. $0.50. From: 1730 M St., N.W.,
Washington, D.C. 20036.

A compendium of information and legislation on local, state, and federal food programs. Outlines both the responsibilities of governmental groups to implement these programs and the rights of participants. Valuable for schools and day care centers, as well as for welfare groups.

G17 **GUIDE TO SCHOOL LAW** By M. Chester Nolte. West Nyack,
N.Y., Parker Publishing, 1969. $12.95.

Reference text for school administrators which provides legal guidance on issues related to schools, based on the premise that state laws and court decisions are becoming increasingly similar. Chapters cover the school administrator's legal status, as well as rights and responsibilities of school employees and school districts. Includes a glossary of legal terms, an index of cases by state, and a subject index.

G18 **A HANDBOOK OF STATE LAWS AND POLICIES AFFECT-
ING EQUAL RIGHTS FOR WOMEN IN EDUCATION** By
Jessica Pearson. Denver, Colo., Education Commission of the
States, 1975. $2. (Report 62 from the Equal Rights for Women in
Education Project.) From: 1860 Lincoln St., Denver, Colo. 80203.

A state-by-state compilation of laws, executive orders, regulations, guidelines, structures, and procedures affecting equal rights for women in education, covering labor laws, employment practices, antidiscrimination agencies, recent and pending legislation, status of the Equal Rights Amendment, policies in elementary and secondary education, and state commissions on the status of women. Its format allows easy reference and comparison between states. Charts at the end offer a quick overview of the findings.

A *Digest of Federal Laws on Equal Rights* (Report 61) is available free from the same source. It is a conveniently arranged summary, digest, and content analysis of federal laws, executive orders, and interpretative guidelines, arranged and synthesized for easy consultation.

G19 **HIGH SPOTS IN STATE SCHOOL LEGISLATION** An Annual Compilation, January 1–August 31, 1972. Compiled by
National Education Assn. Washington, D.C., 1936– . $2.
Annual compilations of selected state legislation based on reports
submitted by state education associations in response to the NEA Research
Division's annual questionnaire; supplemented by such sources as state
education journals, legislative bulletins, and texts of bills. The odd cutoff
date corresponds with the end of legislative sessions in most states. Varies
in size, since most legislative sessions are held in even-numbered years.
   This book is in part a score card on the goals of state educational
associations: the first category is "major achievements and defeats,"
arranged by state. Other areas, categorized by goals and enactments,
include school finance; teacher salaries, tenure, contracts, certification,
professional standards and practices, leaves of absence, professional
negotiation and related legislation, retirement, and social security;
textbooks, instruction, and curriculum; pupil transportation; education
of exceptional children; school buildings and sites; school district reorganization; local school administration; state school administration; and
higher education. A final page cross-indexes states with topics.

G20 **HOW TO FIND U.S. STATUTES AND U.S. CODE
CITATIONS** By U.S. House Committee on the Judiciary. 2nd
Edition, Revised. Washington, D.C., U.S. Government Printing
Office, 1971. $0.10.
A useful tool for an inexperienced, but determined, legal researcher.

G21 **JOURNAL OF COLLECTIVE NEGOTIATIONS IN THE
PUBLIC SECTOR** Edited by Dr. Harry Kershen. Farmingdale,
N.Y., Baywood Publishing, 1972– . Quarterly. $25/year; two-year
cumulative index.
This publication deals with an increasingly important aspect of law and
administration: public negotiation and public sector mediation. As a
forum for ideas and information, it includes varying viewpoints, theoretical discussions, and practical treatment of such topics as accountability
and performance level as they relate to the concepts of collective
negotiation.

G22 **JOURNAL OF LAW AND EDUCATION** Silver Spring, Md.,
Jefferson Law Book Co., 1972– .Quarterly. $25.00/year; foreign
and Canada, $27.50/year.
The *Journal of Law and Education* was designed to inform, predict, and
collate information in the burgeoning area of education law. The bulk of
this publication is devoted to serious, well-researched articles on such

issues as public sector strikes, curriculum control, elementary school law, and loyalty oaths; that is, any area where law and education impinge upon each other. Two continuing sections are "Legislation," which provides updates on significant legislation, and "Notes on Recent Cases," which provides judicial decisions in education.

G23 **LEGISLATION, ACHIEVEMENTS AND PROBLEMS IN EDUCATION** A Survey of the States, 1972. By Education Commission of the States. Denver, Colo., 1972. $2. (Out-of-Print)
A comprehensive report, based on a well-designed survey, that was sent to all state departments of education (with replies from 46). Contains legislation (proposed and enacted), achievements, and problems in education as reported by state departments of education, legislative reference bureaus, and other education organizations. This information is compiled under 12 major headings: accountability; administration; early childhood education; financing of public education; higher education; nonpublic, private, and parochial education; pupil personnel; special education; teachers and school personnel; and vocational education. Headings are subdivided for further access, with a good overall index. Appendixes include a list of legislative reference bureaus and state departments of education. Subsequent surveys are being released as research briefs on specific topics.

G24 **1972 LEGISLATION AND ACHIEVEMENTS RELATED TO TEACHERS AND OTHER SCHOOL PERSONNEL** By Doris M. Ross. Denver, Colo., Education Commission of the States, 1973. $2. (Research Brief No. 4)
A concise, well-organized summary of topical state legislation in 1972, based on a survey of state education agencies and legislative service agencies. Areas covered include evaluation, certification and professional practices of teachers and professional staff, collective bargaining, utilization of personnel, tenure, and training, but omit salaries, benefits, and retirement (which are adequately covered elsewhere by NEA and AFT). Arranged by subject, then by states, this book contains legislative citations, statute citations of summaries, and status of each bill. The last four pages provide current lists of state education agencies and legislative service agencies. No central index, but well cross-referenced.

G25 **LEGISLATION BY THE STATES: Accountability and Assessment in Education** By Phyllis Hawthorne. Revised Edition. Denver, Colo., Co-operative Accountability Project, 1973. Free. From: 1362 Lincoln St., Denver, Colo. 80203.
A state-by-state analysis of state legislation in accountability, based on

documents collected for the Co-operative Accountability Project and maintained in the State Education Accountability Repository (SEAR) (N22).

G26 **A LEGISLATOR'S GUIDE TO SCHOOL FINANCE** By Anthony Morley et al., prepared for the National Legislative Conference Special Committee on School Finance. Denver, Colo., Education Commission of the States, 1972. $2.

This booklet contains a brief analysis of four alternatives for state systems on school funding, together with a concise conceptual framework for approaching the subject of school finance reform. Since the booklet was prepared as a practical guide for state legislators, it focuses on concrete issues of reform in the context of each state's political atmosphere. States studied were Minnesota, Michigan, Kansas, and New York, but the book is valuable to any state seeking an understandable introduction to the problems of school finance. Similar *Research Briefs,* published in 1975 and available from the same source for $2 each, are *A Legislator's Guide to the Year-Round School, A Legislator's Guide to Education Accountability, A Legislator's Guide to Teacher Tenure,* and *A Legislator's Guide to Collective Bargaining in Education.*

G27 **NEA REPORTER** Washington, D.C., National Education Assn., 1962– . 8 issues/year; membership only.

Issued monthly from September through May, except in December, this newsletter analyzes federal education legislation and lists research and program resources. Available only to members of NEA, together with *Today's Education.*

G28 **STATE BLUEBOOKS AND REFERENCE PUBLICATIONS** A Selected Bibliography. 2nd Edition. By Council of State Governments. Lexington, Ky., 1974. $3.

This book, arranged by state (with territories at the end), provides titles and availability of (mostly ongoing) state publications in three major categories: legislature and general state government, digests or summaries of legislative action, and general guides and statistics. An extremely helpful tool for anyone studying states or state legislative actions. It is compiled by the Council of State Governments and checked for accuracy by state legislative reference bureaus. A quarterly *Legislative Research Checklist,* prepared by the same agency, lists reports by legislative service agencies and other study committees in the states.

G29 **STATE CONSTITUTIONAL PROVISIONS AND SELECTED LEGAL MATERIALS RELATING TO PUBLIC SCHOOL FINANCE** Edited by Linda E. Perle and Barrie L. Goldstein for the U.S. Office of Education. Washington, D.C., U.S. Government Printing Office, 1973. $1.30.
A reference work outlining state constitutional structures for school finance reform purposes.

G30 **STATE CONSTITUTIONAL PROVISIONS RELATING TO STATE BOARDS OF EDUCATION AND STATE SUPERIN-TENDENTS** Lexington, Ky., Council of State Governments, 1971. $2.50.
An analytical and comparative study of constitutional provisions presented in table format with summary texts. Charts include method of selection, term of office, compensation, qualifications, power and duties, and removal of the Chief State School Officer. Others deal with the number, selection, ex officio members, qualifications, terms of office, compensation, powers and duties, and removal of state school board members.

G31 **STATE DEPARTMENTS OF EDUCATION, STATE BOARDS OF EDUCATION, AND CHIEF STATE SCHOOL OFFICERS, 1972** Prepared by Sam P. Harris for U.S. Office of Education. Washington, D.C., U.S. Government Printing Office, 1973. $2.50.
Provides information on structure, organizations, and constitutional and/or statutory basis of education in the 50 states.

G32 **STATE GOVERNMENT NEWS** Lexington, Ky., Council of State Governments, 1970– . Monthly. $5/year.
Covers significant items from individual states, legislation, reorganization in state governments, etc. The bulk of this publication is often devoted to actions in Washington which affect the states.

G33 **STATE LAW AND THE EDUCATION OF HANDICAPPED CHILDREN; Issues and Recommendations** By Frederick J. Weintraub, Alan R. Abeson, and David L. Braddog. Reston, Va., Council for Exceptional Children, 1971. $3.60.
Statement of major issues and recommendations relating to government and to education of the handicapped. Covers the right to an education, identification and placement, planning, administrative responsibility, services, and personnel. A final section proposes two model state laws.

G34   **A STUDY OF STATE LEGAL STANDARDS FOR THE PROVI-
      SION OF PUBLIC EDUCATION**   Prepared by the Lawyers'
      Committee for Civil Rights Under Law for the National Institute of
      Education. Washington, D.C., National Institute of Education,
      1974. Free. From: NIE, Washington, D.C. 20208.

A summary and comparison (mostly in chart form) of state laws and
regulations relating to education, based on a study of 37 areas (ranging
from accountability to vocational education), with comparative charts for
20 of these areas. Includes a bibliography of other legal studies involving
the 50 states, a list of state contacts, and a bibliography of state source
materials and summaries.

   Conducted by the Lawyers' Committee for Civil Rights Under Law, this
study collected, categorized, and compared current laws on elementary
and secondary school education in the 50 states. Three thousand pages of
summaries, organized by state and by subject area, are being incorporated
into the ERIC system, and are available from the National Institute of
Education and the Lawyers' Committee for limited printing and dissemination. These materials are now being used for a further Lawyers'
Committee project designed to develop model legislative and administrative standards for public education.

G35   **THE TEACHER'S DAY IN COURT: Review of 1971**   Washing-
      ton, D.C., National Education Assn., Research Div., 1939–1972.
      $3.

An annual report which digested decisions of state and federal courts
where teachers and other certificated school personnel were plaintiffs or
defendants. It provided summaries of court decisions on legal issues of
importance to teachers, covering such issues as certification, salaries,
contracts, tenure, school desegregation, civil rights, teacher-school board
negotiations, and liability for pupil injury. Still a convenient shortcut for
research (this is the last of these reports to be published).

   A Pupil's Day in Court, published by the NEA Research Division, covered
student rights and case law.

G36   **WASHINGTON REPORT ON LEGISLATION FOR CHIL-
      DREN: And What You Can Do About It**   By American Parents
      Committee, Inc. Washington, D.C., 1947– . "Issued from time to
      time when Congress is in session." $10/year, members. From: 52
      Vanderbilt Ave., New York, N.Y. 10017.

A mimeographed newsletter, issued approximately four times a year (to
members only) by the Washington office of the American Parents

Committee, that provides a good overview of the entire range of legislation concerning children—not only education, but child welfare, child health, nutrition, child labor, juvenile delinquency, and all other areas that affect children. It is well-organized, in accordance with goals of the American Parents Committee, and offers concise summaries of legislation, as well as tables, charts, and explicit information on funding.

G37 **YEARBOOK OF SCHOOL LAW, 1974** Edited by Floyd G. Delon et al. Topeka, Kan., National Organization on Legal Problems of Education, 1974. Annual. $9.95.

This yearbook has been produced under varied auspices and has been published by various publishers since 1933; however, since 1972, it has been edited, produced and published through NOLPE. The *Yearbook* reviews the previous year's major cases of school law, with chapters—authored by individual specialists—covering governance of education, liability, school property, school finance, teachers and other employees, pupils, and higher education. A tremendous increase in class action suits has been noted in recent years. NOLPE and its other publications are discussed in greater detail in N19.

FEDERAL FUNDS

Sources of information on federal funds to a large extent overlap those on law and legislation. This section includes two types of supplemental printed sources: original documents—relatively inexpensive and available to the general public—which can be tedious and difficult to decipher; and relatively high-priced information services or newsletters, which scan the public records and probe their own private sources. The latter vary widely in price and quality. Only those exhibiting a high level of accuracy and relevance have been included here.

Since the *Federal Register* (G15) is obliged to print guidelines, regulations, and agency rules, it may be the best source to follow for the implementation of legislation.

The U.S. sources listed in Chapter 15 (both regional and central) are responsible for providing information pertaining to their agencies and policies. If federal sources, however, fail to provide such information, federal coordinators in state departments of education, depending on their information sources, may be worth contacting.

G38 **ANNUAL REGISTER OF GRANT SUPPORT, 1975-76**   Edited by Jean L. Aroeste. 8th Edition. Chicago, Marquis Who's Who, Academic Media, 1975. $47.50.

A well-organized, well-indexed survey of currently available grants, which, unfortunately, does not appear until September or October of each year. The eighth edition includes 1,580 grant support sources: government, foundations, business, labor unions, and professional organizations. It is arranged by broad subject categories such as humanities, social sciences, health and medicine, area studies, and environment. Provides such information as organization, purpose, eligibility, financial data, and duration of grant support. Indexes are by subject, organization, geographical region, and personnel (trustees, directors, award committee members).

G39 **CAREER EDUCATION: A Handbook of Funding Resources**   By Charles W. Ryan. Boston, Houghton Mifflin, 1973. $1.

A handy guide to funding sources (local, state, federal, and foundation) available for elementary and secondary programs in career education. Includes a glossary on career education and a sample research proposal.

G40 **CATALOG OF FEDERAL DOMESTIC ASSISTANCE**   By Office of Management and Budget. Washington, D.C., U.S. Government Printing Office,1965– . Annual. $14.50/year (including basic catalog and supplementary material for an indefinite period); $3.65 additional for foreign mailing.

A loose-leaf guide to the complexities of federal, social, and economic assistance programs for states, communities, private groups, and individuals, roughly classified by bureau functions. It describes more than 1,000 programs administered by approximately 60 federal agencies and departments, and contains authorizing statute, nature of program activities, eligibility and restrictions, deadlines, and local and Washington contacts, as well as detailed indexes. A valuable directory resource for local agency addresses and services. This publication was formerly issued by the Office of Economic Opportunity.

G41 **CATALOG OF FEDERAL EDUCATION ASSISTANCE PROGRAMS, 1974**   By U.S. Office of Education, Office of Management. Washington, D.C., U.S. Government Printing Office, 1974. $5.55. (DHEW Publication No. [OE] 74-01600)

This education catalog stems from the larger *Catalog of Federal Domestic Assistance*. It contains brief descriptions of education-related federal programs—including all Office of Education programs—and other federal programs supporting educational services, professional training, and library services. Programs, arranged by number, offer clearly worded and well-formatted descriptions which include agency, authorization, objectives, types of assistance, uses and use restriction, applicant eligibility, application and award process, financial information, regulations and guidelines, and information contacts. Its scope covers all types of grants, loans, scholarships, and other financial assistance; assistance in the form of property, facilities, goods, or services; and technical assistance, counseling, and professional training. Includes an Index by Program Names, an Authorization Index (by name of Act), a Public Law Index, a U.S. Code Index, an Administering Agency Index, and a Beneficiary Information Index.

G42 **EDUCATION FUNDING NEWS** Edited by Erna Ferlanti. Washington, D.C., Education Funding Research Council, 1971– . Biweekly. Membership only.

An excellent publication about sources of federal aid to education, slanted toward the needs of public schools and focusing on lawmakers and federal regulations. Summaries include relevant dates and appropriate federal offices to contact, usually with names and phone numbers of individuals. Articles and reviews are informative. A more detailed discussion of the Education Funding Research Council can be found in Chapter 15.

G43 **FEDERAL AID INFORMATION SERVICE** By National School Public Relations Assn., Arlington, Va., 1973– . $90/year. From: 1801 N. Moore St., Arlington, Va. 22209.

Designed for local school districts participating in federal aid activities, this service includes several publications. The *Federal Aid Fact Book,* published each January, lists and describes the major aid-to-education programs, including type and purpose of assistance, authorizing legislation, use restriction, related programs, guidelines and regulations, information contacts, and how to apply. The weekly newsletter, *Washington Monitor,* provides updates on federal agencies, changing guidelines, actions by Congress, etc., every Monday. A three-times a year *Federal Aid Planner* contains detailed explanations of assistance programs relevant to the needs of local school districts. Price includes two copies of the *Fact Book,* three sets of the newsletter, a set of loose-leaf binders for all publications, and cumulative indexes in July and December of all three publications.

G44 **FEDERAL FUNDS FOR DAY CARE PROJECTS** Compiled by Beatrice Rosenberg, U.S. Department of Labor, Women's Bureau. Washington, D.C., U.S. Government Printing Office, 1972. $1.

An overview of federal funds, from all sources, which can be used for day care programs. Provides a detailed listing by departments and agencies, including information on authorizing law, source of funds, who is eligible, and whom to contact.

**G45 GETTING INVOLVED; YOUR GUIDE TO GENERAL REV-
ENUE SHARING** By Department of the Treasury, Office of Revenue Sharing. Washington, D.C., U.S. Government Printing Office, 1973. $0.40.

"The purpose of this booklet is to provide information about the general revenue sharing program, especially about its aspects which directly encourage public involvement in decision making." [From its Introduction.]

G46 THE GUIDE TO FEDERAL ASSISTANCE FOR EDUCATION By Robert E. Horn. Washington, D.C., Appleton-Century-Crofts Educational Div., 1973. 2 Vols. $375/set; annual supplements, $225.

Both the contents and indexes of this loose-leaf compilation (with dated pages) are updated extensively each month. Contents are arranged by lettered sections, with large tabs. Areas covered include programs, regional and state offices, and an "in process" section with full how-what-why information on grants and eligibility criteria. The contents are indexed by individuals, school levels, state agencies, laws, federal funds, and deadlines.

G47 GUIDE TO FUNDING NEW CAREERS PROGRAM By New Careers Training. 2nd Edition. New York, 1972. $5. From: New Human Services Institute, 184 Fifth Ave., New York, N.Y. 10010.

Covers more than 180 federal grant-in-aid programs offering funds to support some aspect of career development. Eligible applicants include public schools, colleges, antipoverty and other nonprofit agencies, and local and state governments. A section on private foundations and on strategies of grantsmanship also is included. A full bibliography of publications on paraprofessionals and career development is available from the institute.

G48 GUIDE TO OE-ADMINISTERED PROGRAMS, Fiscal Year 1975 By Education Division, U.S. Department of Health, Education, and Welfare. Washington, D.C., U.S. Government Printing Office, 1975. Annual. Multiple copies, $0.25 each; single copies free from American Education, P.O. Box 9000, Alexandria, Va. 22304. (Reprinted from *American Education*.)

Presents data on financial and technical assistance for the coming fiscal year in chart form (see Figure 6), grouped to indicate either types of institutions or nature of support; that is, for research, construction, etc. Categories include type of assistance, authorizing legislation, purpose, appropriation in dollars, who may apply, and where to apply.

G49 **GUIDE TO PROGRAMS** By National Endowment for the Arts. Washington, D.C., U.S. Government Printing Office, 1973. Multiple copies, $0.95 each; single copies free from National Endowment for the Arts.

This publication outlines programs of the National Endowment for the Arts under which grants are available and tells how and when to apply.

TYPE OF ASSISTANCE	AUTHORIZING LEGISLATION	PURPOSE	APPRO-PRIATION (dollars)	WHO MAY APPLY	WHERE TO APPLY [1]
GROUP III: FOR RESEARCH					
1 Handicapped research and related activities	Education of the Handicapped Act, Title VI-E, (PL 91-230)	To promote new knowledge and teaching techniques applicable to the education of the handicapped	9.566.000	State or local education agencies and private educational organizations or research groups	OE's Bureau of Programs for Handicapped, Division of Innovation and Development
2 Physical education and recreation for the handicapped	Education of the Handicapped Act, Title VI-E, (PL 91-230)	To perform research in areas of physical education and recreation for handicapped children	350.000	State or local education agencies, public or nonprofit private educational or research agencies and organizations	OE Bureau of Programs for Innovation and Development
3 Vocational education curriculum development	Vocational Education Act of 1963, as amended, Part "I"	To develop standards for curriculum development in all occupational fields and promote the development and dissemination of materials for use in teaching occupational subjects	4.000.000	State and local education agencies, private institutions and organizations	OE Application Control Center, Office of Adult, Vocational, Technical and Manpower Education
4 Vocational education research (developing new careers and occupations)	Vocational Education Act of 1963, as amended, Part C	To develop new vocational education careers and to disseminate information about them	9.000.000	Education agencies, private institutions and organizations	OE Application Control Center, Office of Adult, Vocational, Technical, and Manpower Education
5 Vocational education research (innovative projects)	Vocational Education Act of 1963, as amended, Part D	To develop, establish and operate exemplary and innovative projects to serve as models for vocational education programs	8.000.000	State boards of education	OE Office of Adult, Vocational, Technical and Manpower Education, Division of Research and Demonstration
6 Vocational education research (meeting vocational needs of youth)	Vocational Education Act of 1963, as amended, Part C	To develop programs that meet the special vocational needs of youths with academic and socio-economic handicaps	9.000.000	Education agencies, private institutions, and organizations	State boards of education
7 Vocational education research (relating school curriculums to careers)	Vocational Education Act of 1963, as amended, Part D	To stimulate the development of new methods for relating school work to occupational fields and public education to manpower agencies	8.000.000	State boards of education, local education agencies	DHEW Regional Offices
8 Library demonstrations	Higher Education Act, Title II-B	To promote library and information science research and demonstrations	1.425.000	Institutions of higher education and other public or private nonprofit agencies, institutions, and organizations	OE Division of Library Programs
GROUP IV: FOR CONSTRUCTION					
1 Public schools	School Aid to Federally Impacted and Major Disaster Areas (PL 815)	Aid school districts in providing minimum school facilities in federally impacted and disaster areas	19.000.000	Local school districts	DHEW Regional Offices
2 Vocational facilities	Appalachian Regional Development Act of 1965	Construct area vocational education facilities in the Appalachian region	24.000.000	State education agencies in Appalachian region	OE Division of Vocational and Technical Education

1 OE (Office of Education)
2 Includes $2,000,000 in appropriated excess foreign currencies, $300,000 from the Bureau of Postsecondary Education
3 At least ten percent for handicapped
4 Represents total funding figure for Title IV of Civil Rights Act
5 Taken from a total $3,000,000 in appropriated excess foreign currencies

DISCRIMINATION PROHIBITED
Title VI of the Civil Rights Act of 1964 states: "No person in the United States shall, on the ground of race, color, or national origin, be excluded from participation in, be denied the benefits of, or be subjected to discrimination under any program or activity receiving Federal financial assistance, or be so treated on the basis of sex under most education programs or activities receiving Federal assistance." All programs cited in this article

FIGURE 6 The chart format of the *Guide to OE-Administered Programs* provides a quick overview of federal financial support for educational purposes.

Areas include art, environment, dance, literature, museums, media, and music.

G50 **SOURCES OF INFORMATION ON FUNDS FOR EDUCA-
TION: An Annotated Bibliography**   Edited by Helen Daetz, Mary Jo Hall, and Robert E. Frank. 2nd Edition. Corvallis, Ore., Federal Relations Book, 1971. $5. From: Office of Federal Relations, Extension Hall Annex, University Campus, Corvallis, Ore. 97331.

A handbook for educational agencies and individuals who need to research and analyze all available information on possible sources of financial support. Identifies and analyzes these "major sources of information" used by professional monitors in the statewide Office of Federal Relations in Oregon to locate information on all levels of education, in all subject areas. Alphabetically lists approximately 260 publications (newsletters, periodicals, compilations) with source, price, address, and informative annotations. Also contains a subject index and a listing of agencies and associations. May be out-of-print.

G51 **THE UNITED STATES BUDGET IN BRIEF: Fiscal Year
1976**   By U.S. Department of Commerce, Bureau of the Budget. Washington, D.C., U.S. Government Printing Office, 1975. Annual. $1.15.

Provides the most understandable account of the U.S. budget available to nonfiscal individuals. It offers an overall view—broken down and analyzed by function—with color charts and tables, excerpts from the President's budget message, and an analysis of possible effects of this budget to 1977 and beyond.

   Two, more detailed, annual budget analyses are *The Budget of the U.S. Government* (Fiscal Year 1976, $3.45) and the *Special Analysis of the Budget of the U.S. Government* (1976, $2.70), both available from the U.S. Government Printing Office or local government bookstores.

G52 **THE VICE-PRESIDENT'S HANDBOOK FOR LOCAL OF-
FICIALS**   By Office of the Vice President. Washington, D.C., U.S. Government Printing Office, 1967. $2.

This interagency guide to federal assistance was written to aid local government officials. Although some of it may be of historical interest only, it is well-written and clear. Its introduction provides an excellent overview of federal assistance.

FOUNDATIONS

The Foundation Center and its regional libraries (N 10) are the best sources for obtaining information not available in the *Foundation Directory* (G57), *Foundation News* (G58), or *Annual Register of Grant Support* (G38).

A handy overall list of foundations which apply major portions of their assets to education can be found on pages 359 to 371 of *Educator's World* (B39). Although the foundations were selected and listed in 1971, this comprehensive list tells when information became available, and includes officers, purposes, limitations, and publications.

ANNUAL REPORTS: The annual reports of foundations, generally available on request, include policy statements, recent grants, and, sometimes, requirements and application procedures. Many of these are on file at The Foundation Center.

INTERNAL REVENUE SERVICE FORM: Since the Tax Reform Act of 1969, foundations have had to face stringent requirements for reporting income, assets, and contributions to the Internal Revenue Service (Form 990A). The public information portion of these forms, which includes names of officers and directors, foundation assets, and a listing of yearly grants, are on file at The Foundation Center—at least for larger foundations—while additional copies of Form 990A are on file at appropriate regional depositories and can be obtained on microfiche.

STATE RECORDS: Most states generally have an office, such as the Registrar for Charitable Trusts, charged with the responsibility for regulating (and hence compiling information on) all state foundations. These files, or at least parts of them, are generally treated as public documents, which may be inspected, at least on-site. The attorney general's office of each state is a good starting place to locate these records, as is the telephone directory for the capitol city.

An increasing number of state agencies and private individuals or groups are compiling guides and directories of their state foundations. For example, the New England Foundation Research Project, operating out of Eastern Connecticut State College in Willimantic, Connecticut, has embarked on a continuing series of state guides to the private foundations of New England states.

The recently discontinued *Foundation Center Information Quar-*

terly reviewed a number of state foundation directories in its 1974 issues. Directories compiled for California, Connecticut, District of Columbia, New Hampshire, and Ohio were reviewed in its January 1974 issue; Michigan, Oregon, and Vermont, in the April 1974 issue.

Copies of subsequent local directories undoubtedly will be available at the various libraries of The Foundation Center, discussed in Chapter 15 (N10).

Materials listed in this section include sources for locating information on foundations, and guides to using this information effectively. More sources are available in Chapter 15.

G53 **THE BREAD GAME: The Realities of Foundation Fundraising** Compiled by Regional Young Adult Project and Pacific Change. Revised Edition. San Francisco, Glide Publications, 1974. $2.95 (paperback).
An unorthodox "how to" for proponents of social change. Includes advice on how to develop and prepare a proposal, sample proposals for small- and large-budget projects, advice on forming tax-exempt organizations, simplified accounting procedures and worksheets, hypothetical grant agreements and reports, what to do while you are waiting, and a Third World perspective on funding.

G54 **A COMPREHENSIVE GUIDE TO SUCCESSFUL GRANTSMANSHIP** By William Hill. Littleton, Colo., Grant Development Institute, 1972. $24, prepaid. From: 2140 S. Holly St., Denver, Colo. 80222.
Covers the entire grant-seeking procedure, from original idea to proposal presentation, for both foundations and government agencies. Includes a bibliography and addresses of sources. A one-year subscription to the monthly *Grant Development Digest* (otherwise $5) is included in the purchase price.

G55 **DIRECTORY OF EUROPEAN FOUNDATIONS** Prepared by Giovanni Agnelli Foundation. Torino, Italy, Giovanni Agnelli Foundation and Russell Sage Foundation, 1969. $9.
Describes 301 nonprofit European foundations concerned with scientific and cultural research; arranged by country. Includes address, year of establishment, founder, purpose, and a description as of 1967. An extended introduction provides much background information on foundations in Europe, nation-by-nation.

G56 **THE $$ GAME: A Guidebook on the Funding of Law-Related Educational Programs** Edited by Charles J. White, III. Chicago, Special Committee on Youth Education for Citizenship, American Bar Assn., 1975. Single copies free. 2–25 copies, $2.00 each; 26–50 copies, $1.75 each; more than 50 copies, $1.50 each.

A practical how-to compilation for developing and sustaining support for legal and political education projects, prepared by the staff of the Youth Education for Citizenship, with suggestions on identifying funding sources, securing community support, and institutionalizing programs. Includes a checklist of addresses of sources of information, and a bibliography of funding materials—books, periodicals, and articles—useful for law-related citizenship education programs.

G57 **FOUNDATION DIRECTORY** Edited by Marianna O. Lewis and Patrick Bowers. 5th Edition. New York, Foundation Center, 1975. $30, including four supplements. Distributed by Columbia University Press.

The eligibility criteria for inclusion in the latest edition of this national directory were that total foundation grants for the year amounted to $500,000 or more, or that foundation assets were $1,000,000 or more. (For previous editions, the criteria were as low as $10,000 and $200,000 for these two categories.) The *Directory* lists approximately 2,200 foundations, arranged by states and indexed by names. Information for each foundation listed includes the legal name, address, and founding date; donors, officers, trustees, and administrators; purposes and fields of interest; limitations and assets; the person(s) to contact; and the number of grants.

Supplements, to be issued in July and December 1975 and in 1976, will provide updates and list approximately 25,000 foundations for which descriptive data (in hard copy or microfiche) are available through The Foundation Center.

G58 **FOUNDATION NEWS** *The Journal of Philanthropy.* Edited by Patrick W. Kennedy. New York, Council on Foundations, 1960– . Bimonthly. $15/year. From: Box 783, Old Chelsea Sta., New York, N.Y. 10011.

This publication changed its contents and format in 1973 to include a removable, self-contained section—*The Foundation Grants Index,* a product of The Foundation Center—which reports on grants of $5,000 or more by state, foundation, and recipient (approximately 1,000 grants per issue) and indexes them by subject. Other sections include news from Washington and the state capitols which could affect philanthropy, as well as in-depth articles on issues, trends, and programs concerned with raising and dispensing revenues.

G59 **GIVING USA: Annual Report** By American Assn. of Fund-Raising Counsel, Inc. New York, 1956– . Annual. $2.50; full subscription, $15.00. From: 500 Fifth Ave., New York, N.Y. 10036.

The annual report issue of *Giving USA* provides an inexpensive overview of the previous year's philanthropy. It covers individuals, bequests, foundations, and corporations, with concise summaries of statistics and trends in religion, health, social welfare, arts, humanities, public affairs, international affairs, and education. Includes good tables, as well as references that lead to other sources. Other issues of *Giving USA* summarize trends in giving and note compilations and reference sources.

G60 **GRANT APPLICATION GUIDE** By Council of Planning Affiliates. Seattle, Wash., 1969. $0.75. From: United Way of King County, 700 Lowman Bldg., 107 Cherry St., Seattle, Wash. 98104.

Designed to help social service agencies seeking funds for innovative proposals, this 15-page guide covers the development of a proposal, locating funding, proposal review, applications to federal agencies, and information on basic grant resources.

G61 **HOW TO PREPARE A RESEARCH PROPOSAL: Suggestions for Those Seeking Funds for Behavioral Science Research** By David R. Krathwohl. Syracuse, N.Y., Syracuse University Bookstore, 1966. $1.

A classic work on proposal writing—using a checklist as a table of contents—intended for behavioral scientists who write research proposals; but the sections covering statement of the problem, objectives, end product, personnel, facilities, and budget are widely applicable to other areas.

G62 **MONEY...YOU CAN GET IT** By Lee Sproull. *Learning Magazine*, *1*(7): 12-13, May 1973.

Offers some helpful suggestions for teachers who want to raise small amounts of money for local education projects, with recommendations on how to contact small foundations, local colleges, universities, and service organizations.

G63 **THE PROPOSAL WRITER'S SWIPE FILE** Edited by Jean Brodsky. Washington, D.C., Taft Products, Inc., 1973. $5.50.

Contains 12 professionally written grant proposals, originally prepared to obtain foundation funding for various organizations—now printed in one book as a source of ideas. Useful for browsing for ideas on concepts, organization, and format.

G64 **TAFT INFORMATION SYSTEM: A Method for Keeping Current on Foundations** By Taft Products, Inc. Washington, D.C., 1971– . $250. From: 1000 Vermont Ave., N.W., Washington, D.C. 20005.

This system provides detailed information on the wealthier foundations and comes in several parts. The *Foundation Reporter* of 1972-1973 listed information on 150 foundations and added an additional 20 with each quarterly supplement: its five indexes are by foundation, state, individuals, fields of interest, and types of grant; its *News Monitor of Philanthropy* is a monthly supplement on grants, appointments, and events; and *Hot Line* (a news service) comes out periodically. In addition to the standard identification of the foundations—with histories, types of grants, geographic areas, officers and trustees, and recent grants—these publications provide details on the decision makers and the characteristics of successful grant requests.

Educational Products
and Curricular Resources

The materials included in the following five chapters are designed primarily to assist educators and administrators who are selecting materials to be used in the schools—for curriculum, instruction, testing, libraries, and media centers. Other materials that deal with these disciplines, but are more appropriate for research purposes or overall discussion of subject areas, were included in the first seven chapters.

Chapter 9 lists tools and methods for selecting instructional materials, and includes some books that evaluate sources, others that list selected materials, and a few that set standards for the process of selection.

Chapters 10 to 13 divide sources of information on instructional materials into several parts. Those collections, compilations, and selection tools dealing with specific curricular areas and teaching methods are included in Chapter 10, Curriculum Materials and Activities; those emphasizing nonprint instructional materials, in Chapter 11, Guides to Nonprint Instructional Materials; and those concerned with children's books, in Chapter 12. While Chapter 13, Tests and Assessment Instruments, is academic in part, its major orientation is the selection of tests and assessment instruments for school use, rather than the theoretical bases of tests and measurements.

Although there is some unavoidable overlap, this arrangement sorts the sources into browsable areas; the items listed in Chapter 9 were too general to fit into more specific categories.

9 | *Selecting Instructional Materials*

This chapter is largely concerned with aiding educators in selecting and evaluating instructional materials and tools. Some factors to consider are timeliness, quality, cost, relation to curriculum, appropriateness for community and students, and, in recent years, selecting instructional materials free from racial and sexist bias. The guides listed here include several which should prove valuable for the latter purpose.

Additionally, guidelines which have been developed by publishers to aid authors in avoiding obvious sexist bias also can be used by educators in evaluating textbooks and other teaching materials. McGraw-Hill's *Guidelines for Equal Treatment of the Sexes in McGraw-Hill Book Company Publications,* which has been extensively reprinted, is available from the Public Information and Publicity Department, McGraw-Hill, 1221 Avenue of the Americas, New York, N.Y. 10020. *Guidelines for Improving the Image of Women in Textbooks* is available from Patricia Forester, Research Information Division, Scott, Foresman, 1900 East Lake Avenue, Glenview, Illinois 60025. Elizabeth Burr, Susan Dunn, and Norma Farquhar have prepared a 12-page pamphlet, *Guidelines for Equal Treatment of the Sexes in Social Studies Textbooks,* which is available for $0.50 from Ms. Farquhar, 12709 Dewey Street, Los Angeles, California 90066.

H1   **THE BOOKLIST AND SUBSCRIPTION BOOKS BUL-
      LETIN**   Edited by Paul L. Brawley. Chicago, American Library
      Assn., 1969– . $20/year.

A compilation of professional reviews of print and nonprint current
media productions—selected, recommended, and evaluated by an organization of professional librarians. The "other media" cover a wide
range, but frequently include slides, multimedia kits, maps, and picture
sets. Frequent bibliographic essays add depth to the impressive breadth
and selectivity of coverage. This is a most important tool for selecting
current materials for libraries and other resource centers. The evaluative
annotated reviews—arranged in broad classifications consistent with the
Dewey Decimal Classification—provide accurate citations, price, subject
indexing, Library of Congress catalog card numbers, and Library of
Congress and Dewey Decimal Classifications. There is an author/title
index in each issue, separate sections on books for young people, and
selections for the small library. A separate cumulative index is published
every six months as part of the subscription.

H2   **BOOKS AND NON-BOOK MEDIA: Annotated Guide to Selec-
      tion Aids for Educational Materials**   By Flossie L. Perkins.
      Urbana, Ill., National Council of Teachers of English, 1972. $4.25
      (paperback).

A comprehensive listing of more than 250 guides and selection aids for all
kinds of educational materials: books, pamphlets, films, records, and
some government sources. Arranged alphabetically by title, with price
and bibliographic information. Annotations are thorough, if unevalua-
tive, and include purpose, scope, subjects, special features, usefulness,
and comparative tools. Contains author/title and publisher indexes, with
separate classified listings of selection aids: for children, for teen-agers,
for college students and adults, for teacher-parent background, and for
librarians. As is almost inevitable, some useful items are omitted and a few
editions are not updated. The original edition, *Book Selection Media,* was
published in 1967, and provides an excellent, although dated, list of book
selection tools.

H3   **CATALOG OF FREE TEACHING MATERIALS, 1973-
      1976**   By Gordon Salisbury. 8th Edition. Riverside, Calif.,
      Rubidoux Printing, 1973. $3. From: P.O. Box 175, Ventura, Calif.
      93001.

A well-indexed guide to available free materials (booklets, charts, posters,
maps, etc.) related to the curriculum, "evaluated by accredited teachers."
Contains approximately 8,000 items. Annotations, including grade level,
type of item, and number of copies which may be acquired free, are listed

in the first section; the second section lists the names and addresses of approximately 1,000 organizations.

H4   **CEDaR CATALOG OF SELECTED EDUCATIONAL RE-SEARCH AND DEVELOPMENT PROGRAMS AND PROD-UCTS**   4th Edition. Denver, Colo., CEDaR Information Office, 1974. 2 Vols. $14.50. From: P.O. Box 3711, Portland, Ore. 97208.
A single source for current information on what is happening in educational laboratories and research centers. This edition describes the programs and products of 9 educational laboratories and 10 research centers: 250 completed products, arranged by subject categories, are described in Volume 1; approximately 162 ongoing research programs are described in Volume 2. Information on completed projects includes target audiences and teachers' materials, as well as information on overall philosophy and development procedures. The program sheets discuss ongoing programs and provide expected completion dates. Subject areas include school organization and administration, early childhood education, elementary and secondary school education, higher education, teacher education, basic research, urban education, and vocational education. Reader service cards are included to assist users in requesting publication lists and further information on individual products. Subsequent annual editions are planned.

This is a comprehensive catalog for specific sources, but is not evaluative, since descriptions supplied by the educational laboratories and research and development centers were edited only for style. Addresses provide direct access both to sources of ongoing research and to completed projects. The CEDAR Council is discussed in M7.

H5   **EDUCATOR'S PURCHASING GUIDE**   5th Edition. Philadelphia, North American Publishing, 1973. $29.50/single copy; bulk and standing order rates available.
A comprehensive guide, based on producers' catalogs, which indexes sources of instructional materials, equipment, and supplies, including textbooks and other printed materials, audiovisual materials, atlases, globes, maps, tests, teaching aids, and services. Equipment and supplies cover art education, athletic and physical education equipment, graphic arts equipment, and science laboratories equipment for use in libraries, learning centers, music instruction, and vocational education. Materials and equipment are indexed by grade, subject, and trade name. Producers are listed alphabetically; dealers and distributors geographically. Good for browsing and for the school purchasing agent. Contains no independent evaluations, but does provide good leads to many sources.

H6 **ELIMINATING ETHNIC BIAS IN INSTRUCTIONAL MATERIALS: Comment and Bibliography** Edited by Maxine Dunfee. Washington, D.C., Assn. for Supervision and Curriculum Development, 1974. $3.25.
Bibliography by Max Rosenberg; includes a practical guide for evaluating instructional materials for racism and sexism. Other sections include descriptions of current programs, projects, and curriculum guides; background readings for teachers; bibliographies of materials for children and young people; and materials supporting cultural pluralism.

H7 **EVALUATING EDUCATIONAL PROGRAMS AND PRODUCTS** Edited by Gary D. Borich. Englewood Cliffs, N.J., Educational Technology, 1974. $12.95.
Incorporates the works of many prominent evaluators in one handbook. Its three sections cover roles and contexts, models and strategies, and methods and techniques. Includes an interesting directory chart which relates chapter contents to readers' occupational roles.

H8 **FREE AND INEXPENSIVE EDUCATIONAL AIDS** By Thomas J. Pepe. 4th Edition. New York, Dover Publications, 1970. $2.
This edition lists 1,800 educational aids (mostly print items) selected from more than 7,000 items examined. The author, who is the Supervisor of Regional School District 15 in Connecticut, used the following criteria for selection: objectivity; educational soundness; whether the aid was simple to incorporate in the classroom, research project, or individual study; whether the presentation was without company sales influence or political bias; and whether the cost was $0.25 or less (82 percent of the items are free; 9 percent are under $0.25). Materials are arranged by broad subject areas, beginning with a list of other teaching aid catalogs. Subjects include agriculture; arts, crafts, and hobbies; business, management, and labor; communications; conservation, energy, and fuels; government; guidance and careers; health and hygiene; homes and homemaking; language arts; manufacturing; music; nutrition and diet; pets; safety; science, weather, and climate; social studies; and transportation. Useful annotations and adequate descriptions are provided for all items. Appendixes include names and addresses of companies, an index of audiovisual aids, and a more detailed subject index.

H9 **FREE AND INEXPENSIVE LEARNING MATERIALS** By George Peabody College for Teachers, Division of Surveys and Field Service. 17th Edition. Nashville, Tenn., 1974. $3.50 (paperback); quantity discount.

Published biennially since 1941, this seventeenth edition includes the titles of more than 2,800 instructional aids, of which 1,400 are new or substantially revised. Materials included are evaluated by the staff of George Peabody's Division of Surveys and Field Service on the basis of content, timeliness, utility, and availability. Items (many annotated) are arranged in 100 well-chosen subject categories.

H10 **GUIDE TO REFERENCE BOOKS FOR SCHOOL MEDIA CENTERS: Sources for Print and Non-Print Media** By Christine L. Wynar. Littleton, Colo., Libraries Unlimited, 1973. $17.50.
A timely guide to reference materials, designed to fit the needs of elementary and secondary media centers. Evaluates and annotates 2,500 titles, with complete bibliographical data, price, and references to original reviews. Includes evaluations of specialized selection tools for print and nonprint media in all subjects. Arranged by subject, with an author-title-subject analytic index.

H11 **IMPROVING MATERIALS SELECTION PROCEDURES: A BASIC "HOW TO" HANDBOOK** New York, Educational Products Information Exchange Institute, 1973. (EPIE Educational Product "In Depth" Report Number 54.) Members, $5; nonmembers, $10; quantity discount.
A brief, comprehensive summary of recommendations for rationalizing and systematizing selection procedures. Covers the roles and requirements of both schools and producers. Also covers methods for developing, applying, and following through on appropriate criteria, with a useful criterion checklist.

H12 **NEW EDUCATIONAL MATERIALS, 1970** Compiled by Lois Markham. 4th Edition. New York, Citation Press, 1970. $3.75.
The final edition of this classified guide to elementary and secondary curriculum-related materials, which annotated approximately 500 new items per year. Arranged by grade level, it includes resource articles as well as annotations of selected films, recordings, multimedia kits, filmstrips, transparencies, teaching/learning games, professional guides, posters, study prints, tapes, laboratory kits, charts, and maps. All four volumes are still usable and still in print.

H13 **NONSEXIST CURRICULAR MATERIALS FOR ELEMENTARY SCHOOLS** Edited by Laurie Olsen Johnson. Old Westbury, N.Y., Feminist Press, 1974. $5.
This practical 96-page packet includes background materials for the teacher (on white numbered pages) and classroom materials (on gold

numbered pages), arranged unbound so items can be removed, rearranged, or photocopied for classroom use. The first section includes easily used checklists for evaluating overt or covert sex bias in teaching materials and situations, as well as references and statistics. The second section includes model curricular units on personalities such as Susan B. Anthony, a workbook on sex-role stereotypes, a brief bibliography, and a reply form which invites comments, suggestions, and revisions.

H14　**THE SEED CATALOG: A Guide to Teaching-Learning Materials**　Edited by Jeffrey Schrank. Boston, Beacon, 1974. $12.95; paperback, $5.95.

Similar in format to the *Whole Earth Catalog*, but more compact (8" × 11"), this guide to underground educational resources is arranged by type of media and includes publications, organizations, periodicals, audio, film, video, games, multimedia, and such educational devices as timers and metric scales. A highly personal compendium, mostly for high school and adult levels, with emphasis on the humanities, communications, and media. It includes many worthwhile items not apt to appear in standard educational catalogs; some are carefully evaluated, and others are represented through producers' blurbs. Subject/title index.

H15　**SELECTING INSTRUCTIONAL MATERIALS FOR PUR-CHASE: Procedural Guidelines**　By Joint Committee of the National Educational Association and Association of American Publishers. Washington, D.C., National Education Assn., 1972. $2 (paperback).

A simple, but comprehensive and thorough, handbook which considers legal and administrative factors (laws, school boards, administrators), means of organizing and selecting materials, guidelines for expenditures, and changing conditions affecting procedures.

H16　**SELECTING NEW AIDS TO TEACHING**　By Richard I. Miller. Washington, D.C., Assn. for Supervision and Curriculum Development, 1971. $1. From: National Education Assn. 1201 16th St., N.W., Washington, D.C. 20036.

Thoroughly but concisely outlines the steps that should be taken and the criteria that should be followed in selecting instructional units.

H17　**SENSITIZING TEACHERS TO ETHNIC GROUPS**　By Gertrude Noar. New York, Anti-Defamation League of B'nai B'rith, 1973. $0.35.

An excellent little pamphlet, not specifically intended for materials selection, but very satisfactory for this purpose. Includes a brief but sensitive discussion of various minority groups in the United States, with an explicit discussion of biases and offending attitudes. The Anti-Defamation League (discussed in Chapter 16) is a major source for research studies and publications concerned with treatment of minorities and women in educational materials. The Council on Interracial Books for Children (1841 Broadway, New York, N.Y. 10023) is another group concerned with promoting children's literature that is free from racial and sexist bias, with some publications directed to the publishing industry.

H18 **SEXISM AND YOUTH**   Compiled by Diane Gersoni-Stavn. New
       York, R. R. Bowker, 1974. $12.95.
A definitive compilation of 47 articles that explore sexism in children's literature, education, games, and home life. Sections include Socialization/Indoctrination, Dear Old Sexist School Days, Books, Propaganda and the Sins of Omission, Media Mix, and the Games Children Play.

H19 **SHARPER TOOLS FOR BETTER LEARNING**   By National
       Association of Secondary School Principals. Reston, Va., 1973. $2;
       quantity discount. From: 1904 Association Dr., Reston, Va. 22091.
The purpose of this compact little pamphlet is to help administrators establish policies for selecting materials. It includes a sample criterion checklist that considers administrative, curricular, pedagogical, and evaluation requirements.

H20 **SOURCES OF TEACHING MATERIALS**   By Catherine M.
       Wilson. Columbus, Ohio State University, 1971. $3 (paperback).
The first part of this guide—on developing a strategy for locating information—is a narrative description of 190 basic reference and research sources, with complete entries at the end of the section. Other parts cover media, broad curricular areas, publishers, and distributors, as well as references to materials and methods of instruction. Provides many other references (some obsolete) and a detailed table of contents, but no index.

10 | *Curriculum Materials and Activities*

This chapter discusses some collections, compilations, and selection tools dealing with specific curricular areas and teaching methods. Other relevant materials can be found in Chapters 9, 11, and 12.

Nonprinted aids to selecting curricular sources are discussed in Chapter 16. Chapter 19, State Library Services to Educators, discusses directory information on a few state curriculum libraries and curriculum sources. Educational Products Information Exchange (EPIE) (O12) is a prime source of information on almost any topic. ERIC clearinghouses, through their announcements, newsletters, and services, also can provide good information on new developments in their various curricular fields.

Some yearbooks of educational associations, such as those of the National Council for the Social Studies (NCSS) and the Association for Supervision and Curriculum Development (ASCD), provide recent, comprehensive guides to materials. Other monograph series, such as those discussed in Chapter 4, also can be quite helpful. Many associations (listed in *Educator's World,* B39), as well as interest groups of all types (some included in Chapters 14 and 16), are valuable sources of curriculum information and evaluation in their subject fields.

Subject periodicals such as *Social Education, Mathematics Teacher, English Journal,* and *Journal of Environmental Education,* grade-level publications such as *Instructor* and *Scholastic Teacher,* and comprehensive publications such as *Learning Magazine* and *School Media Quarterly* provide news, reviews, and evaluations. More than 2,000 educational journals are listed in *Educator's World,* many containing comprehensive curricular information. *Education Index* (F8) and *CIJE* (F5) can be used to locate curricular ideas and materials in indexed periodicals.

If the user has access to a computer search of ERIC, the descriptor "Curriculum Guides" can be cross-searched with a specific area of interest to obtain a custom bibliography of abstracts describing curriculum guides in that field.

It is also wise to be aware of local sources. School, school district, county office, and state department of education librarians or curriculum consultants may already have compiled such a bibliography. One or more of these sources may have summaries, evaluations, or compilations of curriculum materials for consultation or free distribution; they also may have their own curricular materials on microfiche or may have acquired one or more curriculum collections in microfiche format.

Manufacturers catalogs often may be helpful in apprising educators of new materials. Some distributors, such as the Social Studies Schools Service (10000 Culver Boulevard, Culver City, California 90230), produce valuable annotated catalogs devoted to specific curriculum areas, with rather objective descriptions of materials from many sources.

Public libraries, of course, should be a major resource for teachers at all levels. The book selection tools discussed in Chapter 12 also are relevant, as are library-compiled bibliographies, which can be particularly valuable for contemporary issues. The holdings of a school or public library should be checked by personal visit or phone call before sending classes out with library assignments.

I1 **ACTIVE LEARNING: Games to Enhance Academic Abilities** By Bryant J. Cratty. Englewood Cliffs, N.J., Prentice-Hall, 1971. $7.95; paperback, $4.50.
Written by an expert in movement education, this book describes more than 100 active learning games designed to improve coordination while teaching geometry, numbers, letters and letter sounds, language arts, skills, memory, and concentration. Includes clear instructions and helpful suggestions for dealing with clumsy children.

I2 **ADULT BASIC EDUCATION: An Evaluation of Materials** By Southwestern Cooperative Educational Laboratory. Albuquerque,

N.M., 1970. 3 Vols. $7. From: Catalog Sales, Southwestern Cooperative Educational Laboratory, c/o University of Albuquerque, Albuquerque, N.M. 87108.

Provides detailed teacher evaluations on a wide variety of adult, basic education, curriculum materials such as English as a second language, English, reading, mathematics, and science. Its well-designed checklist and evaluation sheet could be extended to other curricular areas. Basic "criteria" include title, author, publisher, objectives, criterion measures, instructional components, learner prerequisites, teacher requirements, reliability, cost, and time, plus (for their purposes) usefulness of these materials for Spanish-speaking adults.

I3   **AFRICA, SOUTH OF THE SAHARA: A Resource and Curriculum Guide**   By Barry K. Beyer. New York, Crowell, 1969. $6.95; paperback, $3.95.

An expanded version of Project Africa's original work, which includes an analysis and full bibliography on teaching about Africa; an analysis of how students view this region; a set of guidelines and objectives; pretests with answer keys to measure student attitudes and knowledge; a well-arranged annotated listing of written, audio, and visual materials with sources and 1969 prices; and a directory of agencies, embassies, and trade organizations representing Africa south of the Sahara.

I4   **AGRICULTURAL EDUCATION IN A TECHNICAL SOCIETY**   An Annotated Bibliography of Resources. By Mary R. Brown et al. Chicago, American Library Assn., 1973. $10.

This comprehensive bibliography was designed as a selection tool for educators at the secondary school level and higher. It covers books, periodicals, government documents, pamphlet sources, media materials, and agribusiness organizations, first by format and then by subject, with asterisks denoting first purchase recommendations. Areas covered include conservation, forestry, veterinary science, fisheries, and food processing, as well as gardening and crop production.

I5   **ALCOHOL AND ALCOHOL SAFETY: A Curriculum Manual for Junior High Level**   By Peter Finn and Judith Platt for the National Highway Traffic Safety Administration and National Institute on Alcohol Abuse and Alcoholism. Washington, D.C., U.S. Government Printing Office, 1972. 2 Vols. Vol. 1, $3.75; Vol. 2, $8.00.

A collection of more than 200 activities for grades seven to nine, covering all major areas of alcohol and alcohol safety, and incorporating many concerns (attitudes, problems, etc., in educational language), teaching methods, and evaluations. Volume 1 is an instructional handbook which classifies activities by objectives to help teachers develop their own curricula. Volume 2 is a loose-leaf collection of individual learning activities, prepunched for insertion in a three-ring notebook.

A similar manual for the elementary school level, *Alcohol and Alcohol Safety: A Curriculum Manual for Elementary Level* (Washington, D.C., U.S. Government Printing Office, 1972. 2 Vols. Vol. 1, $3.50; Vol. 2, $5.25), is more concerned with traffic and pedestrian safety.

16   **ALTERNATIVE HIGH SCHOOLS: Some Pioneer Programs** By Suzanne K. Stemnock. Washington, D.C., Educational Research Service, 1972. $3. (ERS Circular 4, 1972) From: Suite 1012, 1815 N. Fort Myer Dr., Arlington, Va. 22209.

Contains descriptions of 47 high school programs serving students in 38 school systems. Although not comprehensive, it includes a good proportion of programs that operated in the 1971-1972 school year, especially in the larger school systems. Criteria for selection included a school system enrollment of more than 12,000 and a program involving voluntary enrollment—an alternative approach rather than enrichment or electives. Based on a questionnaire developed by ERS (from information supplied by the schools), this paper was prepared by ERS and verified by the schools. Also includes a brief bibliography and an index to facilities and programs.

17   **AMERICAN GOVERNMENT INFORMATION UNIT: Curriculum Alternatives for Secondary Schools** By Nancy C. Adelson and Sandra G. Crosby. San Francisco, Far West Laboratory for Educational Research and Development, 1971. $7.95 (paperback). From: Universal Research Systems, Suite 107, 363 S. Taaffe St., Sunnyvale, Calif. 94086.

Describes, analyzes, and compares nine secondary school programs on American government, politics, and social issues in parallel fashion, with one-page summaries followed by detailed reports on goals, costs, and training: a package intended to help teachers and school districts reach decisions on appropriate curricula.

18   **AMERICAN INDIAN TEACHING MATERIALS: Films, Filmstrips, and Tapes** By Robert L. Brown and J. Johnson Russell. Arcata, Calif., Humboldt State University, 1972. $1.50 (paperback).

A guide to media materials about the American Indian, available for purchase, loan, or rental. The listing for 16-mm films includes an alphabetical title list—which provides a synopsis of bibliographic information and source—and a subject index. Similar information is provided for filmstrips and tapes, but without subject indexes. Includes a directory of 130 distributors and a few free loan sources.

I9   **ANALYSES OF BASIC AND SUPPLEMENTARY READING MATERIALS**   By Educational Products Information Exchange Institute. New York, 1974. (EPIE Education Product "In Depth" Report Number 64.) Members, $5; nonmembers, $10; quantity discount.

This report uses an "Instructional Design Analysis" system to analyze and evaluate 76 commercially marketed reading series. Materials are arranged alphabetically by category (general audiences, grade levels, supplementary materials). Each analysis includes product descriptions, instructional design (objectives and scope, sequence, methodology, evaluation), and a final evaluative EPIEcomment. A separate section, arranged in the same sequence as the main text, lists approximate prices (as supplied by the producers in 1974). The Instructional Design Analysis system used here is described fully in EPIE Product Report Number 62/63, *Selecting and Evaluating Beginning Reading Materials—A How-to Handbook,* available for $10.

I10   **AN ANNOTATED LIST OF NEW SOCIAL STUDIES PROJECTS**   Compiled by Merle M. Knight. Boulder, Colo., Social Science Education Consortium, 1970. Microfiche, $0.75; hard copy, $1.85 (plus postage). (ED 041 815) From: ERIC Document Reproduction Service, P.O. Box 190, Arlington, Va. 22210.

Provides comparative information on 34 social studies projects, updating those listed in I36.

I11   **A BIBLIOGRAPHY FOR TEACHERS OF SOCIAL STUDIES**   Social Studies Sources. By Raymond A. Ducharme, Jr. et al. New York, Teachers College Press, 1968. $1.75 (paperback).

An annotated guide to guides in various social studies areas, which almost eliminates the need to research this area prior to 1968. Provides approximately 225 references covering social studies, history, geography, economics, political science, sociology, anthropology, area studies, and educational technology at the elementary and secondary school levels. Bibliographic information includes prices (as of 1968); annotations are brief but informative.

I12   **BIBLIOGRAPHY OF LAW-RELATED CURRICULUM MATERIALS: Annotated**   By Special Committee on Youth Education for Citizenship, American Bar Assn. Chicago, 1974. Single copies free; multiple copies, $1.75 for 2–25; quantity discount.

This bibliography covers a variety of commercial and noncommercial printed materials dealing with law-related education and successful pedagogical approaches, including textbooks, nontexts, and novels that are adaptable to the classroom, and teachers' materials. More than 400 annotated items, with information on price, source, grade level, presence of teachers' guides, etc., are included. Major categories are origins and concepts of law, the Constitution, the Bill of Rights, current issues, the political process, practical law, and teaching of law, with a separate list of series publications.

The Special Committee on Youth Education for Citizenship, discussed in Chapter 16, also has compiled a media list, *Media: An Annotated Catalogue of Law-Related Audio-Visual Materials*, reviewed in Chapter 11.

113 **BIBLIOGRAPHY OF SCIENCE COURSES OF STUDY AND TEXTBOOKS—K-12** Compiled by National Science Teachers Assn. Washington, D.C., 1973. $2.50 (paperback).
A convenient listing of major curriculum projects, courses of study available through state and local school departments of education, and science textbooks—kindergarten to grade 12.

114 **BILINGUAL-BICULTURAL EDUCATION AND ENGLISH-AS-A-SECOND-LANGUAGE EDUCATION** A Framework for Elementary and Secondary Schools. By Bureau of Publications, California State Department of Education. Sacramento, 1974. $0.50.
Adopted as a policy guideline by the California State Board of Education on July 12, 1973, this handbook includes definitions, assessment goals, recommendations for staff, staff development, instruction, and community involvement; an exposition and comparison of instructional methods for bilingual students; and a thoughtful, well-organized section on methods and suggested criteria for selecting instructional materials for bilingual education. As of January 1975, the Bureau of Intergroup Relations of the California State Department of Education also had issued a working draft of a promising "Guide to Ethnic Heritage Curriculum Analysis," which will provide checklists and outlines for evaluation of materials.

115 **BLUEPRINTS FOR BETTER READING** School Programs for Promoting Skill and Interest in Reading. By Florence Damon Cleary. 2nd Edition. Bronx, N.Y., H.W. Wilson, 1972. $14.
An idea book for use by teachers and librarians to improve reading programs. Part I is devoted to identifying areas involved in improving reading guidance programs. Part II suggests means for using the library and lists criteria for selecting and evaluating learning materials. Part III

describes programs, procedures, activities, and devices for teaching critical reading, both for acquiring information and for building values and appreciation. Eleven charts outline goals and procedures for acquiring information and locating materials. Extensive bibliographies throughout.

I16   **CALIFORNIA CURRICULUM GUIDES, 1974** Compiled by Curriculum Materials Depository, San Mateo County Office of Education. Redwood City, Calif., San Mateo Educational Resources Center, 1974– . $3.50 for 1974; free to subscribing agencies. From: 333 Main St., Redwood City, Calif. 94063.

This is a yearly catalog of curriculum guides prepared by California county and local educational agencies and submitted to a Curriculum Materials Depository, which serves as a statewide collection and dissemination agency to distribute materials available in microfiche. The catalog is arranged by subject, institution, and CM (curriculum microfiche) number, with brief resumés under the last category. Individual microfiche cards (each containing approximately 40 to 70 pages of text) are available at $0.50 per fiche; standing orders—for the whole collection—are $0.35 per fiche, effective July 1975. The first catalog indexes 418 items, with strengths in ethnic education and individualized instruction.

I17   **CAREER EDUCATION FOR RURAL SCHOOL ADMINIS-TRATORS** By Everett D. Edington and Howard K. Conley. Washington, D.C., Education Resources Div., Capitol Publications, 1973. $4 (paperback).

A mass of ideas and strategies for rural schools can be found in this book by two authors from the ERIC Clearinghouse on Rural Education and Small Schools. It includes lists of community organizations, firms that produce or distribute free and low-cost career education materials, and a bibliography of career education books. Outlines what a student needs to know to make an informed career decision, provides 70 suggestions for incorporating career education in the elementary classroom, and includes a list of criteria for high school students doing their own career research.

I18   **CAREER EDUCATION MICROFICHE COLLECTION CATALOG** By Career Education Task Force. Sacramento, Calif., State Department of Education, 1975. $0.50. From: State Publications Office, P.O. Box 271, Sacramento, Calif. 95802.

An index to a career education microfiche collection of more than 500 items, housed in the San Mateo Educational Resources Center. Materials are arranged by grade level and title, under subject headings. Use and number of pages are indicated, and a supplementary institution index also is included. Individual microfiche from this collection can be obtained from 333 Main Street, Redwood City, California 94063: $0.50 to individuals whose counties do not participate in the services of the San Mateo Educational Resources Center; less to those who do. Most of the materials were produced by California educators, institutions, and school districts in an effort to infuse career education into school programs.

I19 **CAREER EDUCATION RESOURCE GUIDE** Edited by James
  E. Bottoms et al. Morristown, N.J., General Learning, 1972. $5.70.
Provides overviews, lesson plans, and classroom activities for career education at three levels: kindergarten/elementary, middle/junior high, and high school/adult. A useful introduction to current thinking, rather than a total career education curriculum.

I20 **CAREER EDUCATION SURVIVAL MANUAL** By Larry
  McClure. Salt Lake City, Utah, Olympus, 1974. $2.95 (paperback).
Originally compiled by Northwest Regional Educational Laboratory as part of a final report to the National Institute of Education, this handbook provides a quick overview of career education programs, with appropriate references. It is well-designed for conveying comprehensive information in an easy-to-read, easy-to-assimilate format.

I21 **CATALOG OF METRIC INSTRUCTIONAL MATERIALS**
  Compiled by Metric Studies Center, American Institutes for Research. Palo Alto, Calif., 1974. $1.50, prepaid; $2.00 if billing is requested. From: P.O. Box 1113, Palo Alto, Calif. 94302.
This catalog integrates the metric instructional materials of 41 suppliers under seven major headings, with descriptions of their significant features.

  The Metric Studies Center also has produced a report, *Going Metric* (available for $5.40, prepaid), summarizing the experiences of five nations in converting to the metric system, and is producing a newsletter, *Air Metri-Gram,* devoted to the educational implications of metrication. Subscriptions are available at $6 for five issues; a sample copy will be sent on request.

I22 **CHINA: A Resource and Curriculum Guide** Edited by Arlene
  Posner and Arne de Keijzer. Chicago, University of Chicago Press,
  1973. $6.50; paperback, $2.95.
Prepared under the auspices of the National Committee on United States-China Relations (more fully described in Chapter 16), this work includes an introduction by Edwin Reischauer, plus three substantive essays on teaching about China at the secondary school level. It is a

scholarly guide that provides a detailed analysis of approximately 25 curriculum units and other instructional materials on China—mostly at the secondary school level and beyond, although no limits are specified. Includes title, source, and costs; the professional background of the author; the teaching approach; scope and emphasis; the contents of the curriculum unit; an overall evaluation of the unit; and outstanding contributions of the unit.

Also includes a 75-page annotated guide to selected audiovisual materials—films and filmstrips, slides and photographs, audiotapes and records—with full descriptions covering source, price, length, and audience; plus a similarly competent selective annotated guide to printed materials on China: books, packets, periodicals, newsletters, Chinese publications, and selected articles; and a final list of resource groups, summer programs on Asia, and publishers. Materials are fully described with source and price, while basic purchases are asterisked. While it is skimpy on materials at the lower levels, it is an outstanding guide for high school age and up.

I23 **CLASSROOM IDEAS FOR ENCOURAGING THINKING AND FEELING** By Frank E. Williams. Buffalo, N.Y., D.O.K. Publications, 1971. $7.50. From: 71 Radcliff Rd., Buffalo, N.Y. 14214.
Categorizes 387 classroom ideas by subject matter and learning strategies. Designed to encourage fluent thinking, flexible thinking, original thinking, and elaborate thinking, as well as curiosity, risk-taking, complexity in general thinking and emerging feeling, and imagination. A highly stimulating book that teachers can use to design and extend their own programs. (See Figure 7.)

I24 **CONFLICT: A Guide to Selected Curriculum Materials** By Center for War/Peace Studies. New York, 1973. Single copy free; multiple copies, $0.50 each.
Includes extremely useful, detailed evaluations by teachers of 17 available social studies units, and materials that deal in various ways with interdependence, change, power, and conflict. The center, a prime source of materials on war and conflict, is discussed more fully in Chapter 16.

I25 **CONSUMER INFORMATION** An Index of Selected Federal Publications of Consumer Interest. By Consumer Product Information. Washington, D.C., 1973– . Quarterly. Free.
An annotated subject listing (appliances, automobiles, clothing, food, etc.) of many federal agency publications, covering all aspects of consumer education: how to buy and use products, child care, family budgeting, house repairs, and financing.

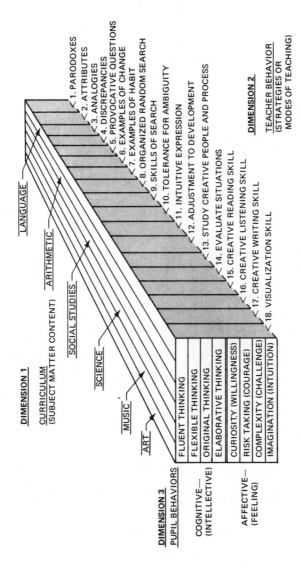

FIGURE 7 Dr. F. E. Williams' *Classroom Ideas for Encouraging Thinking and Feeling* uses this cube to locate classroom exercises according to subject content, teaching strategy, or pupil behavior.

I26 **CURRICULUM ACTIVITIES GUIDE TO WATER POLLU-
TION AND ENVIRONMENTAL STUDIES**   By U.S. Environ-
mental Protection Agency. Washington, D.C., U.S. Government
Printing Office, 1972. 2 Vols. Vol. 1 – Activities, $2.25; Vol. 2 –
Appendixes, $2.25.

This high-school level curriculum guide, which was partially funded by
the Ford Foundation, provides a series of field activities based on
observation and first-hand investigation. Volume 1 covers the hydrologic
cycle, human activities (farming, sewage treatment, dams, etc.), and social
and political factors. Includes for each activity, ways to introduce the
activity, suggested grade level, equipment, discussion questions, and
bibliographies. Volume 2 provides equipment lists, basic experiments,
reference sources, and other information.

I27 **CURRICULUM DEVELOPMENT IN ELEMENTARY
MATHEMATICS**   By Kathleen Devaney and Lorraine Thorn.
San Francisco, Far West Laboratory for Educational Research and
Development, 1974. $7.95.

An informed, helpful exposition and comparison of nine of the new
elementary mathematics curricula, eight developed with U.S. government financing and by the Nuffield Mathematics Project in England.
Provides overviews, content focus, classroom actions, costs of implementation, evaluation, date developed, source, etc. A very helpful guide for
elementary teachers choosing mathematics curricula.

I28 **CURRICULUM GUIDES: A Selective Bibliography**   By Council for Exceptional Children. Reston, Va., 1972. Microfiche, $0.75;
hard copy, $1.85 (plus postage). (ED 065 959) From: ERIC Docu-
ment Reproduction Service, P.O. Box 190, Arlington, Va. 22210.

A bibliography of 100 abstracts dealing with curricula for gifted and
handicapped children, from the files of the ERIC Clearinghouse on
Handicapped and Gifted. Items included were selected on the basis of
currency, author's reputation, information value, contents, and availability of documents. This paper includes subject and author indexes, as well
as forms for ordering documents.

I29 **CURRICULUM GUIDES FOR FAMILY LIFE AND SEX
EDUCATION**   By E. C. Brown Foundation. Eugene, Ore., 1972.
$2. From: 1802 Moss St., Eugene, Ore. 97403.

An annotated listing of more than 100 family life and sex education
guides, arranged by state, city, and school district. The E.C. Brown
Foundation also publishes a bimonthly newsletter which reports on
educational programs and recent publications dealing with marriage and
the family.

130 **CURRICULUM GUIDES IN ART EDUCATION** By National
Art Education Assn. Reston, Va., 1970. $2.50. From: 1916
Association Dr., Reston, Va. 22091.
A listing, with descriptions, of selected art curriculum guides for
kindergarten through high school. Other publications by this association
cover art education for preprimary through higher education.

131 **CURRICULUM MATERIALS, 1974** Compiled by Richard D.
Kimpston and Joan Black. Washington, D.C., Assn. for Supervision and Curriculum Development, 1974. Annual. $2.
Although descriptions are not included, this annual catalog provides
access to a large number of current noncommercial curricula displayed at
the annual ASCD (spring) conference. The latest issue lists approximately
800 resources in 15 curriculum areas, mostly by state and local school
districts. The subject arrangement is subdivided by grade level and
subject; subsequent arrangement is by state and issuing agency (whether
district, state, or other agency). Information includes title; date; developer; source, with address; and price, if available. Microfiche copies of
Selected Guides from the ASCD Exhibit for 1970 on were reproduced by
Kraus-Thomson Organization, Limited, Microform Division, Route 100,
Millwood, New York 10546. Prices vary. Approximately 100 selected
ASCD guides for 1972 were priced at $110 (for all 100).

132 **CURRICULUM PROJECTS AND MATERIALS IN ELEMEN-
TARY SCHOOL BEHAVIORAL SCIENCES: Summary
Sheets** By APA Clearinghouse on Precollege Psychology and
Behavioral Sciences. Washington, D.C., 1972. Free. From: Rm.
209, 1200 17th St., N.W., Washington, D.C. 20036.
A convenient loose-leaf compilation of summary sheets on elementary
school behavioral science curricula, updated as new curricula are located.
Projects and materials are selected for inclusion when the study of human
behavior is a central focus, and when the target audience includes
kindergarten to grade six. Original packet included 26 programs meeting
these criteria. Information includes name of project, director or author,
publisher, financer(s), educational level, curriculum materials available,
and comments.

133 **DARCEE CURRICULUM GUIDES** By Demonstration and
Research Center for Early Education. St. Louis, CEMREL, Inc.,
1970– . $1.75 each.
A series of guides—developed mostly by the Demonstration and Research
Center for Early Education of George Peabody University—that introduce instructional activities into the preschool curriculum. Some units,
such as *Home and Family, Plants, Winter, Forest Animals,* and *Neighbors and*

Community, include activities, activity extensions, and suggestions for evaluation. Others merely suggest instructional activities.

I34   **DIRECTORY OF AMERICAN POETS**   By Poets and Writers, Inc. Revised Edition. New York, 1975. $12; paperback, $6. From: 201 W. 54th St., New York, N.Y. 10019.

The first edition of this work, *A Partial Directory of American Poets,* listed poets who were available for work in the schools—a resource pool for curriculum planners. This enlarged edition includes names and addresses (arranged by state) of more than 1,500 poets available for readings, workshops, and other assignments; all bona fide poets published either in book form or in national periodicals. The *Directory* supplies current addresses (two or more addresses for transient authors), phone numbers, titles of recent books, the poets' preferences for assignments (elementary, teacher-training, etc.), and their ability, if any, with foreign languages. Includes a list of 450 organizations which have sponsored poetry readings and workshops, plus bibliographies or guides to recordings and tapes, anthologies, little magazines, grants and awards, literature projects, and bookstores. There is an overall alphabetical index to poets, and a classified index of those poets representing or writing for various minority groups. An updating CODA, *Poets and Writers Newsletter,* available at no extra cost, provides information on contemporary poets between editions. A handy tool for creative teachers from school districts with funds available for the arts.

I35   **A DIRECTORY OF SELECTED RESOURCES IN SPECIAL EDUCATION**   Compiled by Merrimack Education Center. Chelmsford, Mass., 1975. $0.75. From: 101 Mill Rd., Chelmsford, Mass. 01824.

An excellent, compact annotated guide to hard-to-locate but valuable products designed to meet the needs of children with different learning styles through diverse programs and materials. Provides a partial guide to agencies, as well as a directory of resources covering home-school communications, classroom techniques, testing and assessment, media and materials, teacher training materials, and other bibliographies.

I36   **DIRECTORY OF SOCIAL STUDIES CURRICULUM PROJ-ECTS**   Compiled by Robert Wingert. Harrisburg, Pa., Pennsylvania State Department of Public Instruction, Bureau of General and Academic Education, 1969. Microfiche, $0.75; hard copy, $4.20 (plus postage). (ED 041 814) From: ERIC Document Reproduction Service, P.O. Box 190, Arlington, Va. 22210.

Covers 84 projects in anthropology, civics, government, conservation, economics, geography, sociology, U.S. history and culture, world affairs, and world history. Information includes name of project, director, address, summary, and grade levels.

I37 **DRUG EDUCATION: A Bibliography of Available Inexpensive Materials** Compiled by Dorothy P. Wells. Metuchen, N.J., Scarecrow Press, 1972. $5.
This guide to materials for the school with budget problems, lists and describes 400 items, including some teaching guides, posters, charts, glossaries, and comic books. Publications are sorted into general, government, and reprint categories, and are arranged by publisher. Contains separate title, author, and subject indexes. Information on individual items includes title, date, number of pages, price, author, brief description, publisher, and address. No materials on alcoholism are included, but other areas are well-covered.

I38 **DRUG EDUCATION (PREP Kit 36)** Edited by Stanley Chow et al., for Far West Laboratory for Educational Research and Development. Washington, D.C., U.S. Government Printing Office, 1973. $1.
Reports on 6 national curriculum packages and 11 case studies of school district drug education efforts.

I39 **EARLY CHILDHOOD INFORMATION UNIT** By Far West Laboratory for Educational Research and Development. San Francisco, 1973. Multimedia unit (two publications, nine filmstrip-and-audio-cassette presentations, in vinyl case), $88.50; if prepaid, $79.65. From: EPIE Institute, 463 West St., New York, N.Y. 10014.
A comprehensive, decision-making information unit to assist teachers, parents, administrators, and community groups evaluate 15 early childhood programs. Includes an introductory filmstrip-and-audio-cassette presentation of major trends in early childhood education, detailed descriptions of eight early childhood programs (written form, filmstrip, and audio), summary descriptions of seven other early childhood programs, EPIE guidelines for evaluative techniques, and an extensive bibliography. Developed with the assistance of a panel of approximately 150 teachers, administrators, and parents who reviewed and evaluated the descriptive and evaluative materials. A print-only version of this unit, *Early Childhood Education* (PREP Report No. 37), is available from the U.S. Government Printing Office for $0.60.

I40   **EDUCATION OF CHILDREN AGED ONE TO THREE: A
      Curriculum Manual**   Edited by Paul H. Furfey. Washington,
      D.C., Catholic University of America, School of Education,
      Catholic Curriculum Development Center, 1972. $2.50. (Out-of-
      Print)

A compilation of techniques for the intellectual stimulation of young
children, culled from months of intensive home instruction of inner-
city babies. The first part provides a background in child development;
the second part, on curriculum, is a "how to" section covering sensory
and motor skills, music, games, dramatic play, numbers, books, and
science. The third part includes five illustrative case histories. The
final part provides a list of recommended and available materials: books,
toys, music, puzzles.

I41   **ELEMENTARY SCIENCE INFORMATION UNIT**   By Far
      West Laboratory for Educational Research and Development.
      San Francisco, 1971. Six reports, seven color filmstrips, seven
      audiotapes, one review booklet, one instruction booklet, $75.
      From: Universal Research Systems, Suite 107, 363 S. Taaffe St.,
      Sunnyvale, Calif. 94086.

This multimedia package examines and compares six elementary science
curricula in parallel fashion, for the purpose of providing school
personnel with enough background information to select the right
curriculum for their schools, while simultaneously training them in
decision making. The characteristics examined include grade level,
subject areas, suggested use, teacher and student materials, goals, sample
topics, student evaluation, unit sequencing, instructional strategy, teacher
preparation, cost, and availability.

I42   **ENCOUNTERS IN THINKING: A COMPENDIUM OF CUR-
      RICULA FOR PROCESS EDUCATION**   By Albert Seferian
      and Henry P. Cole. Buffalo, N.Y., Creative Education Foundation,
      n.d. Free. From: Bishop Hall, 1300 Elmwood Ave., Buffalo, N.Y.
      14222.

Prepared sometime around 1971 by the Eastern Regional Institute for
Education, this document contains descriptive or annotated listings of 45
curricula presumed appropriate for "process" education; that is,
generalized and adaptive behaviors that enable individuals to learn, solve
problems, and produce. These curricula meet eight criteria designed by
ERIE, including availability, research base, and grade level for all children
from preschool through sixth grade. Also includes sources, descriptions,
and (sometimes) references and/or evaluations.

143 **ENERGY CHOICES FOR NOW: SAVING, USING, RE-NEWING** By National Education Assn. Washington, D.C., 1974. Student Edition, Teachers' Manual, and Energy Chart. $3.50 for examination set of Teachers' Manual and Student Edition; quantity discount for classroom sets. From: NEA Publications Order Department, Academic Bldg., Saw Mill Rd., West Haven, Conn. 06516.

The competent Teachers' Manual includes objectives, background, activities, presentations, and lists of materials. The student edition is attractive and well-illustrated, and includes charts, vocabulary lists, a table of predictions, and references for further study on such topics as the sun, current energy sources, and nuclear energy. Appropriate for middle-grade students.

144 **THE ENERGY CRISIS: Aids to Study** Compiled by Margaret McDaniel. Lincoln, Mass., Hatheway Environmental Education Institute, 1974. $0.60. From: Hatheway Environmental Education Institute, Massachusetts Audubon Society, Lincoln, Mass. 01773.

An annotated bibliography covering books, pamphlets, reports, magazine articles, audiovisual aids, curriculum guides and units, simulations, and other bibliographies, with addresses of sources. Items appropriate for elementary grades are asterisked.

145 **ENVIRONMENTAL EDUCATION** By Martha T. Henderson. Boulder, Colo., Social Science Education Consortium, 1973. $1.80.

Provides an excellent selective sampling of environmental education programs—kindergarten to grade 12—which incorporates social studies viewpoints. Reviews six programs encouraging individual inquiry, seven programs stressing interaction between humans and their environments, six programs emphasizing field work, and five programs incorporating values and ethics in a curriculum of law, politics, and/or economics. A bibliography of source books and less familiar periodicals also is included.

146 **ENVIRONMENT AND POPULATION: A Sourcebook for Teachers** By Kathryn Horsley et al. Washington, D.C., National Education Assn., 1972. $5.25; paperback, $3.75. From: NEA Publications Order Department, Academic Bldg., Saw Mill Rd., West Haven, Conn. 06516.

This handbook includes discussion materials, classroom activities, reference works, and recommended audiovisual materials relating population variables to social and natural pressures. Explicit concepts at the junior high and high school levels are provided for incorporating population and environment into such existing curricula as science, social studies, family life, and contemporary issues.

I47   **ENVIRONMENT MEDIA GUIDE**   By Environment Informa-
      tion Center, Inc. New York, 1973. Free. From: Environment
      Information Center, Inc., Media Services Dept., 124 E. 39th St.,
      New York, N.Y. 10016.
A comprehensive directory of environmental books and films.

I48   **ESP CURRICULUM GUIDE**   By Robert A. McConnell. New
      York, Simon and Schuster, 1970. $2.40.
This curriculum guide for high school and college students was developed by a university scientist actively engaged in research on ESP. It
includes experimental suggestions and a well-annotated listing of 15
books (out of more than 800 published) that the author considered
appropriate for an orthodox, scientific research and experimental study
of ESP.

I49   **AN EVALUATION OF INSTRUCTIONAL MATERIALS: EN-
      GLISH, SPELLING, HANDWRITING AND LITERATURE
      ADOPTED IN CALIFORNIA, JUNE 1974**   Coordinated by Dr.
      Curtis May. Redwood City, Calif., San Mateo County Office of
      Education, 1974. $3.50. From: 333 Main St., Redwood City, Calif.
      94063.
A substantial compilation of teacher evaluations—approximately 150
individual items and packages—intended to narrow teacher choices for
instructional materials. Models (matrices), developed by the Educational
Products Information Exchange, cover types of materials (textbooks,
systems, kits, etc.), approach (programmed, thematic, oral language,
eclectic, etc.), and emphasis, plus a rating scale grade and a detailed
overall evaluation. Well-indexed and universally applicable in the selection of curriculum materials.

I50   **FEMINIST RESOURCES FOR SCHOOLS AND COLLEGES:
      A Guide to Curriculum Materials**   Edited by Carol Ahlum
      and Jacqueline M. Fralley. Old Westbury, N.Y., Feminist Press,
      1973. $1 (paperback), plus postage and handling. From: Distribu-
      tion Office, Feminist Press, 10920 Battersea Lane, Columbia,
      Md. 21044.
A preliminary annotated bibliography, in newsletter format, that includes
books, pamphlets, slide shows, films, and tapes, with prices and ordering
information. The publisher also maintains (since 1970) a Clearinghouse
on Women's Studies, providing both descriptions of courses and names of

teachers. For additional information, contact the Editorial Office, Feminist Press, Box 334, Old Westbury, N.Y. 11568.

I51 **FOR STORYTELLERS AND STORYTELLING** Bibliographies, Materials, and Resource Aids. Chicago, Ill., Children's Services Div., American Library Assn., 1968. $1.50 (paperback).
This compilation by experienced storytellers of the American Library Association is old, but storytelling is an ancient art.

I52 **FREE AND INEXPENSIVE MATERIALS ON WORLD AFFAIRS** By Leonard S. Kenworthy and Richard A. Birdie. 3rd Edition. New York, Teachers College Press, 1969. $1.95.
An excellent selection of more than 1,000 items—costing $0.85 or less—dealing with all aspects of world affairs and current policies. Includes general subjects such as education, food, maps, travel, war and peace, and women; materials on U.S. foreign policy; special materials for teachers and group leaders; materials on world regions and individual countries; and materials on international organizations. Most of these items are pamphlets, maps, and books, but some audiovisual materials, kits, and film guides also are listed.

I53 **GOOD READING FOR POOR READERS** By George D. Spache. Revised Edition. Champaign, Ill., Garrard Publishing, 1974. $5.75 (paperback).
The first four chapters discuss choosing books to match children's abilities and needs, and present a survey of readability formulas. The next eight chapters list 1,800 titles for remedial reading, arranged under broad categories, with brief annotations and bibliographic descriptions, omitting price but including reading and interest levels. Materials are comprised of trade books, simplified books, textbooks, magazines, series, programmed materials, games, and visual aids. Appendixes include Spache's Readability Formula, author and title indexes, and a directory of publishers.

I54 **GUIDELINES: CURRICULUM DEVELOPMENT FOR AESTHETIC EDUCATION** By Manuel Barkan, Laura Chapman, and Evan Kern. St. Louis, CEMREL, Inc., 1970. $10.80.
This publication was the result of a joint effort by CEMREL, Inc. and Ohio State University to produce rational, aesthetic education guidelines for grades kindergarten to 12; to help students develop skills of discrimination and judgment; and to refine attitudes, patterns of thought, and actions. The book divides naturally into two parts—handbook and appendixes. The handbook provides concepts and methods; sections deal

with units of instruction and their relationships, procedures for designing units of instruction, courses and programs, and guidelines for evaluating effects. The appendixes introduce working tools, and include a well-researched thesaurus, definitions in context, a concepts section of 1,195 indexed references and quotations (arranged under bibliographic citations and thoroughly indexed by subject and aesthetic categories), and a workbook section, with checklists.

I55   **A GUIDE TO SECURING AND INSTALLING THE PARENT/CHILD TOY-LENDING LIBRARY** By Far West Laboratory for Educational Research and Development. Washington, D.C., U.S. Government Printing Office, 1972. $0.60.
A guide to securing and installing the Toy-Lending Library, developed by the Far West Laboratory as a tool to promote positive self-concepts and intellectual growth in three- and four-year-old children while simultaneously contributing to parents' understanding of, and positive reactions to, child-related activities.

I56   **HALF-HOUR NOTICE: 50 Mini-Lessons for High School Substitutes** By Mary Glenn Haskins. New York, Citation Press, 1974. $4.95 (paperback).
Teachable lessons, designed by an experienced writer and high school substitute teacher, covering most areas of high school curriculum: English, science, math, history, government, art, music, foreign languages, and physical education, plus a general group of lessons for achievers and some good introductions to research skills. These self-contained lessons, all less than one hour long, are supplemented by lists of follow-up activities and related readings.

I57   **HANDY KEY TO YOUR NATIONAL GEOGRAPHICS: Subject-Picture Locator** Compiled by Charles S. Underhill. 11th Edition. E. Aurora, N.Y., C.S. Underhill, 1974. $3 (paperback); quantity discount.
The latest edition of this popular guide indexes *National Geographics* from 1915 through 1973. Arranged by subject, it indexes articles, colored illustrations, and paintings.

I58   **HUMANITIES PROGRAMS TODAY** Edited by Richard Adler. New York, Citation Press, 1970. $3.65.
Presents case studies of 35 humanities programs offered in elementary and high schools in 1970, providing valuable information on philosophies and practices, grouping procedures, teaching methods, etc., in relation-

ship to variables such as student abilities, grade levels, and available resources.

I59 **IMPROVING READING IN EVERY CLASS: A Sourcebook for Teachers** By Ellen Lamar Thomas and H. Alan Robinson. Boston, Allyn and Bacon, 1972. $17.95; abridged edition, $6.95.
Provides high school teachers with a wide variety of practical methods on how to improve reading skills (for information-gathering purposes) in nine curricular areas: mathematics, science, industrial arts, typing and business education, foreign languages, home economics, music, fine arts, and physical education, with a fine supply of practical examples and procedures, sample lessons, tests, checklists, and worksheets. Additional chapters provide background for reading instruction and library use. A subject index, helpfully placed at the beginning of the book, cross-indexes all parts of the book by curricular areas. Convenient to use, with many practical suggestions.

I60 **INSTRUCTIONAL AIDS IN MATHEMATICS: 34th Yearbook** By National Council of Teachers of Mathematics. Washington, D.C., 1973. $12.
This outstanding guide covers criteria for selecting and evaluating such instructional aids as textbooks and other printed materials, models and manipulative devices, teaching machines and computers, and projection devices, including adequate historic background, educational objectives, and intelligent detail. Well-illustrated and useful for classroom teachers at all levels.

I61 **INSTRUCTIONAL AIDS, MATERIALS AND SUPPLIES** By Educational Development Center Follow Through Program. Newton, Mass., Educational Development Center, Inc., 1970. $1.
A list of possible materials for an open classroom.

I62 **INSTRUCTIONAL RESOURCES FOR TEACHERS OF THE CULTURALLY DISADVANTAGED AND EXCEPTIONAL** By Robert M. Anderson. Springfield, Ill., Charles C. Thomas, 1969. $11.
Selected listing of 1,000 items (books, games, records, films, ditto sheets, etc.) appropriate for handicapped students—chosen because the authors and/or other experienced teachers found them good teaching resources in practice. Materials are arranged by curriculum areas that include such categories as "Listening and Speaking" and "Motor Learning," as well as standard subject areas. In each section, entries are arranged by type of

material and include series title, publisher, author, cost, interest level, and type of handicap. Although these materials were initially carefully selected on practical criteria, the descriptions are neither evaluative nor extensive. A list of sources (primarily publishers) and a bibliography on teaching the disadvantaged are included.

I63   **INSTRUCTIONAL STRATEGIES AND CURRICULUM UNITS FOR SECONDARY BEHAVIORAL SCIENCES** Plattsburgh, N.Y., State University of New York, 1973. $2.25. From: James M. Johnson, Department of Psychology, State University of New York, Plattsburgh, N.Y. 12901. (Checks should be made payable to Research Foundation of SUNY.)

This manual, compiled by participants in a two-week workshop, is devoted primarily to high school curriculum units: "Language and Communication," "Non-Verbal Communication," "Study of Small Groups," "How to Develop a Community Classroom," "Experimental Sociology: The City as a Resource," "Micro-Society," "Operant Conditioning," and "Esthetics." These units, in a variety of formats, usually include suggested activities for students and relevant resources.

I64   **INSTRUCTOR: Cumulative Index, August 1966-1971** By Judith Jenkins. Littleton, Colo., Libraries Unlimited, 1972. $8.50.

Since the *Instructor* is a prime source of curricular tips and practical ideas, this detailed analytical index could prove extremely useful to elementary school teachers. Articles are indexed by author, title, and subject, with cross-references to related subjects. Headings include general areas such as art education, and specific themes such as "Thanksgiving."

I65   **INTERCOM** New York, Center for War/Peace Studies, 1959– . 3 to 5 issues/year. $6.00/4 issues; $1.50–$2.50/single copy; quantity discount. From: 218 E. 18th St., New York, N.Y. 10003.

A resource tool for teachers and community leaders that focuses on global problems of war, peace, conflict, and social change, with the aim of promoting constructive alternatives consistent with democratic values. Each issue concentrates on a single subject—Spaceship Earth, Multinational Corporations, and Population are some recent examples. A typical issue on a key area—southern Africa for example—includes a map; thumbnail sketches of the countries; an overview of their problems in relation to the United States; a listing of liberation movements and publications; suggested issues for discussion; comprehensive guides to organizational resources, films, and bibliographies; plus an evaluation sheet for the entire issue. The selected annotated resource guides—to organizations, audiovisual materials, and printed materials—are of consistently high quality; the subjects are current and usually of interest to high school and college students, although some issues, for example that on Spaceship Earth (November 1972), have included materials (such as games) for the upper elementary grades. The format has been changed recently to include additional charts and visual aids.

I66   **MATERIALS FOR CIVICS, GOVERNMENT, AND PROB-
LEMS OF DEMOCRACY: Political Science in the New Social
Studies**   By Mary Jane Turner. Boulder, Colo., Social Science
Education Consortium, 1971. $5.95; paperback, $3.95.
A comparative survey of 49 political science curriculum packages. Includes systematically presented information on cost, availability, contents, educational objectives, teaching strategies, and evaluations.

I67   **MATERIALS FOR OCCUPATIONAL EDUCATION: An Annotated Source Guide**   By Patricia Schuman. New York, R.R.
Bowker, 1971. $10.75.
This well-organized tool was compiled to meet the needs of educators and librarians. Since the majority of relevant materials is obtained from professional and trade associations, governments, agencies, and private businesses, all of which change frequently, this source lists 600 organizations (selected from 3,000) that supply books, periodicals, manuals, and other media for 63 occupational areas. Entries include types of materials and specific titles, with ordering information. Emphasis is on materials relevant to two-year college instructional programs. Further sources of information appear under the subject categories. Two chapters provide annotated lists of publishers and professional organizations.

I68   **MATERIALS FOR THE OPEN CLASSROOM**   Edited by Skip
Ascheim. New York, Dell, 1973. $3.
A stimulating guide to a limited number of well-selected (mostly manipulative) items appropriate for elementary level open classrooms.

I69   **MITRES, LITRES, AND GRAMS: Introducing Metrification in
the Primary School**   Compiled by Great Britain Schools Council
for Curriculum and Examinations. New York, Citation Press,
1971. $1.35.
A British guide for elementary school teachers—with work cards, sample exercises, and illustrations—designed to introduce the metric system. One of a comprehensive series of British publications intended to involve teachers in curricular changes. This one is particularly applicable to our approaching metric conversion.

170   **MULTIMEDIA MATERIALS FOR AFRO-AMERICAN STUDIES**   A Curriculum Orientation and Annotated Bibliography of Resources. Edited by Harry Alleyn Johnson et al. New York, R. R. Bowker, 1971. $21.50.

A highly selective, annotated listing of more than 700 films and a substantial number of other media materials, such as filmstrips, recordings, audio and video tapes, and approximately 100 paperback books relating to Afro-Americans and Africa. The book begins with position papers presenting the views of four Black educators on relevant education for minority students. It ends with directories of distributors. Bibliographically complete and accurate.

171   **MUSIC CURRICULUM GUIDES**   By H. W. Arberg and S.P. Wood. Washington, D.C., U.S. Government Printing Office, 1964. (Out-of-Print)

A comprehensive bibliography of curriculum guides for music educators, as of 1964. Includes 491 annotated items, covering both philosophy and practice in music instruction. Part I, arranged primarily by grade level, is then subdivided alphabetically by title under each state. Part II, general curriculum guides, is arranged alphabetically by title. Although the indexes and most of the materials listed are no longer available for consultation, this guide is still useful for historic research and for suggesting the possibilities of music curricula.

172   **NEW IN-DEPTH EVALUATIONS OF SOCIAL STUDIES CURRICULAR PROJECTS, PROGRAMS, AND MATERIALS**   *In: Social Education, 37*(7):711-798, November 1972. $1.50. From: National Council for the Social Studies. 1201 16th St., N.W., Washington, D.C. 20036

This section in a special issue of *Social Education* provides an up-to-date, in-depth evaluation of 26 well-known social studies projects (from Amherst to Utah). Each discussion includes an introduction, information on rationale and objectives, product characteristics, content, methodology, conditions for implementation, and evaluation. A convenient overview table includes information on subject areas, materials, format, and guidelines of the National Council for the Social Studies. The issue is a joint production of NCSS and the Social Science Education Consortium in Colorado, with SSEC contributing much of the writing, as well as the articles concerned with analyzing, selecting, and evaluating curricular materials. A-plus issue of this fine periodical.

173   **NEW INSTRUCTIONAL MATERIALS FOR AGRICUL-TURAL EDUCATION, 1974-1975** By American Vocational Assn., Curriculum Materials Committee, Agricultural Education Div. Washington, D.C., 1975. Annual. Free. From: Vocational Agricultural Service, 434 Mumford Hall, Urbana, Ill. 61801.

An annual collection of noncommercial curriculum materials for agricultural education, developed by vocational educators in agriculture. The 1974-1975 issue includes 187 items that are available. These items are fully described, with information on source and price, and cover such areas as field crops, horticulture, forestry, animal science, soils, diseases and pests, agricultural engineering, agricultural economics, agricultural education, and professional readings.

174   **NINE MODEL PROGRAMS FOR YOUNG CHILDREN** By Benjamin F. Quillian, Jr. and Kathryn S. Rogers. St. Louis, Mo., CEMREL, Inc., 1972. Vol. 1, $8; Appendix, $6. From: 3120 59th St., St. Louis, Mo. 63139.

Compares basic philosophy, goals, and techniques of nine preschool programs (representative of open, individualized, structured, and noninstructional types). Sample lesson materials also are included.

175   **OCCUPATIONAL OUTLOOK HANDBOOK, 1974-75** By U.S. Department of Labor. Washington, D.C., U.S. Government Printing Office, 1974. $6.85.

Published annually, this basic career education guide provides up-to-date, accurate, occupational information on 800 occupations and 30 major industries, including requirements, advancements, outlook, working conditions, and sources of further information for each. It is based on findings of the Bureau of Labor Statistics. In recent issues, related occupations are intelligently arranged in close proximity to each other. An invaluable source for high school counselors, with much directory information.

176   **OPEN EDUCATION AT EDC: Films and Publications** By Educational Development Center. Newton, Mass., 1973. Free. From: EDC Publications, 55 Chapel St., Newton, Mass. 02160.

An annotated bibliography of 40 films and 50 publications on open education, available for sale or rent. Although bibliographically poor, it is well-annotated and interrelated; includes prices, titles, and authors of selected materials to assist teachers and administrators in implementing open education programs.

177 **OPTIONS AND PERSPECTIVES: A Sourcebook of Innovative Foreign Language Programs in Action, K–12** Edited by William Love and Lucille Honig. New York, Modern Language Assn. of America, 1973. $3.50 (paperback).

Reviews 51 (from a wide variety of) elementary and secondary school foreign-language programs, including individualized instruction, foreign-language camps, magnet schools, and foreign study.

178 **POPULATION EDUCATION RESOURCES** By Zero Population Growth. Washington, D.C., 1974. $1.50; single copies free to teachers, upon written request on school letterhead.

A convenient packet (reflecting ZPG viewpoints) that includes charts, fact sheets, descriptions, and source guides for audiovisual materials and books at the elementary and secondary school levels, as well as teaching suggestions and activities for classrooms and community groups.

179 **THE PSYCHOLOGY TEACHER'S RESOURCE BOOK: First Course** By American Psychological Assn. 2nd Edition. Washington, D.C., 1973. $3 (paperback).

A comprehensive source book for psychology teachers, first published as *Teaching of Psychology in the Secondary School*, this recently completed revision is both current and thorough. It includes brief reviews and comparisons of introductory textbooks, reading books, and laboratory manuals; a tabulated list of journals, including name, address, cost(s), reading levels, typical article length, descriptions, and recommendations; a list of nontechnical books (novels, case studies, biographies) for high school students, classified by problem area; comprehensive sections on audiovisual materials and reference materials; lists of animal, equipment, and supply sources; and addresses of organizations able to provide information or materials suitable for psychology students or teachers. Approximately 1,000 items are covered, including films and audiovisual sources.

180 **READER DEVELOPMENT BIBLIOGRAPHY** Compiled by Philadelphia Free Library. Syracuse, N.Y., Readers Press, 1974. $2.50.

This guide, intended to meet the needs of young adults and adults who cannot read above the eighth grade level, provides annotations and bibliographic data for 600 books, arranged by interest categories, including leisure reading; community and family life; jobs; reading, writing, and arithmetic; science; and the world and its people. Provides an author index and the reading level (Gunning Fog Index) for each book. Current plans are to update annually and to provide cumulative editions every three years.

181   **READ FOR YOUR LIFE: Two Successful Efforts to Help People Read and an Annotated List of Books that Made Them Want To** By Julia R. Palmer. Metuchen, N.J., Scarecrow Press, 1974. $15.

An annotated list, arranged by subject, of 1,500 book titles proved popular and successful in reading programs. The descriptive annotations note content, reader popularity in reading programs, and interests and reading levels (kindergarten to adult), plus an author-title index.

Ms. Palmer has had extensive experience in reading programs, as a volunteer in New York City schools and also in a pilot project in the Bushwick-Bedford Stuyvesant area of Brooklyn. The book includes an outline of these two programs, with teaching tips derived from this experience.

182   **READING MATERIALS HANDBOOK: A Guide to Materials and Sources for Secondary and College Reading Improvement** By Allen Berger and Hugo Hartig. Oshkosh, Wis., Academia Press, 1969. $2 (paperback).

Annotates materials, texts, and workbooks for individual and classroom use, as well as references for teachers, references on evaluation, and audiovisual materials. Subjects covered include developmental reading, remedial reading, special education, and reading research.

183   **RECOMMENDED ENGLISH LANGUAGE ARTS CURRICULUM GUIDES K–12** And Criteria for Planning and Evaluation. Edited by Sr. Rosemary Winkeljohann. Urbana, Ill., National Council of Teachers of English, 1974. $0.75 (paperback). From: 1111 Kenyon Rd., Urbana, Ill. 61801.

An annotated list of a small number of recommended or exemplary curriculum guides, selected (and reviewed since 1970 by a review committee) from those voluntarily submitted to the Committee on Curriculum Bulletins of the National Council of Teachers of English; updated annually in November. The guides listed are available, either free or for purchase. A detailed list of review criteria is printed at the end of the book. This paper should be required reading for individuals selecting English curricula.

184   **REFERENCE ENCYCLOPEDIA ON THE AMERICAN INDIAN** Volume 1, Edited by Barry T. Klein; Volume 2, Edited by Dan Icolari. 2nd Edition. Rye, N.Y., Todd Publications, 1974. 2 Vols. $17.50 each.

This substantial work can be used for research as well as for curriculum planning. Volume I consists of a comprehensive, 2,500-entry, annotated bibliography of books dealing with the American Indian (with young people's titles asterisked), including complete bibliographic information and subject and publisher indexes. Other mediaographies, arranged by type of materials, cover such items as films, picture sets, songbooks, maps, charts, and records, with contents notes, sources, and prices. Additional lists cover government publications and periodicals. Directory sections include associations, reservations and tribal councils, government agencies, museums and libraries, arts and crafts shops, and college courses, all arranged alphabetically within geographical areas. Volume II consists of hard-to-find biographical sketches of prominent living Indians, with a few biographies of non-Indians currently active in Indian affiars.

185 **REPORT OF THE INTERNATIONAL CLEARINGHOUSE ON SCIENCE AND MATHEMATICS CURRICULAR DEVELOPMENTS** Edited by J. David Lockard. 8th Report. College Park, Md., University of Maryland, 1972. $3. From: Science Teaching Center, College Park, Md. 20742.

An excellent, inexpensive summary of new science and mathematics curriculum projects throughout the world. This was a joint project of the Science Teaching Center of the University of Maryland and the American Association for the Advancement of Science, with the advice and cooperation of UNESCO. Questionnaires were edited, and intelligent summaries were prepared, providing background information, project title, headquarters, staff, products, evaluation, prospects, language(s), teacher training requirements, and future plans for each project. Varied indexes, by country, grade level, and subjects, comprise the introduction to this valuable catalog.

186 **SCIENCE CAN BE ELEMENTARY: Discovery-Action Programs K–3** By Barbara S. Waters. New York, Citation Press, 1973. $8.50; paperback, $3.85.

This is an intelligent analysis of the philosophy and recommendations of six federally funded science curriculum development programs—especially helpful for elementary school teachers who may have little or no science training. It includes detailed descriptions of activities from each program, which can be easily adaptable to average kindergarten through grade three classrooms. Appendixes provide an excellent compendium of science sources in education: an evaluative annotated directory and bibliography of science curriculum programs, sources of materials, professional organizations, and federal programs.

187 **SCIENCE MATERIALS FOR CHILDREN AND YOUNG PEOPLE** Edited by George S. Bonn. *In: Library Trends,* 22(4), April 1974. $2.50.

The April 1974 issue of *Library Trends* is comprised of a series of commissioned articles by distinguished authors, editors, reviewers, librarians, and science teachers to assist parents, librarians, and teachers in selecting and evaluating all types of science materials. It includes outstanding lists of science periodicals, science reference books, and science media materials, as well as explicit criteria for selection.

188 **SELECTIVE GUIDE TO MATERIALS FOR MENTAL HEALTH AND FAMILY LIFE EDUCATION** Compiled by MHMC Information Resource Center. New York, Mental Health Materials Center, 1972. $35; supplementary newsletter service available at $12/year. From: 419 Park Ave., S., New York, N.Y. 10016.

Contains summaries, authoritative evaluations, suggested audiences, and uses for more than 500 program aids (mostly publications and films) in mental health and family life education. Materials are arranged by subjects which include child growth and development; adolescence; family life, including sex education and aging; intergroup relations; community resources and programs; and such problem areas as alcoholism, drug abuse, mental illness, and suicide prevention. A useful tool for adult educators, health personnel, and community groups, as well as for schools. A good buying aid for school nurses and counselors. The MHMC Information Resource Center produces and distributes a wide variety of materials on mental health. A free list, available on request, describes other publications on mental health and family life education.

189 **SHORT-SPAN ACTIVITIES: Ideas for Utilizing Spare Minutes in the Classroom** By Lynne Miller and Carol Batten. New York, Citation Press, 1973. $0.95 (paperback).

Source book for the elementary school teacher, which includes more than 80 suggestions on how to get the most out of unexpected spare minutes through games and activities for different time spans, subject areas, and grade levels. Arrangement is by subjects, which include language arts, social studies, math, art, science, current events, and "fun games." It also could be used by parents or group leaders.

190 **SIMULATION GAMES FOR THE SOCIAL STUDIES CLASSROOM** By William A. Nesbitt. 2nd Edition. Washington, D.C., Foreign Policy Assn., 1971. $2.50.

Although there are more extensive lists of simulation games, this one is slanted toward the needs of the social studies teacher. Includes a discussion of effective classroom uses of games, as well as a bibliography of readings on games.

I91   **SOCIAL ISSUES RESOURCES SERIES**   Edited by Eleanor C. Goldstein. Washington, D.C., Exotech Systems, 1972– . $30/set; $25/set for three or more sets.

Each *Social Issues Resources* publication is a loose-leaf notebook containing reprints of approximately 60 selected articles from a wide variety of sources—magazines, newspapers, government documents, technical journals—dealing with a single important topic. Reprints are in clear typeface, on good paper, with a table of contents, an introduction, and a teacher's guide. These current anthologies deal with drugs, pollution, population, minorities, corrections, transportation, women's lib, welfare, urbanization, poverty, and similar topics. Most could be excellent curriculum units on contemporary social studies issues at high school, college, and adult levels.

I92   **SOCIAL STUDIES CURRICULUM MATERIALS DATA BOOK**   By Social Science Education Consortium. Boulder, Colo., 1971-1973. 2 Vols., including supplements. $40. Annual subscription (for two subsequent supplements) $15.

An ongoing evaluative summary of three types of curriculum materials: project materials from nationally funded projects, innovative textbooks, and games and simulations. Thus far, more than 215 products have been evaluated. Data sheets on project materials include an overview, description of the format, and elements (cost and time, information on the rationale, intended users), as well as a section on evaluation and use, with references. Subject areas are comprised of traditional studies, as well as multidisciplinary and interdisciplinary studies. Loose-leaf format; updated in March and October.

Packets of 10 to 15 data sheets on specific subject areas from this book are available for $1.50 each. Currently, packets are available for Elementary Social Studies; Intermediate Social Studies; Secondary American History; Civics/Government; Conflict Analysis, Minority Education, Urban Problems; Anthropology, Sociology, Psychology; and World History and World Cultures.

SSEC's *Profiles of Promise* offers 30 newsy briefs each year on selected innovative social studies practices, with descriptive information on the objectives, planning, personnel, communication, and evaluation of these practices (30 issues/year, $10).

I93   **SOCIAL STUDIES EDUCATION PROJECTS: An ASCD Index**   Compiled by Bob L. Taylor and Thomas L. Groom. Washington, D.C., Assn. for Supervision and Curriculum Development, 1971. $1.

A nonevaluative, nonexhaustive index compiled primarily from existing directories and materials of the Social Science Education Consortium in Boulder, Colorado, with updated information (obtained via survey) for 53 of the 111 projects it lists alphabetically. Summary information includes grade level, subject area, purpose, directors, and relevant published materials, plus an index of directors and projects. Not a categorized or definitive listing, but a helpful pragmatic attempt to keep current with curriculum developments in the social studies.

I94 **A SOURCEBOOK OF ELEMENTARY CURRICULA, PRO-GRAMS AND PROJECTS: From the ALERT Information System** Edited by Samuel N. Henrie et al. San Francisco, Far West Laboratory for Educational Research and Development, 1972. $5.75. From: U.S. Government Printing Office, Washington, D.C. 20540.

Although somewhat heavy on products of regional laboratories such as Far West and other federally funded research and development centers, this compilation is a good starting source for information on innovative elementary school curricula. Arranged alphabetically by subject, the *Sourcebook* is a sampler providing adequate to ample information on more than 300 selected, innovative elementary curricula, training programs, projects, and resources (that is, bibliographic and curriculum guides and handbooks). First priority was given to research and development products; second, to new non-research and development programs that have demonstrated their value through field trials; and third, to other new programs which ". . . show internal evidence of good quality and represent important alternatives to traditional practice."

Subject coverage is excellent (although the treatment is uneven), including the basic subjects, neglected traditional subjects such as aesthetic education, and topical and trendy areas such as affective education, drug education, environmental education, and ethnic education.

Information on individual programs and curricula is comprehensive and readable. For each program listed, the *Sourcebook* presents—in clear useful format—information on source, developer, price, address, availability, subject area, target audience (including grade level), sample topics, goals, instructional methods and sequencing, length of time required, student and teacher roles, special equipment and facilities, student testing, program evaluation, etc. Also includes additional charts, as needed, of materials, equipment, services, and costs for some programs and curricula. One uncommon, but convenient, feature is the notation: "Information current as of   ." The resource items are not so good, and although they include many useful references, they represent an almost random and far from comprehensive sampling.

195   **SPARKS—SCIENCE PROJECTS: Avenues of Research and Keys to Science**   Edited by Suzanne K. Gray. Boston, Boston Public Library, 1971. $1. From: Information Office, Boston Public Library, P.O. Box 286, Boston, Mass. 02117.

A well-annotated bibliography of an assortment of more than 100 source books for science projects, mostly at the junior high and high school levels, with a few ranging down to the elementary grades; most books listed are guides to experiments and sources of materials. Areas covered include astronautics, electronics, geology, meteorology, astronomy, physical sciences, life sciences, and general science. Provides complete bibliographic information, with prices; annotations contain appropriate grade levels and useful detailed descriptions. Excellent for independent and individualized study at all levels.

196   **SUGGESTED GUIDELINES FOR CONSUMER EDUCATION, GRADES K–12**   By President's Committee on Consumer Interests. Washington, D.C., U.S. Government Printing Office, 1972. $0.65.

This committee's working aid for implementing consumer education programs; includes a comprehensive listing of agencies involved in consumer education.

197   **SURVIVAL KIT FOR SUBSTITUTES: Activities that Work in Elementary Classrooms**   By Vita Pavlich and Eleanor Rosenast. New York, Citation Press, 1974. $3.65 (paperback).

Written by two experienced Los Angeles substitute teachers, this source book contains a useful introduction and hundreds of activities in language arts, social studies (including international projects), art with limited materials, holidays, rainy days, and mathematics, with a special chapter on day-long activities (one-day murals, one-day newspapers). Projects rank high on interest, cognitive content, and relation to elementary school curriculum.

198   **SYNOPSIS OF SELECTED CAREER EDUCATION PROJECTS**   Edited by Robert Morgan et al. Raleigh, N.C., National Center for Occupational Education, North Carolina State University, 1972. Free. From: P.O. Box 5096, Raleigh, N.C. 27607.

An overview of 39 kindergarten through twelfth grade career education projects in 30 states, selected from 250 nominated. Information for each, gathered by on-site visits and perusal of the literature, includes grade levels, objectives, in-service training needed, community involvement, and evaluation procedures.

I99 **THE TEACHER'S ALMANAC: Practical Ideas for Every Day of the School Year** By Dana Newmann. New York, Center for Applied Research in Education, 1973. $8.95. (Distributed by Prentice-Hall.)

Arranged by month, this elementary school teacher's resource book of practical ideas suggests activities for all curriculum areas, with calendars that include holidays and historical events, birthdays of and quotations by famous men and women born during the month, bulletin board ideas, timely games, and appropriate seasonal activities.

I100 **TEACHER'S PACKET OF GEOLOGICAL MATERIALS** Compiled by U.S. Geological Survey. Reston, Va., 1970– . Free.

This substantial packet, containing 49 items of geological materials, provides a variety of teacher-tested lists, brochures, pamphlets, and information sheets, including guides to maps and other sources of information; for teachers of topology, earth science, and geology. Especially useful at the high school level.

I101 **TEACHING ABOUT ASIA** By American Society for Eastern Arts. San Francisco, Calif., 1972. 5 Pamphlets. $3.75. From: 425 Bush St., San Francisco, Calif. 94108.

This attractive packet of pamphlets includes listings of sources and resources, film annotations, bibliographies, discographies, and essays for teachers teaching about Asia.

I102 **TEACHING AFRICA TODAY: A Handbook for Teachers and Curriculum Planners** By E. Jefferson Murphy. New York, Citation Press, 1973. $3.85 (paperback).

Intended for grades 5 through 12, this guide covers curriculum units and courses on a wide range of African studies, and has copious annotated listings of print and media materials for each section—geography; pre-European history; colonial history; and cultural, economic, and political aspects—are included. The final chapter provides guidelines for selecting curriculum materials—255 items.

I103 **TEACHING HUMAN BEINGS: 101 Subversive Activities for the Classroom** By Jeffrey Schrank. Boston, Beacon Press, 1972. $7.95; paperback, $3.45.

A young teacher not only denounces current teaching practices, but does something about it. This book consists of 101 highly interesting classroom activities dealing with such unorthodox areas as sense education, hidden assumptions, violence and the violated, chemicals and the body, learning about death, and, of course, subversive activities. The exercises are interesting and appropriate for a wide range of age levels from elementary school up. The hidden assumptions—curricula dealing with stereotypes and ways and means of ferreting out culture-bound assumptions—might be good for teachers themselves. Includes suggestions for background reading and lists of related materials: books, films, and filmstrips.

I104 **TEACHING TOMORROW** A Handbook of Science Fiction for Teachers. By Elizabeth Calkins and Barry McGhan. Dayton, Ohio, Pflaum/Standard, 1972. $2.50.

Essentially, the second part of this guide is a series of lists intended to bring science fiction into the high school English curriculum. Lists include 200 recommended novels (annotated), as well as book dealers and publishers, science-fiction conventions, organizations, indexes, motion pictures, and amateur and professional magazines. The first part includes hints, strategies, study guides, and case studies for the teacher.

I105 **TOWARD QUALITY EDUCATION FOR MEXICAN AMERICANS: Mexican American Education Study** By U.S. Commission on Civil Rights. Report VI. Washington, D.C., 1974. Free.

Part of a series based on conditions and practices in the schools of five southwestern states—Arizona, California, Colorado, New Mexico, and Texas. Analyzes curriculum, pupil placement, teacher education, counseling, and equal education; recommends actions for government and education.

I106 **UNIPACS** Originated by Gardner Swenson. Salt Lake City, Teachers UNIPAC Exchange, 1967– . Various prices: $0.10/page, plus $5.00 for each mailing; lifetime fee, $99.00, plus $0.10 per page; or exchange basis. From: 1653 Forest Hills Dr., Salt Lake City, Utah 84106.

UNIPACS are formatted learning packages that include plans for single-concept individualized lessons designed for student use (approximately 7,300 items as of June 1975). Each UNIPAC includes 10 elements: a pretest, statement of primary concept, component parts to be learned, behavioral objectives, instructions for selecting activities, diversified activities, self-test, post-test, opportunities for related learning (Quest), and a field test of the packages. Produced by teachers who participate in UNIPAC workshops, and distributed by a national UNIPAC bank. Lists or catalogs are available for the following subject areas:

Reading (all levels)
Primary (all subjects)
Social Studies (elementary and secondary)*
Language Arts (elementary and secondary)*
Art (all levels)
Science (elementary and secondary)*
Business Education (all levels)
Foreign Languages (all levels)
Mathematics (elementary and secondary)*

Dance (all levels)
Health (all levels)
Home Economics (all levels)
Library Science (all levels)
Industrial Arts (all levels)
Driver Education (all levels)
Music (all levels)
Physical Education (all levels)
Inservice (adult)
Counseling (all levels)
Career Education (all levels)

* (Separate lists available for elementary and secondary levels for some subjects.)

UNIPACs have been reproduced on microfiche by various groups, starting with the Kettering Foundation. Microfiche copies can be obtained from San Mateo County's Educational Resources Center (see Chapter 19) and from Connecticut's Area Cooperative Educational Services, 12 Village Street, North Haven, Connecticut 06473, for approximately $0.35 per UNIPAC.

A more detailed discussion of UNIPACs and other learning packages can be found in *Learning Packages in American Education* by Philip G. and Miriam B. Kapfer (Englewood Cliffs, N.J., Educational Technology, 1973).

I107   **VALUE EDUCATION NEWSLETTER** By Consultants Clearinghouse Service. Campbell, Calif., Value Education Publications, 1973– . 9 issues/year. Free. From: P.O. Box 947, Campbell, Calif. 95008.
Provides news on trends, programs, and consultants, as well as evaluations of materials and curricula.

I108   **WHAT IS A CITY? A Multi-Media Guide on Urban Living** Edited by Rose Moorichian. Boston, Boston Public Library, 1969. $2. From: P.O. Box 286, Boston, Mass. 02117.
An annotated directory of well-chosen books, pamphlets, periodicals, films, filmstrips, loops, recordings, and realia dealing mostly with the contemporary rather than with the historic city. Provides complete information (except for price), with a one-paragraph review. Materials are for all ages—preschool through high school.

A companion volume, *What Is a City? Young People Reply,* compiled by Dianne Farrell and Ruth M. Hayes in 1969, is available from the same source for $1.

I109 **WOMEN IN THE WORK FORCE: Development and Testing of Curriculum Materials** By Louise Vetter and Barbara Sethney. Washington, D.C., U.S. Government Printing Office, 1973. $0.95.
A package of curriculum materials designed to assist high school girls in considering alternatives when making plans for labor force participation and adult female roles.

I110 **THE WORLD OF WORK: An Annotated Bibliography for the Primary Grades** By Patricia R. Myren. Guilderland, N.Y., Guilderland Central School District, 1972. Free. From: State Farm Rd., Guilderland, N.Y. 12084.
Materials in this annotated list include books, filmstrips, pictures, records, and other media, classified by broad work areas. It is interesting, attractive, informative, technically competent, and suitable for primary school children.

I111 **YELLOW PAGES OF LEARNING RESOURCES** Edited by Richard S. Wurman. Cambridge, Mass., MIT Press, 1972. $1.95.
"This book is an invitation to discover the city as a learning resource. It provides a selection of typical firsthand learning resources that can be found in almost any city and outlines the avenue to follow to make these sources accessible." The resources involved are: learning from 70 people, learning at 29 places, and learning about 13 processes. The grade level is precollege. Contains some interesting tables comparing cities and outlining sources (useful for any social studies teacher). The book concludes with an *ad hoc* partial directory of programs using these or similar resources.

11 | *Guides to Nonprint Instructional Materials*

The guides in this chapter, unlike those listed in the previous two chapters, are primarily media-oriented rather than general or subject-oriented. "Media," in this chapter, includes simulation games, microforms, programmed instruction, and other nonprint materials. Some of the organizations, depositories, and information exchanges listed and discussed in Chapter 16 also can provide guidance in the use and selection of media materials.

The wide selection of competent guides discussed in this chapter is indicative of a fairly recent trend. Traditionally, although expenditures for media equipment and materials constitute a large educational expense (more than $2 billion a year—53 percent for 16-mm films and equipment), many school districts have selected and purchased them with distinctly limited thought and evaluation, due partly to the shortage of useful guidance tools, as well as failure to use existing tools.

Educational Products Information Exchange (EPIE) (O12), for instance, in spite of its efforts to provide independent, objective tests and evaluations of educational materials, equipment, and systems for the educational community, has been underused and, as a single organization, cannot always make necessary evaluations of products and services in time for useful dissemination.

The Library Technology Program of the American Library Association (O24) also has conscientiously and thoroughly evaluated many kinds of equipment, but has lacked the financial support required to disseminate the results of its evaluations broadly enough.

175

Many of the software guides—designed by producers' organizations or relying on producers' information—have failed to provide the bibliographic or descriptive information needed for intelligent evaluation and purchase; sometimes such information has been provided in awkward or badly indexed formats. Some producers and distributors tend to give glowing accounts of their products, but omit or misrepresent significant items such as production dates and audience levels.

In recent years, however, existing guides have refined and improved their formats and contents, while experienced library publishers increasingly have used their bibliographic skills to produce selected and comprehensive indexes of media materials.

Although we have not yet achieved the "complete guide" to our burgeoning media materials—one that is competent, comprehensive, inexpensive, up-to-date, evaluative, well-written, bibliographically complete, and easy to use—the guides listed in this chapter meet at least some of these criteria, and can be considered the most valuable of the hundreds investigated.

Guides to Educational Media (J22) provides rather complete details on media guides as of 1971. The ERIC Clearinghouse on Information Resources (O17) has produced a paper, *A Comparison of Guides to Non-Print Media,* which evaluates nonprint indexes. The reference section of *Audiovisual Marketplace* (J2) is perhaps the prime source for additional information.

Educational journals, newsletters, and services often include reviews or notices of nonprint materials in their areas of interest. Following are a few helpful sources:

American Biology Teacher   *Instructor*
Audiovisual Instruction   *Learning Magazine*
Balance Sheet   *Mass Media*
Behavioral Science Teacher   *Mathematics Teacher*
*Booklist   **Media and Methods*
Clearinghouse Review   **Periodically*
Contemporary Psychology   *PTA Magazine*
*EFLA Evaluations   *Scholastic Teacher*
*English Journal   **Science and Children*
Exceptional Children   *Science News*
Grade Teacher   **Science Teacher*
Horn Book   *Sightlines*

*Social Education
Social Studies
* Particularly valuable items.

Some state media services, dealing with state library services to educators, are included in Chapter 19.

Those users who lack access to media materials through a school system may be able to locate them through public libraries or library networks. The *Directory of Film Libraries in North America* (New York, Film Information Council, 1971) is a geographic directory of public libraries in the United States that circulate nonprint materials.

J1 **AUDIO-VISUAL EQUIPMENT DIRECTORY, 1975-1976**
Edited by Sally Herickes. Fairfax, Va., National Audio-Visual Assn., 1975. Annual. $11.25, prepaid; $12.50, if billed. From: 3150 Spring St., Fairfax, Va. 22030.

This attractive guide, issued around May of each year, is now in its 21th edition. It is based on information supplied by manufacturers, rather than on independent ratings. More than 2,000 models of audiovisual equipment are listed—by type of equipment (74 categories), then alphabetically by company name, and, finally, numerically or alphabetically by model. There is a picture of each piece of equipment, as well as such information as price, operation, dimensions, weight, and electrical requirements. Includes a list of manufacturers with addresses and phone numbers, and a geographical listing of dealers. Not comprehensive, but clear and useful, especially for those who know the field well.

This compilation of comparative data from manufacturers can be checked against the feedback and objective evaluations of EPIE and the technology tests of the American Library Association.

J2 **AUDIO VISUAL MARKETPLACE: A Multimedia Guide 1974-75** 5th Edition. New York, R.R. Bowker, 1974. Biennial. $21.

An authoritative, useful directory issued every other Spring. It lists producers and distributors, equipment, associations, conventions, film festivals, events, and manufacturers, and contains sections covering reference publications, serials and review services, and services and dealers (cataloging, film services, repair services, etc.). This edition includes subject classification indexes for media, manufacturers, and production companies, as well as a subject index to the whole book. An introductory foreword discusses trends in the audiovisual field.

J3   **AUDIO VISUAL QUICK LISTS** By Baker and Taylor Co.,
      Audio Visual Div. Momence, Ill., 1973– . Free. From: P.O. Box 230,
      Momence, Ill. 60954.
"Single source" buying guides which can be used effectively as selection
aids and reference sources. For single subjects, approximately 25 media
formats are covered: films, games, flash cards, globes, slides, and
recordings, among others. Entries, by title, include grade level, technical
description, a code for media formats, producer, release date, brief
description, price, and a recommendation code. Some of the titles in this
series are *Newbury/Caldecott Awards, Career Education, Environmental
Studies, Library Science,* and *Bilingual Education.* The lists are updated by a
new professional publication, *MediaCenter* (J35).

J4   **A CATALOG OF UNITED STATES GOVERNMENT PRO-
      DUCED AUDIOVISUAL MATERIALS** By National Au-
      diovisual Center, General Services Administration. Washington,
      D.C., 1974. Free.
Contains 4,500 audiovisual items available for sale or rental from the
center, which was established in 1969 to provide government agencies
and the general public with one central source from which to obtain
instructional and promotional audiovisual materials produced for or by
agencies of the executive branch of government. Many of the films were
used originally as training films and are very suitable for vocational and
technical education, as well as for secondary school students and adults;
a few are appropriate for younger children. Subject range is wide, and
prices are relatively low.

J5   **CATALOGUE OF REPRODUCTIONS OF PAINTINGS 1860
      TO 1973** By UNESCO. Paris, UNESCO, 1974. $13.20. From: Uni-
      pub, P.O. Box 433, New York, N.Y. 10016.
A helpful guide to high-quality reproductions of the world's great
paintings, selected by international art experts for excellence and
importance. For each work chosen, it provides a full description of both
the painting and its print and a black-and-white photograph of the
original work. Information includes name of artist (with dates of birth
and death), title, date, size, medium, and location of original painting, as
well as the size, price, printer/publisher, and printing process for the
reproduction. Contains a special section for organizing exhibitions on
special themes, such as Impressionism, North American abstracts, and
others.

J6   **CHILDREN ARE CENTERS FOR UNDERSTANDING MEDIA** Edited by Monroe D. Cohen and Susan Rice. Washington, D.C., Assn. for Childhood Education Intl., 1974. $3.95.

This cooperative project of the Association for Childhood Education International and the Center for Understanding Media is designed to remove media from the passive watching stages. The book is full of child-tested, active media projects and programs for elementary school children. Specific activities are well-illustrated and deal with sound, film, animation, and storyboarding, among others. Provides an annotated bibliography of the new media, plus film lists and source notes.

J7   **CONTEMPORARY GAMES** A Directory and Bibliography Covering Games and Play Situations or Simulations Used for Instruction and Training by Schools, Colleges and Universities, Government, Business, and Management. Compiled by Jean Belch. Detroit, Mich., Gale Research, 1973. 2 Vols. Vol. 1 – *Directory*, 1973, $42; Vol. 2 – *Bibliography*, 1974, $38.

A directory of games and simulations compiled by the head of the Curriculum Materials Center of the University of Washington. It includes "decision-making and problem-solving exercises having sufficient intellectual content to be used for educational purposes." The directory consists of more than 900 games—preprimary through adult levels—arranged alphabetically by title, in a well-chosen, easy-to-read format, with indexes by subject area and grade level. For most games, the entry includes broad subject categories, age or grade level, playing time, number of players, date originated, designer and/or producer, source, price, a brief description of the game and how it is played, and (sometimes) bibliographical citations. Also contains a separate directory of producers.

Volume 2, a *Bibliography* (of references) is less useful for teachers, but is fine for serious students of games. It contains 2,400 citations, most with annotations, from 1957 to 1973.

J8   **A CORE MEDIA COLLECTION FOR SECONDARY SCHOOL LIBRARIES** By Lucille G. Brown. New York, R. R. Bowker, 1975. $16.95.

Provides details on 2,000 recommended nonprint items for grades 7 to 12. All items are selected on the basis of favorable reviews in professional journals or on prior inclusion in outstanding media collections. Entries are arranged alphabetically by title under Sears library subject headings. Information for each entry includes a brief description, grade level, producer and distributor, order number, Dewey Decimal Classification (if available), release date, price, and recommending sources. Highly recommended items are asterisked. Contains an author/title index, plus a directory of procedures and distributors.

J9   CREATING A SCHOOL MEDIA PROGRAM   By John T. Gillespie and Diana L. Spirit. New York, R.R. Bowker, 1973. $11.50.
In-depth guidance for organizing and administering school media programs at all levels—from single schools to statewide programs. Includes discussions of recent national standards, as well as functions, staffing, supervising policies, and means of maximizing use of media programs at all levels—local, regional, district, and state—with attention to topics such as policymaking and budgeting. Also includes case studies, successful media programs, media characteristics, and criteria for selection.

J10   DIRECTORY OF FILMS FOR DATA EDUCATION   Compiled by Arthur H. Pike. Northfield, Vt., Society of Data Educators Publishing Office, 1972. $2.25 (paperback).
Lists and describes approximately 300 films on data education for high school students and adults. Films are arranged alphabetically by title. Information includes resume, date of release, whether in color or black-and-white, rental prices, running time, and least expensive sources, but omits millimeters and audience level of films.

J11   DRUG ABUSE FILMS   By National Coordinating Council on Drug Education. 3rd Edition. Chicago, American Library Assn., 1973. $5.
Contains evaluative reviews and synopses of films and other audiovisual productions; evaluated by a panel of reviewers comprised of students and assorted experts. Evaluations report the strong and weak points of each work, using (largely) the criteria of accuracy, approach, and realism. Asterisked items are first choices; objectionable works also are signalled. The book is divided into sections on film and other audiovisual aids, including filmstrips, recordings, slides, and transparencies: each of these groups is arranged alphabetically by subject. Bibliographic information includes production date, producer, length, and price, as well as target audience. Subject index at end. No entries on alcohol.

J12   EDUCATIONAL MEDIA YEARBOOK   Edited by James W. Brown. New York, R.R. Bowker, 1973– . Annual. $19.95.
This reference series contains articles by media experts, and covers such areas as publishing trends and equipment. Includes a directory of approximately 500 media organizations; a listing of foundations and federal grant agencies which have funded media projects in the last two

years; lists of media periodicals, award-winning films, and schools offering media doctoral programs; and an annotated multimedia resources directory, arranged by title. The *Yearbook* also contains an excellent, cross-referenced index, with a separate directory of publishers, producers, and distributors.

J13 **EDUCATORS PROGRESS SERVICE, INC.** Randolph, Wis. 53956.
This publisher offers a series of guides containing selected, annotated listings of free materials, which are arranged by title under subject headings, with teacher reference, title index, subject index, and (sometimes) demonstration curriculum units incorporating free materials. (The pages of each section are of different colors.) While not highly selective, the guides are easy to use, provide clear ordering instructions, and are updated annually. Recent editions discuss materials available for Canadian educators. Some current titles are:

Educators Guide to Free Films. 34th Edition. 1974. $12.75. Lists approximately 5,000 films—mostly 16-mm; more than 1,000 are new.
Educators Guide to Free Filmstrips. 26th Edition. 1974. $9.25. Lists approximately 500 titles; arranged by curriculum areas.
Educators Guide to Free Guidance Materials. 13th Edition. 1974. $9.75. Lists approximately 1,500 items in all media.
Educators Guide to Free Health, Physical Education and Recreation Materials. 7th Edition. 1974. $10.00. Lists approximately 2,500 items; arranged first by type of media and then by subject.
Educators Guide to Free Science Materials. 15th Edition. 1974. $10.25. Lists approximately 2,000 items; arranged by type of media, with several demonstration units.
Educators Guide to Free Social Studies Materials. 14th Edition. 1974. $10.50. Lists approximately 3,000 items—many new; arranged by type of media, then by social studies topic.
Educators Guide to Free Tapes, Scripts, Transcriptions. 21st Edition. 1974. $10.50. Lists approximately 1,000 items, including video tapes from varied sources, with informative annotations; arranged by subject.
Elementary Teachers Guide to Free Curriculum Materials. 31st Edition. 1974. $10.75. Lists nearly 2,000 items; arranged by subjects, with some demonstration curriculum units.

J14 **ENVIRONMENTAL FILM REVIEW: A Critical Guide to Ecology Films** By Environment Information Center. New York, 1972. $20.
A subject classified listing and review covering all major aspects of environment, including pollution and contamination, energy, food and

drugs, land use, population planning, waste disposal, wildlife, and weather modification.

J15 **THE EVALUATION OF MICROPUBLICATIONS** A Handbook for Librarians. By Allen Veaner. Chicago, American Library Assn., 1971. $3.25 (paperback).
Written simply and clearly, this book describes types of microforms and criteria for evaluating them. Includes a useful bibliography.

J16 **THE FAMILY GUIDE TO CHILDREN'S TELEVISION: What to Watch, What to Miss, What to Change, and How to Do It** Compiled by Evelyn Kaye for Action for Children's Television (Boston, Mass.). New York, Pantheon (Random House), 1974. $8.95; paperback, $2.95.
This comprehensive activists' guide to children's television is appropriate for educators as well as for parents. It provides basic information on the techniques and economics of television broadcasting: professional opinions on the value and harm of television, effects of TV violence on children, and the influence of commercials. Contains an interesting workbook section for children to use in determining their own viewing habits—rating programs, evaluating viewing environments and commercials, and creating their own productions—as well as an annotated guide to TV programs by the National Association for Better Broadcasting.

J17 **FEATURE FILMS ON 8 MM AND 16 MM** Edited by James L. Limbacher. 4th Edition. New York, R.R. Bowker, 1974. $16.50.
An index and booking source for more than 15,000 commercial films available for sale or rent in the United States, ranging from early film classics to 1973 releases. Entries provide information on running time, studio, director, actors, and distributors. Contains a geographical index to film distributors, indexes to directors and film series, and a useful bibliography of film reference works. The editor estimates that this volume covers 95 percent of all feature films available in the United States.

J18 **FILM GUIDE FOR MUSIC EDUCATORS** By Donald J. Shelter. 2nd Edition. Washington, D.C., Music Educators National Conference, National Education Assn., 1968. $2.50. (Out-of-Print)
Covers 560 films and 50 filmstrips, mostly for the secondary school level. Arranged by title under categories that include performance, history and biographies, band, orchestra, music education, and visual interpre-

tations of music. Also contains subject and title indexes, a bibliography, and a directory of producers and distributors.

J19 **FILMS FOR EARLY CHILDHOOD: A Selected Annotated Bibliography** By Mariann Pezella Winnick. New York, Early Childhood Education Council of New York City, 1973. $3.50. From: 197 Bleecker St., New York, N.Y. 11237.

This bibliography of approximately 400 films and film series for early childhood teachers is arranged by subject under such categories as development, current trends, program planning, curriculum, parent education, teacher training, comparative education, children, and series. Originally part of a film course on early childhood education, this guide is designed for locating and booking films. It includes title, running time, information on whether the film is in color or black-and-white, rental and purchase price, a four-star rating system—from one star (adequate) to four stars (excellent), a title index, and a directory of distributors and producers.

Two other publications dealing with early childhood materials have been produced by the Early Childhood Education Council: one on evaluating art materials, the other on nonsexist materials.

J20 **FILMS ON THE FUTURE** By Marie Martin. Washington, D.C., World Future Society, 1974. $3.95.

A selective, annotated listing of films, topically arranged and covering such areas as forecasts, food, population, human values, and science fiction, with information on length, source, and rental costs. The *Futurist,* a monthly periodical of the World Future Society, lists and reviews materials dealing with the future, mostly at the high school and adult levels, and offers discounts on certain books through a book service.

J21 **FILMS—TOO GOOD FOR WORDS: A Directory of Nonnarrated 16 mm Films** By Salvatore J. Parlato, Jr. New York, R.R. Bowker, 1973. $12.50.

An interesting directory that lists and describes approximately 1,000 films which rely on their pictorial qualities rather than on narration or dialogue. Appropriate for all age levels from elementary school to adult, it is arranged by subjects covering the arts, other places and customs, science, nature, expression, city and suburb, values, fun, action, war and peace, fantasy, and literature. Information—which includes awards won—is complete, except for price. An invaluable tool for selecting films for media students, for bright students who find narratives patronizing, for aurally handicapped students, for foreign-speaking students, and for students with low-language ability.

J22 **GUIDES TO EDUCATIONAL MEDIA** Edited by Margaret I. Rufsvold and Carolyn Guss. 3rd Edition. Chicago, American Library Assn., 1971. $3. (Out-of-Print)
An annotated bibliography of reference books and bibliographies on films and filmstrips. It includes catalogs extant in 1971, 66 catalogs that were no longer available in 1971, 10 professional organizations, and 33 periodicals. Annotations cover scope, number of entries, arrangement of entries, and special features, plus an author's note. Information is complete and easy to understand.

J23 **A GUIDE TO DRUG ABUSE EDUCATION & INFORMATION MATERIALS** By National Institute of Mental Health. Washington, D.C., U.S. Government Printing Office, 1972. $0.50. Stock No. 1724-0216. Single copies free from NIMH, 5600 Fishers Lane, Rockville, Md. 20852.
This attractive booklet covers drug education materials in various media for all levels: elementary schools, community colleges, teachers groups, therapeutic groups, etc. Although it provides an effective visual display of NIMH materials, it generally omits bibliographic details. Contains ordering information and a current list of state lending libraries.

J24 **GUIDE TO FREE-LOAN FILMS ABOUT FOREIGN LANDS** (Formerly *Guide to Foreign Government Loan Films.*) Alexandria, Va., Serina Press, 1975. $14.95.
Comprised of synopses of more than 3,000 films (arranged by country) that are available on a free-loan basis from more than 75 foreign governments. Includes some excellent resources on art and history, plus films dealing with customs, culture, international relations, travel, science, music, sports, personalities, etc. Most films have English sound tracks; others could be useful for foreign-language classes. (Lists of materials available from foreign governments also can be obtained by direct application either to the embassies or to such agencies as the National Film Board of Canada.)

J25 **THE GUIDE TO SIMULATIONS/GAMES FOR EDUCATION AND TRAINING** By David W. Zuckerman and Robert E. Horn. 2nd Edition. Hicksville, N.Y., Research Media, 1973. $23, prepaid; $2 extra for billing.
The second edition of this comprehensive source book discusses 613 currently available simulations and games either designed or useful for

educational purposes, ranging in price from $1.95 to $15,000. Games and simulations are arranged alphabetically by title and producer. Business games represent the largest single category, with 185 games; other categories are mathematics, history, language skills, urban/ community issues, education, and economics—generally the whole range of curriculum, for all ages from preschool through college. Two hundred fifty of the games can be used for preschool through grade eight (50 in math, 36 in language skills, 33 in history, 18 in social studies, and the remainder in college, adult education, vocational education, etc.). Data on each game includes name of developer (with date developed), age level, playing time, preparation time, number of players required, materials required, a summary description, comments, costs, and source—all clearly presented. Other features include an annotated guide to literature and gaming groups by Paul A. Twelker and Kent Layden; some useful articles on introducing and preparing simulation games by Robert Hall; addresses and persons to contact at relevant organizations; and a list of 473 games not chosen, with reasons for their exclusion. Future editions will be issued at approximately 18-month intervals.

J26 **HANDBOOK OF GAMES AND SIMULATION EXERCISES**
Edited by G.I. Gibbs. Beverly Hills, Calif., Sage, 1974. $12.
A brief guide to 2,000 games and simulations, with brief descriptions of contents and audiences, plus a directory of suppliers, including many outside the United States. Games range from preschool to postgraduate levels.

J27 **INDEX TO COMPUTER ASSISTED INSTRUCTION** Edited by Helen A. Lekan. 3rd Edition. New York, Harcourt, Brace, Jovanovich, 1971. $21.50 (paperback).
A comprehensive index to 1,264 computer programs—mostly for senior high school level or higher—in 70 subject areas. Arranged by subject; cross-referenced by processor, computer language, logic, and source. Full descriptions include name, author, source, contents, prerequisites, level (preschool to graduate), type of student, completion time, logic and use of program, supplementary materials, availability, sponsor, program language, processor, and terminal descriptions. Recommended only for educational agencies which have available (or contemplate) computer terminals and telephone lines.

J28 **INDEX TO INSTRUCTIONAL MEDIA CATALOGS** New York, R.R. Bowker, 1974. $19.95.
Subject index to approximately 650 educational media catalogs for kindergarten through grade 12, arranged by subject and media. In-

cludes approximately 40 types of media—filmstrips, audiotapes, periodicals, multimedia kits, workbooks, recordings—in 150 subject areas. Entries provide information on instructional-level methodology and producer or publisher. Contains a directory of firms, as well as a separate index to suppliers of related equipment and services.

J29 **INTERNATIONAL INDEX TO MULTIMEDIA INFORMATION** (Formerly *Film Review Index.*) Edited by Wesley A. Doak and William J. Speed. Pasadena, Calif., Audio-Visual Associates, 1970– . Quarterly. $36/year.

This publication has been transformed into a quarterly review which indexes approximately 100 publications that carry reviews of media materials. Indexing is performed by librarians and teachers. It is divided into four sections: a *review* section, arranged by title, which cites the film or media and the reviewing source and provides brief extracts of reviews, designed to indicate the scope of the work; a *subject index,* which lists materials by title under subject categories; a *publications directory,* which lists the reviewing sources and addresses, frequency of publication, and prices; and a *producers and distributors* directory, with addresses. Citations in the title section are complete if the original review is complete. With recent changes in format and content, the *International Index* is becoming a valuable and reasonably current aid to securing information on media materials.

J30 **INTERNATIONAL JOURNAL OF INSTRUCTIONAL MEDIA** Farmingdale, N.Y., Baywood Publishing Co., 1973– . Quarterly. $25/4 issues. From: 43 Central Dr., Farmingdale, N.Y. 11735.

Provides a long-needed philosophical basis and appraisal of the relationship of educational media to educational goals; covers practical aspects such as collection building and facilities design.

J31 **LANDERS FILM REVIEWS** Los Angeles, Calif., 1956– . Annual. 9 issues/year, plus binder and index. $35/year. From: P.O. Box 69760, Los Angeles, Calif. 90069.

Each issue of this major source of ongoing evaluations reviews approximately 80 to 85 films (approximately 800/year). The reviews, with full bibliographic information, include description, audience level, and, sometimes, evaluative or critical comments. Also contains some multimedia kits, as well as lists of media catalogs. Title and subject indexes in each issue; both are cumulated in the last issue of each volume, which includes a convenient binder and a yearly source directory. Subscription price also includes a "Research Service" for locating hard-to-find films and distributors through the Landers reference collection.

Other compilations by this publisher include a *Foreign Language Audiovisual Guide* (2,000 items in 12 languages, for $1).

J32   **LA RAZA IN FILMS: A List of Films and Filmstrips**   Compiled by Cynthia Baird. Oakland, Calif., Latin American Library, Oakland Public Library, 1973. Free. From: Latin American Library Center, 1449 Miller Ave., Oakland, Calif. 94601.

An annotated directory of 270 films and filmstrips—English-language and Spanish for all levels, children through adults—dealing with Mexico, Latin America, and Spanish-Speaking Americans. Information includes title, physical description, language, price, and distributor. No index, although titles are listed in the table of contents, with a directory of distributors at the end.

J33   **LEARNING WITH GAMES: An Analysis of Social Studies Educational Games and Simulations**   Edited by Cheryl L. Charles and Ronald Stadsklev. Boulder, Colo., Social Science Education Consortium, 1973. $4.95.

Emphasis is on 70 social studies games for kindergarten to grade 12, using ssec's parallel analysis technique. Also includes annotated bibliographies on simulation design and games, directories of games and simulations, descriptions of game developers, listings of newsletters and journals dealing with games, and a guide to 80 producers of social studies educational games and simulations—altogether a good guide for its field.

J34   **MEDIA: An Annotated Catalogue of Law-Related Audio-Visual Materials**   Edited by Susan E. Davison. Chicago, Special Committee on Youth Education for Citizenship, American Bar Assn., 1975. Single copies free; multiple copies $2 each for 2 – 25 copies; quantity discount.

One of a series of directories and catalogs issued by the American Bar Association's Special Committee on Youth Education for Citizenship (yefc). It lists more than 400 films, filmstrips, audio cassettes, video tapes, and media kits in a classified format. Major content areas cover origins and basic concepts of law, the Constitution, the Bill of Rights, current issues, political process, practical law, and references on the teaching of law for teachers and administrators. Within each section, materials are further divided by subtopic and arranged alphabetically by title. Information for each entry is comprised of recommended grade level, type of material (including length), price, source, and useful annotations. Includes an excellent index and a directory of distributors. For additional information about the publications of this agency, see O42.

J35 **MEDIACENTER** New York, Baker & Taylor, 1975– . $8/8 issues
during school year. From: Baker & Taylor Cos., 1515 Broadway,
New York, N.Y. 10036.
Annotated listings of current audiovisual materials, with independent
departments and feature articles. The first issue (May 1975) contains
excellent articles on and recommendations for women, as well as on
sexism in education.

J36 **MEDIA PROGRAMS: District and School** (Formerly *Standards
for School Media Programs*, 1969.) By American Assn. of School
Librarians (AASL) and Assn. for Educational Communications and
Technology (AECT). Chicago, American Library Assn.; Washington,
D.C., AECT, 1975. $3.
Represents a consensus of opinions by professionals in library and
information science, educational technology, and related fields. Includes
many performance guidelines, and a chapter on "collections," which
covers selection policies and procedures. Other areas cover program
patterns and relationships, personnel, program operation, and facilities.

J37 **MICROFORM RETRIEVAL EQUIPMENT GUIDE** By National Archives and Records Service. Washington, D.C., U.S.
Government Printing Office, 1970. $0.65.
This compilation explains microfiche use and equipment. One of a
handy series of publications from the Office of Records Management of
the National Archives and Records Service.

J38 **MOVIES FOR KIDS** By Edith Zorrow and Ruth M. Goldstein.
New York, Avon/Discus, 1973. $1.65.
A guide to films for children between the ages of 9 and 13, with an initial
chapter on "How to Look at a Movie." The major part of the book
consists of an annotated listing of 125 feature films (approximately
200-word annotations), a briefly annotated listing of 75 short films, and
a supplementary listing of appropriate feature films. Includes names of
distributors, organizations, books about films, and recommended film
periodicals.

J39 **MULTI-MEDIA REVIEWS INDEX** Edited by C. Edward Wall.
Ann Arbor, Mich., Pierian Press, 1970– . Annual. $39.50, including
monthly and tri-quarterly supplements; $25.00 for annual only.
This index attempts to keep current with media reviews. It contains four
separate title lists of films, filmstrips, records and tapes (sometimes listed
by composer or performer), and miscellaneous media (slides, kits,
transparencies, prints, radio scripts, maps, posters, and simulation

games). Arranged by titles, the *Index* provides bibliographic descriptions of reviews, plus citations and overall ratings by reviewers.

J40 **MUSEUM MEDIA** A Biennial Directory and Index of Publications and Audiovisuals Available from United States and Canadian Institutions. Edited by Paul Wasserman and Esther Herman. Detroit, Mich., Gale Research, 1973. $48.

Calls attention to a variety of media materials issued by museums, historical societies, and similar institutions in the United States and Canada. Arranged alphabetically by state, it lists the institutions and their productions (mostly print), including books, pamphlets, catalogs, films, filmstrips, maps, and realia, among others. These productions are interesting, inexpensive, and often related to education, but the guide (based on a questionnaire) unfortunately lists the productions of only 732 museums (out of more than 2,000 queried). Contains indexes by title, keyword, subject field, and geographic area.

J41 **NATIONAL CENTER FOR AUDIO TAPES CATALOG, 1970- 72** By National Center for Audio Tapes. Boulder, Colo., 1972– . Triennial. $4.50; foreign, $5.40. From: Stadium Bldg., University of Colorado, Boulder, Colo. 80302.

A compact catalog of approximately 12,000 audio tapes, selected on the basis of "curricular relevance and production quality"; arranged by broad subject areas (arts, education, language and literature, mathematics – science, physical – recreational activities, social studies, vocational – technical), and then by series, including many well-known radio series such as the Calvacade of America. Entries provide subject codes (Library of Congress), grade levels (primary through adult), series title and description, name, code, date, running time, and series stock number. These tapes can be purchased from the National Center starting at $2.40 a reel.

J42 **NATIONAL INFORMATION CENTER FOR EDUCATIONAL MEDIA (NICEM)** University of Southern California, University Park, Los Angeles, Calif. 90007. (213) 746-6681

This information center, operating from a computer data bank of 400,000 media listings, produces an expensive, comprehensive, and continually expanding series of publications which serve as checklists for titles in a wide variety of media and in some currently important subject fields, adding approximately 50,000 items per year. Despite their ambitious scope, this series of paperback directories is difficult to use, bibliographically inadequate, and short on needed information. Individual volumes attempt—with varying degrees of success—to list materials by title and subjects, but generally omit price and date, and provide source only by a complex code. Similarly, NICEM's catalogs omit publication dates. The indexes to films and filmstrips, however, now in their fifth editions, are widely used and consulted. Other NICEM indexes are topically valuable. Microfiche editions are available for most of their publications. A bimonthly *Update of Nonbook Media* ($106/year), available in book form and microfiche, updates all directories listed below and forms part of several discount packages offered by NICEM.

Index to Black History and Studies (Multimedia). 2nd Edition; 1975; $19.50. Lists and briefly describes more than 10,000 titles.

Index to Ecology (Multimedia). 2nd Edition; 1973; $19.50. Lists 11,000 titles. See series description above.

Index to Educational Audio Tapes. 3rd Edition; 1974; $42.50; microfiche, $28.50. Lists and describes 24,000 audio tapes under 2,000 headings. Includes the release date and grade level, but not the publication date or price.

Index to Educational Overhead Transparencies. 4th Edition; 2 Vols.; 1974; $68.50; microfiche, $49.50. Lists and describes approximately 50,000 educational transparencies.

Index to Educational Records. 3rd Edition; 1974; $42.50; microfiche, $28.50. Lists approximately 22,000 record titles using curriculum-oriented subject headings. Omits age, availability, prices, and, most often, year of release and grade level. Not well cross-referenced. See series description above.

Index to Educational Slides. 2nd Edition; 1975; $38.50; microfiche, $26.50. Covers 18,000 slide sets and slides, with annotations, number of slides per set, year of release, audience level, size, color, producer, and distributor codes.

Index to Educational Video Tapes. 3rd Edition; 1974; $26.50; microfiche, $18.50. Lists and describes 12,000 video tapes. See series description above.

Index to 8-mm Motion Cartridges. 4th Edition; 1974; $42.50; microfiche, $28.50. Lists and describes approximately 22,000 motion cartridges. See series description above.

Index to Health and Safety Education (Multimedia). 2nd Edition; 1975; $26.50. Indexes 18,000 entries in seven media (filmstrips, film cartridges, films, video tapes, discs, audio tapes, and transparencies). Major categories covered are health, home economics (which includes heating, nursing, and consumer education), safety, physical education, and natural sciences. Some of the entries are astonishingly far afield from the subjects listed.

Index to Producers and Distributors. 3rd Edition; 1974; $19.50; microfiche,

$12.50. An alphabetical listing of 10,000 producers and distributors, including names, addresses, codes, and media.

Index to Psychology (Multimedia). 2nd Edition; 1975; $26.50; microfiche, $18.50. Lists and describes approximately 18,000 titles in psychology and related areas such as special education, counseling and guidance, sexual behavior, smoking, drugs and alcohol, attitudes, and opinions. It includes the usual media mix, for audience levels ranging from preschool to adult. Descriptions include title, size and physical description, length, color code, producer and distributor, year of release, and LC catalog card number. Levels are included in the subject section, but not in the title section. See series description above.

Index to 16-mm Educational Films. 5th Edition; 1975; 3 Vols; $99.50; microfiche, $79.50. Contains 90,000 briefly annotated entries. See series description above.

Index to 35-mm Filmstrips. 5th Edition; 1975; 2 Vols.; $78.50; microfiche, $59.50. Lists and describes 52,000 filmstrips. See series description above.

Index to Vocational and Technical Education (Multimedia). 2nd Edition; 1975; $26.50; microfiche, $18.50. This edition covers 18,000 titles in seven media areas, mostly for the high school level and up (although codes are provided for kindergarten up to professional). Most titles are in the standard industrial-mechanical-construction areas of the old vocational schools. Prices still are not included. See series description above.

J43 **101 FILMS FOR CHARACTER GROWTH** By Jane Cushing. Notre Dame, Ind., Fides Publishers, 1969. $1.50.

Provides an interesting analysis and discussion of 101 films concerned with character, originally prepared for a film guidance course aimed at junior high school levels and up. Its table of contents organizes these films as they illuminate desirable attitudes and goals, which include individual fulfillment, healthy self-image, self-motivation, integrity versus expediency, conflicting loyalties, and war versus peace. Individual films are analyzed by rating, topic, synopsis, age level, remarks, and questions for discussion. Sources, prices, running time, and bibliographic information are given at the end in an alphatetical index.

J44 **PICTURE SOURCES** A Joint Publication of the Special Libraries Association and the American Society of Picture Professionals. Edited by Ann Novotny and Rosemary Eakins. 3rd Edition. New York, Special Libraries Assn., 1975. $17.

An index to pictures available to researchers; could be helpful to teachers, curriculum specialists, and audiovisual users. Includes all kinds of pictures—original photographs, black-and-white prints, color transparencies, original drawings, greeting cards, art reproductions, architectural drawings, cartoons, advertisements, illustrated books, negatives, and positives—in all sizes and shapes—all of which can be used for publication, television and films, or for research purposes. Sources indexed include museums, libraries, government agencies, historical societies, etc. Thoroughly indexed by subject and location.

J45 **PREVIEWS: Non-Print Software & Hardware News & Reviews** New York, R.R. Bowker, 1972– . Annual; 9 issues/year. $5.00/year for subscribers to *School Library Journal* and *Library Journal;* $7.50/year for others.

This journal combines both the descriptive guide to forthcoming cross-media materials that appeared in *School Library Journal's* semiannual "Audiovisual Guide" and the evaluative media reviews that appeared in *School Library Journal* and *Library Journal.* The "Audiovisual Guide" to forthcoming materials appears in the September and March issues of *Previews,* with descriptive listings—based on producer-compiled materials—arranged under subject categories. Lists approximately 3,000 items per year. The review sections of both *SLJ* and *LJ* have been incorporated and expanded into a media- and subject-arranged compilation of evaluative reviews of all media fields—approximately 150 items an issue; four times as many as the two journals previously covered. Feature articles explore trends and controversies and provide special subject compilations. The bibliographical information is complete and accurate; reviews are intelligent, although they vary in emphasis. The only possible defects of this review journal are that it does not lend itself too readily to browsing and that it lacks reference indexes in the individual issues.

J46 **PROGRAMMED LEARNING AND INDIVIDUALLY PACED INSTRUCTION: Bibliography** By Carl H. Hendershot. 5th Edition. Bay City, Mich., Hendershot Programmed Learning, 1973-1976. Basic volume, $30; with 8-month supplements to 1976, $58. From: 4114 Ridgewood Dr., Bay City, Mich. 48706.

This comprehensive loose-leaf source book lists approximately 3,500 learner-paced texts and other individualized programmed learning units in many formats, with detailed information on study time, length, grade level, prerequisites, price, and appropriate descriptive information. It is arranged by 222 subject areas ranging through the entire academic curriculum to adult education and interest areas such as boating and bridge. Sections on instructional systems and pictures of devices are new features in this edition. *Supplements,* issued every eight months, keep information current.

J47 **RECORD AND TAPE REVIEWS INDEX** Compiled by Antoinette O. Maleady. Metuchen, N.J., Scarecrow Press, 1972– . 1971, $8.50; 1972, $13.50; 1973, $20.00; 1974, $20.00.

An index to reviews of recordings of classical music and readings of poetry, drama, etc., by the music librarian of Sonoma State College, covering discs, tapes, and cassette recordings from major U.S. and British reviewing media. Entries, arranged by composer, provide complete information on review source and identification. Contains separate sections for music in collections and for spoken recordings; could be quite valuable in prepurchase evaluation of records, tapes, or cassettes.

J48 **RECORDED VISUAL INSTRUCTION, 1976 Edition** By Great Plains National Instructional Television Library. Lincoln, Neb., 1973. Single copy free. From: P.O. Box 80669, Lincoln, Neb. 68501.

Catalogs a library of 150 recorded televised courses for all grade levels via videotape, video cassette, and 16-mm film. Arranged by subject and grade levels, and fully described down to lesson outlines. Courses from this catalog can be leased from the Great Plains National Instructional Television Library or can be duplicated by them to meet user specifications.

J49 **RECORDINGS FOR CHILDREN: A Selected List of Records and Cassettes** By New York Library Assn., Children and Young Adult Services Section. 3rd Edition. New York, 1972. $3. From: Carol Cox Book Co., 20 Booker St., P.O. Box 717, Westwood, N.J. 07675.

One of a series of annotated listings of materials selected by librarians for excellence and appeal. Other titles are *Films for Children, Films for Young Adults,* and *Records and Cassettes for Young Adults.*

J50 **A REFERENCE GUIDE TO AUDIOVISUAL INFORMATION** By James L. Limbacher. New York, R.R. Bowker, 1972. $14.95.

A guide to sources of information on nonprint media: films, filmstrips, theatre, dance and music, radio, television, and recordings. Includes an annotated listing of 400 audiovisual reference books (with 50 asterisked as basic reference sources); an annotated listing of 110 periodicals, ranging from fan magazines to scholarly journals; and a glossary of 300 terms. Intended for reference librarians and/or instant experts on media, and includes information on setting up card files for hard-to-answer reference questions. A good section on background reading in media fields is arranged in classified order. A few useful titles are omitted, but this guide can be helpful for media people who are not familiar with reference tools, as well as for librarians who need more background on media.

J51　**RESOURCES FOR LEARNING: A Core Media Collection for Elementary Schools**　Edited by Roderick McDaniel. New York, R. R. Bowker, 1971. $16.50.

An alphabetically arranged and graded subject index of audiovisual materials for elementary schools (kindergarten to grade six). Total list includes 4,000 recommended titles in all types of media, selected from approved lists, reviews, and school collections. For each title, information includes author, release date, media, producer, grade level, price, annotation, and who it was recommended by. There are 575 asterisked titles (first choice), available for $5,000 (without films); with films the price would be $24,000. Some free items also are included.

J52　**SEX EDUCATION ON FILM: A Guide to Visual Aids and Programs**　By Laura J. Singer and Judith Buskin. New York, Teachers College Press, 1971. $3.95 (paperback).

A well-arranged, evaluative guide to 110 films, filmstrips, slides, and transparencies on many aspects of sexual development. Categories cover family relationships, childbirth, masculinity and femininity, premarital behavior, marriage, and problem areas (venereal disease, family planning, premarital pregnancy). Entries provide adequate ordering and bibliographic information, as well as information on availability of teachers' guides. The annotations realistically indicate such things as moralistic approaches and limitations. Includes a model program in sex education, using some of these materials. Also includes lists of pamphlet sources and a directory of distributors.

J53　**SLIDE BUYERS GUIDE**　By Nancy DeLaurier. Kansas City, Mo., College Art Assn., 1974. $3.00; addenda sheet, $0.20. From: Nancy DeLaurier, University of Missouri, Kansas City, Mo. 64110.

This compendium of information on art slide sources is intended primarily for art museums and college art departments, but can be used to good advantage by high schools and elementary schools.

J54　**TEACHERS GUIDE TO TELEVISION**　By National Assn. of Broadcasters. New York, n.d. Semiannual (October and February). $3.50/year; discount for four or more subscriptions to the same address.

An excellent source of information on commercial programs of educational value, with advance notices of programs for the coming semester. The package includes a schedule of programs "of educational value" on major networks and on Public Broadcasting Service, a Classroom TV Calendar suitable for bulletin board placement, and *Teachers Guides* for "outstanding" programs on ABC, CBS, and NBC. These guides provide lesson plans—aims, synopses, suggestions for activities, discussions before and after the selected programs, and bibliographies of supportive materials; a reading list of children's and young adult books compiled by the American Library Association; and a film list compiled by the Association for Educational Communications and Technology.

J55 **TEACHER TRAINING FILMS: A Guide, Pre-Service and In-Service** Compiled by Carole M. Kirkton. Urbana, Ill., National Council of Teachers of English, 1971. $0.75.
One of the few available selected listings of teacher training audiovisual materials. Although it concentrates on areas related to language, literature, reading, dramatics, and oral and written expression, some of the films selected deal with broader educational topics, such as teacher-student relationships, educational innovations, and student behavior.

J56 **TELEVISION INSTRUCTION CATALOG: GUIDE BOOK** By National Instructional Television Center. Bloomington, Ind., 1974. Annual. Free. From: Box A, Bloomington, Ind. 47401.
This annual catalog describes television and film courses for both open and closed television stations and for instructional television. Also provides order, rental, and preview information. Courses are for all levels, from preschool through adult, and include teacher training materials.
In the fall of 1973, the National Instructional Television Center became a division of the newly incorporated Agency for Instructional Television, a nonprofit American-Canadian agency, which also will operate a Council for Instructional Television through which prospective users can participate in the selection and direction of instructional television materials. Regional offices are located in Arlington, Virginia, Atlanta, Georgia, Wauwatosa, Wisconsin, and San Mateo, California.

J57 **TOY REVIEW MAGAZINE** By American Teaching Toys, Inc. Newton, Mass., 1972– . Quarterly. $2/year. From: 383 Elliot St., Newton, Mass. 02164.
Reviews toys in such classifications as infant, preschool, make believe, outdoors, dolls and friendly creatures, stocking stuffers, fun and learning, crafts and kits, science and nature, games and puzzles, put togethers, and unclassifiables. Indexed by type, but not by title. Includes

articles on toys, some critical reviews, and some reviews by children of children's books. A useful guide rather than a consumer report.

J58 **UNESCO ART EDUCATION SLIDES** Paris, UNESCO, 1960– .
Sets #1–9 (30 slides/set), $18.50 each; sets #10–12 (100 slides), $45 each. From: Unipub, P.O. Box 433, New York, N.Y. 10016.

These attractive boxed slide sets, accompanied by texts, are intended to illustrate contemporary concepts and methods of art education throughout the world. All sets, except sets #10–12, consist of 30 slides each.

1. Play, Explore, Perceive, Create.
2. Three-dimensional Art for the Adolescent.
3. Visual and Plastic Stimuli in Art Education.
4. The Art of the Child in Japan.
5. Industrial Design.
6. Modern Architecture.
7. Graphic Design.
8. African Children's Art.
9. Latin American Children's Art.
10. Arts and Man (100 slides, in color and black-and-white).
11. Arts as Environment (100 slides).
12. Continuity of Forms: Crafts, Industrial Design and Architecture (100 slides).

J59 **UNESCO ART SLIDES** Paris, UNESCO, 1960– . 28 sets (30 slides/set), $18.50 each. From: Unipub, P.O. Box 433, New York, N.Y. 10016.

A series of 28 sets of high-quality color transparencies, intended to make known some relatively unknown public masterpieces of world art.

1. Egypt: Paintings from Tombs and Temples.
2. Yugoslavia: Mediaeval Frescoes.
3. India: Paintings from the Ajanta Caves.
4. Iran: Persian Miniatures, Imperial Library.
5. Spain: Romanesque Paintings.
6. Norway: Paintings from the Stave Churches.
7. Masaccio: Frescoes in Florence.
8. Australia: Aboriginal Paintings from Arnhem Land.
9. Ceylon: Paintings from Temple, Shrine and Rock.
10. Nubia: Masterpieces in Danger.
11. U.S.S.R.: Early Russian Icons.
12. Mexico: Pre-Hispanic Paintings.

13. Japan: Ancient Buddhist Paintings.
14. Czechoslovakia: Romanesque and Gothic Illuminated Manuscripts.
15. Greece: Byzantine Mosaics.
16. Israel: Ancient Mosaics.
17. Ethiopia: Illuminated Manuscripts.
18. Turkey: Ancient Miniatures.
19. Bulgaria: Mediaeval Murals.
20. Tunisia: Ancient Mosaics.
21. Romania: Painted Churches of Moldavia.
22. Cyprus: Byzantine Mosaics and Frescoes.
23. Poland: Fifteenth Century Painting.
24. Austria: Mediaeval Murals.
25. Monte Alban, Mitla: Two Cities of Ancient Mexico.
26. Copan: A Maya Site in Honduras.
27. Tepotzotlan: Baroque Architecture in Mexico.
28. Brazil: Colonial Religious Art.

12 | *Children's Books*

There are many fine tools for selecting children's books which are relatively unused by teachers when selecting books for classes or planning individual reading programs. Included in this chapter are a few of the selection tools that are most applicable for school use. They were originally designed mostly for and by librarians and rate from good to excellent in the criteria of selection, annotations, and bibliographic information.

Booklist (H1) is a good source for keeping current with the latest books, as are the *Center for Children's Books Bulletin* (K9), *Instructor* (J64), *Scholastic Magazine,* published by Citation Press (C4), and *School Media Quarterly,* published by the American Association of School Librarians (O1). Current bibliographies of children's books can be found in *Education Index* (F8) and *Library Literature* (F31), as well as through ERIC—although not as easily. The Children's Book Council and the Information Center on Children's Cultures, among others discussed in Chapter 16, also should be consulted. Some book lists on particular topics and books for remedial reading are included among the Curriculum Materials and Activities in Chapter 10.

Both school and public libraries, naturally, are good sources for current reading lists, subject-oriented lists, and collections of materials. For those who want to go beyond the sources listed here, *Books and Non-book Media* (H2) and *Children's Literature* (K11) are good guides to guides. Bonnie M. Davis' *A Guide to Information Sources for Reading* (D4) deals with professional sources of reading information. Materials on reading in Chapter 10 also are relevant.

Two books that might prove helpful to teachers who wish to extend their uses of books are *Children's Literature in the Curriculum* by Dewey W. Chambers (Chicago, Rand McNally, 1971), which contains many ideas for using literature in reading, social studies, science, creativity, etc., and *Down the Rabbit Hole* by Selma Lanes (New York, Atheneum, 1971), an affectionate but nonsentimental discussion of children's literature by a Black writer and book reviewer. It includes a delightful personal list of recommended titles for children between the ages of two to seven—mostly recent titles reviewed by Ms. Lanes.

Two books on selection materials for children are particularly valuable for teachers and librarians: *Issues in Book Selection* (New York, Bowker, 1973), a collection of essays—mostly from *Library Journal* and *School Library Journal*—provides helpful guidance on such topics as sexuality, stereotypes, books on the occult, etc.; and *Matters of Fact*, by Margery Fisher (New York, Crowell, 1972), an exposition and demonstration of appropriate criteria for selecting factual "information books."

K1   **AMERICAN DIVERSITY: A Bibliography of Resources on Racial and Ethnic Minorities for Pennsylvania Schools** By Pennsylvania Department of Education. Harrisburg, Pa., 1969. Free. From: Box 911, Harrisburg, Pa. 17126.

A comprehensive annotated bibliography of preschool through teacher references, with approximate grade levels indicated. Includes fiction, nonfiction, and some audiovisual materials covering Afro-Americans, American Indians, Jewish Americans, Mexican Americans, Oriental Americans, Pennsylvania Germans, Puerto Ricans, other Americans, and multiethnic materials.

K2   **AMERICAN INDIANS: An Annotated Bibliography of Selected Library Sources** By Minnesota University Library Services Institute for Minnesota Indians. St. Paul, Minnesota State Department of Education, Indian Education, 1970. Free, while supply lasts. From: Publisher, St. Paul, Minn. 25101. OR Microfiche, $0.75; hard copy, $6.58. (ED 040 004) From: ERIC Document Reproduction Service, P.O. Box 190, Arlington, Va. 22210.

This extensive annotated bibliography of books, pamphlets, newspapers, magazines, and audiovisual materials was compiled by teachers and librarians under the direction of Indian educators. It was rated "superior" by the American Library Association's Subcommittee on Materials for American Indians. Contains approximately 300 annotated titles for elementary and junior high school levels, and *many* senior high school titles and materials, including arts and crafts.

K3   **APPRAISAL: Children's Science Books**   By Children's Science Book Review Committee. Cambridge, Mass., 1968– . $4/year; 3 issues/year. From: Appraisal, Children's Science Book Review Committee, 13 Appian Way, Cambridge, Mass. 02138.

This unusual evaluation source is published by the Children's Science Book Review Committee, a nonprofit organization sponsored by the Harvard Graduate School of Education and the New England Round Table of Children's Librarians, dedicated to the belief that science books deserve the same careful evaluation as do literary works. It implements its belief by combining in one attractive format, evaluative annotations and ratings by science specialists and children's librarians (see Figure 8). Interesting reading; an inexpensive tool for locating high-quality relevant books for all grade levels.

K4   **THE BEST IN CHILDREN'S BOOKS, 1966-1972**   Edited by Zena Sutherland. Chicago, University of Chicago Press, 1973. $9.95.

Well-written reviews of 1,400 children's books published between 1966 and 1972. These were discriminatingly selected by the advisory committee of the Center for Children's Books (see K9) primarily on the basis of literary quality, with subject representation a secondary consideration. Reviews are arranged alphabetically by author and then title, with many indexes to make the book especially useful for teachers and librarians: one on developmental values (adaptability, cultural awareness, etc.); another for curricular use (Africa, anthropology, etc.); a detailed subject index; a reading-level index, from two years old to grade 12; a title index; and an index by type of literature (poetry, drama, etc.).

K5   **BIBLIOGRAPHY OF BOOKS FOR CHILDREN**   Edited by Sylvia Sunderlin. Revised Edition. Washington, D.C., Assn. for Childhood Education Intl., 1971. $2.25 (paperback).

Provides annotations of more than 1,000 well-chosen, generally inexpensive books for preschool and elementary school children, selected by a committee of librarians and teachers. It is arranged by classification, based both on library categories (fantasy, poetry, religion) and curriculum. There is a useful section (printed on colored paper) of representative reference books. The *Bibliography* contains an author and title index, plus a directory of publishers. Other compilations of ACEI include a list of children's books priced at $1.50 or less, and a guide to children's magazines. For more information on the publisher, see C1.

Webster, David. *How To Do a Science Project;* illus. with photographs and diagrams. Franklin Watts, 1974. 61 p. $3.95. "A First Book."

Age 9 up.

EX LIBRARIAN: What a fine book! Mr. Webster, after years of teaching and working with children, knows exactly what they want to find out, how disorganized most of them are, and how hard it is for them to follow through on a project. Bits of other children's reports, notes, drawings and charts are used in this book which puts the whole concept in the proper perspective for the young person looking for ideas and methods. Mr. Webster gives wise advice about sloppy writing, attention in detail, giving credit where it is due, not becoming discouraged, neatness and confidence in presentation—all done in a positive and encouraging way. There is an extensive list of "Books with Project Ideas," a good index, and credit given to the pupils whose work he has used for illustration. One cannot adequately say how helpful this book is!   H.K.

F   SPECIALIST: There is too much credence attributed here to the analogy of science projects with science research. The book tries to make this point instead of presenting projects as an enjoyable activity for some students, and an alternate way to learn for others, but not necessarily profitable for all students. Science fairs are no longer in vogue in some parts of the country and this should not be used to justify the use of science projects. The rest of the book presents useful examples and valuable suggestions for project ideas. Topics included planning, sources of error, oral and written reports, and visual display techniques. There is too little on safety, humaneness with animals, sources of information, measurement techniques, and true research methodology which utilizes test and control design and repeatability. There is an admirable list of 47 books with project ideas suitable for young investigators.   J.R.P.

FIGURE 8   Librarians and subject specialists present separate ratings and evaluations in *Appraisal,* a publication of the Children's Science Book Review Committee.

K6   **BIBLIOTHERAPY** Methods and Materials. Edited by Eleanor
      Phinney for Assn. of Hospital and Institution Libraries, Commit-
      tee on Bibliotherapy and Subcommittee on the Troubled Child.
      Chicago, American Library Assn., 1971. $6.50 (paperback).

A joint product of two committees, this book is a simple but competent
introduction to bibliotherapy, which indicates some uses of books for
aiding troubled children. The last 100 pages consist of descriptions and
annotations of approximately 250 books useful in this field. Areas
covered include physical handicaps, sibling and peer relationships,
parents with troubles, parent-child conflicts, nature books (for release of
tension), sex education, self-discovery, self-realization, gangs, and youth.
The titles are well-chosen and annotated; special attention is given to
theme, audience, reading level, and interest level. Most of the books are
for students above the fourth grade.

K7   **THE BLACK EXPERIENCE IN CHILDREN'S BOOKS** By
      Augusta Baker. Revised Edition. New York, New York Public
      Library, 1971. $0.50. From: Office of Children's Services, NYPL, 8
      E. 40th St., New York, N.Y. 10016.

Annotates approximately 250 titles, selected by children's librarians, to
provide all children between ages 4 and 11 with an "unbiased, well-
rounded picture of Black life in some parts of the world." Books were
chosen on the basis of language, theme, illustrations, and freedom from
stereotyping. Subject organization is by geographic area; the United
States is divided by age groups, subject, and type of literature (folklore,
music, biography, civil rights, etc.).

K8   **BOOKS FOR SECONDARY SCHOOL LIBRARIES** By Na-
      tional Association of Independent Schools Library Committee.
      4th Edition. New York, R.R. Bowker, 1971. $8.95.

An excellent list for a small library or learning center, arranged by
Dewey Decimal Classification, with brief annotations. Fully indexed by
author, subject, and title, including a good selection of foreign titles.
First through third editions were published under the title: *4,000 Books
for Secondary School Libraries.*

K9   **CENTER FOR CHILDREN'S BOOKS BULLETIN** Edited by
      Zena Sutherland. Chicago, University of Chicago Press, 1945– .
      Monthly, except August. $8/yr. From: 5801 Ellis Ave., Chicago,
      Ill. 60637.

Provides reviews and annotations of current children's books selected by
an advisory committee of the University of Chicago Graduate Library
School. Reviews are evaluative and include grade levels as well as specific
recommendations for purchase and use.

K10 **CHILDREN'S BOOKS IN PRINT, 1974** 6th Edition. New
York, R.R. Bowker, 1975. $20; quantity discounts.
A comprehensive bibliography, revised annually in December or
January, that lists all children's books in print, including paperbacks.
Approximately 40,000 titles, with author, title, and illustrator indexes.
Grade levels are preschool to grade 12, using levels assigned by the
publisher. Entries are bibliographically complete, with author, title,
price, publisher, grade level, binding, illustrator, and catalog card
number. Includes a directory of approximately 500 publishers. A basic
tool for book purchasers.

K11 **CHILDREN'S LITERATURE: A Guide to Reference Sources,
First Supplement** Compiled by Virginia Haviland and Margaret
N. Coughlan. Washington, D.C., U.S. Library of Congress, 1972.
$3. From: Superintendent of Documents, U.S. Government Print-
ing Office, Washington, D.C. 20542.
Published approximately every five years, this guide contains an annotated bibliography of information sources on children's literature. Included in this edition are books, pamphlets, and articles published
mostly between 1966 and 1969, although a few earlier items are included.
All sources can be found in the Library of Congress. Areas covered in
depth include history and criticism, authorship, illustrations, books and
children, minority treatment, libraries, national and international
studies, and bibliography. A valuable reference source, especially for
librarians and reading teachers. The original edition, *Children's Literature: A Guide to Reference Sources* (1966), is still available for $2.50 from
the U.S. Government Printing Office.

K12 **THE CHILD'S FIRST BOOKS** A Critical Study of Pictures and
Texts. By Donnarae MacCann and Olga Richard. New York,
Wilson, 1973. $10.
Presents criteria for judging children's books (ages two to seven) which
should be extremely helpful for early childhood educators. Contains 39
examples of art from recently published children's books. Ten chapters
discuss necessary literary and graphic elements when selecting books for
young children.

K13 **ELEMENTARY SCHOOL LIBRARY COLLECTION** By Mary
V. Gaver. 9th Edition. Newark, N.J., Bro-Dart Foundation, 1974.
$25. 1975 Supplement.
Frequently reissued and updated, this is a good evaluation tool—
primarily for books, but also for media materials. Contains more than
10,000 titles (9,000 books, 100 periodicals, 1,700 media products),
classified under the Dewey Decimal Classification and well-indexed.

Also provides recommendations for first, second, and third purchase. A good buying tool for elementary school libraries; equally useful for elementary school teachers selecting materials to meet the individual interests of students. Appendixes include "Media for Pre-School Children" and suggested books for independent reading.

K14   **EL-HI TEXTBOOKS IN PRINT, 1974**   5th Edition. New York, R.R. Bowker, 1970– . Annual. $19.95; quantity discounts.

Revised annually in the spring, this useful index to more than 18,500 elementary, junior high, and high school textbooks and supplementary readers is arranged under 20 curriculum subjects. Entries include author, title, grade level, publication date, price, publisher, and related teaching materials. Contains indexes to authors and titles, as well as a new index to textbook series arranged by curriculum areas, plus the usual list of publishers and addresses. Excellent tool for textbook ordering.

K15   **A GUIDE TO POPULAR GOVERNMENT PUBLICATIONS For Libraries and Home Reference**   By Linda C. Pohle. Littleton, Colo., Libraries Unlimited, 1972. $9.50.

Describes approximately 2,000 government publications covering more than 100 topics—most of them relevant to the needs of students and teachers. Emphasis is heaviest on current topics such as ecology, consumer education, and civil rights, but books and pamphlets are included on almost any topic of general interest. Indexed by subject.

K16   **IN BLACK AND WHITE: Afro-Americans in Print**   A Guide to Afro-Americans Who Have Made Contributions to the United States of America from 1619 to 1969. Edited by Mary Mace Spradling. Kalamazoo, Mich., Kalamazoo Library System, 1971. $3 (paperback).

A handy and unusual index to biographical data on Black Americans, living and dead. Arranged alphabetically by last name, entries contain year of birth and death, as well as citations to sources of information. Also includes an occupational index and a bibliography of source materials. Comprehensive, compact, and usable—although it could use more cross-references to and from nicknames and adopted names.

K17   **INDIAN BIBLIOGRAPHY: Professional Library Collection**   By National Indian Training Center. 2nd Edition. Brigham City, Utah, 1972. Free. From: Professional Library, National Indian Training Center, P.O. Box 66, Brigham City, Utah 84302.

A printed catalog of a substantial collection of books on the American

Indian, arranged by Dewey Decimal Classification. Listed items are available for five-week interlibrary loan.

K18 **I READ, YOU READ, WE READ; I SEE, YOU SEE, WE SEE; I HEAR, YOU HEAR, WE HEAR; I LEARN, YOU LEARN, WE LEARN** By American Library Assn., Library Service to the Disadvantaged Child Committee. Chicago, American Library Assn., 1971. $2.

Despite the somewhat confusing title, this list (an outgrowth of a previous booklist prepared for the Office of Economic Opportunity) is excellent for any child, but especially for the disadvantaged child. Books, chosen for appeal to children who think they hate books, are categorized into four broad age levels: preschool, 5 to 8, 9 to 11, and 12 to 14. Within these groups, the books are divided into poems, stories, films, and recordings—mostly titles up to 1970. Titles are generally in print or available in libraries. Appendixes include program aids for adults, as well as directories of film and record distributors.

K19 **LATIN AMERICA** An Annotated List of Materials for Children. By Information Center on Children's Cultures. New York, 1969. Free. From: 331 E. 38th St., New York, N.Y. 10016.

Compiled by nationals, residents, librarians, and teachers, this comprehensive list (as of the date of publication) of English-language materials for children includes excellent annotations of approximately 500 titles selected for good clear writing, attractive illustrations, accurate and current contents, and an uncondescending tone. Sections on Puerto Rico and Mexico include books on the cultures of these areas available in the United States. One of many excellent and usually free bibliographies compiled by this center, which is discussed in O22.

K20 **LITERATURE BY AND ABOUT THE AMERICAN INDIAN: An Annotated Bibliography for Junior and Senior High School Students** By Anna Lee Stensland. Urbana, Ill., National Council of Teachers of English, 1973. $3.65.

This descriptive bibliography of 350 books by and about American Indians starts with an 18-page essay which covers stereotypes and selection criteria. The main section, arranged by subject, is excellent for Indian myth and legend.

K21 **LITTLE MISS MUFFET FIGHTS BACK: Recommended Non-Sexist Books About Girls for Young Readers** By Feminists on Children's Media. Revised Edition. New York, 1974. $1. From: Feminist Book Mart, 162-11 Ninth Ave., Whitestone, N.Y. 11357.

An attractive little list of "non-sexist" children's books, most of which have appealing, yet capable, heroines—approximately 300 titles, both fact and fiction. Briefly annotated and classified by reader and literary type, with supplementary articles on children's book publishing and sexism.

K22 **A MULTIMEDIA APPROACH TO CHILDREN'S LITERATURE** A Selective List of Films, Filmstrips, and Recordings Based on Children's Books. By Ellin Greene and Madalynne Schoenfeld. Chicago, American Library Assn., 1972. $3.75 (paperback).

Provides a list of selected media useful for introducing books to children—from preschool to grade eight. It lists 425 books alphabetically by title, with related films, filmstrips, and recordings separately described under the book title: a total of 174 16-mm films, 175 filmstrips, and 300 disc and tape cassette recordings. A useful tool which provides short annotations of the items, including price, bibliographic information, and grade level. Covers picture books, traditional and folk literature, fairy tales, fiction, drama, and poetry, as well as a few background books on children's authors and illustrators. The introduction contains a briefly annotated list of recordings, selection aids, program aids, and realia for storytelling and children's book programs. Separate indexes by authors, film titles, filmstrip titles, media on authors and illustrators, record titles, and subjects are provided at the end.

K23 **PAPERBACK BOOKS FOR CHILDREN** Compiled by American Assn. of School Librarians. New York, Citation Press, 1972. $0.95 (paperback).

Conveniently arranged by subjects, this inexpensive guide lists and annotates more than 700 well-recommended books for elementary school children—all of them now available in quality paperback editions; particularly valuable for financially constrained groups seeking quality books at the elementary school level. All titles chosen for inclusion were originally recommended by widely used selection aids; paperback editions were individually reviewed and evaluated on the basis of clear readable print, original illustrations or suitable alternates, and whether there had been any significant changes from the original works. A few additional titles, included because of worth and timeliness, were individually reviewed by experienced school librarians. Each entry includes author, publisher, price, suggested grade levels, and, where appropriate, the illustrator. Contains author and title indexes, plus a directory of publishers.

K24 **PICTURE BOOKS FOR CHILDREN** Edited by Patricia Jean Cianciolo. Chicago, American Library Assn., 1973. $5.95.

The books listed in this annotated bibliography were selected by the Picture Book Committee of the National Council of Teachers of English to develop an understanding and appreciation of beauty and creativity in the graphic arts, as well as to provide literary experiences for children from preschool to junior high school levels. Titles listed (hardbound and mostly recent) are grouped into broad categories: Me and My Family, Other People, The World I Live In, and The Imaginative World. Annotations include grade level as well as bibliographic data and price. Author, title, and illustrator indexes.

K25 **THE READER'S ADVISER AND BOOKMAN'S MANUAL** Edited by Sarah L. Prakken. 12th Edition. New York, R.R. Bowker, 1974-1976. 3 Vols. Vol. 1, $23.50; Vols. 2 and 3 not yet priced.

Although primarily designed to assist librarians and others in planning systematic individual programs for adults, this manual could be invaluable for individualizing instruction or curriculum planning at the high school level. Volume 1 covers American and British literature—including poetry but excluding drama. Volume 2 covers drama and foreign literature from Greece, Rome, Europe, Asia, and Africa, with brief, thorough, fascinating accounts and evaluations of authors and titles. Volume 3 (highly recommended by the *Whole Earth Catalog*) is a "layman's guide to the best in print in general biography, history, bibles, world religions, philosophy, psychology, sciences, folklore, the lively arts, communications and travel." An authoritative sourcebook and reference tool.

K26 **READING LADDERS FOR HUMAN RELATIONS** Edited by Virginia M. Reid. 5th Edition. Washington, D.C., American Council on Education, 1972. $9.00; paperback, $3.95. From: National Council of Teachers of English, 1111 Kenyon Rd., Urbana, Ill. 61801.

Hilda Taba and Margaret Heater edited previous editions of this annotated reading list for elementary and secondary school students, designed "to extend sensitivity towards people, their values, and way of living." This edition, published in cooperation with the National Council of Teachers of English, selects books that emphasize cultures and how to cope with change. The books are indexed by theme and age; the annotations indicate possible uses by teachers and librarians.

K27 **SENIOR HIGH SCHOOL LIBRARY CATALOG** 10th Edition.
New York, H.W. Wilson, 1972. With five annual supplements—
1973 to 1977. U.S. and Canada, $30; foreign, $35.
Similar in intent to the *Elementary School Library Collection* (K13), this is a
selective and evaluative tool for the high school library, with emphasis on
grades 10 through 12. While it is still a bit timid in selecting fiction titles
and books that accurately describe current high school mores, the titles
related to academic programs and to curriculum enrichment are extremely well-selected, well-annotated, and popular with students. Lists
approximately 5,000 titles arranged conveniently by Dewey Decimal
Classification, with an excellent analytic author, title, and subject index
in one alphabet. A valuable and timesaving tool for preparing subject
and interest reading lists for students in this age range, as well as for
using public library resources. For an additional $5, this book is available
with a bound-in *Catholic Supplement,* which lists additional books selected
by a committee of the Catholic Library Association. A *Children's Catalog*
(12th Edition, 1971, $25) and a *Junior High School Library Catalog* (2nd
Edition, 1970, $30) also are available from the publisher.

K28 **SOURCES OF READING MATERIALS FOR THE VISUALLY
HANDICAPPED** By American Foundation for the Blind. New
York, 1971. $1.50.
Comprised of 21 leaflets in a folder on such topics as talking books,
books in braille, and other materials appropriate for blind and visually
handicapped children and adults.
   The Division for the Blind and Physically Disabled, Library of
Congress, Washington, D.C. 20542, also provides many helpful source
guides for the blind and visually handicapped.

K29 **SUBJECT GUIDE TO CHILDREN'S BOOKS IN PRINT
1974** A Subject Index to Children's Books in 8,500 Categories.
5th Edition. New York, R.R. Bowker, 1975. $20.
Revised annually in December or January, this companion volume to
Children's Books in Print (K10) is a cross-referenced index under Sears
(standard school library) subject categories. Provides complete ordering
information, as well as such information as price, publisher, edition,
illustrator, and grade level.

13 | Tests and Assessment Instruments

This chapter on measurement instruments is included in the Educational Products and Curricular Resources section to emphasize that the major purpose of testing within the context of schools is educational rather than experimental or theoretical. Tools included were selected on this basis, although the basic assortment of compilations, indexes, and bibliographies should provide a good starting place for anyone interested in a more extended study of measurement theory. The basic sources listed in Chapters 2 through 7 are, of course, still important here.

The major relevant indexes are *Psychological Abstracts* and *Education Index,* although many others might be helpful. Tests and measurement information are frequently found in *Psychological Abstracts* in the section on EDUCATIONAL PSYCHOLOGY under the "Test" and "Test Construction" headings, Personality and Abilities category. In *Education Index,* the heading "Tests and Scales" and its cross-references and subheadings will locate most relevant periodical articles in education journals. The ERIC descriptors are not as satisfactory, although they are the only ones available for *Resources in Education.* Many academic references are so scattered through *Dissertation Abstracts International* that a DATRIX search might be the best approach.

Some important collections discussed in Chapter 16 are the Test Collection of the Educational Testing Service (ETS) (O13) and the ERIC Clearinghouse on Tests, Measurement, and Evaluation (O19), which is also part of ETS. Two large data banks of test materials are Project TALENT (P12) and the National Assessment of Educational Progress (M26). While the Center for the Study of Evaluation is not a service agency, its test materials are relevant for educators, as are those of the closely related Instructional Objectives Exchange (O23).

A few test reviews can be found in Macmillan's *Education Yearbook* (C6). The best sources for keeping current with reviews of tests are the *Journal of Educational Measurement* and the *Journal of Counseling Psychology*. Prime sources for reviews of current books on testing include the *British Journal of Educational Psychology, Contemporary Psychology,* and *Educational and Psychological Measurement.*

Additional assessment instruments for schools and school districts are included at the end of this chapter; most of them cannot be located through the guides listed in this book.

L1   **CSE-ECRC PRESCHOOL/KINDERGARTEN TEST EVALUATIONS** By Center for the Study of Evaluation, UCLA Graduate School. Los Angeles, 1971. $5. From: 145 Moore Hall, University of California, Los Angeles, Calif. 90024.

Attempts a critical and objective evaluation of published instruments for assessing and diagnosing preschool and kindergarten children, keyed to educational objectives and evaluated by measurement experts on meaningfulness, appropriateness, administrative feasibility, and standardization. Includes useful tables and charts.

L2   **CSE ELEMENTARY SCHOOL HIERARCHICAL OBJECTIVES CHARTS** By Center for the Study of Evaluation, UCLA Graduate School. Los Angeles, 1970. 20 charts, $12.50. From: 145 Moore Hall, University of California, Los Angeles, Calif. 90024.

These 17″ x 22″ charts are somewhat difficult to handle, therefore could get relegated to a back shelf. If they can be mounted for use, they provide a convenient means for matching broad goals with specific behavioral objectives. For this purpose, CSE has categorized education goals into 41 broad areas and 104 subgoals.

L3   **CSE ELEMENTARY SCHOOL TEST EVALUATIONS** Edited by Ralph Hoepfner. Los Angeles, Center for the Study of Evaluation, UCLA Graduate School, 1971. $5. From: 145 Moore Hall, University of California, Los Angeles, Calif. 90024.

This study reviews and evaluates approximately 1,000 tests to determine their suitability for first, third, fifth, and sixth grade students and school situations. Tests are organized by 145 major educational goals, and are evaluated in terms of a quantified test evaluation, MEAN. Despite its sophistication, this book is designed for school use rather than for research and contains very convenient and easy-to-use evaluative tables.

L4 **CSE ELEMENTARY SCHOOL TEST PRICE LIST, 1973** By Center for the Study of Evaluation, UCLA Graduate School. Los Angeles, 1973. $0.50. From: 145 Moore Hall, University of California, Los Angeles, Calif. 90024.

Updated at intervals, this publication contains prices of elementary school tests evaluated in *CSE Elementary School Test Evaluations* (L3).

L5 **CSE PRESCHOOL/KINDERGARTEN TEST PRICE LIST, 1973** By Center for the Study of Evaluation, UCLA Graduate School. Los Angeles, 1973. $0.50. From: 145 Moore Hall, University of California, Los Angeles, Calif. 90024.

Contains that necessary ingredient—price—for the preschool and kindergarten tests evaluated by CSE (L1).

L6 **CSE SECONDARY SCHOOL TEST EVALUATIONS** By Center for the Study of Evaluation, UCLA Graduate School. Los Angeles, 1974. 3 Vols. $22. From: 145 Moore Hall, University of California, Los Angeles, Calif. 90024.

An organized evaluation of more than 1,100 standardized tests used in junior and senior high schools, carefully rated by measurement experts, curriculum specialists, and high school teachers for meaningfulness according to specific goals, appropriateness for particular student groups, usefulness for administrative and decision-making purposes, and overall quality of technical excellence and standardization.

L7 **DEVELOPMENTS IN EDUCATIONAL TESTING** Edited by Karlheinz Ingenkamp. New York, Gordon and Breach, 1969. 2 Vols. $24.50 each; $19.60, prepaid.

A compilation of papers from an international conference on educational testing held in Berlin in May 1967; valuable for anyone interested in educational trends in countries other than the United States, since 20 introductory papers describe a wide range of educational tests in the United States, Europe, Africa, Asia, Australia, and South and Central America. The remainder of the high-quality articles cover the entire theoretical and practical bases of testing, often with substantial bibliographies.

L8 **GUIDELINES FOR TESTING MINORITY GROUP CHIL-DREN** New York, Anti-Defamation League of B'nai B'rith, 1973. $0.35.

This reprint of a 1964 article explains the conditions that prevent disadvantaged children from demonstrating their full mental potentialities in school-administered intelligence tests.

L9 **MANUAL FOR QUANTITATIVE ANALYSIS OF TASKS OF ONE-TO-SIX-YEAR-OLD CHILDREN** By Burton L. White and Barbara Kaban. Cambridge, Mass., Harvard Pre-School Project, 1971. Mimeographed. $5. From: B.L. White, Graduate School of Education, Appian Way, Cambridge, Mass. 02138.

This is one of a series of mimeographed manuals for testing various abilities in preschool children, stemming from the research of the Harvard Pre-School Project; all contain detailed instructions, examples, and tables of contents. Others are: *Manual for Abstract Ability Tests* by Bernice Shapiro (1971, $3.25), *Manual for Assessing Social Abilities of One-to-Six-Year-Old Children* by Daniel Ogilvie and Bernice Shapiro (1970, $3.00), *Manual for Assessing the Discriminative Ability of One-to-Three-Year-Old Children* by Barbara Koslowski and Bernice Shapiro (1972, $1.50), and *Manual for Testing the Language Ability of One-to-Three-Year-Old Children* by Janice Marmor (1972, $3.00).

L10 **MEASURES OF INFANT DEVELOPMENT: An Annotated Bibliography** By P.D. Guthrie and Eleanor V. Horne. Princeton, N.J., Educational Testing Service, 1971. Free. From: Headstart Test Collection, ETS, Princeton, N.J. 08540.

Forty-one measures of infant development from birth to 24 months, with annotations providing information on the purposes of the tests, the groups for whom the tests are intended, what is tested and how, and information on scoring and standardization.

L11 **MEASURES OF SOCIAL PSYCHOLOGICAL ATTITUDES** By John P. Robinson and Philip R. Shaver. Revised Edition. Ann Arbor, Mich., Institute for Social Research, 1974. $15; paperback, $10.

One of a series of three excellent volumes prepared by the University of Michigan's Survey Research Center; together, the three volumes constitute a much-needed guide to empirical instruments for measuring attitudes. The revised edition of this volume, which includes a section on self-esteem, may be the most valuable for educators; the other two volumes, *Measures of Political Attitudes* and *Measures of Occupational Attitudes and Occupational Characteristics,* are equally well-done. All three volumes contain valuable introductions to each section. Scales and tests in each section are conveniently arranged. For each scale, the editors include a clear description, plus information on samples, location, administration data (including time), validity, reliability, homogeneity, results and comments, and references for further reading.

L12 **MEASURES PERTAINING TO HEALTH EDUCATION** III. Alcohol, An Annotated Bibliography. By P. D. Guthrie. Princeton, N.J., ERIC Clearinghouse on Tests, Measurement, and Evaluation, 1972. Hard copy, $1.85; microfiche, $0.75. (ED 068 570) (TM Report 10) From: ERIC Document Reproduction Service, P.O. Box 190, Arlington, Va. 22210.

This annotated bibliography describes 117 instruments designed to assess attitudes, behavior patterns, practices, knowledge, and correlates of alcohol—some designed for students and adults in general, others for those with alcohol problems. Clear descriptions include information on test purpose, appropriate groups, and what is tested, as well as information on administration, scoring, interpretation, and standardization. A table in the front of the book, arranged by title, classifies tests by range and assessment. Two other reports in the series—ED 060 042 and ED 068 569, also available from EDRS—report on 30 instruments related to smoking and 90 instruments assessing attitudes, knowledge, and behavior related to drugs.

L13 **MIRRORS FOR BEHAVIOR: An Anthology of Classroom Observation Instruments** Edited by Anita Simon and E. Gil Boyer. Philadelphia, Research for Better Schools, 1967 to 1971. 17 Vols., including supplements. Price not available.

Contains complete information on 92 classroom observation systems designed to study verbal and nonverbal interactions in classrooms, small groups, and counseling and therapy groups; some systems applicable as well for anthropological or industrial research. The 15th volume is a useful synthesis and summary of information provided in the first 14 volumes.

L14 **PERSONALITY TESTS AND REVIEWS** Edited by Oscar K. Buros. Highland Park, N.J., Gryphon Press, 1970. $45.

There are approximately 7,000 reviews of personality tests in this comprehensive inventory—all from the first six *Mental Measurements Yearbooks* (L20), including updating of 408 tests, plus information about 80 tests not included in any yearbook. Includes an author index, a comprehensive 513-page bibliography, a scanning index to all personality tests, and a directory of publishers of personality tests.

L15 **READING TESTS AND REVIEWS**   Edited by Oscar K. Buros. Highland Park, N.J., Gryphon Press, 1968. $15.

A comprehensive bibliography representing all reading tests reviewed in the first six *Mental Measurements Yearbooks* (L20) and 33 tests not listed in any yearbook. Includes an index to 292 reading tests and a master classified index to the first six *Mental Measurements Yearbooks,* as well as a directory of publishers and indexes of titles and names (authors, test designers, etc.).

L16 **READING TESTS FOR THE SECONDARY GRADES: A Review and Evaluation**   Edited by William Blanton, Roger Farr, and J. Jaap Tuinman. Newark, Del., International Reading Assn., 1972. $2. From: 6 Tyre Ave., Newark, Del. 19711.

Intended primarily for classroom teachers concerned with selecting reading tests for high school students, this book analyzes 14 of the most commonly used reading achievement tests for content and statistical characteristics. A useful table provides comparative information on these tests, with access to further discussion in Buros' *Mental Measurements Yearbooks* (L20) and *Reading Tests and Reviews* (L15). One of a fine series of books published by IRA, designed to provide guidance for all aspects and levels of reading instruction.

L17 **SCHOOL ACHIEVEMENT OF CHILDREN BY DEMOGRAPHIC AND SOCIOECONOMIC FACTORS**   By National Center for Health Statistics. Washington, D.C., U.S. Government Printing Office, 1971. $1.

Using data from the National Health Survey, this report correlates findings from the Wide Range Achievement Test reading and arithmetic subtests with age, sex, race, region of the United States, size of place of residence and population change, family income, parents' education, and grade in school—shown in raw scores, standard scores, and grade equivalents.

L18 **SELECTED REFERENCES IN EDUCATIONAL MEASUREMENT**   By Educational Testing Service (ETS). 3rd Edition. Princeton, N.J., 1970. Free. From: ETS, Princeton, N.J. 08540.

An interpretive, annotated guide to books and reference volumes in educational measurement. Books cover measurement theory and methods, measurement in education and guidance, test construction, commentaries on testing, and other relevant areas. Also provides a selected annotated list of test publishers and relevant professional journals. Information is bibliographically complete, but omits prices. An excellent reference source.

L19 **SELF-DIRECTED SEARCH FOR EDUCATIONAL AND VO-CATIONAL PLANNING** By John L. Holland. Palo Alto, Calif., Consulting Psychological Press, 1971. 2 booklets and Counselor's Guide. Specimen set, $2; discount on class sets. From: 577 College Ave., Palo Alto, Calif. 94306.

Two simple booklets, *Self-Directed Search* and *Occupations Finder,* allow students above the junior high school reading level to match their interests and characteristics with appropriate occupations. This self-directed search method, extensively researched at the Johns Hopkins Center for the Study of Social Organization of Schools, covers 431 occupations (approximately 95 percent of the labor force). This method also can be used with younger students, with appropriate guidance. A professional manual for testers or teachers is available for $3.

L20 **THE SEVENTH MENTAL MEASUREMENTS YEAR-BOOK** Edited by Oscar K. Buros. Highland Park, N.J., Gryphon Press, 1972. 2 Vols. $55.

This yearbook, as were six earlier yearbooks (issued irregularly from 1938 to 1972), is designed to assist test users in making more intelligent use of standardized tests in education, psychology, and industry, especially commercial tests sold in the United States. Prepared by a husband and wife team, without benefit of grants or outside support, it is an impressive and comprehensive work. *The Seventh Mental Measurements Yearbook,* which supplements rather than supplants previous volumes, devotes 1,532 pages to tests and reviews, 314 pages to books and reviews, and 140 pages to indexes. The test and review section covers 1,157 tests, and includes 798 original test reviews by 439 reviewers, 181 excerpted test reviews from 39 journals, and 12,372 references to specific tests—55 percent greater than the number of references in the sixth edition. The reviews themselves are explicitly concise and critical. Excerpted reviews are carefully selected and edited. The book section lists practically all books on testing and assessment techniques published between 1933 and 1970. The book review index covers 664 new books on testing issued mostly between 1964 and 1970. Indexes include directories of periodicals and publishers, indexes of book and test titles, an index of names, and classified indexes of tests and reviews.

L21 **STANDARDIZED SCIENCE TESTS: A Descriptive Listing** Compiled by Lee Summerlin and Janet Wall. Washington, D.C., National Science Teachers Assn., 1973. $1.50.

An inexpensive little book that provides sources and descriptions for almost all standardized elementary and secondary science tests.

L22 **STANDARDS FOR EDUCATIONAL AND PSYCHOLOGICAL TESTS AND MANUALS** By a Joint Committee of the American Psychological Assn., American Educational Research Assn., and National Council on Measurement in Education. Revised Edition. Washington, D.C., American Psychological Assn., 1974. $5; $3 to members.

A cogent, brief, but well-organized set of guidelines that should be read by everyone who uses tests or evaluation instruments. It is a clearly written, categorized guide which provides criteria and standards for users as well as producers of tests. (It is particularly important for the former to know what is *not* being measured on the chosen instruments.) Areas covered include interpretation, dissemination of information, and standards for reliability and validity—for interest inventories, personality inventories, and projective devices, as well as for more standard tests. The index, like the text, is clear and helpful.

L23 **STATE EDUCATIONAL ASSESSMENT PROGRAMS** By Educational Testing Service, with Education Commission of the States and Educational Resources Information Center. 2nd Edition. Princeton, N.J., Education Testing Service, 1973. Free. From: ETS, Princeton, N.J. 08540.

Attempts to incorporate into one document, detailed information concerning educational assessment programs and plans for all the states as of 1973—based on a survey conducted by the Educational Testing Service staff, with the initial assistance of the Education Commission of the States. The report is in two parts: the first is an overview of state-by-state assessment, with a presentation of the purposes and methods of the survey; the second is a state-by-state report of the assessment activities of the states and the District of Columbia, arranged in alphabetical order. The interview guide is in the appendix.

L24 **STATE TESTING PROGRAMS: Status, Problems and Prospects** By Robert L. Ebel. Princeton, N.J., Educational Testing Service, 1974. Free. From: ETS, Princeton, N.J. 08540.

A useful overview of state testing programs which provides insight into current topics, a capsule history, and references to other studies of state testing programs.

L25 **TESTS FOR SPANISH-SPEAKING CHILDREN: An Annotated Bibliography** By Pamela Rosen and Eleanor V. Horne. Princeton, N.J., Educational Testing Service, 1971. Free. From: ETS, Princeton, N.J. 08540.

With the supplement, contains 34 tests for Spanish-speaking children;

fully annotated, with grade or age levels indicated. Part of the Head Start Test Collection described in O13.

L26   **TESTS IN PRINT—II: An Index to Tests, Test Reviews, and the Literature on Specific Tests**   Edited by Oscar K. Buros. 2nd Edition. Highland Park, N.J., Gryphon Press, 1974. $70.

The second edition of this index to approximately 2,500 tests and 70,000 documents relating to tests is useful for the educator who requires factual rather than evaluative information. Includes test titles, parts and subtests, copyright dates, groups for whom the tests are intended, number of scores, publication dates, authors, and publishers. Contents are arranged by type of test; tests are cross-referenced to test reviews and citations of the *Mental Measurements Yearbooks* (L20). Indexes include personal names and test titles, as well as a directory of test publishers.

L27   **TESTS IN THE ARTS**   By Thomas J. Johnson and Robert J. Hess. St. Louis, Mo., CEMREL, Inc., 1970. $5.10. From: CEMREL, Inc., 3120 59th St., St. Louis, Mo. 63139.

Intended as a comprehensive index of research and assessment instruments in the arts, it abstracts 235 tests in the fields of art, dance, literature, music, and creativity. (Drama and film also were researched, but tests specifically related to these areas were not located.) Includes, for each test given, information on format; scoring methods; normative data; information on validation, reliability, and statistical backup for claims; as well as author, title, and source, but not price. Arranged by categories, with author index, permuted index, and abstracts for each section. Elaborate response taxonomies and nested response constructs are given for each field.

ADDITIONAL ASSESSMENT INSTRUMENTS

L28   **CRITERIA FOR ASSESSING SCHOOL READING PROGRAMS: Kindergarten through High School**   By Connecticut Assn. for Reading Research (CARR). Hartford, Conn., Connecticut State Department of Education, 1970. $3. From: Nora D. Adams, 269 Academy Rd., Cheshire, Conn. 06410.

This series of instruments was designed by CARR to assist elementary school staffs improve reading instruction, after field-testing in 12 school systems. Nine sections of objective questions identify areas that may need improvement: system background, individual school background, individual staff background, preprimary and kindergarten programs, elementary reading programs, content-area reading programs, independent reading programs, remedial and corrective reading programs, summary evaluations, and recommendations. Comprehensive and easy to administer.

L29 **DESIGN FOR A SCHOOL RATING OR CLASSIFICATION SYSTEM** By Bayla F. White. Washington, D.C., The Urban Institute, 1970. $1.50 (paperback).

A succinct and well-thought-out school classification system designed for use in assessing performance within a local school system. Provides simple but logical means for identifying and classifying schools—using (largely) records that are already available. The end result is a method for determining what each school is accomplishing for its students in relationship to other schools with similar student populations.

L30 **ELEMENTARY SCHOOL EVALUATION: Administrator's Guide to Accountability** By Eugene J. Bradford, Albert F. Doremus, and Clifford R. Kreismer. West Nyack, N.J., Parker, 1972. $15.

Handbook and guide providing a full discussion of evaluative criteria selections and examples of assessment instruments; recommended by individuals who know the field.

L31 **HOW TO CONDUCT LOW COST SURVEYS: A Profile of School Survey and Polling Procedures** By National School Public Relations Assn. Arlington, Va., 1973. $4.75.

Provides a rationale and practical guidelines for conducting accurate, economical surveys. NSPRA also distributes *Polling and Survey Research* (produced by the ERIC Clearinghouse on Educational Management) which quotes pro and con research on research means, such as interview guides and questionnaires, as well as various ways of constructing questions and analyzing data.

L32 **INFORMATION FOR PARENTS ON SCHOOL EVALUATION** By Robert Feldmesser and Esther Ann McCready. Princeton, N.J., ERIC Clearinghouse on Tests, Measurements, and Evaluations, 1974. (TM Report 42) Free. From: ETS, Princeton, N.J. 08540.

A thoughtful literature review of evaluation guides (going back to 1954) which could be used by parents or other citizen groups to obtain comparative data on schools and to evaluate schools for quality. Valuable for pointing out the shortcomings of these guides and their basic agreement on certain dimensions of evaluation.

L33 **KNOW YOUR SCHOOLS** By League of Women Voters Education Fund. Washington, D.C., League of Women Voters of the United States, 1974. $1. From: 1730 M St., N.W., Washington, D.C. 20036.

Designed to assist citizen groups in surveying and analyzing local school systems, with the aims of furthering communication between citizens and their schools and of strengthening public understanding of school objectives and needs. Well-organized and thorough, it covers organization, operation, and planning, as well as educational programs. An attempt is made to consider and incorporate current educational concerns (such as funding and community control) within the fundamental context of public education. The major parts of the guide deal with school systems and school programs: the first part, with the scope and content of the school program; the second part, with administration, teaching staff, plant, financing, and community relationship. The volume includes a useful bibliography. This guide can be used for a comprehensive survey of a district or for studying a single area (such as administration) or a single school. The primary purpose of the league is to carefully and objectively assess government functions; in education, this includes many state departments of education as well as individual school systems.

L34 **A LOOK INTO YOUR SCHOOL DISTRICT** By Charles F. Kettering Foundation. Englewood, Colo., 1972. $0.40. From: Phi Delta Kappa, 8th and Union Sts., Bloomington, Ind. 47401.

A manual to guide public opinion surveys of local school districts.

L35 **SEXISM IN SCHOOLS: A Handbook for Action** By Nina Rothchild. Mahtomedi, Minn., Author, 1973. $2. From: 14 Hickory St., Mahtomedi, Minn. 55115.

A handbook, by a school board member of a small Minnesota district, designed to assess "structures and personalities" in school districts for action against sex discrimination. Areas covered include school athletic budgets, sex stereotyping in children's books, differential expectations for boys and girls in classrooms and counseling, attitudes, and women as subordinates among school personnel—as they affect children's definitions of their roles in life.

PART IV
Nonprint Sources

Directory and Institutional Information Sources
Nonprint Sources of Government and Financial Information
Institutional Sources of Product and Curricular Information
Computerized Retrieval Sources
Gaining Access to Educational Information and Materials
State Library Services to Educators

14 | *Directory and Institutional Information Sources*

Directory information and descriptions of 32 institutional information sources, covering all areas of education other than educational financing and government (see Chapter 15) and educational curricula and materials (see Chapter 16), are discussed in this chapter. These sources can answer specific questions and/or provide printed materials in many broad interest areas, including educational bibliographies and bibliographic systems, educational sociology, child welfare, day care, educational research, educational administration, educational facilities, educational counseling, public relations, special education, higher education, and international education.

Various types of organizations also are included: professional associations, advocacy and volunteer organizations concerned with the problems of particular children or youth, special libraries, microfiche depository and distribution systems, government agencies, and others.

Other worthwhile information sources can be found through the directories listed in Chapter 3 and through references in educational literature. Some of the monograph sources listed in Chapter 4 also can supply answers to specific queries in their areas of coverage.

M1 **AMERICAN COLLEGE PUBLIC RELATIONS AS-SOCIATION** Suite 600, 1 Dupont Cir., N.W., Washington, D.C. 20036. (202) 293-6360

Subject areas of its library collection cover higher education, public relations, fund raising, and institutional management. Holdings include 1,000 books, 2,000 pamphlets, 5,000 documents, 25 periodicals, and approximately 100 microfiche. The library is open to college and university public relations and fund raising officials. Publications include *Education Abstracts* (F7), *College and University Journal,* and a *Microfiche Library* of conferences and workshops ($75/year).

M2 **BIBLIOGRAPHIC SYSTEMS CENTER (BSC)** Case Western Reserve University Library, School of Library Science, University Cir., Cleveland, Ohio 44145. (216) 368-3500

A resource center for classification schemes, thesauri, and subject heading collections designed primarily for special libraries, but helpful to users who would like to organize subject collections of books or documents and to eliminate the difficulties of standard classification schemes. Its collection covers all subject areas and includes approximately 40 to 50 education items, plus many more in social and behavioral sciences.

The center will search its collections for classification schemes and vocabulary lists to fit user needs, and will loan relevant materials for approximately one month if more than one copy is available. For efficient service, inquirers are asked to describe their area of interest, projected ultimate size of the collection, and types of users and documents. With this information, preliminary lists of relevant materials are sent to the inquirer, from which a selection can be made. Borrowers can photocopy any or all of these materials; BSC will copy limited amounts at $0.15 per page, plus a $1.00 handling charge. Mail and phone requests are accepted; no charge for loans or inquiries at the present time.

M3 **BLACK CHILD DEVELOPMENT INSTITUTE, INC.** Suite 514, 1028 Connecticut Ave., N.W., Washington, D.C. 20036. (202) 659-4010

Organized in 1970 to serve as advocates of Black children across the nation, the institute's main thrust is to assist in the development of quality child-centered programs in Black communities for children of working mothers. Its publication, *The Black Child Advocate* (bimonthly), and an occasional newsletter, *Black Flash,* both deal with information on programs, legislative developments, and local efforts relating to child development. The *Flash* is dispatched immediately to inform subscribers of significant changes in rules, regulations, or legislative matters at all levels.

M4 **CENTER FOR VOCATIONAL AND TECHNICAL EDUCATION** Ohio State University, 1960 Kenny Rd., Columbus, Ohio 43210. (614) 486-3655

The subject areas of this center are (increasingly) career education plus technical and vocational education. The basic responsibility of the center is to strengthen the capacity of state educational systems in providing occupational education programs. The affiliated *AIM/ARM* project and the center library are the information storage sections of the center.

Centergram is a newsletter published by the center. Another publication is *Abstracts of Instructional and Research Materials in Vocational and Technical Education (AIM/ARM)* (F1). Tapes of these abstracts are part of a computerized data base, which can be consulted through state research coordinating units as well as some commercial services (see Chapter 17), or which can be purchased from the center for $150/year (user providing tapes). A recent product, designed to simplify research for vocational educators, is the *ERIC Instructional Package for Vocational Educators* (group model or independent study model), which provides search exercises and explanations for some ERIC retrieval tools. The approximately 350 publications of the center are available in five series: research and development, leadership training, bibliography, information, and center-related. These are listed and indexed in a substantial publications list, which is available on request, complete with updates.

Library holdings include approximately 30,000 books and documents, 1,500 dissertations, nearly 500 periodicals, almost 900 microfilms, and a complete ERIC microfiche collection, available to visiting professional personnel who are sponsored by senior staff members of the center. Facilities include viewers and duplicators for microfiche and microfilms. The center offers contract services in research, development, information, program planning, and evaluation.

M5 **CHILD WELFARE LEAGUE OF AMERICA** Dorothy L. Bernhard Library, 67 Irving Pl., New York, N.Y. 10003. (212) 254-7410

The league is a membership organization of public and private welfare agencies in the United States and Canada, which was organized to promote improved services to deprived, neglected, or dependent children. One of its many publications, *Child Welfare* (monthly), attempts a multidisciplinary approach to the problems of children. Its well-staffed special library (with three professionals and two nonprofessionals) deals with child development, child welfare, social work, and social welfare; it houses approximately 3,000 books, 600 documents, 85 periodicals, and 75 vertical files. Open during business hours to professionals, researchers, and graduate students.

M6 **CLEARINGHOUSE FOR SOCIOLOGICAL LITERATURE** Department of Sociology, Northern Illinois University, DeKalb, Ill. 60115. (815) 753-1194

Founded in 1965, this clearinghouse is somewhat similar in concept to ERIC (M12), although its subject areas cover sociology and related social sciences, and its size is considerably smaller. It is a combination depository and publication system dealing directly with authors, who pay a fee to have documents entered into the system, but subsequently receive royalties on sales. Documents are reproduced photographically and are available both in microfiche and photocopies ($0.40 per microfiche of 28 pages, or $0.10 per full-page printout). All documents are abstracted in *Sociological Abstracts* (F22).

M7 **COUNCIL FOR EDUCATIONAL DEVELOPMENT AND RE- SEARCH, INC. (CEDaR)** Information Office, Suite 206, 1518 K St., N.W., Washington, D.C. 20005. (202) 638-3193

The council, presently limited to university-based educational research and development centers and educational regional laboratories, is an interest group whose aim is to advance the level of educational research and development and to demonstrate its importance to educational audiences in the United States.

CEDAR's information office, the public information agency of this group, functions as a clearinghouse for information about the council and its members and answers queries on the projects and products of its members. This is accomplished primarily through two publications, the *D & R Report* (an irregularly published newsletter, available on request), which presents highlights of the activities of supporting institutions, and the *CEDaR Catalog* (H4), which provides almost yearly compilations of the products and current projects of council members. Direct access to these research sources is sometimes valuable to teachers, administrators, and researchers interested in innovations in particular areas. The information office can be contacted for names, addresses, and areas of interest, after which complete publication lists can be obtained from the individual agencies.

M8 **DAY CARE AND CHILD DEVELOPMENT COUNCIL OF AMERICA, INC. (DCCDCA)** 1012 14th St., N.W., Washington, D.C. 20005. (202) 638-2316

A national, nonprofit, voluntary organization—highly successful in keeping current with the changing scene—whose purpose is to simultaneously extend and upgrade child care programs. It is an advocacy group whose interests include the social, physical, emotional, and intellectual development of the child, policymaking roles for parents, and adequate training and pay for staff. Membership is comprised of educators, parents, interested citizens, and a variety of child specialists, including day care center staff, child psychologists, pediatricians, nurses, and nutritionists. Membership fees range from $7 for students or day care parents to $50 for agencies.

Services include technical assistance, which consists of a wide variety of on-site and written consultations for child care projects or community organizations, and provision of public education materials for improving the quality and quantity of child care programs.

The council is a primary source of data and information for all aspects of child care and a major disseminator of publications relating to its interests, some of which are *VOICE for Children,* a monthly magazine (available to members only) providing thorough child care coverage; frequent *Bulletins,* covering important events and legislative/regulatory activities related to child care; and *Resources for Day Care,* an impressive selection of materials selected or commissioned by DCCDCA for distribution and available on request (see Figure 9). The council distributed more than 50,000 books at cost during 1974. Other activities include national and state workshops and meetings.

M9　**EDUCATIONAL FACILITIES LABORATORIES** Library, 477 Madison Ave., New York, N.Y. 10022. (212) 751-6215

A nonprofit corporation established in 1958 to encourage experimental, innovative, yet economical, changes in school and college facilities. It has been highly active in encouraging new products; in applying industrialized building systems to schools; and in developing joint occupancy plans, schools without walls, multiple-use schools, and other innovative systems. Since 1958, more than 2,000,000 copies of reports have been distributed to decision makers in the education construction industry.

Its inexpensive reports and films deal with most innovative types of school facilities: career education, early childhood facilities, environmental education, found spaces, high schools, libraries, student housing, children's centers, and others. A new report, *Fewer Pupils/Surplus Space,* based on a survey of 100 districts in 40 states, offers the essentials of a shrinkage plan to school districts experiencing declining enrollment. A brochure and order lists are available without charge.

Library holdings include 7,000 books and pamphlets and 100 periodicals on the design, planning, and construction of—as well as alternate uses for—educational facilities. Open to educators and architects by appointment.

child development

A-1 CHILD CARE BULLETIN NO. 1, SUBJECT: DAY CARE: RESOURCES FOR DECISIONS. (OEO). DCCDCA, 1971. 24 pp. $.50.
In her "Preface," reprinted in this Bulletin, Dr. Edith Grotberg surveys basic questions and existing gaps in our knowledge of child development in the context of day care. Dr. Jerome Bruner's "Overview of Development and Day Care," also reprinted here, provides a detailed introduction to, and a critique of, child development research. The Bulletin also contains the table of contents of the entire volume edited by Dr. Grotberg for OEO (See A-10).

B-5 EARLY CHILDHOOD EDUCATION: HOW TO SELECT AND EVALUATE MATERIALS. Educational Products Information Exchange Institute, 1972. 110 pp. $4.00.
A consumer's guide to curricula and educational materials and kits marketed by major businesses which are entering the early childhood field. This report gives valuable assistance to child care programmers in matching materials with their own philosophy of child development.

8 GUIDELINES FOR OBSERVATION AND ASSESSMENT: AN APPROACH TO EVALUATING THE LEARNING ENVIRONMENT OF A DAY CARE CENTER. Ilse Mattick and Frances J. Perkins, DCCDCA, 1972. 42 pp. $1.75.
After a fruitless search for an adequate, thorough evaluation model for a child care program, Ms. Mattick of Wheelock College and Ms. Perkins of Brandeis University decided to prepare their own. This guidebook includes an introduction which outlines their comprehensive premises for effective evaluation and their three-part evaluation model. They focus on physical, interactional, and program settings. Highly recommended.

9 EVALUATING CHILDREN'S PROGRESS: A RATING SCALE FOR CHILDREN IN DAY CARE. Southeastern Day Care Project. Reprinted by DCCDCA, 1973. 50 pp. Illustrated. $2.00.
Using developmental standards agreed upon by parents as well as professionals in child development and early childhood education, this manual provides rating scales, related to specific ages, for use in gaining feedback about individual children and groups. The format of these rating scales is clear and easy to use. Instructions are included.

14 A GUIDE FOR TEACHER RECORDING IN DAY CARE AGENCIES. Lola B. Emerson, CWLA, Revised 1970. 23 pp. $.75.
The basic purpose of this guide is "to consider what it is that we look for and note at various stages of the child's adjustment and growth while under day care." A concise booklet on how to do the above and why it is important that this is done. Would be extremely helpful for those programs that do self-evaluations.

27 THE PRIMER. National Capital Area Child Day Care Association, 1972. 30 pp. $1.50.
This is an introduction to *practical* child development, especially designed for newcomers to work in day care centers. Based on Head Start training materials, it expands easy to understand wisdom about working with children in day care and makes delightful reading.

38 PRESCHOOL BREAKTHROUGH: WHAT WORKS IN EARLY CHILDHOOD EDUCATION. National School Public Relations Association, 1970. 48 pp. $4.00.
Designed to help school personnel prepare for preschoolers by discussing experimental approaches to teaching and explaining many individual programs which have proved successful in raising achievements in language and numerical skills.

15

FIGURE 9   Sample page from *Resources for Day Care,* a catalog of publications distributed by the Day Care and Child Development Council of America (M8), assembled from many sources.

M10 **EDUCATION RESEARCH LIBRARY** National Institute of Education, 1832 M St., N.W., 6th Fl., Washington, D.C. 20208. (202) 254-5060

This recently opened library includes the entire collection of the former HEW Departmental Library and a rare book collection which includes children's books, textbooks, and treatises dating back to 1489; approximately 80,000 books and 10,000 documents. The periodical collection provides 1,110 current titles and 25,000 bound volumes, including a large collection of early nineteenth century journals. Other resources include the complete ERIC microfiche collection, as well as *Congressional Information Service* and *Newsbank* on microfilm. Through the Educational Reference Center, this library provides HEW on-line access to 18 data bases. Services for outside agencies include interlibrary loan and photo-duplication. A computerized book catalog listing all of the library's materials—presently in the planning stage—may make this library's resources more widely available.

M11 **ENTELEK CAI/CMI INFORMATION EXCHANGE** Entelek, Inc., 42 Pleasant St., Newburyport, Mass. 01950. (617) 465-3000

A membership organization, active since 1965, which collects and disseminates information on current activities in computer-assisted instruction and computer-managed instruction.

Members (for $150/year) are entitled to a monthly book of tear-out card sheets (which can be filed either as books or as cards) containing abstracts and specifications of literature, programs, and facilities dealing with computer-assisted and computer-managed instruction, as well as an annual survey and synthesis of CAI/CMI data. Members also receive a microfiche collection containing the data prepared and distributed by ENTELEK from 1965 to date, complete with author, subject, and supplementary indexes.

M12 **ERIC (Educational Resources Information Center)** National Institute of Education (NIE), Washington, D.C. 20208. (202) 254-5555

ERIC is a national bibliographic network, originally designed and supported by the U.S. Office of Education, to organize and disseminate otherwise fugitive research materials: results of exemplary programs, research and development efforts, professional papers, committee reports, and other educational information. Its principal contributions have been the publication of these materials in microfiche format and their indexing in *Resources in Education (RIE)* and a variety of other tools. Its other major product is an index to educational periodicals, *Current Index to Journals in Education (CIJE)*. Both are discussed in detail in Chapter 7.

ERIC now operates out of the National Institute of Education. Its components are a varying number of clearinghouses (16 at present, but subject to change), the ERIC Processing and Reference Facility (a clearinghouse for the clearinghouses), and a variety of public and commercial distribution channels (see Figures 10 and 11). There are approximately 600 ERIC microfiche collections (see B32) throughout the world, generally open to serious researchers.

Individual copies (microfiche and hard copy) of uncopyrighted microfiche documents are available from ERIC Document Reproduction Service (EDRS), Computer Microfilm International Corporation, P.O. Box 190, Arlington, Virginia 22210. (Hard copies can be purchased for approximately $1.20 to $1.50 per 25 pages, based on a sliding scale; microfiche copies cost approximately $0.15 each, with a minimum charge of $0.75.) Other tools designed to provide access to these documents are available from the U.S. Government Printing Office.

Magnetic tapes of document indexes and abstracts are available from ERICTAPES, Leasco Systems and Research Corporation, Suite 303, 4833 Rugby Avenue, Bethesda, Maryland 20014. Chapters 17, 18, and 19 of this book include some research and resource services and some libraries that search the ERIC data base at varying rates. Information on states performing this service is included in Chapter 19. Some ERIC clearinghouses also provide search facilities.

The bulk of ERIC's work is performed at specialized clearinghouses (usually established at ongoing professional organizations, universities, and other institutions). In addition to acquiring, assessing, reviewing, and abstracting the documents and periodicals listed each month in *RIE* and *CIJE*, they prepare bibliographies and interpretations of research and (sometimes) commission original papers. Some of the ERIC clearinghouses answer requests for information in their particular fields; others confine their communications to printed newsletters, research summaries, and bibliographies. Because the grantee organizations and/or institutions operating the ERIC clearinghouses and ERIC headquarters have frequently changed, there has been a disconcerting lack of continuity in their operation. In some cases, clearinghouses were discontinued just when they gained expertise; typically, transition problems occur at each change. Listed below, in alphabetical order, are descriptions of some of the ERIC clearinghouses; still others are classed and listed in Chapter 16, namely:

ERIC Clearinghouse for Reading and Communication Skills (O16)
ERIC Clearinghouse for Social Studies/Social Science Education (O41)
ERIC Clearinghouse on Information Resources (O17)
ERIC Clearinghouse on Languages and Linguistics (O18)

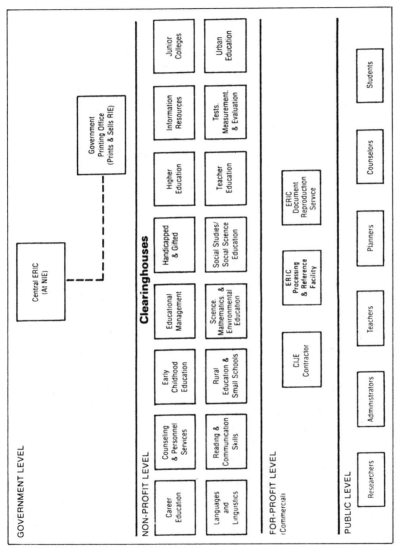

FIGURE 10 Organization chart of the Educational Resources Information Center (ERIC).

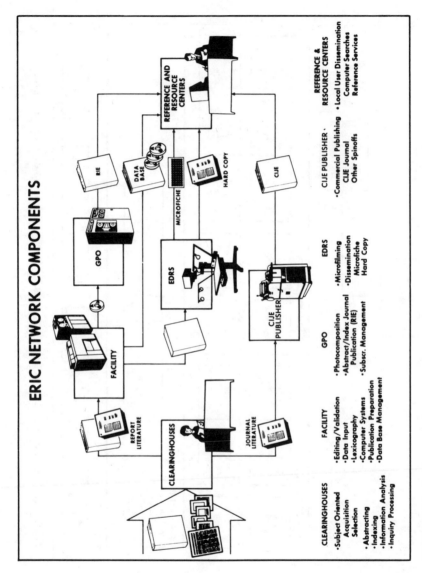

FIGURE 11   ERIC network components.

ERIC Clearinghouse on Tests, Measurement, and Evaluation (O19)
ERIC Information Analysis Center on Science, Mathematics and Environmental Education (O20)

ERIC, of course, is interested in receiving relevant materials—two legibly typed or printed copies—which can be submitted to the appropriate clearinghouse.

M13 **ERIC CLEARINGHOUSE FOR JUNIOR COLLEGES (ERIC/ JC)** 96 Powell Library, University of California, Los Angeles, Calif. 90024. (213) 825-3931

Subject areas cover public and private community and junior colleges, including studies about students, staff, curricula, programs, libraries, and community services. Its publications include a monograph series, published by the American Association of Junior Colleges, available at $2 each; and a series of topical papers dealing with such topics as Black studies and instructor evaluation, free while the supply lasts. Lists are available on request. Library holdings consist of approximately 2,200 documents and a complete ERIC microfiche collection. The library is open to the public from 8:00 a.m. to 5:00 p.m., Monday through Friday. The clearinghouse will perform free manual searches on subjects related to junior college education; it has no computer facilities.

M14 **ERIC CLEARINGHOUSE IN CAREER EDUCATION (ERIC/ CICE)** 204 Gurler St., Northern Illinois University, DeKalb, Ill. 60115. (815) 753-1251

This new clearinghouse, which replaces two others (Adult Education and Vocational-Technical Education), is responsible for enriching and integrating the areas of formal and informal adult and continuing education at all ages and in all settings; vocational and technical information, including new subprofessional fields; and all facets of career education, including attitudes, general and specific knowledge, decision-making skills, and life roles. Its products include data reviews, state-of-the-art papers, bibliographies, and syntheses. Resources include library holdings of 200 books, 200 pamphlets, and 400 documents, and an ERIC computer-search capability. Manual literature searches are free; a fee of $5 is charged for computerized bibliographic searches using the QUERY system.

M15 **ERIC CLEARINGHOUSE ON COUNSELING AND PER- SONNEL SERVICES (ERIC/CAPS)** University of Michigan, 2108 School of Education Bldg., Ann Arbor, Mich. 48104. (313) 764-9492

Subject areas include preparation, practice, and supervision of counselors at all educational levels and in all settings; theoretical development of counseling and guidance; use and results of personnel procedures such as testing, interviewing, disseminating, and analyzing such information; group work and case work; nature of pupil, student and adult characteristics; and personnel workers and their relation to career planning, family consultations, and student orientation activities. Information is disseminated through an annual newsletter, *CAPS Capsule,* available free; *Searchlights,* annotated bibliographies on topics of current interest (21 available; $1.00–$1.50/issue); and special monographs and papers focusing on high-interest topics. Library holdings consist of 1,600 books, 9,000 documents, and a complete ERIC microfiche collection (106,000 microfiche). The library is open to administrators, practitioners, researchers, students, interested laypersons, and various groups of individuals who request orientation sessions. Approximately 25 packets of resumés are available.

M16 **ERIC CLEARINGHOUSE ON EARLY CHILDHOOD EDU-CATION (ERIC/ECE)** College of Education, University of Illinois, 805 W. Pennsylvania Ave., Urbana, Ill. 61801. (217) 333-1386

This clearinghouse is concerned with areas pertaining to early childhood education and development, focusing primarily on educational theory, research, and practices related to children from birth through age 12. Papers collected include research studies, program reviews, curriculum guides, literature reviews, reports on educational standards, and other monographs. The clearinghouse publishes timely bibliographies and position papers, which can be ordered from the Publications Office at the above address, at prices ranging from $0.50 to $4.00. A list of these publications can be obtained free from ERIC/ECE. Also available from the same address is the quarterly *ERIC/ECE Newsletter* ($2.00/4 issues), which reports on current programs, practices, and publications. The clearinghouse provides a question-answering service (both telephone and written requests are welcome) and offers computer searches of the ERIC data base for a moderate fee. Its library, open to the public, contains the complete ERIC microfiche collection, plus many books, pamphlets, and periodicals relative to the education and development of children.

M17 **ERIC CLEARINGHOUSE ON EDUCATIONAL MANAGE-MENT (ERIC/CEM)** Library, South Wing, University of Oregon, Eugene, Ore. 97403. (503) 686-5043

The subject areas of this clearinghouse are administration, educational organization, and facilities at the elementary and secondary school levels (including finance and planning); it is oriented towards collection and dissemination of information. Its *Newsletter,* which might cease publication because of federal printing regulations, has been a prime source of information on other compilations and sources of information. ERIC/CEM produces many commissioned papers, including substantial assessments and reviews such as its current *Politics of Education* ($2.50), and has jointly published a useful monograph series on school law with the National Organization on Legal Problems of Education (N19), a series of subject resumés of ERIC documents with the National Association of Secondary School Principals (C10), and currently is working with the National Association of Elementary School Principals (NAESP) to produce monthly analytic reports of current trends in such areas as class size and community schools. These are available from NAESP, P.O. Box 9114, Arlington, Virginia 22209, for $24/year.

School Management Information Retrieval Service (SMIRS), its latest information service, is designed to provide clients with needed information, primarily in the areas of educational management and facilities. Depending on queries, clients are referred to specific research reviews or bibliographies or to other organizations which can supply the information. If clients wish, computerized searches of *RIE* and *CIJE* can be arranged through Lane Intermediate Education District. For each computerized information search from SMIRS, send a check for $16, made payable to Lane IED, together with a carefully stated and defined question, including, if possible, a list of ERIC descriptors or other search terms, to: User Services Coordinator, SMIRS, ERIC Clearinghouse on Educational Management, University of Oregon, Eugene, Oregon 97403 (telephone 503/686-5052). Output will include up to 130 ERIC abstracts.

M18 **ERIC CLEARINGHOUSE ON HANDICAPPED AND GIFTED (ERIC/EC)** CEC Information Center on Exceptional Children, 1920 Association Dr., Reston, Va. 22091. (703) 620-3660

The Council for Exceptional Children (CEC), a professional organization active since 1922, operates this ERIC clearinghouse, which covers the entire scope of special education: mental retardation, physical handicaps, homebound and hospitalized children, visually handicapped, children with learning disabilities, children with communication disorders, gifted children, and teacher training for special education. Its subdivisions—for members interested in particular phases of special education—are professional organizations that charge dues, plan their own programs, and offer a great deal of professional assistance to their members.

An extensive series of high-quality publications includes *Exceptional Child Education Abstracts* (F10); *Exceptional Children* (8 issues/year, $8.50);

the *Exceptional Child Bibliography Series,* partially computer-generated, which includes many directory issues as well as other publications dealing with aspects of teaching exceptional children ($4.00 each); *ERIC ExCErpt; Teaching Exceptional Children* (quarterly, $7.50/year); CEC Tape Cassette Library; and many helpful and authoritative monographs. Publications range from scholarly and research-oriented to (particularly in recent years) practical guides for teachers and administrators. Its publication program for 1974-1975 includes many items on gifted education. A descriptive brochure giving further details can be obtained upon written request.

Library holdings include 5,000 books, 5,000 pamphlets, 2,000 documents, 3,000 periodicals, a complete ERIC microfiche collection, and the computerized data base for the printed *Exceptional Child Education Abstracts.* The library is open to the public from 8:00 a.m. to 4:00 p.m.; computer searches are performed as needed, at $35 for the first 100 abstracts. Individual information requests receive specific answers, literature packets, or referrals (including computer searches, when appropriate). Turnaround time is two weeks; replies are to-the-point and helpful. For best results, the problem, handicapping condition, and general age range should be provided. All individuals concerned with handicapped and gifted children are eligible for service.

M19 **ERIC CLEARINGHOUSE ON HIGHER EDUCATION (ERIC/HE)** George Washington University, Suite 630, One Dupont Cir., Washington, D.C. 20036. (202) 296-2597

Areas of interest are higher education (except junior college education and teacher education, which have their own clearinghouses) and English-language education. Its *Higher Education Research Report Series* (10 issues/year) is published by the American Association for Higher Education. Library holdings include approximately 4,000 documents, 25 periodicals, and an ERIC microfiche collection. The library is open from 9:00 a.m. to 5:00 p.m., Monday through Friday.

M20 **ERIC CLEARINGHOUSE ON RURAL EDUCATION AND SMALL SCHOOLS (ERIC/CRESS)** Box 3AP, New Mexico State University, Las Cruces, N.M. 88001. (505) 646-2623

ERIC/CRESS's primary interests are in American Indian education, Mexican-American education, migrant education, and outdoor education, as well as rural education and small schools. Collection includes literature covering the social and cultural characteristics of American (and international) rural populations. Its helpful quarterly, *ERIC/CRESS Newsletter,* free on request, is filled with cogent review articles, interesting sources, and lists of materials in its areas of interest. Monographs, synthesis papers, yearly updated subject bibliographies, curriculum guides, speeches, and journal articles emerge in large numbers from the clearinghouse. Some of its more interesting workshops involve collaboration with other groups, such as a four-week institute for librarians working with Mexican-Americans and American Indians, and similar joint workshops with teacher education groups.

Library holdings consist mostly of brochures and information pamphlets, a collection of local documents, copies of materials from other clearinghouses, and a complete ERIC microfiche collection. ERIC computer searches can be arranged for a $4 set-up fee, plus actual costs for computer and reproduction time. A full-time computer programmer is a member of its staff.

A satellite center of this clearinghouse, located at the University of North Dakota (Grand Forks, North Dakota 58201), holds copies of ERIC/CRESS publications and also acquires documents for ERIC Central.

M21 **ERIC CLEARINGHOUSE ON TEACHER EDUCATION (ERIC/SP)** Suite 616, One Dupont Cir., N.W., Washington, D.C. 20036. (202) 293-7280

Subject areas cover the selection, preparation, in-service training, and retirement of education personnel, including those in health, physical education, and recreation (but excluding those in outdoor education). Publications include a newsletter, as well as monographs available through the ERIC system. Also conducts workshops and seminars relating to ERIC and to teacher education.

Library holdings consist of 1,000 books, pamphlets, and documents, and a complete ERIC microfiche collection. While only a limited number of free ERIC computer searches are performed through this clearinghouse, on a first-come, first-served basis, users receive assistance in preparing or framing questions for computerized retrieval or are referred to other computer services—generally Systems Development Corporation—at an average cost of $20.

M22 **ERIC CLEARINGHOUSE ON URBAN EDUCATION (ERIC/ CUE)** Teachers College, Columbia University, Box 40, 525 W. 120th St., New York, N.Y. 10027. (212) 678-3437

Primary areas of interest are education of urban children and youth who have been handicapped by virtue of their economic, cultural, ethnic, or social status. The *IRCD Bulletin* ($4/year, four times/year) carries an analytic or review article and bibliography devoted to a single subject, the aim being to synthesize and formulate concepts and practices which will improve the development and educational achievement of urban children and youth, especially Blacks, Puerto Ricans, and Asian Americans. Copies or listings of the *Urban Disadvantaged Series* and the *Doctoral Research Series* also are available for $2.50 each. The former consists of state-of-the-art papers, brief reviews, and annotated bibliographies, often of documents available through the ERIC system. Each item in the series summarizes the existing literature about an aspect of the psycho-educational development of diverse urban populations. The latter is a group of annotated bibliographies of doctoral dissertations dealing with various aspects of the education of minority groups. Its *Equal Opportunity Review* presents, in ways that can be usefully implemented, brief over-views of research and practices relating to the education of diverse urban populations. They also point to trends in educational issues that can help to keep both the professional and lay communities informed.

Mail requests for publications are answered mostly by bibliographic compilations, but also by materials and referrals. Free manual and computerized searches for pertinent questions are performed on a limited basis.

Library holdings include 15,500 books and documents, 65 periodicals, and the entire ERIC microfiche collection. The library is open from 10:00 a.m. to 4:00 p.m. on Wednesdays and Fridays.

M23 **EUROPEAN DOCUMENTATION AND INFORMATION SYSTEM FOR EDUCATION (EUDISED)** Documentation Centre for Education in Europe, Council of Europe/Conseil de l'Europe, 67006 Strasbourg Cedex, France. Telephone 356,440
A multinational, multilingual, European counterpart to ERIC, which began in Strasbourg in 1968 with a meeting of representatives from Council of Europe states who were using or planning to use electronic computerized systems for processing educational information. EUDISED is intended to be a comprehensive, but decentralized, network to coordinate a wide variety of educational information, especially information relating to innovations and educational development.

Projects, thoughtfully designed to coordinate with and facilitate use of existing systems, include surveys of existing information systems and abstracting services, national projects, organization of networks for exchange of materials and information, standardization and coordination of record formats and computer systems, and development of national committees and of special or national educational documentation centers as needed.

EUDISED reports on its activities through an *Information Bulletin* and a newsletter, *EUDISED News*, as well as through an excellent series of *EUDISED Technical Reports*, issued yearly, and fairly accessible in scholarly education libraries. Its *EUDISED Multilingual Thesaurus* (Paris and The Hague, Mouton Publ., 1973) is available in French, English, and

German. Other publications (free or low-cost) can be obtained from its Strasbourg office. As a facilitation center, it is a good source to contact for information on national, multinational, and international organizations of related scope and interests, such as the Council for Educational Technology for the United Kingdom, the European Bureau of Adult Education (EBAE), and the International Bureau of Education. Its cross-cultural, multilingual approach has much potential for American education.

M24 **HUMAN RELATIONS AREA FILES (HRAF)** 755 Prospect St., New Haven, Conn. 06520. (203) 777-2334
This substantial data bank and research tool, designed for cross-cultural research in anthropology and related behavioral disciplines, is an important research aid for anyone interested in researching the cross-cultural aspects of education and topics related to education. HRAF is a unique, direct-access, social science information retrieval system based on a complete line-by-line, page-by-page analysis and classification of nearly 3,000,000 page references for more than 4,000 selected sources, covering some 300 nations and cultures. The files are arranged first by culture and then by 710 numeric subject categories (79 broad subjects), based on George P. Murdock's *Outline of Cultural Materials* (4th Revised Edition, New Haven, Conn., 1969), with extensive cross-referencing. Section 87 deals with formal education; other sections, which constitute a rich lode for educational research, include 85 – Infancy and Childhood, 86 – Socialization, 88 – Adolescence, and 15 – Behavior Process and Personality. The files are not designed for current information, but are a resource file of substantive descriptive data, largely ethnographic accounts of nonwestern cultures. While these are continuously expanded, the time lag between original publication and integration into the files is at least one year. The complete files, in 5″× 8″ paper format, are distributed to HRAF's 24 supporting member institutions. The HRAF-Microfiles, a limited version of material from the paper files, on 3″ × 5″ microfiche, are distributed in annual series of approximately 100,000 file pages to some 200 associate member institutions throughout the United States and around the world. Although hours and accessibility vary, these collections are generally open to researchers and educators. A list of available files may be obtained from HRAF upon written request.

M25 **INFORMATION CENTER OF INSTRUCTIONAL TECHNOLOGY** Academy for Educational Development, 1424 16th St., N.W., Washington, D.C. 20036. (202) 265-5576 and 265-3336
Sponsored by the Academy for Educational Development, this center is

a resource facility for educators in newly developing countries who are interested in applications of educational technology. Its library collection includes films, filmstrips, and radio and television tapes, as well as books, reports, and other documents. The center is creating an international clearinghouse for exchange of information and materials on educational technology, with areas of expertise ranging through training sources, media sources, and financial sources, as well as professional and trade associations. It invites visitors and welcomes requests for information. A directory, *Sources of Information and Assistance on Educational Technology for Development* (available free, on request), provides names, addresses, and brief descriptions of more than 100 organizations involved in educational reform projects in newly developing countries.

M26 **NATIONAL ASSESSMENT OF EDUCATIONAL PROGRESS (NAEP)** Education Commission of the States, 200 Lincoln Tower, 1860 Lincoln St., Denver, Colo. 80203. (303) 893-5200

An annual survey of the knowledge, skills, understanding, and attitudes of 80,000 to 100,000 young Americans ages 9, 13, and 17 and young adults between the ages of 26 and 35, which began to collect information in 1969. Its goals are to gather and make available comprehensive data on the educational attainments of young Americans and to measure the growth and/or decline in subject-area attainments. Ten subject areas are currently under assessment (two each year under a revolving plan): citizenship, science, writing, music, mathematics, literature, social studies, reading, art, and career and occupational development. Achievements are matched by geographic region, community size and type, sex, color, and parental education. An NAEP newsletter reports current activities and is available free from the above address. Both national and group reports of results in science, citizenship, writing, and reading, ranging in price from $1.00 to $1.75, are available from the U.S. Government Printing Office. These are listed in the *Education Price List* (D19) and are noted in NAEP publications and in the *Monthly Catalog of United States Government Publications. Update on Education: A Digest of the National Association of Educational Progress* (1975, $5.75) presents summaries and in-depth reports on NAEP assessments in science, social studies, music, literature, reading, writing, and citizenship. To get on its mailing list, write for a copy of *Questions and Answers About NAEP.*

A Department of Utilization Applications has been created to collect and disseminate information on how results are used, which information can be valuable for local and state assessment projects, curriculum design, instructional materials development, and teacher education.

Since early 1975, national assessment data has been made available on magnetic computer tape for use or purchase by individuals or institutions outside the NAEP system. These tapes, broken down by NAEP variables—sex, color (black and white), level of parental education, geographic region, and size and type of community—are available at $78 each for the separate age levels (9, 13, 17, and young adults 26 to 35) participating in NAEP surveys. Tapes can be ordered through EDSTAT-Tapes, National Center for Education Statistics, Room 3069, FOB-6, 400 Maryland Avenue, S.W., Washington, D.C. 20202.

M27 **NATIONAL COMMISSION ON RESOURCES FOR YOUTH, INC. (NCRY)** 36 W. 44th St., New York, N.Y. 10036. (212) 682-3339

This nonprofit organization, founded in 1967, collects and disseminates information about innovative programs which enable youth to become active participants in their communities and schools through involvement in decision making and through provision of services to others. NCRY distributes how-to-do-it information about youth participation programs on film, videotape, and in print; it also develops model programs. Youth Tutoring Youth and the Youth Helper in Day Care programs are two models which have been implemented broadly. To learn more about NCRY materials and programs, write for its free quarterly newsletter, *Resources for Youth.*

M28 **NATIONAL COUNCIL FOR ACCREDITATION OF TEACHER EDUCATION (NCATE)** 1750 Pennsylvania Ave., N.W., Washington, D.C. 20006. (202) 298-7118

A nonprofit, voluntary accrediting body devoted exclusively to the evaluation and accreditation of teacher education programs; the only national agency in this field. NCATE cooperates and shares information with six regional accrediting agencies. It is the current source of information on the accreditation status of teacher education programs and will make available up-to-date information on different aspects of these programs. Its *Annual List,* free on request, is a convenient listing—by state—of the names of all accredited teacher education institutions, with the accreditation status of each shown by symbol in appropriate columns; based on accreditation visits, which usually take place every 10 years.

M29 **NATIONAL EDUCATION ASSOCIATION (NEA)** Staff Library, 1201 16th St., N.W., Washington, D.C. 20036. (202) 833-5473

Designed primarily to serve the staff of NEA, this library is open for public use. Its collection, which includes 20,000 books, 10,000 pamphlets, 700 periodicals, and a complete ERIC microfiche collection, embraces all aspects of public education in the United States and is particularly strong on statistics, legislation, and teacher-centered materials. A good source for interlibrary loan.

M30 **NATIONAL INSTITUTE OF MENTAL HEALTH (NIMH)** National Clearinghouse for Mental Health Information, Communication Center, 5600 Fishers Lane, Rockville, Md. 20852. (301) 443-4278

Subject areas of this mental health collection of 7,000 books and 500 periodicals (plus NIMH documents and bibliographies and mental health reports) include psychiatry, psychology, sociology, and other biomedical, social, and behavioral sciences related to public health. Services are primarily for the NIMH staff, but at the discretion of the librarian are available to nongovernmental students and researchers engaged in professional study or research. Computer searches of data banks are performed for professionals only. Data banks used include those of the National Clearinghouse for Mental Health Information and the National Library of Medicine (MEDLARS and MEDLINE). The institute is a prime source of information on the mental health aspects of education. A free list of publications, as well as single free copies of publications, will be sent upon written request.

M31 **NATIONAL REFERRAL CENTER** Science and Technology Div., Library of Congress, 10 First St., S.E., Washington, D.C. 20540. (202) 426-5670

This agency of the Library of Congress is a guide to individuals and institutions with specialized subject knowledge and/or experience which can be used as sources of information, especially in fields of science, social science, and technology. It also compiles information on agencies, etc., which can provide various types of information. Its holdings include 9,000 records of information sources in science, technology, and social sciences, maintained on a current basis and indexed by subject. A referral service is available, which refers inquirers to relevant institutions, individuals, and services. Requests may be made in person, by mail, or by telephone. Replies are rapid and to-the-point. For best results, the center's Request for Referral Service form (see Figure 12) should be used; requests should be as specific as possible. The center is user-oriented and maintains an ongoing evaluation of its services through an appraisal form.

　　Publications include a six-volume *Directory of Information Resources in the United States;* the *Social Sciences* volume (B34) and the *Federal Government* volume (B33) are discussed in Chapter 3. Other volumes cover *Water, General Toxicology, Physical Sciences and Engineering,* and *Biological Sciences.*

NATIONAL REFERRAL CENTER FOR SCIENCE AND TECHNOLOGY
Library of Congress, Washington, D. C. 20540

_____
(Date)

REQUEST FOR REFERRAL SERVICE

(Please print or use typewriter and fill in as completely as possible.)

PERSON SUBMITTING: _____ TITLE: _____

NAME OF ORGANIZATION: _____

ADDRESS: _____

_____ TEL: _____

REQUEST: (Please be precise in stating your area of interest and the information
desired. Specific requests are more satisfactorily answered than are general
requests. Also, our response will be expedited if you use a separate form for
each request, and if you give any information which will affect the search for
resources.)

_____

_____

_____

_____

_____

_____

_____

RESOURCES ALREADY CONTACTED OR CONSULTED: (Without this guidance, either general or
specific, the Center may suggest resources already well known to you.)

_____

_____

_____

SPECIAL QUALIFICATIONS: (Inquirers are referred to resources only when it is expected
that they meet whatever qualifications or limits the resources may place on their
services. Please indicate if you are participating in a Government contract, are
affiliated with a recognized research project, hold membership in a professional
society or trade association, or have other special relationships that may apply.)

_____

_____

_____

TYPE OF REPLY WANTED: Letter _____ Telephone _____ Wire _____ Personal Pickup _____

83-42 (8/64)

FIGURE 12 The National Referral Center's Request for Referral Service form,
which is used to obtain detailed background information.

From time to time, it issues selected list(s) of information resources. Some recent titles in this series of interest to educators are *Selected Information Resources and Materials for Environmental Education, Selected Information Resources on Vocational Education,* and *Selected Information Resources on Science Education.*

M32   **NEXUS**   American Assn. for Higher Education, Suite 780, One Dupont Cir., N.W., Washington, D.C. 20036. (202) 785-8480

A telephone referral system dealing with all aspects of postsecondary education. A "people bank," NEXUS uses the telephone to connect people who need information with people who can provide it. Call or write for a detailed brochure.

M33   **U.S. BUREAU OF EDUCATIONAL AND CULTURAL AF-FAIRS**   U.S. Department of State, Office of Public Information and Reports, Room 4323, 2201 C St., N.W., Washington, D.C. 20520. (202) 632-3175

Under the Fulbright-Hays Mutual Educational and Cultural Exchange Act of 1961, the Bureau of Educational and Cultural Affairs was made responsible for leadership and coordination of international, educational, scientific, and cultural exchange activities throughout the Federal Government. Its own exchange activities involve students, teachers, professors, government officials, and leaders in science, education, labor, the arts, and other fields. It also provides encouragement and, in some cases, financial assistance to private organizations involved in similar activities. In effect, it is the center of a network of private and governmental "people-to-people" programs, and can serve as a guide or directory to related organizations and programs.

Its pamphlet library is open from 8:45 a.m. to 5:30 p.m. Publications, available on request, include an annual report, *International Exchange; Partners in Exchange,* a discussion and classified listing of some of the organizations involved in exchange programs; and *A Word of Caution,* which discusses sources of information on educational summer opportunities abroad.

15 | Nonprint Sources of Government and Financial Information

This chapter lists prime sources of information on finance and government (including legislation) in education—official bodies, special libraries, and federal agencies. Also included are a few advocacy agencies, although they are not information agencies per se; their concern with certain issues requires that they keep fully informed and that they make use of this information. The few federal organizations, offices, and bureaus listed in this chapter (N23 and N24) are responsible for answering inquiries or referring individuals to other sources of information. Information leading to other federal agencies can be found in the directories listed in Chapter 3. The *Directory of Information Sources: Federal Government* (B33) is a prime and current source for federal agencies, as is the National Referral Center (M31). The *United States Government Manual* (B48) also can lead to sources and documents. Other directories listed lead to state personnel and state agencies.

Research tools most useful in the fields of government and finance in education are discussed within the texts, annotations, and introduction to Chapter 8.

Two advocacy organizations, the Black Child Development Institute (M3) and the Day Care and Child Development Council of America (M8), are good sources of information on legislation in their areas of interest. Their newsletters provide excellent in-

depth reports on national and local legislation and funding. The
Council for Exceptional Children, listed as an ERIC clearinghouse
(M18), is considered the prime source of information on legisla-
tion concerned with handicapped children.

N1   **ADVISORY COMMISSION ON INTERGOVERNMENTAL
     RELATIONS (ACIR)**   726 Jackson Pl., N.W., Washington, D.C.
     20575. (202) 382-4953
This commission, established in 1959, is a 26-member, bipartisan,
permanent national body that monitors the operations of the federal
system concerning intergovernmental issues. Its membership consists of
representatives from legislative and executive branches of federal, state,
and local governments and the general public. It is financed largely
through congressional appropriations, plus token contributions from
some states and large cities; also will accept foundation grants for special
projects.
   In addition to commission policy reports and its state legislative
program, ACIR services include background and information publications and an annual report on the state of the federal system; preparation and wide distribution of four-page summaries of major findings;
periodic information bulletins and an information interchange service;
plus an intergovernmental relations library. Its publications are distributed through the U.S. Government Printing Office and the National
Technical Information Service. Single free copies often are available
directly from the commission. Titles of interest to individuals concerned
with educational administration and financing include *State Action on
Local Problems, Who Should Pay for the Public Schools?, Federalism and the
Academic Community,* plus many well-researched reports on such areas as
revenue sharing.

N2   **AMERICAN PARENTS COMMITTEE, INC. (APC)**   52 Van-
     derbilt Ave., New York, N.Y. 10017. (212) 685-4400; and 1346
     Connecticut Ave., N.W., Washington, D.C. 20036. (202) 785-3169
Incorporated in 1947, this is a membership, nonprofit, nonpartisan
public service association working for the enactment of federal legislation to benefit the nation's 75 million children. Although it is a lobby
group rather than an information organization, it is thoroughly aware of
all aspects of federal legislation that affects children. Its board of
directors adopts yearly Federal Legislative Goals on Behalf of Children,
while APC works for congressional action on these goals, concentrating
on obtainable measurements. Its *Washington Report on Legislation for
Children* is discussed in G36.

N3   **BILL STATUS SYSTEM**   Committee on House Administration, 2401-A Rayburn House Office Bldg., Washington, D.C. 20515. (202) 225-1772; 51772 for congressional users.

The Bill Status System, a computerized system which began operations in February 1973, is designed to record, store, and disseminate legislative information on bills and resolutions introduced in Congress. Intended primarily for congressional and committee offices, this service can provide either printed or verbal legislative status reports on bills or resolutions introduced in either house. The printed "hard copy" reports (see Figure 13) are computer printouts detailing the status of each bill to date. These are available to individuals connected with Congress, on-demand, or automatically if a congressman or a committee requests updating of particular bills. Although the service is oriented to congressional needs, any individual can telephone the Bill Status Office and receive, at no cost, current information on the official status of any bill. To facilitate queries, it is desirable to provide some of the following information: number or official title of the bill, date of introduction, sponsor, and committee title. For an informative pamphlet on this new system, write: Director, House Information Systems, 1632 Longworth House Office Building, Washington, D.C. 20515.

N4   **CALIFORNIA SCHOOL BOARDS ASSOCIATION (CSBA)**   Policy Reference Library, Suite 201, 800 9th St., Sacramento, Calif. 95814. (916) 443-4691

A policy reference library comprised of more than 900 California school district policy manuals and other related materials. Services to CSBA members include classes in district policy development, mailing of sample school district policies on specific topics requested, and reviews of California school district employer-employee relations. The library and classes are intended primarily for school board members, but may be open to teachers, administrators, and private citizens on request.

N5   **CITIZENS CONFERENCE ON STATE LEGISLATURES**   Research Library, 4722 Broadway, Kansas City, Mo. 64112. (816) 531-8104

The primary function of this organization is to study state legislatures, which increasingly are setting educational policies. The research library includes books, news articles, pamphlets, periodicals, brochures, etc., relating to state legislatures and to other important state and national issues such as education and state finance. Its competent staff will answer questions and perform research relating to state legislation for legislative groups, other government groups, or individuals.

```
MARCH 18, 1974              BILL STATUS OFFICE                 PAGE   1
                       U.S. HOUSE OF REPRESENTATIVES

                    DETAIL STATUS PROFILE FOR   H.R.9639


SPONSOR........... PERKINS

DATE INTRODUCED... JUL 26, 73

HOUSE COMMITTEE... EDUCATION AND LABOR

SENATE COMMITTEE.. AGRICULTURE AND FORESTRY

TITLE............. A BILL TO AMEND THE NATIONAL SCHOOL LUNCH AND
                   CHILD NUTRITION ACTS FOR THE PURPOSE OF PROVIDING
                   ADDITIONAL FEDERAL FINANCIAL ASSISTANCE TO THE
                   SCHOOL LUNCH AND SCHOOL BREAKFAST PROGRAMS

    JUL 26, 73 REFERRED TO HOUSE COMMITTEE ON EDUCATION AND LABOR.

        SEP  6, 73 FIRST DAY OF COMMITTEE CONSIDERATION AND MARK-UP
                   SESSION.

        SEP  6, 73 FINAL DAY OF COMMITTEE CONSIDERATION AND MARK-UP
                   SESSION.

        SEP  6, 73 ORDERED TO BE REPORTED WITH AMENDMENTS.

        SEP 11, 73 REPORTED TO HOUSE WITH AMENDMENTS BY HOUSE COMMITTEE
                   ON EDUCATION AND LABOR.   REPORT NO: 93-458.

    SEP  6, 73 RULES COMMITTEE HEARING REQUESTED.

    SEP 11, 73 PLACED ON UNION CALENDAR, NO: 210.

    SEP 12, 73 RULES COMMITTEE HEARING REQUESTED.

    SEP 13, 73 HEARINGS HELD BY COMMITTEE ON RULES.

    SEP 13, 73 RULE ORDERED TO BE REPORTED PROVIDING AN OPEN RULE WITH
               1 HOUR OF DEBATE.   PARTIAL WAIVER OF POINTS OF ORDER.

    SEP 13, 73 RULES COMMITTEE RESOLUTION H.RES.543 REPORTED TO HOUSE.

    SEP 13, 73 RULE PASSED HOUSE.

    SEP 13, 73 PASSED HOUSE (AMENDED) BY YEA-NAY VOTE: 389 - 4.

    SEP 17, 73 REFERRED TO SENATE COMMITTEE ON AGRICULTURE AND
               FORESTRY.

        SEP 21, 73 REPORTED TO SENATE WITH AMENDMENTS BY SENATE
                   COMMITTEE ON AGRICULTURE AND FORESTRY.   REPORT NO:
                   93-404.

    SEP 24, 73 PASSED SENATE WITH SENATE AMENDMENTS BY YEA-NAY VOTE: 83
```

FIGURE 13   Computer printouts such as this from the Bill Status System are available to individuals connected with Congress. Information also can be obtained via telephone.

N6   **COUNCIL OF STATE GOVERNMENTS**   Iron Works Pike, P.O. Box 5577, Lexington, Ky. 40505. (606) 252-2291

A joint agency of all state governments—created, supported, and directed by them. It conducts research on state programs and problems; maintains an information service available to state agencies, officials, and legislators; assists in state-federal liaison; promotes regional and state-local cooperation; and provides staff for affiliated organizations.

The council has the resources, willingness, and expertise to search and collate information in areas related to the states. It issues a variety of publications on legislation, state government, and finance, including *Book of the States* (G2) and *State Government News* (G32), which are backed by extensive collections of unpublished data. A publications list is available on request. Complimentary copies of publications are available to state officials and legislators.

The major office of the Council of State Governments is located in Lexington, Kentucky, and most materials are available from that office. Local offices, which can be extremely helpful, are located in New York City, Chicago, Atlanta, Washington, D.C., and San Francisco.

Eastern: 36 West 44th Street, New York, New York 10036, (212) 687-0559.

Midwestern: 203 North Wabash Avenue, Chicago, Illinois 60601, (312) 236-4011.

Southern: 3384 Peachtree Road, N.E., Atlanta, Georgia 30326, (404) 266-1271.

Washington: 1150 17th Street, N.W., Washington, D.C. 20036, (202) 785-5610.

Western: 85 Post Street, San Francisco, California 94104, (415) 986-3760.

N7   **EDUCATION COMMISSION OF THE STATES**   ECS Resource Center, 300 Lincoln Tower, 1860 Lincoln St., Denver, Colo. 80203. (303) 893-5200

An outgrowth of the National Governor's Conference of 1965, the Education Commission is an extremely important source of information—one of the few that covers the interests of legislators, educators, and school officials. It now has 47 members (45 states and 2 territories), with an operating body consisting of seven representatives from each member state (including the governor), two members of each state legislature, and four persons active in education. Since its function is to provide communication among states on educational matters, it collects information on all the states; authorizes studies; collects, analyzes, and disseminates current educational finance information; and is a clearinghouse for information on existing and proposed education legislation.

Its resource center is a special library of more than 500 subjects, both within the framework of education and legislation, as well as where the two intersect. Holdings include more than 4,000 cataloged items: books, speeches, reports, monographs, and pamphlets, including many state documents not widely available elsewhere. Also included are 590 newsletters by state departments of education, state legislative councils, state NEA's and AFT's, higher education agencies, and other national educational and governmental organizations, plus 150 periodicals. ERIC and *CIJE* computer searches are performed for its staff. Although the library is open to the general public, it is primarily intended for use by ECS staff. Self-service facilities are available to a limited number of competent researchers; library staff members are most helpful with specific queries.

Publications include state-by-state analyses of major education legislation, two free newsletters (see G11 and G12), bibliographies prepared by the resource center prior to their annual meeting, the *State Education Leaders Directory* (B5), and others which can be found through the index of this *Directory*. A complete publication list is available on request.

The Education Commission is the operating agent for the National Assessment of Educational Progress (M26) and a major source of information on higher education.

N8   **EDUCATION FUNDING RESEARCH COUNCIL (EFRC)**   752
National Press Bldg., Washington, D.C. 20004. (202) 347-6342
This is a nonprofit membership organization, established in May 1971, to serve school administrators and others needing accurate and current information on federal education funding. Full membership ($176/year) or associate membership ($96/year) affords access to a number of publications and services. The associate membership includes *Education Funding News* (biweekly on Fridays), an excellent publication providing information on federal aid to education, slanted toward the needs of public schools; and *Federal Register Watch* (biweekly), which thoroughly scans the *Federal Register* for relevant regulations, rules, and deadlines. Both of these publications specialize in understandable summaries, relevant dates, and complete information (including phone numbers and names of individuals) on the federal offices which should be contacted. Full membership includes both of these publications, plus a more personalized and more mechanized retrieval service. A five-minute weekly taped summary of what is happening vis-à-vis Congress and education is available to members 24 hours a day by calling a special EFRC congressional report telephone number. An information HOTLINE, also available to members by telephone, covers the entire range of education funding and procedures at the federal levels: who's doing what, how much money is available, laws, guidelines, regulations, and

referral to other sources. A retrieval service locates information and materials requested by phone or letter. Extra services include proposal research at $18 an hour (minimum charge of two hours); proposal kits, for such subjects as career education and funding for the handicapped, available at various prices starting at $45; and seminars related to EFRC's areas of interest.

N9 **FEDERAL INFORMATION CENTERS** U.S. General Services Administration, 18th and F Sts., N.W., Washington, D.C. 20405. (202) 755-8660

There are, as of January 1975, approximately 60 Federal Information Centers, located in 34 states. These centers, a joint venture of the U.S. General Services Administration and the U.S. Civil Service Commission, act as focal points for local, national, and international federal information and, in some instances, can provide information on local or state governments. As clearinghouses or information coordinators of federal information, they answer some questions directly and refer others to appropriate local sources or to individuals in one of the government agencies. The Washington office can provide telephone numbers and locations of local offices, which sometimes can provide information on local educational jurisdictions, activities, and funding.

N10 **THE FOUNDATION CENTER** 888 Seventh Ave., New York, N.Y. 10019. (212) 752-1433; 1001 Connecticut Ave., N.W., Washington, D.C. 20036. (202) 347-1400; The Chicago Community Trust, Suite 840, 280 S. LaSalle St., Chicago, Ill. 60604. (312) 372-3356

This major source of information on foundations includes three reference libraries which specialize in collecting and analyzing materials on foundations. The Foundation Center, which has always provided good tools for learning about philanthropy and foundations, lately has been introducing improved indexing and disseminating tools, including a computerized Foundation Grants Data Bank. Library catalogs include information on more than 20,000 foundations, listed alphabetically by name. Files include the Internal Revenue Service's IRS 990-A forms from 1962 to 1969, which list officers, assets, grants, foundation reports, newsletters, and newspaper clippings. From 1970 on, the IRS 990 forms are in indexed microfilm and microfiche format. *Foundation News* includes the *Foundation Grants Index* which, from 1973 on, indexes grants of $5,000 or more. These are listed geographically (by state), then by foundation name, with keyword indexes. The reference collection consists of books and articles on philanthropy and foundations. Reference libraries are open to the public from 9:00 a.m. to 5:00 p.m.,

Monday through Friday. Services include factual data on foundations and are furnished via mail, Xerox copies, or phone. IRS forms are supplied on microfiche (15 pages for $0.15) and in hard copy ($0.25/ page). The New York headquarters office can arrange for a $15 custom computer search of its Foundation Grants Data Bank.

The Data Bank, established in 1972, is a computerized file of approximately 20,000 foundation grants, which adds approximately 1,000 items every two months. It does not include information on structure, personnel, assets, or philosophies of the foundations. Custom searches may be made for a minimum fee of $15 per search for up to 50 grant records; $0.20 per grant thereafter. The file can be searched by subject, key term, and foundation or recipient name. The printout can be arranged alphabetically by foundation or recipient name, geographically by state, or in order of increasing or decreasing dollar amount. Other custom searches can involve statistical data, frequency data, or searches omitting certain categories. A custom search request form, available on request, is reprinted in the October 1973 *Foundation Center Information Quarterly.*

Major publications include the *Foundation Directory* (G57) and *Foundation News* (G58), which now incorporates the *Foundation Grants Index.*

In accordance with the center's policy to expand its public service through regional collections, a number of collections have recently been established. Following is a list of all collections to date, with their addresses and geographical coverage. National collections covering the entire United States are located at The Foundation Center libraries in New York City and Washington, D.C., and at The Chicago Community Trust.

State	Name	Geographical Coverage
Alabama	Birmingham Public Library 2020 Seventh Avenue, North Birmingham 35203	Alabama
Arkansas	Little Rock Public Library Reference Department 700 Louisiana Street Little Rock 72201	Arkansas
California	University Research Library Reference Department University of California Los Angeles 90024	Alaska, Arizona, California, Colorado, Hawaii, Nevada, Utah
	San Francisco Public Library Business Branch 530 Kearny Street San Francisco 94108	Alaska, California, Colorado, Hawaii, Idaho, Montana, Nevada, Oregon, Utah, Washington, Wyoming

State	Name	Geographical Coverage
Colorado	Denver Public Library Sociology Division 1357 Broadway Denver 80203	Colorado
Connecticut	Hartford Public Library Reference Department 500 Main Street Hartford 06103	Connecticut, Massachusetts, Rhode Island
Florida	Jacksonville Public Library Business, Science and Industry Department 122 North Ocean Street Jacksonville 32202	Florida
	Miami-Dade Public Library Florida Collection One Biscayne Boulevard Miami 33132	Florida
Georgia	Atlanta Public Library 126 Carnegie Way, N.W. Atlanta 30303	Alabama, Florida, Georgia, Kentucky, Mississippi, North Carolina, South Carolina, Tennessee, Virginia
Hawaii	Thomas Hale Hamilton Library Social Science Reference 2550 The Mall Honolulu 96822	California, Hawaii, Oregon, Washington
Illinois	The Newberry Library 60 West Walton Street Chicago 60610	Illinois, Indiana, Michigan, Minnesota, North Dakota, South Dakota, Wisconsin
Iowa	Des Moines Public Library 100 Locust Street Des Moines 50309	Iowa
Kansas	Topeka Public Library Adult Services Department 1515 West Tenth Street Topeka 66604	Kansas
Kentucky	Louisville Free Public Library Fourth and York Streets Louisville 40203	Kentucky
Louisiana	New Orleans Public Library Business and Science Division 219 Loyola Avenue New Orleans 70140	Louisiana

State	*Name*	*Geographical Coverage*
Maryland	Enoch Pratt Free Library 400 Cathedral Street Baltimore 21201	Maryland
Massachusetts	Associated Foundation of Greater Boston One Boston Place, Suite 948 Boston 02108	Connecticut, Maine, Massachusetts, New Hampshire, Rhode Island, Vermont
	Boston Public Library Copley Square Boston 02117	Massachusetts
Michigan	Henry Ford Centennial Library 15301 Michigan Avenue Dearborn 48126	Michigan
	Grand Rapids Public Library Sociology and Education Department Grand Rapids 49502	Michigan
Minnesota	Minneapolis Public Library Sociology Department 300 Nicollet Mall Minneapolis 55401	Iowa, Minnesota, North Dakota, South Dakota
Mississippi	Jackson Metropolitan Library 301 North State Street Jackson 39201	Mississippi
Missouri	Linda Hall Library Science and Technology 5109 Cherry Street Kansas City 64110	Kansas, Missouri
	The Danforth Foundation Library 222 South Central Avenue St. Louis 63105	Iowa, Kansas, Missouri, Nebraska
Nebraska	Omaha Public Library 1823 Harney Street Omaha 68102	Nebraska
New Hampshire	The New Hampshire Charitable Fund One South Street Concord 03301	New Hampshire
New Jersey	New Jersey State Library Reference Section 185 West State Street Trenton 08625	New Jersey

State	Name	Geographical Coverage
New York	New York State Library State Education Department Education Building Albany 12224	New York
	Levittown Public Library Reference Department One Bluegrass Lane Levittown 11756	New York
	Rochester Public Library Business and Social Sciences Division 15 South Avenue Rochester 14604	New York
North Carolina	William R. Perkins Library Duke University Durham 27706	North Carolina
Ohio	The Cleveland Foundation Library 700 National City Bank Building Cleveland 44114	Michigan, Ohio, Pennsylvania, West Virginia
Oklahoma	Oklahoma City Community Foundation 1300 North Broadway Oklahoma City 73103	Oklahoma
Oregon	Library Association of Portland Education and Psychology Department 801 S.W. Tenth Avenue Portland 97205	Alaska, California, Hawaii, Oregon, Washington
Pennsylvania	The Free Library of Philadelphia Logan Square Philadelphia 19103	Delaware, New Jersey, Pennsylvania
	Hillman Library University of Pittsburgh Pittsburgh 15213	Pennsylvania
Rhode Island	Providence Public Library Reference Department 150 Empire Street Providence 02903	Rhode Island

256

State	Name	Geographical Coverage
South Carolina	South Carolina State Library Reader Services Department 1500 Senate Street Columbia 29211	South Carolina
Tennessee	Memphis Public Library 1850 Peabody Avenue Memphis 38104	Tennessee
Texas	The Hogg Foundation for Mental Health The University of Texas Austin 78712	Arkansas, Louisiana, New Mexico, Oklahoma, Texas
	Dallas Public Library History and Social Sciences Division 1954 Commerce Street Dallas 75201	Texas
Utah	Salt Lake City Public Library Information and Adult Services 209 East Fifth Street Salt Lake City 84111	Utah
Virginia	Richmond Public Library Business, Science & Technol- ogy Department 101 East Franklin Street Richmond 23219	Virginia
Washington	Seattle Public Library 1000 Fourth Avenue Seattle 98104	Washington
West Virginia	Kanawha County Public Library 123 Capitol Street Charleston 25301	West Virginia
Wisconsin	Marquette University Memorial Library 1415 West Wisconsin Avenue Milwaukee 53233	Illinois, Indiana, Iowa, Michigan, Minnesota, Ohio, Wisconsin
Wyoming	Laramie County Community College Library 1400 East College Drive Cheyenne 82001	Wyoming

N11 **FUNDING SOURCES CLEARINGHOUSE, INC. (FSC)** 2600 Bancroft Way, Berkeley, Calif. 94704. (415) 548-5880; and 116 S. Michigan Ave., Chicago, Ill. 60603. (312) 346-2521

A private, nonprofit research organization founded in 1971 for the express purpose of matching grant seekers with grant makers. Its files of more than 50,000 grant programs (updated daily from a perusal of 3,700 periodicals and 600 major newspapers) are in computer format. Approximately 500 grant programs—from foundations, government, corporate, and private funding sources—are added each month. Membership ($50 annually) is limited to educational, cultural, research, and community organizations and other nonprofit groups. Members are entitled to unlimited computerized searches for their projects. Structured search application forms (one for each project) are computer-matched with donors in 6 to 10 areas, including interests, purposes, funding levels, geographical considerations, and types of grant awards. Prospective reports on potential donors average three to five pages in length and cost $1.85 per page. These include summary sheets, basic information, contact person, financial data, current priorities, recent representative grants, and application information. Biographical profiles are compiled on foundation officers and trustees for $1 each. Membership also includes an excellent biweekly newsletter, *Grants Daily Monitor,* which covers recent developments relating to grants, and provides reference services and "How To" guides covering all types of development, including proposal writing.

N12 **JOINT REFERENCE LIBRARY** 1313 E. 60th St., Chicago, Ill. 60637. (312) 947-2162

A clearinghouse on public administration for research staff of other agencies. Its specialized collection includes 20,000 books, 60,000 pamphlets, and 500 periodicals. A good source of information on local documents dealing with government issues. Its semimonthly publication, *Recent Publications on Governmental Problems* ($15/year), provides current information on governmental areas, including education, and is a guide to other sources.

N13 **LAWYERS' COMMITTEE FOR CIVIL RIGHTS UNDER LAW** Suite 520, 733 15th St., N.W., Washington, D.C. 20005. (202) 628-6700

A committee of lawyers formed in 1963 at the request of President Kennedy for the purpose of promoting enforcement, protecting civil rights, and assisting the American legal profession in discharging its responsibilities to racial minorities and the poor. It is a source of information on education litigation (and a part of the litigation in some cases); recently assisted in the compilation of an impressive comparative study of education laws of the United States and of the fifty states (G34).

N14 **LEAGUE OF WOMEN VOTERS OF THE UNITED STATES** 1730 M St., N.W., Washington, D.C. 20036. (202) 296-1770

This is the headquarters of the League of Women Voters, a volunteer, nonpartisan citizens' organization (now open to men) whose major expertise is in the evaluation of governmental functions and activities, national governments through a national league, and state and local governments through state and local leagues. The school survey developed by the league is reviewed in Chapter 13. As of 1973, approximately 33 state leagues had ongoing "positions" in education, which involved, in most cases, thorough studies and reports on state and local educational administration and functions. These reports generally are highly competent, accurate, time-saving compilations of basic information, well-organized for action and comprehension. A list of state league programs can be checked against a list of state league offices to locate those currently studying state policies. Both lists are available from the national league at no cost.

N15 **METROPOLITAN ASSOCIATION FOR PHILANTHRO-PY** 607 N. Grand Blvd., St. Louis, Mo. 63103. (314) 535-9956

An informal clearinghouse for eight St. Louis foundations, with information on others in the area.

N16 **NATIONAL CLEARINGHOUSE FOR LEGAL SERVICES** Suite 2220, 500 N. Michigan Ave., Chicago, Ill. 60611. (312) 943-2866

This clearinghouse is the publications center and information exchange of the National Legal Services Corporation. It provides a central repository of poverty law materials produced by legal services lawyers and distributes these to legal services attorneys and others. Library holdings include 500 books, 1,000 pamphlets, 150 periodicals, and 17,000 indexed pleadings, legal memoranda, briefs, decisions, and practice handbooks. Original texts of all materials are cataloged and numbered. Civil rights cases include many relating to students and education, as well as many concerning legal areas peripheral to education, such as adoption, consumer law, dependent children, employment, environment, freedom of speech, health, Indians, juveniles, legislation, mental health, migrant workers, and women's rights. Copies are available at a nominal cost. For more information, see *Clearinghouse Review* (G3).

N17 **NATIONAL ENDOWMENT FOR THE ARTS** 2401 E St., N.W., Washington, D.C. 20506. (202) 634-6369

An independent agency of the Federal Government which awards grants to individuals and nonprofit organizations concerned with the arts, in the fields of architecture, environmental arts, dance, education, expansion arts, crafts, literature, museums, music, public media, theatre, and the visual arts. Grants to organizations must be matched dollar for dollar; grants to individuals carry no matching proviso. Its Artists-in-Schools program is described in *Artists in Schools,* co-authored by the National Endowment for the Arts and the U.S. Office of Education (Washington, D.C., U.S. Government Printing Office, 1973; $2.50). Write to its Program Information Office for a current briefing on publications and availability of funds.

N18 **NATIONAL INSTITUTE OF EDUCATION (NIE)** U.S. Department of Health, Education, and Welfare, 1200 19th St., N.W., Washington, D.C. 20208. (202) 254-5800

The National Institute of Education was created by Congress in 1972 to help solve the problems of American education through research and development. Institute policy is set by the National Council on Educational Research, a panel of distinguished citizens appointed by the President.

Now in its fourth year, the institute has developed a problem-oriented program responsive to the concerns of Congress and the education community. Programs, focused on both academic and administrative problems of schools, are being conducted through competitive contracts and grants with research institutions, state education agencies, schools or school districts, universities, and individuals throughout the United States.

NIE's six program areas are Basic Skills, Education and Work, Finance and Productivity, School Capacity for Problem Solving, Educational Equity, and Dissemination. A brochure describing these programs is available from the institute's Office of Public Affairs.

N19 **NATIONAL ORGANIZATION ON LEGAL PROBLEMS OF EDUCATION (NOLPE)** 825 Western Ave., Topeka, Kans. 66606. (913) 357-7242

Established in 1954, this is a membership organization of school board attorneys, professors of law and administration, administrators, teachers, and others interested in school law. It does not take official positions on policy questions, but attempts to provide broad information concerning current issues in school law. It issues an excellent series of publications (priced considerably lower for members). The following publications are included in the $25 membership.

NOLPE School Law Reporter (bimonthly) cites or discusses all school law cases reported by state and federal courts of record in the United States. Cases are reported under categories similar to those in the *Yearbook of School Law* (G37).

NOLPE Notes (monthly) is a newsletter containing information on important case filings, administrative decisions, legislative developments, new publications, and school law conferences.

NOLPE School Law Journal (semiannual) is a review journal concentrating on basic issues and significant trends (such as police-school cooperation, equal protection, and state educational finance).

Other publications include *Legal Problems of Education Series,* published in conjunction with W. H. Anderson Company: books dealing with education law for specific administrators or for specific subject; for example, *Law of Guidance and Counseling* or *Legal Problems of School Boards. NOLPE Monographs,* a joint venture with the ERIC Clearinghouse on Educational Management (M17), deals with student control and student rights, and with legal aspects of school administration.

NOLPE's library, concerned primarily with school law, is open to "anyone interested." According to its constitution, it is a "clearinghouse for information on research and publications"; but generally is not prompt in responding to requests from nonmembers.

N20 **NATIONAL SCHOOL BOARDS ASSOCIATION (NSBA)** 800
State National Bank Plz., Evanston, Ill. 60201. (313) 869-7730
Founded in 1940, this organization represents approximately 80 percent of the nation's more than 96,000 school board members and school districts with 96 percent of the public school children in the United States. Its basic purposes are to assist state school boards associations and local school districts which are NSBA Direct Affiliates and to represent the perspective of local citizen control of education wherever school governance is an issue at the national level.

A variety of publications are issued by NSBA. A monthly magazine, *The American School Board Journal* ($18.00), keeps school board members informed on current issues; it has won many awards for excellence. Quarterly research reports cover such topics as *Impact of Collective Bargaining on Curriculum-Instruction* ($3.50); *Women on School Boards* ($2.50); and *Class Size/Open Plan Schools/Flexible-Modular Scheduling* ($1.50). *Washington Fastreport,* the direct line between school board leaders and education's fast-changing national pace, is issued fortnightly as part of the Direct Affiliate Program. *School Boards* is a bimonthly newsletter published in conjunction with state school boards associations.

Educational Policies Service (EPS/NSBA) is a subscription service which includes complex reference tools, an on-call reference service for members, and monthly publications. The NSBA annual convention attracts more than 20,000 school board members, administrators, and others from all parts of North America and is the largest meeting of elected public officials held in North America.

The Council of School Attorneys consists of attorneys who are serving as counsel for local public school districts, state school boards associations, or state departments of education. Members of the council meet annually just prior to NSBA's annual convention.

The Council of Big City Boards of Education is composed of school board members from the nation's 50 largest cities, with a core population of 300,000 or more. The council meets annually just prior to NSBA's annual convention.

NSBA's library (closed to the public, but open to reasonable telephone and mail requests) is concerned with education and educational administration, and includes materials on curriculum and educational reform. It has the most complete collection of state school boards association publications, which often are not available in other libraries. Its collection now consists of approximately 1,000 books and 400 periodicals.

Training materials for school board members include two training packages, "OnBoard" and "BOARD ACTION," with 16-mm color-sound films, as well as cassette series covering boardmanship, collective bargaining, legal responsibilities, and policy and public issues. The School Board Academy offers a continuing series of seminars on a changing variety of topics of interest to school board members and administrators.

N21 **NEW JERSEY EDUCATION ASSOCIATION RESEARCH LIBRARY (NJEA)**   180 W. State St., Trenton, N.J. 08608. (609) 599-4561

This special library in education, intended for the NJEA professional staff, covers negotiations, instruction, educational research, educational innovations, and New Jersey school law. Holdings include 600 books, 17 four-drawer files of pamphlets, 150 legal documents (United States and New Jersey), and 250 periodicals. The library answers requests for information on educational topics from staff and membership and prepares materials packets for members on such current topics as middle schools, open classrooms, and teacher accountability. It also indexes and abstracts decisions by the New Jersey Commissioner of Education and prepares the index to NJEA's periodical, *NJEA Review.* An SDI (Selective Dissemination of Information) service is being introduced for NJEA staff; reports, such as *Criteria for Class Size and Specialists,* are compiled; and financial aid studies are performed. Its "Guide to Programs" provides up-to-date information on current projects and programs. The library is open to students and the general public; no borrowing privileges.

N22 **STATE EDUCATIONAL ACCOUNTABILITY REPOSITORY (SEAR)** Wisconsin Department of Public Instruction, 126 Langdon St., Madison, Wis. 53702. (608) 266-1344

SEAR is a library of reports and articles on accountability, published by states and outlying possessions; one of the features of the Cooperative Accountability Project (CAP), financed through ESEA Title V funds. As of 1975, approximately 900 publications were on file in SEAR; most are annotated in the August 1974 edition of the *Bibliography of the State Educational Accountability Repository.*

SEAR was established to provide state and local agency personnel and other interested persons with access to a central source of materials and reports on accountability, which deal with statutes and models, assessment and evaluation programs, educational goals and performance objectives, copies of test instruments, performance indicators, and other aspects of accountability. In addition to its basic bibliography, which will be updated in 1975 or 1976, other publications cover state legislation, state goals, educational indicators, costs of accountability, roles of the participants, dissemination systems, and developing assessment programs. Reports are available on request. Its library is open for drop-in service or by appointment.

N23 **U.S. OFFICE OF CHILD DEVELOPMENT (OCD)** U.S. Department of Health, Education, and Welfare, 400 6th St., S.W., Washington, D.C. 20201. (202) 755-7724; Children's Bureau: Rm. 5801, (202) 755-7418; Head Start Program: Rm. 2030, (202) 755-7782. (Mailing address: P.O. Box 1182, Washington, D.C. 20013.)

The U.S. Office of Child Development, since 1973 part of HEW's Office of Human Development, now includes the Children's Bureau, founded by Congress in 1912, and the Head Start Program, originally launched by the Office of Economic Opportunity (OEO) in 1965. It focuses on the nation's children, from conception to early adolescence, with emphasis on the formative first five years and on children who are high-risk because of special circumstances: children of low-income families, abused or neglected children, migrant and native American children, children in institutions, children requiring day care, and adoptive services or family services. Other foci include early childhood development, legislation affecting children, education for parenthood, and long-range and conceptual planning related to child welfare. Traditionally, the Children's Bureau has collected and disseminated information relating to children. OCD has a variety of publications covering its areas of interest. These include a bimonthly, *Children Today* ($6.10/year), which contains feature articles, news and reports, and a good review section. Other publications include research studies, useful bibliographies, and informative, readable pamphlets. A complete list of publications (and single copies of many) are available without charge on request.

N24   **U.S. OFFICE OF EDUCATION (OE)**   400 Maryland Ave., S.W., Washington, D.C. 20202. (202) 245-8707 – Publications/Information Office.

The Office of Education was created by Congress in 1867 as an independent agency, was transferred to the Department of the Interior in 1869, and to the Federal Security Agency in 1939, which was amalgamated into the Department of Health, Education, and Welfare (HEW) in 1957. Together with the National Institute of Education (N18), the National Center for Educational Statistics (E1), the Fund for the Improvement of Postsecondary Education, and the Federal Interagency Committee on Education, it is part of HEW's Education Division under the Assistant Secretary for Education and is headed by its own commissioner.

OE, which began with a staff of four and a budget of $25,000 in 1867, had, in 1975, 3,000 employees and a budget of more than $6 billion. It administers more than 100 programs, mostly through state and local education agencies, and affects virtually all students in the nation's 16,000 school districts, 3,000 universities, and 10,000 occupational schools. Its expressed goals are to improve the quality and relevance of American education; to equalize opportunities for individuals and groups handicapped by physical or mental handicaps or by economic, racial, or geographic conditions; and to provide financial support to a variety of educational agencies, including libraries, adult education agencies, and higher education, as well as state and local educational agencies.

The attached chart (Figure 14) shows the current reorganization of OE. The Publications/Information Office is the basic source for information on current programs and publications. Other information sources within the agency include the following Bureaus and offices.

_____**BUREAU OF EDUCATION FOR THE HANDICAPPED (BEH)**
7th and D Sts., S.W., Washington, D.C. 20201. (202) 245-9661 (Mailing address: 400 Maryland Ave., S.W., Washington, D.C. 20202.)

BEH is concerned with all aspects of educating the handicapped, gifted, and talented, including technical assistance to states, training of teachers and other educational personnel, and providing media services and

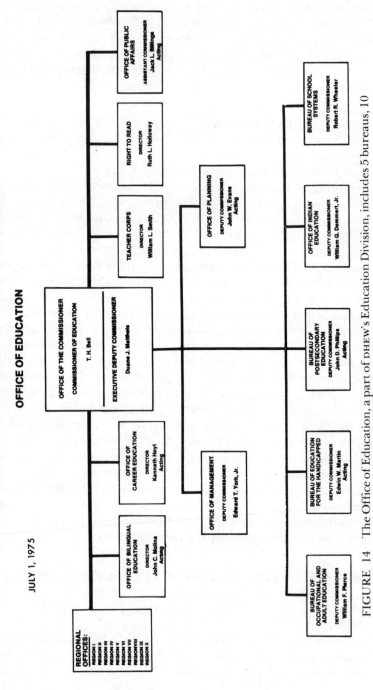

FIGURE 14   The Office of Education, a part of DHEW's Education Division, includes 5 bureaus, 10 regional offices, and several staff offices.

captioned films for the deaf. Its information service attempts to answer all questions, including those dealing with financial assistance for services involving the handicapped. The Division of Research answers queries from individuals involved with special education and those working with the handicapped, or refers them to other sources of information. A packet of materials on its programs can be obtained upon written request.

_____BUREAU OF OCCUPATIONAL AND ADULT EDUCATION
400 Maryland Ave., S.W., Washington, D.C. 20202. (202) 245-8166
This bureau is concerned with all aspects of adult, vocational, and technical education; manpower training and development; and development of area vocational school facilities. It answers queries and makes referrals to other sources of information, especially to relevant individuals in the 10 regional offices. It has a small reference library containing laws, regulations, and other materials in its fields and publishes regulations, guidelines, curriculum guides, booklets, and reports, as well as statistics and summaries, concerning vocational educational trends.

_____BUREAU OF SCHOOL SYSTEMS Rm. 4111, 400 Maryland
Ave., S.W., Washington, D.C. 20202. (202) 245-8720
Financial and technical assistance is provided by this bureau to state and local education agencies to support programs which benefit migrant, neglected, delinquent, and disadvantaged children. It assists local schools with problems growing out of desegregation and administers funds to help support public education in areas where federal activity has increased school enrollment or removed property from local tax rolls. It helps state departments of education identify problems, evaluate programs, and undertake comprehensive planning; and supports experimental and innovative projects designed to improve education. The bureau allots funds to the states so that they may provide library resources, textbooks, and other instructional materials for elementary and secondary school students; makes grants to states to improve library services in isolated or inadequately served areas; funds development of educational television programs; and makes grants to local and state education agencies, public colleges, and other institutions for noncommercial radio and television equipment.

_____OFFICE OF EQUAL EDUCATIONAL OPPORTUNITY Rm.
2001, 400 Maryland Ave., S.W., Washington, D.C. 20202. (202) 245-8484
This office is interested in all aspects of school desegregation, including

266 NONPRINT SOURCES

training of school personnel and providing aid to school districts to reduce racial isolation. It answers queries, provides consulting services, and publishes reports in the area of school desegregation.

_____OFFICE OF LEGISLATION 400 Maryland Ave., S.W., Washington, D.C. 20202. (202) 245-8180
The Office of Legislation is the OE staff office which coordinates planning and prepares specifications for legislation necessary to carry out the functions and proposed objectives of the Office of Education and for providing OE and HEW staff members with information on the content, status,.and progress of legislation affecting education. While functioning primarily as a service organization for the operating units within the Office of Education, it will answer specific outside inquiries on federal education legislation. It does *not* maintain a mailing list or issue regular publications.

_____USOE REGIONAL OFFICES

Address and Telephone Number	Region	States Served
Regional Commissioner of Education U.S. Office of Education John F. Kennedy Federal Bldg. Government Center Boston, Mass. 02203 (617) 223-7205	I	Connecticut Maine Massachusetts New Hampshire Rhode Island Vermont
Regional Commissioner of Education U.S. Office of Education Federal Bldg. 26 Federal Plz. New York, N.Y. 10007 (212) 264-4370	II	New Jersey New York Puerto Rico Virgin Islands
Regional Commissioner of Education U.S. Office of Education 3535 Market St. Philadelphia, Pa. 19108 (215) 597-1001	III	Delaware District of Columbia Maryland Pennsylvania Virginia
Regional Commissioner of Education U.S. Office of Education 50 7th St., N.E., Rm. 550 Atlanta, Ga. 30323 (404) 526-5087	IV	Alabama Florida Georgia Kentucky Mississippi North Carolina South Carolina Tennessee

Address and Telephone Number	Region	States Served
Regional Commissioner of Education U.S. Office of Education 300 S. Wacker Dr. Chicago, Ill. 60606 (312) 353-5215	V	Illinois Indiana Michigan Minnesota Ohio Wisconsin
Regional Commissioner of Education U.S. Office of Education Federal Office Bldg. 1114 Commerce St. Dallas, Tex. 75202 (214) 749-2636	VI	Arkansas Louisiana New Mexico Oklahoma Texas
Regional Commissioner of Education U.S. Office of Education 601 E. 12th St. Kansas City, Mo. 64106 (816) 374-2276	VII	Iowa Kansas Missouri Nebraska
Regional Commissioner of Education U.S. Office of Education Federal Office of Education Federal Office Bldg., Rm. 9017 1961 Stout St. Denver, Colo. 80202 (303) 837-3544	VIII	Colorado Montana North Dakota South Dakota Utah Wyoming
Regional Commissioner of Education U.S. Office of Education 50 Fulton St. San Francisco, Calif. 94102 (415) 556-4921	IX	Arizona California Hawaii Nevada American Samoa Guam Wake Island Trust Territory of the Pacific Islands
Regional Commissioner of Education U.S. Office of Education 1321 Second Ave. Seattle, Wash. 98101 (206) 442-0434	X	Alaska Idaho Oregon Washington

Figure 15 depicts the regional boundaries and headquarters of the Department of Health, Education, and Welfare.

N25 **URBAN INSTITUTE** 2100 M St., N.W., Washington, D.C. 20037. (202) 223-1950

A nonprofit research organization established in 1968. Independent and nonpartisan, the institute responds to current needs for disinterested

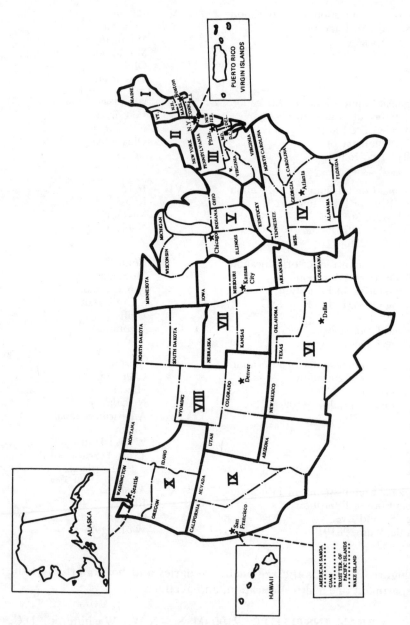

FIGURE 15   DHEW regional boundaries and headquarters.

analysis and basic information. Research findings and a range of interpretive viewpoints are published at low cost as an educational service. Areas covered include education (primarily school finance and evaluation), evaluation and analysis, employment and manpower, housing, welfare, urban finance, state and local government, health, and transportation. Specific questions within its range of interests are answered promptly and intelligently. A catalog of publications is available on request.

16 | *Institutional Sources of Product and Curricular Information*

Listed in this chapter are some of the institutions and organizations that can assist teachers, counselors, purchasing agents, media personnel, and librarians who wish to select, organize, develop, locate, or borrow educational materials or resources for schools or for educational purposes. These include tests, media materials, curricular materials, equipment, and resource people and consultants.

The agencies listed here supplement the printed sources listed in Chapters 9 through 13. Others can be located through the audiovisual directories listed in Chapter 11 and the basic directories listed in Chapter 3. Newsletters and information sheets, particularly those of various ERIC clearinghouses, can provide current information on additional agencies.

O1   **AMERICAN ASSOCIATION OF SCHOOL LIBRARIANS**   50
        E. Huron St., Chicago, Ill. 60611. (312) 944-6780
Offers introductory literature and competent consultative services in its fields of interest, which include organizing and operating media centers, selecting and organizing educational materials, and information on such current trends as behavioral objectives in librarianship and education.

O2   **AMERICAN INSTITUTE OF PHYSICS**   Education Div., P.O.
        Box 617, Stony Brook, N.Y. 11790. (512) 862-8787

This division of the American Institute of Physics provides consultation services and an information pool for physics education, science education, and physics career information educators. Its library on these subjects includes approximately 600 books, pamphlets, and documents and 20 periodical subscriptions.

O3 **ANTI-DEFAMATION LEAGUE OF B'NAI B'RITH (ADL)** 315 Lexington Ave., New York, N.Y. 10016. (212) 689-7400

A leading human relations agency, founded in 1913, concerned with eradicating racial and religious discrimination against Jews and other minority groups. It is now a vast national agency with 28 regional offices staffed by professional personnel—active in law (legislation), education, human relations, urban affairs, and related areas. Its promotion and production of classroom materials that supply accurate information about minority groups are of primary interest to educators.

It is recognized both for its documented studies of misleading materials and its production of books, pamphlets, and audiovisual materials on racial and ethnic groups, including materials about Puerto Ricans and Mexican Americans, produced under government education grants. Also serves as consultant to teacher-training institutes and school systems developing curricula and methods. Its "simulation game" technique uses filmed situations with specially developed manuals to help school systems recognize and resolve classroom conflicts. Model programs for school systems faced with interracial and social tensions include in-service training for teachers, supervisors, and administrators.

The headquarters office in New York City can supply current catalogs of excellent printed and audiovisual materials designed for school use, plus addresses of its 28 regional offices (which cover most areas of the United States). These regional offices are active community agencies interested in eradicating racial tensions in such areas as education and employment.

O4 **CENTER FOR THE STUDY OF EVALUATION** UCLA Graduate School of Education, 145 Moore Hall, 405 Hilgard Ave., Los Angeles, Calif. 90024.

The Center for the Study of Evaluation began as a university-based research and development center in 1966 and is the only federally sponsored agency working exclusively on educational evaluation. Its two major ongoing programs center on the technology of evaluation and objectives-based evaluation. Although not primarily a service organization, its quarterly (free) journal, *Evaluation Comment,* is a readable and rewarding publication, each issue highlighting specific evaluation topics and providing cogent summaries of significant ideas. Recent issues, for instance, dealt with goal-free evaluation and school accountability laws. The center also sells the test evaluations, goal charts, and monographs which it develops (see Figure 16).

Dissemination Office
Center for the Study of Evaluation
145 Moore Hall
University of California
Los Angeles, California 90024

Gentlemen:

Enclosed is my check (money order, or purchase order), payable to the Regents of the University of California, for the following CSE publications.

CSE Secondary School Test Evaluations
　　　Number of 3 volume sets:_____at $22.00 per set   .   .   .   . $_____
CSE Elementary School Test Evaluations
　　　Number of copies:_____at $5.00 per copy   .   .   .   .   .   . $_____
CSE Preschool/Kindergarten Test Evaluations
　　　Number of copies:_____at $5.00 per copy   .   .   .   .   .   . $_____
CSE/RBS Test Evaluations: Tests for Higher-Order, Cognitive,
　　　Affective, and Interpersonal Skills
　　　Number of copies:_____at $8.50 per copy   .   .   .   .   .   . $_____
CSE Elementary School Hierarchical Goals Charts
　　　Number of sets:_____at $12.50 per set   .   .   .   .   .   . $_____
CSE Preschool/Kindergarten Hierarchical Goals Charts
　　　Number of sets:_____at $10.00 per set   .   .   .   .   .   . $_____
CSE Monograph Series in Evaluation:
　　　No. 1 — Domain-Referenced Curriculum Evaluation: A Technical
　　　Handbook and a Case Study from the MINNEMAST Project
　　　Number of copies:_____at $3.50 per copy   .   .   .   .   .   . $_____
　　　No. 2 — National Priorities for Elementary Education
　　　Number of copies:_____at $3.50 per copy   .   .   .   .   .   . $_____
　　　No. 3 — Problems in Criterion-Referenced Measurement
　　　Number of copies:_____at $3.50 per copy   .   .   .   .   .   . $_____
　　　No. 4 — Evaluation and Decision Making: The Title VII Experience
　　　Number of copies:_____at $3.50 per copy   .   .   .   .   .   . $_____
California residents add 6% sales tax   .   .   .   . $_____

　　　　　　　TOTAL   .   .   .   . $_____

Please send to:

　　Name_____

　　Address_____

　　City   State   ZIP

Please bill to (if different from above):

　　Name_____

　　Address_____

　　City   State   ZIP

FIGURE 16   CSE publications provide practical evaluations and compilations of evaluations.

O5   **CENTER FOR UNDERSTANDING MEDIA**   75 Horatio St.,
New York, N.Y. 10014. (212) 691-2260

A nonprofit organization, incorporated in New York in 1969, specializing
in projects that involve young people and the new media. It is developing
a media study curriculum designed to produce critical and active
consumers of various media forms and is looking for methods to integrate
teaching about media with teaching literature and the arts. Also trains
teachers to teach its new media study curriculum.

Current projects are involved with development of media curricula,
filmmaking by children, a Children's Film Theatre, teacher training,
parent education, a Young Filmmakers' Festival for cable television, a
portable theater, and a Young Peoples' Radio Festival. Publications
include a children's film catalog and a portfolio of media activities for
children. Recently, the center has jointly edited five volumes of film
scripts with Scholastic Books, and has prepared a booklet on media study
in the elementary schools with the Association for Childhood Education
International, reviewed in Chapter 11 (J6). Also collaborates with other
groups and individuals who share its interests, and is a source of
information on activities in media curricula. Its occasional journal,
Medialog, reports on the work of the center and covers facets of the media
studies field.

O6   **CENTER FOR WAR/PEACE STUDIES**   218 E. 18th St., New
York, N.Y. 10003. (212) 475-0850; Claremont Hotel Office Park,
Suite 235, Claremont at Ashby, Oakland/Berkeley, Calif. 94705.
(415) 849-3535

An off-shoot of New York Friends, this educational organization is
concerned with global issues that affect war, peace, conflict, and change,
as well as with evolving constructive alternatives to violence which advance
justice, democratic values, and human dignity. Its interdisciplinary
resources in this area include curricular and resource materials in
economics, ecology, population, human rights, and many areas of social
studies and social sciences.

Publications include *Intercom* (I65), directed towards teachers at all
levels; *War/Peace Report* (bimonthly, $8/year) for college-level materials;
curriculum materials and guides to curriculum materials in its areas of
interest; and four studies, *Global Dimensions in U.S. Education* ($5/set), on
international education at different levels. Holdings and resources of the
center are available to teachers, schools, school systems, and administrators. Regional programs include in-service and pre-service projects.

O7   **CHILDREN'S BOOK COUNCIL**   67 Irving Pl., New York, N.Y.
       10005. (212) 244-2666
A nonprofit organization of children's book publishers, formed in 1945 to
encourage the reading and enjoyment of children's books. It is the donor
organization of the National Book Awards program, and publishes a
useful reference guide, *Children's Books: Awards & Prizes* (1975, $4.95),
produced biennially in the summer. It is the official headquarters of
Children's Book Week, founded in 1919, and provides promotion and
display materials created for this event by well-known illustrators of children's books. Special publications and display materials also are available
for promoting the Summer Reading Program. "PRELUDE: Mini Seminars
on Using Books Creatively," its cassette series, is useful for in-service
teacher education. Another valuable series for teachers is the *Children's
Book Showcase* (an annual selection of excellent graphically illustrated
children's books), which can frequently be related to elementary curriculum. Its year-round reading programs, complete with display and
instructional materials, have specific themes for each year; in 1976, for
example, the theme will be American Bicentennial Reading.
   The council has cooperative programs and working liaison committees
with many other organizations listed in this guide: the Association for
Childhood Education International (C1), the International Reading
Association (C9), the National Council for the Social Studies (C11), and
others.
   It maintains a noncirculating library of examination copies of children's
books published in the previous three years, with a permanent section of
award-winning books, publishers' catalogs, review media, and book
selection aids. The library is open to the public during regular business
hours, 9:00 a.m. to 5:00 p.m. Display materials, reading order forms, and
lists of publications and programs are available on written or personal
request. For complete listings, send a self-addressed mailing label and
$0.20 in postage to the attention of BW Materials Brochure.

O8   **CLEARINGHOUSE ON PRECOLLEGE PSYCHOLOGY AND
       BEHAVIORAL SCIENCE**   American Psychological Assn., Rm.
       209, 1200 17th St., N.W., Washington, D.C. 20036. (202) 833-7592
This clearinghouse of the American Psychological Association was
established in 1970 to collect and disseminate information on the teaching
of psychology in secondary schools and behavioral sciences in elementary
schools. Its resource collection is small and exclusively in these fields.
Holdings include approximately 400 books, plus surveys, curriculum
project materials, guides, and periodical literature on precollege psychology and elementary behavioral sciences, including certification requirements and teacher-training programs.

Specific information and bibliographies in this field are available to both teachers and psychologists. Clearinghouse materials can be used on the premises by appointment. Membership includes nine issues of *Periodically*, a lively, readable, four-page newsletter published the last Friday of each month, September to May, with one page devoted to "gimmickry," another to high-level "pocket reviews," and the remainder to news, course announcements, etc. High school teachers of psychology who affiliate with the American Psychological Association or its Division on the Teaching of Psychology ($2.50 and $2.00, respectively) can subscribe to APA journals at greatly reduced member rates and/or receive the division newsletter.

O9   **CLEARINGHOUSE ON WOMEN'S STUDIES**   c/o Feminist Press, SUNY College at Old Westbury, P.O. Box 334, Old Westbury, N.Y. 11568. (516) 876-3086

Active since 1970, this clearinghouse is an educational project of the Feminist Press, publishers of an interesting variety of feminist literature, much of it directed toward the schools. The clearinghouse collects, compiles, and disseminates information about women's studies at all levels of education. At the college level, its information bank includes in-house information and syllabi from more than 4,000 women's study courses and from more than 100 programs being conducted on U.S. college campuses. It provides a similar information network and curriculum-gathering service for the elementary and secondary school levels, from a collection including curriculum outlines, course materials, and institutional strategies.

Publications include resource guides, curriculum materials, bibliographies, directories, and a newsletter, all designed to provide answers and support for their requests for information. An in-service project for public school teachers provides introductory and advanced courses on the socialization of boys and girls and the teaching of literature and history. Other activities include a nationwide conference on in-service education and sex-role stereotyping for educators.

O10 **CURRICULUM MATERIALS CLEARINGHOUSE (CMC)** Xerox University Microfilms, 300 N. Zeeb Rd., Ann Arbor, Mich. 48106. (313) 761-4700, Ext. 349

This clearinghouse (a subdivision of Xerox University Microfilms) compiles and disseminates microfiche packages of curriculum materials in a wide variety of subjects, from preschool to grade 12 levels. Its purpose is to provide the education community with a centralized pool of curriculum materials, ideas, and information, as well as to provide publishing facilities for curriculum developers who would otherwise be unable to disseminate their own materials. It is currently soliciting curriculum materials, in all areas, from private developers and public agencies.

Its ultimate plan is to compile and distribute, in microfiche format, a set of approximately 500 units, updated each year, in a Curriculum Materials Microfile. The first microfile, issued early in 1974, includes 260 instructional units on 828 microfiche. Future microfiles, of approximately 500 instructional units (100,000 pages) a year, will be issued quarterly for $1,200/year, on a standing order basis. These "practical" instructional units include all information needed for classroom presentations. Subscribers are free to make multiple copies of copyrighted materials for their own use. Microfiche copies of individual units are available at $1 per fiche, with a $10 minimum. The cost of hard copies depends on the number of pages required. CMC offers a 30-percent discount on the purchase of a Xerox 320 microfiche reader, and a copying service which provides microfiche or hard copy of individual instruction units.

Curriculum Briefs and Index, a book accompanying the microfile sets, but which can be purchased separately for $50, provides title, developer, and subject indexes to the original curriculum units, plus a developer's abstract and a brief (50 to 100 words) critical annotation prepared by an independent curriculum consultant.

O11   EDUCATIONAL FILM LIBRARY ASSOCIATION (EFLA)
17 W. 60th St., New York, N.Y. 10023. (212) 246-4533

A nonprofit membership organization founded in 1943, EFLA is a national clearinghouse for information on nontheatrical 16-mm films and other media, and is interested in all aspects of education, the arts, films, and media, including their production, distribution, and use in science, religion, and industry. Annual dues, based on size of members' film collections, ranges from $35 to $100.

EFLA's extensive reference library provides information to members by phone, in person, and by mail. It is open to the public two days a week (Tuesdays and Thursdays) for individual reference and research. Member libraries receive an outstanding evaluation service, *EFLA Evaluations,* consisting of 10 monthly sets of evaluations for films, containing well-formatted bibliographic information and film synopses. Commentary based on ratings by independent reviewing committees covers subject areas, technical treatments, and appropriate age groups. Its quarterly *Sightlines* ($12/year) lists all new releases of 16-mm films, 8-mm films, and filmstrips, together with news, articles, and selected subject lists. Other publications include *A Manual on Film Evaluation* (1974; members, $4; nonmembers, $5); a bibliography, *Museums with Film Programs* (1974; members, $3; nonmembers, $5); many other books and pamphlets on film evaluation; subject lists of films; and a compilation of its evaluations, *Film Evaluation Guide,* which, with supplements, reviews more than 5,700 films from 1946 to 1971 ($54). Order forms and price lists will be sent on request.

Also sponsors workshops on topics such as film evaluation, filmmaking, and film library administration, as well as the American Film Festival, which awards the "Emily."

O12 **EDUCATIONAL PRODUCTS INFORMATION EXCHANGE INSTITUTE (EPIE)** 463 West St., New York, N.Y. 10014. (212) 675-1163

This institute was established in 1967 to serve as a "consumers union" for the nation's schools; it is a nonprofit membership organization whose purpose is to provide independent, objective tests and evaluations of educational materials, equipment, and systems for the educational community.

Its basic information files and subsequent reports on varied educational products are based on thorough and detailed collection, organization, and analysis of producer statements; commissioned product reviews by scholars, researchers, and testing agencies (including its own Product Testing Laboratory); and feedback from a broad sample of users, including teachers, students, and administrators. Its information file is being computerized. EPIE currently maintains data on 800 pieces of educational hardware and is planning to include as many items as are available. Training workshops in materials evaluation are conducted for interested school systems and individuals.

Regular membership ($50/year) includes 6 issues of the *EPIE Report* and 18 issues of the biweekly newsletter, *EPIEgram.* In addition, other services and, from time to time, special reports are available. Nonmembers can purchase individual issues of the *EPIE Report.* Subscriptions to *EPIEgram* ($24/year) are available, and subscribers can purchase issues of the *EPIE Report* at a 50-percent discount.

_____**EPIEgram: THE EDUCATIONAL CONSUMERS' NEWS-LETTER** New York, EPIE Institute, 1972– . 18 issues/year (October through June). Members, free; nonmembers, $24/year.

An informative biweekly publication which includes miniproduct evaluations, purchase advice, reports of conferences, Washington-watching, brief book reports, book notices, product complaints (and occasionally product praise), survey information, many citations, and referrals to further sources (see Figure 17). Invaluable for purchasing agents and audiovisual departments. "Feedback" forms are included for ongoing evaluations, suggestions, and comments.

EPIEGRAM

the educational consumers' NEWSLETTER

NOVEMBER 1, 1975	VOL. 4 NO. 3
EPIE INSTITUTE, 463 WEST STREET, N.Y. 10014	
NONPROFIT ● CONSUMER SUPPORTED ● UNBIASED	

ADVICE

CRITERIA FOR A GOOD AUDIO CASSETTE

PRODUCT REPORT

INADEQUATE INDEXES FROM THE NEW YORK TIMES?

Seven out of nine people who, according to advertisements for The New York Times School Microfilm Collection, endorse the collection have told EPIE that the indexes for the collection are, after all, inadequate or worse. We understand the Times policy on all the news that's fit to print. But are all advertisements fit to print? One librarian was quoted in the Times Company brochure as saying: *"We were very pleased when your indexes arrived, listing the contents of each microfilm reel by subject or topic."* Today she is not sure whether she was misquoted or whether her opinion of the indexes has changed with attempted use--but she is sure that: *"The index is very poor. The collection should have a more definitive subject listing, and more date listings also. The subject headings are too broad, and the index is incomplete. Articles we have in the collection are not listed."*

Another endorser had, in fact, complained to the company about the quality of the index. This librarian was unaware that she was quoted in the Times Company advertising literature. She still agrees with what she has been quoted as saying: *"The fascination of students with the events of the past make this Collection a part of our leisure reading program."* But, she explained to EPIE, though students do use the collection for browsing, *"We would never have put that kind of money into leisure reading alone."* Others pointed out what students miss because of the poor indexes.
        "Trying to use the collection as a research tool is 'death.' Students can't crack the code of the indexes."
        "Our social studies teachers bemoan the lack of indexes. How much is locked in those reels! We should be able to get full use of the collection. . . ." EPIE tried to contact all 18 endorsers featured in the Times Company's advertising --but five had left the school cited, and four had no city listed. We were prompted by a member's letter to the Microfilming Corporation of America (a New York Times Company), complaining that the indexes were incomplete and incomprehensible. He said:
        "Unlike the selected testimonials in your advertising literature, our enthusiasm has turned to frustration . . . Your program concept is probably sound, except that your experts have left out one important dimension--the user."

FIGURE 17   Sample page of *EPIEgram,* the Educational Consumers' Newsletter. This biweekly, published by the Educational Products Information Exchange Institute, is a prime source of evaluation for educational products and processes.

EPIE REPORTS   New York, EPIE Institute, 1967– . 6 issues/year (September/October through July/August). Prices vary from $3 (for inbrief reports) to $20 (for in-depth reports).

Recent issues of *EPIE Report* cover evaluations of 16-mm motion picture projectors, more than 140 pages of analyses of elementary mathematics materials, and an important discussion of electrical safety in schools. Evaluations are thorough, competent, well-organized, and based on well-chosen and expressly stated criteria.

O13 **EDUCATIONAL TESTING SERVICE (ETS)**   Test Collection
(B-016), Box 592, Princeton, N.J. 08540. (609) 921-9000

The Test Collection department of ETS is a source of current information on measures and services, a reference collection, and an archive of tests. Its primary holdings consist of 10,000 tests—cataloged by authors, titles, and subjects—backed by approximately 100 reference books on tests. Included are foreign, domestic, current, out-of-print, commercially available, and experimental tests for all subject areas and for all types of tests. Supplementary files include test publishers (American and foreign), scoring systems and services, state testing programs, test reviews, and sources of information on tests.

Since 1970, ETS has had a contract with HEW's Office of Child Development to identify and collect tests appropriate for children from birth to nine years of age, and now houses the Head Start Test Collection (a bibliographic collection of tests). It is beginning to convert its files to microcopy, and ultimately hopes to have all instruments which it has permission to duplicate available in microfiche.

An impressive amount of research is performed by a staff of four (one semiprofessional and three secretarial). ETS prepares ongoing bibliographies and lists of tests (in given areas), as requested. Its ongoing publications include *Major U.S. Publishers of Standardized Tests* (free, updated as needed); a quarterly digest of information on tests, the *Test Collection Bulletin* ($2/year), which announces new tests and services, new publishers, and new references on tests; and a calendar of testing programs. Several of its excellent annotated bibliographies, available without charge, include *Assessment of Teachers, Attitudes Toward School and School Adjustment (Grades 4–6), Attitudes Toward School and School Adjustment (Grades 7–12), Self-Concept Measures (Grades 7 and Above), Criterion-Referenced Measures,* and *Tests for Educationally Disadvantaged Adults. Head Start Test Collection Reports* now available include: *Measures of Self-Concept, Measures of Infant Development, Measures of Social Skills, School Readiness Measures, Tests for Spanish Speaking Children,* and *Language Development Tests.* These annotated bibliographies are available without charge from the Head Start Test Collection as long as the supply lasts and, subsequently, will be available from the ERIC Document Reproduction Service. The Test Collection is open without charge to persons engaged in education, research, advisory services, and related activities, including students, teachers, and members of school systems and boards of education. The standards of the American Psychological Association, as well as publishers' restrictions, are followed in granting access to the files. Tests on file are for reference use only and may not be copied without the publisher's permission. As of summer 1975, the Test Collection is making available microfiche copies of unpublished tests in the fields of education and psychology. The first set (Set A) of 118 microfiche tests is available for $2 per test or $118 for the entire set. A list of titles can be obtained from the Test Collection. In addition to providing on-site access, the Test Collection staff will answer specific mail or telephone requests without charge, identifying materials or supplying annotated lists.

O14   **EDUCATION DEVELOPMENT CENTER (EDC)**   55 Chapel St., Newton, Mass. 02160. (617) 969-7100

EDC, a leading center for curriculum reform since 1958, is perhaps best described as a conglomerate of 20 projects, each with its own funding, director, and staff. Areas of interest include pre-service and in-service teacher education, community support for educational programs, social studies, science and mathematics, open education, international education, career education, and media programs. Its lively and interesting newsletter, *EDC News,* is free at the present time to educators who would like to keep current with their projects. It includes approximately 16 pages, dealing with its areas of interest, book reviews, and new developments in elementary science, among others.

O15   **ENVIRONMENTAL ACTION COALITION (EAC)**   235 E. 49th St., New York, N.Y. 10017. (212) 486-9550

A nonprofit membership organization concentrating on environmental education and action programs; an excellent source for curriculum ideas and information on urban environmental education. Membership is $10/year for adults, $5 for children, and includes free admission to workshops; special membership teaching aids: for instance, lesson plans and bibliographies on down-to-earth topics such as solid waste disposal; use of the EAC library of books, teaching aids, magazines, and clippings; and two membership newsletters: *Cycle* (monthly) provides background information on current EAC activities and reviews environmental books, and *Eco-News* (10 issues during the school year), an attractive, topical, urban, environmental newsletter for children in the fourth to sixth grades, includes many suggestions for interesting learning activities, plus a teacher's guide for each issue.

O16   **ERIC CLEARINGHOUSE FOR READING AND COMMUNI-CATION SKILLS (ERIC/RCS)**   National Council of Teachers of English, 1111 Kenyon Rd., Urbana, Ill. 61801. (217) 328-3870

This recently combined clearinghouse covers reading, English, journalism, speech, and theatre at all levels and in all institutions. Speech and theatre now include radio, film, television, forensics, interpersonal and small group interaction, theatre, and oral interpretation and are coordinated with the assistance of the Speech Communication Association, Statler Hilton Hotel, New York, N.Y. 10001.

As might be expected from its language specialization, its publications are quite extensive—some issued separately and others in conjunction with organizations such as the International Reading Association and the National Council of Teachers of English, all of whom publish ongoing "ERIC Reports" in their various journals to provide reviews of documents. Offers a series of *Basic Bibliographies*—annotated bibliographies on topics of current interest, such as semantics, dialects, and creative writing. Its *State of the Art Monographs* are commissioned booklet-length studies providing depth and current research in usable form. The staff conducts ERIC workshops at national and regional conferences of professional organizations to explain the ERIC system. Queries from professionals are answered with bibliographies, abstracts, and informal literature searches.

O17 **ERIC CLEARINGHOUSE ON INFORMATION RESOURCES (ERIC/IR)** School of Education, Stanford Center for Research and Development in Teaching, Stanford University, Stanford, Calif. 94305. (415) 497-3345

Areas of interest are educational media, libraries, information science, and instructional technology. Scope encompasses traditional library and print resources, as well as technology-based media. Publications include occasional newsletters and news releases, guides to literature, state-of-the-art papers, occasional papers, listings of ERIC documents, commissioned papers, and brochures on ERIC and on the Stanford clearinghouse.

Its library contains a few hundred books and pamphlets, 200 periodicals, and a complete ERIC collection. A MicroLibrary of selected ERIC materials on educational media and technology has been assembled by this clearinghouse and will be published by Microfiche Publications of New York. The total collection of 2,500 items is priced at $1,000. Separate collections will be available for instructional television, individualized instruction, instructional systems design, media evaluation, and research on instructional media and technology. Supported by financial backing from Stanford University's School of Education, the clearinghouse provides a computerized information retrieval search service for educators, information specialists, businesses, community organizations, and others who require comprehensive reference searches. The information bank includes ERIC materials, *Exceptional Child Education Abstracts, AIM/ARM,* materials from the National Technical Information Service (NTIS) and the National Agricultural Library (NAL), *Psychological Abstracts, Dissertation Abstracts,* and *Social Sciences Citation Index.* Individually designed searches in the interactive mode are priced at approximately $40 to $50 per search.

O18 **ERIC CLEARINGHOUSE ON LANGUAGES AND LINGUIS-
TICS (ERIC/CLL)** Center for Applied Linguistics, 1611 N. Kent
St., Arlington, Va. 22209. (703) 528-4312

The Center for Applied Linguistics has been the site of this clearinghouse
since June 1974. The clearinghouse collects and disseminates information
on foreign-language education, psycholinguistics, bilingual-bicultural
education, English as a second/foreign language, and uncommonly
taught languages. Information about accessions is published regularly in
approximately 40 state and national-language periodicals. The clearinghouse also publishes a series of practical guides for classroom teachers,
state-of-the-art papers, and selected bibliographies under the title
CAL·ERIC/CLL Series on Languages and Linguistics.

O19 **ERIC CLEARINGHOUSE ON TESTS, MEASUREMENT, AND
EVALUATION (ERIC/TM)** c/o Educational Testing Service,
Rosedale Rd., Princeton, N.J. 08540. (609) 921-9000

Associated with the well-known Educational Testing Service, this clearinghouse processes documents related to tests and other measurement
devices, measurement or evaluation procedures and techniques, as well as
documents dealing primarily with evaluative aspects of other programs
and projects.

Its publications include a newsletter, *TM News* issued 10 times/year,
which contains news on tests, book reviews, announcements of meetings
and reprints, and ongoing bibliographies. Its *TM Reports* (free on request,
while supply lasts) are an impressive series of interpretive summaries,
bibliographies, and reviews of research. This series includes summaries of
selected papers from the American Educational Research Association's
annual meetings from 1971 on; a series of excellent summaries on various
aspects of reading research from 1960 to 1970; and surveys of measuring
instruments in assorted fields such as adult learning, alcohol education,
criterion-referenced measurement, test bias, health education, and drug
education. Specific titles include: 28 – *Opening Institutional Ledger
Books—A Challenge to Educational Leadership;* 30 – *Procedures and Issues in the
Measurement of Attitudes;* 31 – *Collection of Criterion-Referenced Tests;* 33 –
Adult Basic Education Programs, Students and Results; 35 – *Evaluation Designs
for Practitioners;* and 36 – *Bias in Testing.* A complete list will be sent on
request.

Its library of approximately 100,000 microfiche covers the areas of
tests, measurement and evaluation, research design, and methodology.
Uses ERIC (DIALOG) to prepare small focused bibliographies in response to
requests for information. The library is open to interested teachers,
administrators, students, and researchers.

O20 **ERIC INFORMATION ANALYSIS CENTER ON SCIENCE, MATHEMATICS, AND ENVIRONMENTAL EDUCATION (ERIC/SMEAC)** 400 Lincoln Tower, 1800 Cannon Dr., Ohio State University, Columbus, Ohio 43210. (614) 422-6717
This clearinghouse deals with science education, mathematics education, and environmental education. It has three excellent and informative free newsletters devoted to specific specialties: *SMEAC Newsletter–Mathematics Education, SMEAC Newsletter–Science Education,* and *SMEAC Newsletter– Environmental Education.* Its library, open to the public, includes more than 100,000 books, pamphlets, journal articles, and microfiche on these topics.

Publications include special bibliographies; reviews of research and trends (such as metrication) in science, mathematics, and environmental education; a *Directory of Projects and Programs in Environmental Education for Elementary and Secondary Schools* ($6.00); and *How to Use ERIC: Mathematics Education* (free), which does a good job of explaining ERIC and listing relevant descriptors.

In addition to processing documents and articles for inclusion in *RIE* and *CIJE,* this clearinghouse has an extensive publication program. Materials include reviews of research prepared in cooperation with the National Association for Research in Science Teaching (NARST), which summarize research efforts within a calendar year at the elementary, secondary, and college levels. Another cooperative venture, started in 1973 with the Association for the Education of Science Teachers (AEST), is the production of the *AEST Yearbook.* Occasional papers include presentations at the annual meeting of NARST and reviews of literature related to specific topics or educational programs. Special bibliographies—aimed primarily at teachers and curriculum personnel—announce availability of documents in selected interest areas. Fact sheets and bulletins also are directed towards specific audiences and needs.

Science educators donate time and talents in preparing critical abstracts and analyses for a new quarterly publication, *Investigations in Science Education* (1974– , $6/year). It is hoped this new publication will help provide comments on and suggestions for preparing research reports, and that it will help improve the writing of science articles.

The ERIC/SMEAC Information Reference Center provides a variety of free and paid services. The free services include fact sheets and bulletins—which must be requested via a standard request form—as well as reference information on the availability of specific publications.

Minimum rates are charged for its publications, and quantity discounts are available. Separate compilations of ERIC abstracts in the fields of science, mathematics, and environmental education have been prepared in cooperation with Education Associates, Inc. of Worthington, Ohio.

These compilations, which facilitate rapid manual searches in each of the separate disciplines, include abstracts, indexes of descriptors, identifiers, authors, and institutions. Compilations are available for 1966-72 and 1973-74. *Science Education 1966-72* costs $22, *Mathematics Education 1966-72* costs $18, and *Environmental Education 1966-72* costs $15.

Computer searches (unscanned) are performed for $10.00 per search. Abstracts can be provided at $4.00 for the first 50 abstracts and $3.50 for each additional 50. Scanned computer searches, also $10.00 minimum, provide relevant abstracts at $7.50 per 50 abstracts and $6.00 for each additional 50 abstracts.

Evaluation of the output of the computer search (for example, what programs are better for our school? which are the most competent research studies?) can be provided at a cost of $10/hour; other consulting services can be negotiated.

O21 **GREAT PLAINS NATIONAL INSTRUCTIONAL TELEVISION LIBRARY** P.O. Box 80669, 1800 N. 33rd St., Lincoln, Neb. 68501. (402) 467-2502

This video tape exchange library was founded with NDEA Title VII funds at the University of Nebraska in 1962, but has been a self-supporting operation since 1966. Its 16-mm and kinescope materials are available on a lease or sales basis. Most can be used either as direct audiovisual presentations in individual classrooms or can be broadcast as television presentations.

Offers approximately 150 complete recorded courses, with related teacher-utilization and in-service materials—at all levels and on all subjects. These can be duplicated via video tape or video cassettes to match the requirements of individual users. Its catalog of *Recorded Visual Instruction* is discussed in Chapter 11 (J48). Other publications include a free, monthly, four-to-six page *GPN Newsletter,* which does a thorough job of discussing topics such as cable television and of reviewing relevant books. Another occasional, free newsletter, *ITV Field Report,* is similarly informative.

O22 **INFORMATION CENTER ON CHILDREN'S CULTURES** United States Committee for UNICEF, 331 E. 38th St., New York, N.Y. 10016. (212) 686-5522

The resources of this UNICEF-sponsored center include 10,000 books; 10,000 photographs; 500 toys, games, and other objects; and 100 periodical titles concerned with children in newly developing countries. Although this center is open to everyone, its primary users are teachers, writers, UNICEF personnel, and media people. It has an impressive assortment of annotated bibliographies covering Africa, Asia, Latin

America, and the Middle East. Other lists include *Children's Art Around the World, Cook Books from Around the World, International Understanding* (K–3, 4–6, or 7–9), and *Spanish and Spanish-English Books*—approximately 100 lists and information sheets, updated annually or every two years. Up to 10 lists will be sent free to requesters who enclose a stamped, self-addressed, legal-size envelope; there is a charge of $1 for more than 10 lists. Other lists are compiled on request, primarily for UNICEF field offices.

O23 **INSTRUCTIONAL OBJECTIVES EXCHANGE (IOX)** P.O. Box 24095, Los Angeles, Calif. 90024. (213) 345-9949
Formerly a project of the UCLA Center for the Study of Evaluation, this organization became a separate agency in June 1970. IOX is a nonprofit educational corporation which has developed a rather impressive collection of instructional objectives, frequently revised, and arranged by subjects, grade levels, and, sometimes, attitudes. Its current *IOX Catalog* lists approximately 50 collections or sets of high-level cognitive and affective instructional objectives (each objective accompanied by one or more illustrative test items). Titles run from *Early Childhood Education* (364 objectives) through *Woodworking* (56 objectives). Other objectives collections include *Self-Concept* (30 objectives), *Judgment: Deductive Logic and Assumption Recognition* (7 objectives), and *Attitude Toward School* (46 objectives). All sets of objectives sell for $8, plus a three-percent charge for postage and handling. Other materials include groups of tests based on objectives ($25) and booklets on evaluating, using, and selecting instructional objectives and related materials. A complete list of publications will be sent on request.

O24 **LIBRARY TECHNOLOGY PROGRAM** American Library Assn., 50 E. Huron St., Chicago, Ill. 60611. (312) 944-6780
Sponsors and executes comprehensive tests for library and media materials, equipment, and supplies. Its test reports are extremely thorough, technically superb, oriented towards the user, and expensive. A current list will be mailed on request.

O25 **MENTAL HEALTH MATERIALS CENTER** 419 Park Ave., S., New York, N.Y. 10016. (212) 889-5760
A nonprofit educational agency, with its main office in New York City, established 20 years ago for the major purpose of evaluating materials (pamphlets, leaflets, films, etc.) which were being used nondiscriminately by mental health professionals. Although the scope and the services of the organization have grown in the last 20 years, its expertise is still in

communication, coordination, and evaluation; it seeks not to add to the body of knowledge, but to spread knowledge, materials, and techniques to those who can best use them.

Some of its services relevant to education are a series of continuing seminars for educators across the country on such topics as mental health education in the schools, effective use of materials in mental health education, and federal programs related to mental health. Its publishing program is small but high-quality: only significant mental health materials which would not be carried by commercial publishers are published. It provides a subscription information service, *Selective Guide to Materials for Mental Health and Family Life Education* (188), and a substantial series of publications on the effective use of materials in mental health education, including *Teach Us What We Want to Know*, which reports verbatim a survey of the health concerns of 5,000 students from kindergarten to grade 12.

Its Information Resources Center, operating from a base of 1,000 pamphlets, offers authoritative information about publications and films for mental health and family life education programs. Also performs specialized bibliographic searches on a contract basis in its areas of interest. Its New York headquarters will provide a list of publications or further information on request.

O26   **MULTICULTURAL RESOURCES**   Fort Mason, San Francisco, Calif. 94123. (415) 493-6729; mailing address: Box 2945, Stanford, Calif. 94305.

This unique and comprehensive collection of multicultural materials, first assembled in 1969 and now owned by HEW's Office of Child Development, has been variously housed in the San Francisco Bay area. Broad in scope, it has been widely shown and well-received on both the east and west coasts. Comprised of more than 5,000 items, the collection includes materials for all ages and all reading levels, from large and small publishers and organizations—not only in the United States, but in Africa, China and other Asian countries, Mexico, the Philippines and Samoa, South America, and Spain. Resources include curriculum ideas, professional literature, bibliographies, and a special section on human relations.

The collection—a gold mine of ideas for teachers—is divided into four major culture areas: Black, Spanish-speaking, Asian-American, and native-American. For each culture area, it includes folktales and legends, books for children, popular reading and high-interest/low-vocabulary materials for all ages, bilingual materials, books, newspapers, periodicals, pictures, and posters, as well as an excellent selection of creative writing by children and young people. Materials were chosen not only to increase understanding and appreciation of various cultures, but to help develop and reinforce a positive self-image in minority youth.

Although its directors are extremely knowledgeable and helpful, this collection is primarily a resource for curriculum development, reference, and research rather than an information center. Products include an ongoing, frequently updated series of inexpensive bibliographies which can be used for materials selection and enrichment. The collection, set up for convenience as a traveling exhibit, can be used for in-service education, as a basis for materials selection, as a resource for college students, and as a source of materials for human relations meetings, ethnic fairs, library conferences, etc.

O27 **NATIONAL ASSOCIATION OF EDUCATIONAL BROAD-CASTERS (NAEB)** 1346 Connecticut Ave., N.W., Washington, D.C. 20036. (202) 785-1100
A membership organization open to educational broadcasters and interested teachers; offers consultant services to teachers.

O28 **NATIONAL AUDIOVISUAL CENTER** Stop 386, Washington, D.C. 20407. (301) 440-7753
The National Audiovisual Center (under the National Archives) was set up as a central clearinghouse, sales and rental agency, and information source for audiovisual materials produced and commissioned by federal agencies. It provides catalog information, plus sales and rental information for approximately 4,000 items—mostly 16-mm films on a wide variety of subjects, many of them valuable for vocational and adult educators—available at rather low fees. A copy of its current catalog is distributed without cost, upon request.

O29 **NATIONAL CENTER FOR AUDIO TAPES** Stadium Bldg., University of Colorado, Boulder, Colo. 80302. (303) 443-2211, Ext. 7341
A resource center comprised of 8,000 16-mm educational films and 14,000 audio tapes (on cassettes or open reels) on all educational topics at all levels from kindergarten to adult. Its primary services are for universities, public, and private schools of Colorado, but it is willing to provide tapes and films to others. Biannual catalogs of educational films and audio tapes are available at $4.50 each. Other activities include media and television production.

O30 **NATIONAL CENTER ON EDUCATIONAL MEDIA AND MATERIALS FOR THE HANDICAPPED (NCEMMH)** Ohio State University, 220 W. 12th Ave., Columbus, Ohio 43210. (614) 422-7596
NCEMMH, founded in 1972 to replace the discontinued Special Education Instructional Materials Centers, is funded by the Bureau of Education for

the Handicapped, U.S. Department of Health, Education, and Welfare. Its purpose is to encourage the use of appropriate educational materials and technology for the handicapped by locating, reviewing, and evaluating materials. The center functions as a liaison agent, surveys the needs of teachers, and provides information on curriculum and instructional products which can be used directly by handicapped children or for parent and teacher education in these fields. It does not provide direct assistance to handicapped persons, but provides information and assistance to state departments of education, teacher education departments in colleges and universities, special centers, and area learning resource centers.

O31 **NATIONAL CLEARINGHOUSE FOR DRUG ABUSE IN-FORMATION (NCDAI)** National Institute on Drug Abuse, Rockwall Bldg., 11400 Rockville Pike, Rockville, Md. 20852. (301) 443-6500

Created in 1970, NCDAI is now the single federal resource for public inquiries on drug abuse programs and related activities. It has two major functions: First, to operate an information bank and referral center containing information on all persons and programs concerned with drug abuse at all levels. Teachers with questions can contact NCDAI and receive information without charge. Second, it produces and distributes publications on drug abuse information, as well as directories of drug abuse resource people. An excellent education packet of selected materials on drug abuse (including school curricula, bibliographies, and catalogs) is available without charge to teachers from: EDUCATION, National Clearinghouse for Drug Abuse Information, P.O. Box 1080, Washington, D.C. 20013. It includes a current *Directory of State Drug Abuse Prevention Officials.*

A computerized information storage and retrieval system for drug abuse materials, NCDAI, features abstracts or descriptions of books, pamphlets, journal articles, posters, films, and other media materials, as well as descriptions of drug abuse treatment and prevention programs, which are assigned subject indexing codes. NCDAI generates bibliographies, selects media materials, and answers questions via mail, personal visits, direct telephone calls, or a 24-hour telephone message service. It has answered more than 2,000,000 queries during its first two years, 100,000 of them requiring complex and detailed responses. A comprehensive collection of information on drug abuse programs throughout the country, PROMIS (Program Management Information System), is a source for information on treatment facilities or drug prevention programs set up to allow retrieval of information on operation, etc. A network of drug abuse information centers, DRACON (Drug Abuse Communications Network), allows decentralized regional access to these materials. Free lending libraries for audiovisual materials have been set up in most states. Specific queries should be directed to the main office.

O32 **NATIONAL COMMITTEE ON UNITED STATES-CHINA RE-LATIONS** Coordinator of Educational Services, 777 United Nations Plz., 9B, New York, N.Y. 10017. (212) 682-6848
Established in 1966, this group is a nonprofit educational organization comprised of members from many professions, with many viewpoints, whose common purpose is to encourage public knowledge and discussion of China. (This group assisted the United States Table Tennis Association in arranging the table tennis exchange venture in April 1972.)

A significant effort on the part of its education and information program is to improve the quality and quantity of secondary teaching by providing educators with information, advice, and materials evaluation, and by cooperating with other educational organizations and teachers. The University Field Staff program consists of 10 field staff offices located throughout the United States, whose China specialist members, mostly professors and graduate students, are willing to volunteer as educational advisors and speakers for schools and community organizations—to organize workshops, evaluate or prepare materials, and arrange conferences or cultural displays.

The New York office can supply additional information; the following local offices can provide local consultation.

Colorado Field Staff
East Asian Studies
Hunter Hall 207
University of Colorado
Boulder, Colo. 80302
(303) 442-5093

Columbia University Field Staff
East Asian Institute
Columbia University
New York, N.Y. 10027
(212) 280-2591

Hawaii Field Staff
Department of History
314 Crawford Hall
University of Hawaii
Honolulu, Hawaii 96815

Michigan Field Staff
Center for Chinese Studies
104 Lane Hall
University of Michigan
Ann Arbor, Mich. 48104
(313) 761-0795

Northern California Field Staff
c/o East Asian Studies
Building 600-T
Stanford University
Stanford, Calif. 94305
(415) 321-2300

Seattle Field Staff
Institute for Comparative and
    Foreign Area Studies
University of Washington
Seattle, Wash. 98105

Seton Hall Field Staff
213 Humanities Hall
South Orange, N.J. 07079
(201) 762-9000, Ext. 505

Southern California Field Staff
393 Kinsey Hall
University of California
Los Angeles, Calif. 90024
(213) 825-1166

Virginia Field Staff
507 Brandon Ave., Apt. 7
Charlottesville, Va. 22903
(703) 295-0668

O33 **NATIONAL EDUCATIONAL FILM CENTER**   Rte. 2, Finks-
burg, Md. 21048. (301) 795-3000
This self-confessed "finest 16-mm library in the world" is composed of
selected films from large U.S. distributors. It is a membership organization offering various bargain rates on film rentals and film-related
materials to teacher members. Its monthly *Sneak Preview* ($8/year) offers
well-written reviews in a psychedelic format, with films of the month and
various cultural bargain offerings all listed together.

O34 **NATIONAL INDIAN TRAINING CENTER**   Professional Library, P.O. Box 66, Brigham City, Utah 84302. (801) 723-8591,
Ext. 328
The holdings of this professional library include a collection of 20,000
books, 1,500 pamphlets, 105 periodicals, 2,800 microfilms, and 2,500
media materials dealing with education and American Indians. Although its work is mostly for the Bureau of Indian Affairs staff, it
publishes an annual *Book Catalog* and an annual *Indian Bibliography,*
which list materials in its collection; available for five-week interlibrary
loan on a nationwide basis.

O35 **NATIONAL MEDICAL AUDIOVISUAL CENTER**   Annex Sta-
tion K, Atlanta, Ga. 30324. (404) 633-3351
An official U.S. center and archive for medical films, somewhat similar in
function to the National Audiovisual Center (O28). Offers two publications of interest to educators: *Mental Health Film Index,* a descriptive
catalog and source guide to approximately 400 titles in the field of mental
health, and *Mental Retardation Film List,* a descriptive catalog and source
list for 150 professional and nonprofessional films on mental retardation.
These and similar catalogs are available to educators on request.

O36 **NATIONAL MULTIMEDIA CENTER FOR ADULT EDUCA-
TION**   Adult Continuing Education Center, Montclair State
College, 848 Valley Rd., Upper Montclair, N.J. 07043. (201) 893-
4353
This center is essentially an information bank for adult education
instruction and curricular materials, including both commercially produced materials and materials generated by teachers. Its collection (5,500
items as of June 1975) includes all types of curricular materials—guides,

textbooks, test kits, workbooks, learning programs, demonstration projects, and reports of successful experiments—classified into 22 curricular areas: English, mathematics, social studies (including minority studies), science, literature, English as a second language, consumer education, career education, health education, family life, prevocational skills, etc.; approximately 100 new items are added each month.

A major feature offered by this center is an abstract service producing approximately 100 5″ × 8″ abstract cards each month—one for each new item in the collection. Cards include information on format, grade level, price, and source, with a one-paragraph description of the content and purpose; cards are cross-indexed by subject and skill, with additional printed quarterly and annual indexes. Sets of these cards are available in every state—in the office of the state director of adult basic education and at state libraries; they also can be obtained through some college and university adult education departments. Complete sets can be purchased for $273; partial sets are available at prorated costs.

The center also produces annotated *Abstract Bibliographies* of its curricular materials, covering topics such as *ESL* (English as a second language), *Consumer Education,* and *Career Education;* each includes approximately 100 abstracts and sells for $2.80. Sets of the materials are available at the center and at the Cooperating National Media Center, Federal City College, 1424 K Street, N.W., Washington, D.C. 20005, (202) 727-2045.

The center offers on-site review of instructional-curricular materials, as well as local and long-distance loans to cooperating groups. Its *NEC Newsletter,* free to subscribers of *Abstract Bibliographies*, covers the field of adult education nationally and internationally, with current news and research findings. It is actively soliciting copies of worthwhile adult education materials and news aout this field.

O37 **NATIONAL SCIENCE FOUNDATION (NSF)** 1800 G St., N.W., Washington, D.C. 20550. (202) 282-7786

The National Science Foundation supports a broad variety of activities aimed at improving education in science, mathematics, and social science, with the general goals of developing scientific literacy (that is, improving children's abilities to understand the concepts, applications, and implications of science) and improving science education for those oriented toward careers in the sciences. Its Division of Pre-College Education in Science supports the development of well-designed curriculum materials, as well as a broad range of activities directed toward administrators, teachers, and educational leaders. It publishes several well-designed pocket directories for different target groups, which include state-by-state listings and thumbnail descriptions of its grant-supported projects. These guides are available without cost.

O38 **NEW SCHOOLS EXCHANGE (NSE)** Pettigrew, Ark. 72752. (501) 677-2300

A casual and competent group whose interests center on educational alternatives, which is "generating a resource library, archives and reference center" on alternative education, and which functions as a clearinghouse for alternative schools in the United States and Canada. Its publications include *Directory of Alternative Schools* (B9) ($3) and a monthly *New Schools Exchange Newsletter* ($10/year). It is a major source of information on individuals and groups active in alternative education, innovative public schools, free universities, networks, and publications.

O39 **POPULATION REFERENCE BUREAU** 1755 Massachusetts Ave., N.W., Washington, D.C. 20036. (202) 232-2288

The Population Reference Bureau is a privately funded organization acting primarily as an information source for scholars, journalists, and educators in the area of national and international population dynamics and the environment. While its information usually is disseminated through its publications, its research staff and library can handle individual requests for information. Membership in the bureau is on a yearly basis ($8/year), with a special membership rate of $5/year for teachers and $2/year for students. Membership includes the following publications: *Population Bulletins, Profiles, PRD Selections,* and *World Population Data Sheets.* Six *Bulletins* are issued yearly; they include studies of a wide range of population issues such as nutrition, affluence, and food resources. Some of its other publications of interest to educators include:

Interchange, a bimonthly newsletter for teachers, administrators, curriculum specialists, and others interested in population education, primarily at the middle and secondary levels. This well-written newsletter, available for $2/year, provides information on projects in process, good reviews of teachers' sources and resources, and reports and announcements of events and activities related to population education.

OPTIONS, published in October 1973, is an 80-page study guide, at the secondary level, to the written and film versions of the report by the Commission on Population Growth and the American Future, available for a $0.50 handling charge.

Its population textbooks include *This Crowded World* (grades 4 to 6, $1.50), *People!* (grades 7 to 9, $1.50), and *The World Population Dilemma* (grades 10 to 12, $2.00). Color slides (35-mm) of maps, graphs, and tables cost $0.50 each.

O40 **RESOURCE CENTER ON SEX ROLES IN EDUCATION**
Suite 603, 1201 16th St., N.W., Washington, D.C. 20036. (202) 833-5426

This information and resource center, a part of the National Foundation for the Improvement of Education, is concerned with sex role stereotyping in elementary and secondary education. It provides technical assistance, training, and research for educational organizations and community groups. Its research holdings, available by appointment, include 30 books, 10,000 pamphlets, 4 periodicals, and 12 newsletters. Its own occasional newsletter, *Research Action Notes,* is available without cost. It also will provide assistance to groups developing other publications as part of an ongoing program.

O41 **SOCIAL SCIENCE EDUCATION CONSORTIUM, INC.
(SSEC)** Resource and Demonstration Center, 855 Broadway, Boulder, Colo. 80302. (303) 492-8155

The Social Science Education Consortium is a not-for-profit organization funded by the National Science Foundation to improve the quality of social science education at all grade levels. To help meet this goal, SSEC maintains a Resource and Demonstration Center—a "hands on" center with new social science project materials, innovative textbooks, multimedia kits, games and simulations, professional library, reference materials, an ERIC microfiche collection, and *Social Studies Curriculum Materials Data Book* (I92) and *Materials for Civics, Government and Problems of Democracy* (I66). The consortium offers a unique visitor workshop program in which individuals and groups are trained in the analysis and use of innovative social science curriculum materials and methods. For those who wish to keep abreast of changes, but are unable to visit the Resource Center, an Information Request Service is available, as well as a Consultation Program whereby SSEC staff, for a fee, will travel to school districts to train educators. The consortium also publishes a variety of items related to social science education, including analyses of curriculum materials, newsletters, books, and occasional papers, some produced jointly with ERIC/ChESS.

SSEC serves as the contracting agent for the ERIC Clearinghouse for Social Studies Education (ERIC/ChESS), the National Institute of Education-supported center that puts social studies material into the ERIC system, and publishes reviews and analytical papers based on that material. Computer services for social science related topics are available from ERIC/ChESS, which is housed in the same building as SSEC. The cost is $15.00 for a computer search that includes up to 50 citations on the printout. Each citation after the first 50 costs $0.10 extra.

O42 **SPECIAL COMMITTEE ON YOUTH EDUCATION FOR CITIZENSHIP (YEFC)** American Bar Assn., 1155 E. 60th St., Chicago, Ill. 60637. (312) 947-4000

This special committee, established in 1971, is supporting the creation and improvement of interdisciplinary programs dealing with our legal system and the democratic process. Its goal is to have law taught systematically at every grade level from kindergarten through high school. It is a national clearinghouse for information, as well as a facilitative agency coordinating with lawyers, representatives of the justice system, educational administrators, teachers, and parents in developing effective law-related programs on a community basis.

Its publications, free to educators, are well-produced directories and catalogs of relevant materials. *Directory of Law-Related Educational Activities* (1974), now in its second edition, provides information on more than 250 law-related projects throughout the United States, a directory of other projects and organizations in the field, and names of local contacts and resource people. *Bibliography of Law-Related Curriculum Materials: Annotated* (1974) lists and describes more than 500 books and pamphlets suitable for use in law-related curriculum. *Media: An Annotated Catalogue of Law-Related Audio-Visual Materials* (1975) is a well-arranged and well-indexed catalog of more than 400 films, filmstrips, audio cassettes, video tapes, and mixed media kits for enriching law-related curricula. Another pamphlet, describing law-related games and simulations, is planned for 1975.

O43 **VANDERBILT TELEVISION NEWS ARCHIVE** Joint University Libraries, Vanderbilt University, Nashville, Tenn. 37203. (615) 322-7311

A nonprofit enterprise of Vanderbilt University providing complete archives of videotapes and audiotapes of evening news broadcasts by the major television networks—ABC, CBS, and NBC—since August 5, 1968, with companion materials including presidential speeches (with accompanying comments), complete coverage of both Democratic and Republican National Conventions in 1968 and 1972, and the 1973 Watergate hearings. Its videotapes are available for use at the archive at $2/hour, and can be rented elsewhere for $15/hour, plus returnable deposit—for Ampex one-inch or EIAJ half-inch formats. Its resources include compilations of specified events: new compilations are performed for $30/hour; existing ones are available at the standard rate. Audiocassettes of full programs rent for $5/hour. A refundable deposit equal to the cost of tapes is required for tapes used outside the library.

Its monthly publication, *Television News Index and Archives,* provides updates and indexes of its materials.

O44 **WOMEN'S ACTION ALLIANCE** 370 Lexington Ave., New York, N.Y. 10017. (212) 685-0800

The Women's Action Alliance is a nonprofit, tax-exempt organization which tries to provide useful tools, resources, and information to women and women's groups, including the development of nonsexist, nonracist, early childhood curriculum. While it is an action group rather than a resource center, it is aware of other groups, activities, and publications in its area of interest, is willing to share information with others through its information and referral section, and has developed a series of inexpensive information packets, including *How to Organize a Child Care Center, How to Organize a Multi-Service Women's Center,* and *Tools to Eliminate Sex Discrimination in State and Local Government,* all of which include resource lists. Its *Non-Sexist Early Childhood Curriculum Manual* includes complete materials lists and parent-teacher consciousness-raising techniques.

17 | Computerized Retrieval Sources

This chapter is given primarily to computer search systems related to education. Many listings are for computer sources searching the ERIC data base—perhaps the best-known and most important, although not the best-designed, computer base for use in the field of education.

Of the computerized sources in education, many share essentially identical data bases with the abstracting and indexing tools discussed in Chapter 7. These include *AIM/ARM* (F1); *CIJE* (F5) and *RIE* (F20)—ERIC tapes; *Dissertation Abstracts International* (F6)—DATRIX (P2); *Exceptional Child Education Abstracts* (F10)—Council for Exceptional Children (M18); *Index Medicus* (F29)—MEDLARS, MEDLINE, and others (P8); *Psychological Abstracts* (F17)—PASAR and PADAT (P13); *Social Sciences Citation Index* (F21)—*Institute for Scientific Information* (P6); *Sociological Abstracts* (F22); and *Weekly Government Abstracts* (F24)—National Technical Information Service.

Other abstract journals discussed in Chapter 7—*Mental Retardation and Developmental Disabilities Abstracts* (F14), for instance—use computer-compatible technology in their preparation, but are not set up for machine searches.

Much the same as other information systems that are designed to handle large quantities of information, computerized information systems have to face and solve certain problems, which include:

1. *The quality of information.* Many information systems include much noninformation and some misinformation.

296

2. *The quality of indexing.* This is the crux of information retrieval. When original indexes are relatively well-designed, such as *Psychological Abstracts* or *Index Medicus,* computer searches will be effective. If indexes are not well-designed (although clever search programming may sometimes help), the speed of the transaction can amplify rather than compensate for sloppy indexing and illogical organization, where the lack of precise terminology, multiplied by rapid computer operation and output, can generate a large unwieldy package.

3. *Access to systems.* This area, which needs much more thought and time, involves knowledge of audiences, establishment of standards to foster compatibility and intersystem use and communications, conversion of existing information sources to machine-readable form, and provision of systems directories.

4. *Products designed for comfort of users and screened for relevance.* Bibliographic citations should be accompanied with means of acquiring printed materials. In the current state-of-the-art, computer products, even without a generous number of irrelevant citations, can be more difficult to use than their standard printed counterparts. Such amenities as upper- and lower-case type and evenness of type densities are frequently overlooked or undervalued, although they are basic to legibility and ultimate communicability.

5. *Interrelationship with other information systems, both printed and computerized.* A computer search cannot be an isolated experience in itself, but must be tied to other sources of educational information to provide adequate assistance. Ideally, the information sources in this book should be part of a simplified integrated system. Computerized systems, like research libraries, need many cross-related tools in their data banks. Researchers in the behavioral aspects of education, for instance, need access to tapes of *Psychological Abstracts* and *Sociological Abstracts* as well as to the obvious ERIC tapes and to printed tools.[1]

---

[1] One promising experiment in integrating computer services with standard public library reference services is currently taking place in San Mateo and Santa Clara counties in California. Under a grant from the Office of Science Information Service of the National Science Foundation, public libraries in Redwood City, San Jose, Santa Clara, and San Mateo, already part of a four-county Cooperative Information Network (CIN), provide facilities for computer terminal access to the vast data bases in Lockheed's DIALOG, while Lockheed coordinates the project and trains librarians in computer retrieval techniques.

Public library clients have been able to use Lockheed's data bases, which, at the project's

6. *Inclusiveness of information.* Because of the casual nature of educational publication, potentially valuable materials often are omitted from existing catalogs, indexes, and systems and are not accessible to computerized retrieval.

Given the sheer quantity of information in education and related fields, computerization is becoming a necessity rather than a luxury. Until the problems listed above are resolved more fully, however, computerization in itself does not automatically guarantee access to appropriate educational information.

The commercial sources of ERIC searches listed here are available to educators and other interested individuals willing to pay commercial fees, which range from $5 to $50 per search. Other data bases tend to be a little higher. To date, no body such as Consumer's Union or EPIE (see O12) has evaluated these searches for either quality or cost-effectiveness.

Unfortunately, the quality of the searches cannot be effectively estimated through printed descriptions. On-line searches, for instance, can be more sophisticated and flexible than batch searches, but the end product is not necessarily superior. In the hands of unskilled or inexperienced computer operators, on-line searches can result in unproductive or expensive products. Careful analysis of the research questions, as detailed in Chapter 1, is equally important for computer searches, where time is translated into money.

Search services of state departments of education are treated in Chapter 19. Typically, these provide services to department staffs, and sometimes to teachers or administrators within the state, often free or for a low fee. More often than not, they offer batch searches—mass-produced searches for which refinements or alterations stop when the search question enters the computer.

Chapter 18 includes a few of the computerized ERIC centers, some of which are located at the Universities of Calgary, Georgia, Illinois, Indiana, Iowa, Minnesota, and Oklahoma, Bradley University, New Mexico University, and Ohio State University. These

---

inception in mid-1974, included approximately 4 million references and abstracts in such areas as ecology, agriculture, energy, pollution, engineering, science, social sciences, psychology, business, technology, and education (at no charge for the first year and half the standard DIALOG price for the second year). This service is backed up by interlibrary loan and library networks.

centers, often working out of education libraries, tend to provide speedier or more custom-tailored searches than do the more general sources. The searches range from free of charge to approximately $10.

Some of the computerized information systems discussed in this chapter offer more data and greater capacity in their computerized forms than in their printed products. A prime example is MEDLARS, which contains far more entries per indexed item than does *Index Medicus,* which is produced from it.

Computerized retrieval search sources discussed elsewhere in this book include the Bill Status System (N3), The Foundation Center (N10), Funding Sources Clearinghouse (N11), Council for Exceptional Children (M18), and National Assessment of Educational Progress (M26). Chapters 14 and 16 provide information on computerized searches performed at varying prices and degrees of sophistication by ERIC clearinghouses dealing with the disadvantaged (M22), educational management (M17), information resources (O17), exceptional children (M18), rural education and small schools (M20), social studies/social science education (O41), teacher education (M21), and career education (M14).

There are many other computerized research services that are occasionally valuable in education—mostly in higher education: those offered by the New York Times, the Institute of Electrical and Electronics Engineers, and the Natural History Information Retrieval System of the National Museum of Natural History, as well as MARC tapes (from the Library of Congress), are all possibilities of marginal value.

Two books that could be helpful to educators are the *Directory of Data Bases in the Social and Behavioral Sciences* edited by Vivian Sessions (B31), the most comprehensive compilation of social science data banks to date; and *Selected Federal Computer-Based Information Systems* compiled by Saul Herner and Matthew J. Vellucci (Washington, D.C., Information Resources Press, 1972), which provides well-written expositions of 35 computer-based information systems throughout the federal government—not designed for education, but possibly good for some research purposes. The *Encyclopedia of Information Systems and Services* (B40) also is worth checking.

The American Society for Information Science has published a detailed analysis of 81 commercially available bibliographic data bases, *Survey of Commercially Available Computer-Readable Biblio-graphic Data Bases,* edited by John H. Schneider, Marvin Gechman, and Stephen Furth (Washington, D.C., 1974).

A recent *Survey of ERIC Data Base Search Services, July 1974* by J.D. Embry et al. (Washington, D.C., National Institute of Education, 1974. ED 095 750) provides a chart analysis, arranged by state, of 120 services which search the ERIC data bases. Information includes audiences, computer services, and costs as of April 1974.

Computerized searches in the behavioral sciences are discussed in Roberta Steiner's "Selected Computerized Search Services in Areas Related to the Behavioral Sciences," *Special Libraries,* *65*(8):319-325, August 1974. Ms. Steiner, librarian for American Institutes for Research, also uses a chart to detail computerized search services that go beyond education and funding to defense documentation, public health, and marriage and family behavior. Her chart also includes costs and time parameters.

A valuable and enlightening account of the life history of one computer-oriented project, EDNET, set up to rationalize educational computer services, appeared in the Summer 1972 issue of *EDUCOM Bulletin.*[2] EDNET was projected to provide persons at all locations with access to computerized resources through a facilitating Educational Information Network (EIN). Actually, the actions and catalog of this agency resulted not in the increased use of existing facilities, but in increased growth of separate systems which borrowed and transplanted features from existing systems.

Educational enterprises interested in acquiring or using computer hardware can get assistance from a recent issue of the *People's Computer Company,*[3] which constitutes an informal buyer's guide to educational hardware, complete with background information on preparing specifications and acquisition of peripheral equipment, systems designs, and summaries of school district experiences, plus a section on evaluating free equipment. The People's Computer Company, whose areas of concern cover public access to computers

[2] LeGates, John. "The Lessons of EIN," *EDUCOM Bulletin,* 7(2):18-20, Summer 1972 (from EDUCOM Interuniversity Communications Council, P.O. Box 364, Rosedale Road, Princeton, New Jersey 08540). EDUCOM itself is an excellent source of information on some aspects of educational computerization.

[3] "PCC Looks at Hardware," *People's Computer Company,* 2(4), March 1974 (from People's Computer Company, P.O. Box 310, Menlo Park, California 94025; yearly subscription, 5 issues/year, $4.50).

and their use in education and recreation, are hoping to issue similar issues in future years.

P1   **DATA USE AND ACCESS LABORATORIES (DUALabs)**   Suite 900, 1601 N. Kent St., Arlington, Va. 22209. (703) 525-1480
DUALabs promotes effective uses of census data and other public data by identifying valuable new files, developing timely solutions to problems of access and use, and disseminating the results of this work as widely as possible. DUALabs' library currently houses approximately 67 statistical data files, including the 1970 Census Summary Tape Files, the 1960 and 1970 Census Public Use Sample Files, and the Census of Governments' Files. Services include tape copying, custom files and extracts, display printouts, analytic reports, seminar programs, and data consultation.

Publications include a newsletter, *Data Access News;* the *Review of Public Data Use,* a quarterly journal focusing on social science research and methodology using publicly available data bases; *1970 Census Technical Bulletins;* the *Census Processing Center Catalog;* and the *1970 Census Data Finder.*

P2   **DATRIX II (Direct Access to Reference Information: A Xerox Service**   University Microfilms, Inc., Ann Arbor, Mich. 48106. (313) 761-4700
A computerized bibliographic file of abstracts of doctoral theses, available in microfilm format, originally listed in the publications *Microfilm Abstracts, Dissertation Abstracts,* and *Dissertation Abstracts International–* 430,000 dissertations in May 1975. DATRIX II offers keyword searching, which is matched against the computer's file of keywords, derived from dissertation titles. The basic fee is $15.00 (prepaid) for a bibliography of up to 150 references; $0.10 for each additional reference (minimum $5.00, prepaid). The research process itself is an interesting exercise in logic and classification.

The DATRIX II printout is arranged in chronological order, beginning with the most recent titles. Each citation indicates the author's name, degree, degree year, and university; appropriate references in *Dissertation Abstracts International (DAI)* or other sources; and the order number for those dissertations that are available from University Microfilms. DATRIX II complements and updates the 37-volume *Comprehensive Dissertation Index* (and its supplements) published by University Microfilms.

A recently published nine-volume *Dissertation Abstracts International Retrospective Index* covers the same data base (up to 1970) with a subject (keyword) arrangement and an author index. It is relatively easy to use in locating doctoral dissertations by subject or author.

P3 **EDITEC, INC.** The Electric Library, 53 W. Jackson Blvd., Chicago, Ill. 60604. (312) 427-6760

An unusual, computer-based information center, which can tap more than 25 million documents from 29 data bases. Major subject areas include business management, financial news and statistics, business and marketing (national and international), government publications, congressional documents, materials cataloged by the Library of Congress, urban affairs, medicine, psychology, agriculture, life sciences, general information, statistics, and education. Data bases relevant to education users include ERIC files, *AIM/ARM, Exceptional Child Education Abstracts, American Statistics Index, Congressional Information Service* and *New York Times* Information Bank (NYTIB) in computer format, with microfiche collections for some of the data banks.

Editec offers a variety of services: individual computer searches of all relevant data banks at $125 each, with contracts at somewhat reduced rates (for example, $100 each for 40 searches). These searches generally include citations and abstracts. Documents can be provided at an additional cost. An SDI (Selective Dissemination of Information) service costs $195 per year for 12 monthly updates in one data base, plus an initial one-time charge of $25 for establishing a "logic" or "profile" of individual interests in order to select new documents each month. Searches are available via TELEX, facsimile, drop-in, computer terminal, or mail, with replies received within one week via mail and more rapidly by computer or electronic means. Its newsletter, *The Editec Letter,* provides users with information about new services and data bases.

P4 **GEORGIA INFORMATION DISSEMINATION CENTER** Office of Computing Activities, Boyd Graduate Study Bldg., University of Georgia, Athens, Ga. 30602. (404) 542-3106

This information center has a wide variety of data bases on tape, including *Psychological Abstracts, Sociological Abstracts, Biological Abstracts, Current Index to Journals in Education (CIJE),* and *Resources in Education (RIE),* plus many more in science and agriculture which also could be valuable to educators—over 6 million documents and citations as of July 1975. It is open to any user, by mail or drop-in, and offers many options in computerized retrieval services. Some of these are:

Search Profiles: Worked out with the help of its staff, can include up to 200 terms (depending on the length of the terms), which can be changed as the user's interests change. These profiles are run against incoming tapes at specified charges per issue.

Current Awareness Searches: Designed to keep users up-to-date on current literature, performed whenever current issues or update tapes are received, and generally mailed out within two days after the tapes are received. Charges for current searches (quarterly) of *CIJE* or *RIE, Psychological Abstracts,* and *Sociological Abstracts* are $10 each per quarter.

Retrospective Searches: Scheduled for two- to three-week delivery and based on a charge per volume. Searches of *CIJE, RIE,* and *Psychological Abstracts* cost $35 per volume; *Sociological Abstracts* cost $50 per volume in 1975.

Search results are printed on standard 8½″ × 11″ paper, which is easier to use than the standard computer printout, and are available on 4″ × 6″ card stock for an additional $0.02 per card. Abstracts can be included on the printouts for $0.10 per abstract. Subscriptions and special searches can be arranged by mail and phone.

P5 **INFORMATION SYSTEM FOR NATIVE AMERICAN MEDIA (ISNAM)** National Indian Education Assn., 3036 University Ave., S.E., Minneapolis, Minn. 55415. (616) 378-0482
Still in a state of development in early 1975, the aim of this long-range project is to provide a computerized evaluative catalog of all media materials used in schools that are by, about, or for native Americans— approximately 15,000 entries are anticipated. The project staff, along with other native-American evaluators, are working on the design of evaluative criteria. A quarterly *Project MEDIA Bulletin* provides updated information on materials and information acquired by the National Indian Education Association, as well as on the progress of ISNAM.

P6 **INSTITUTE FOR SCIENTIFIC INFORMATION (ISI)** 325 Chestnut St., Philadelphia, Pa. 19106. (215) 923-3300
ISI publishes *Current Contents* (F4) and the *Social Sciences Citation Index* (F21) and offers custom-tailored, computerized, current subject searching and citation services at various rates.

Automatic Subject Citation Alert (ASCA) starts at $115 per year for simple profiles (trial rate of 13 weeks for $39). This computer citation service applies a personalized profile of an individual's interest to its data base of 4,500 scientific periodicals (the data base for educational research would be 1,100 periodicals in social and behavioral sciences). The individual profile is worked out jointly by ISI and the user, who would list subject interests, authors, and publications he would like to keep up with, what he has written on the subject, and some authors and books he considers relevant. With the help of a personal telephone call, ISI designs an interest profile for the individual or organization, which is checked via computer each week against the periodicals received by ISI. Beginning with that week, the subscriber receives a weekly list of relevant citations and can, by subscribing to ISI's Original Article Tear Sheet Service (OATS), receive tear sheets of articles (see F4 for a more detailed description of the tear-sheet service).

Social Sciences Citation Index searches also are available from ISI for a minimum of $75 (3 hours of search time). This citation tool indexes journals in educational research, ethnic group studies, sociology, and statistics, as well as publications in social science fields less relevant to education.

P7   **LOCKHEED INFORMATION RETRIEVAL SERVICE (DIALOG)** 1756 Westwood Blvd., Los Angeles, Calif. 90024. (213) 829-5090; 3251 Hanover St., Palo Alto, Calif. 94304. (415) 493-4411; Suite 303E, 200 Park Ave., New York, N.Y. 10007. (212) 682-4630; and 900 17th St., N.W., Washington, D.C. 20006. (202) 872-5971

Lockheed's data base includes tapes of all education files, *Resources in Education (RIE), Current Index to Journals in Education (CIJE), Exceptional Child Education Abstracts, Abstracts of Instructional and Research Materials (AIM/ARM)*, the now discontinued *Current Projects in Education and Field Reader Catalog, Psychological Abstracts,* National Technical Information Service (NTIS), *Social Sciences Citation Index,* and a substantial number of business, agricultural, scientific, medical, technical, and private data bases.

On-line service prices vary, depending on the number of hours, distance from the computer, and type of terminal. The ERIC computer charge per hour is $25 for most data bases, with an additional charge of $0.10 per item for off-line printing. Contracts now are available with no minimum hour requirements. Services are for organizations only; individual searches are not available through Lockheed. (See Figure 18.)

P8   **MEDICAL LITERATURE ANALYSIS AND RETRIEVAL SYSTEM (MEDLARS)** National Library of Medicine, 8600 Rockville Pike, Bethesda, Md. 20014. (301) 496-4000

MEDLARS is the National Library of Medicine's computer-based system that provides rapid access to the journal literature of the health sciences—almost 2.5 million references dating back to 1964. The articles, indexed at a rate of more than 200,000 each year, are taken from 2,300 journals in many languages and medical specialties. The references appear in print each month in *Index Medicus* and also are published in a variety of specialized "Recurring Bibliographies"; for example, *Bibliography on Medical Education, Index to Dental Literature,* and others.

MEDLINE (MEDLARS On-Line) is a nationwide system for directly searching the MEDLARS data base through computer terminals in 350 medical

```
TITLE        CIN DEMONSTRATION
DATE/FILE    5-16-74/11
SEARCHER     O. FIRSCHEIN
REQUESTOR    S
ADDRESS      DEPT. 52/53, BLDG. 201
SET ITEMS DESCRIPTION (+=OR;*=AND;-=NOT)
--- ----- --------------------------------


         EXPAND DYSLEXIC
REF   INDEX-TERM            TYPE ITEMS RT
E1    DYSLECTIC---------------       4
E2    DYSLECTICS--------------       5
E3    DYSLEPTIC---------------       3
E4    DYSLEXIA---------------      611   5
E5    DYSLEXIAS--------------        1
E6    -DYSLEXIC---------------     107
E7    DYSLEXICS--------------       12
E8    DYSLOGIA---------------        2
E9"   DYSLOGIC---------------        2


   1    620  E4-E7
              E6: DYSLEXIC
   2    535  WRITING
   3     27  1 AND2



           TYPE 3/5/5
DOC YEAR: 1973 VOL NO: 49 ABSTRACT NO: 9
4698
    SPECIFIC LEARNING DISORDERS IN CHILDHO
OD.
    GOMEZ, MANUEL R.

    MAYO GRADUATE SCHOOL OF MEDICINE, ROCH
ESTER, MINN.
    PSYCHIATRIC ANNALS   1972 MAY VOL. 2(5
) 49-65
    DEFINES  SPECIFIC  LEARNING  DISORDERS
    AS PARTIAL OR SELECTIVE LIMITATIONS OF
LEARNING  WHICH  ARE  ATTRIBUTABLE  TO
CEREBRAL  IMPAIRMENT.  THEORIES CONCERNING
ETIOLOGY  AND  EDUCATIONAL  REMEDIES  AR
E  BRIEFLY  DISCUSSED.  THE SYMPTOMS AND
TREATMENT  OF  DEVELOPMENTAL  DYSLEXIA,
SPELLING DISABILITY, WRITING DISABILITY,
DYSCALCULIA, DRAWING DISABILITY, AND DYS
PRAXIA ARE CONSIDERED IN DETAIL.
    CLASSIFICATION- 14

    SUBJECT TERMS- DYSLEXIA, LEARNING DISO
RDERS; 15610, 27990
    INDEX  PHRASE-  DYSLEXIA  &  DYSCALCU
LIA  &  SPELLING  &  WRITING  &  DRAWING
DISABILITIES & DEVELOPMENTAL CLUMSINESS,
DEFINITIONS & SYMPTOMS & TREATMENT
SEARCH TIME (MIN.):    6.58
```

FIGURE 18   This typical Lockheed DIALOG printout provides an abstract of an
article in a medical-psychiatric journal dealing with an educational
problem.

institutions around the country. MEDLINE contains approximately 500,000 references to the most recent (two to three years) journal literature. Although MEDLINE primarily serves the health community, it is sometimes appropriate for those engaged in educational research to use MEDLINE; for example, to access the literature on learning disabilities, reading, speech, hearing, and other areas where biology and medicine interrelate with learning.

Other computerized search services of the National Library of Medicine available over the nationwide MEDLINE network are CATLINE, which provides access to books cataloged by the library; TOXLINE, which provides access to the literature of toxicology and pharmacology; and AVLINE, which provides information about audiovisuals used for health science education. Effective July 1975, the cost of searches of all National Library of Medicine on-line data bases is $15 for each hour of computer connect time between 10:00 a.m. and 5:00 p.m., Eastern Time, and $8/hour at all other times. Each page of off-line printout costs $0.10.

P9   **NATIONAL CLEARINGHOUSE FOR MENTAL HEALTH IN-FORMATION (NCMHI)**   National Institute of Mental Health, 5600 Fishers Lane, Rockville, Md. 20852. (301) 443-4517

This clearinghouse collects and disseminates scientific and technical information on all aspects of mental health for mental health professionals, students, and others interested in this field. NCMHI answers telephone and mail requests from a computerized file which included 210,000 abstracts as of August 1975 (incorporating new documents at a rate of 45,000 per year). Other services, for which teachers are eligible, include special bibliographies and referral services. The National Institute of Mental Health distributes single copies of its publications on request, without charge.

P10 **NEW ENGLAND RESEARCH APPLICATION CENTER (NERAC)**   Mansfield Professional Park, Storrs, Conn. 06268. (203) 486-5433

A comprehensive technical information service whose many computerized scientific and technical files cover the fields of biology, chemistry, engineering, metals, textiles, air pollution, and electronics, plus those of the Institute for Scientific Information (P6), MEDLARS (P8), Smithsonian Science Information Exchange (P16), DATRIX (P2), and ERIC (M12). These are backed up by manual searches in the University of Connecticut library, whose resources include 1,000,000 volumes, 20,000 reference books, 7,000 current periodical subscriptions, and the published indexes of *Psychological Abstracts* and *Sociological Abstracts*.

Its on-site computer facility is tailored towards its clients' demands and is not shared with anyone. NERAC performs all the strategy design on searches, with no limit on the number of descriptors. Output is a complete printout of all information, including abstracts. Copies of documents are provided for an average charge of $5.25 per document. The basic charges are *not* by individual search, but are based on access to its total files and prorated according to the "number of people asking questions."

P11 **NORTHWEST REGIONAL EDUCATION LABORATORY** Information Center, 710 S.W. Second Ave., Portland, Ore. 97204. (503) 248-6922

This computerized service uses the DIALOG system to search data bases, including ERIC, *Exceptional Child Education Abstracts, Psychological Abstracts,* NTIS, and *AIM/ARM*. As of April 1975, the price for a search was $7.00 per hour for staff time, plus data base time, which varies from $0.83 per minute for ERIC up to $1.90 per minute for other bases. Additional charges for varying print formats include $0.10 for full citation and abstract and $0.05 for full citation only. Typical searches cost approximately $20 each.

P12 **PROJECT TALENT DATA BANK** American Institutes for Research (AIR), 1791 Arastradero Rd., P.O. Box 1113, Palo Alto, Calif. 94302. (415) 493-3550

Project TALENT's data bank consists of magnetic tape information on a longitudinal study of 400,000 high school students, selected on a stratified random basis (starting in 1960) and subjected to an inventory of tests. The data is available for use in a wide variety of formats at cost. *The Project TALENT Data Bank: A Handbook* (available from the above address for $2.50) contains extensive information on the tests, inventories, procedures, and follow-ups of Project TALENT, as well as the policy guidelines under which the data may be used. The AIR library houses a unique file of AIR technical reports on education.

P13 **PSYCHOLOGICAL ABSTRACTS SEARCH AND RETRIEVAL SERVICE (PASAR)** American Psychological Assn., Office of Communications—Bibliographic Control, 1200 17th St., N.W., Washington, D.C. 20036. (202) 833-7600

Magnetic tapes of *Psychological Abstracts* from 1967 to date are produced as a by-product of its method of composition (see F17 for a description of the contents). Tapes can be leased by an information center through the PATELL (Psychological Abstracts Tape Edition Lease or Licensing) service or hooked up to a computer terminal through PADAT (Psychological Abstracts Direct Access Terminal), a process that allows interaction and a variety of outputs. PADAT subscriptions are available for a minimum of one hour per month, which averages three to four searches at a cost of approximately $90. For the occasional user, PASAR provides mail access. The requesting individual mails a request form to the association's central office for processing through an on-line computer terminal. An information specialist translates and amplifies the request to meet the needs of the requester. An average search costs $40.00 to $60.00, based on a $15.00 processing charge, plus $2.25 per minute of computer time. The total cost is based on the complexity or number of variables or limiting factors in a search, not on the number of references retrieved. The final product is a computer printout of citations and abstracts which can be sorted alphabetically by title or author, or chronologically at a slight extra charge. Because of the high quality of indexing, these well-structured searches produce a high proportion of relevant materials.

Even though its competent information specialists share the responsibility for search strategy and vocabulary, users should consult the index terms in individual volumes of *Psychological Abstracts* or the new *Thesaurus of Psychological Index Terms* (A17) prior to requesting a search. The PASAR Search Request Guidelines (shown in Figure 19) are designed to assist users in constructing useful search statements.

P14 **RESEARCH AND INFORMATION SERVICES FOR EDUCA-**
     TION (RISE) 198 Allendale Rd., King of Prussia, Pa. 19406.
     (215) 265-6056

Sponsored by Montgomery County's Intermediate Unit, RISE provides information services to educators and education students in Montgomery County, Pennsylvania and to the Bureau of Planning in the Pennsylvania State Department of Education; also offers its services to the general public.

Resources, dealing primarily with administration, curriculum, and supportive services for education, include 3,000 books, 18,000 documents, 328 periodical subscriptions, some standard education indexing and abstracting services, a file of 1,040 literature searches, and complete microfiche collections of ERIC, the Curriculum Materials Clearinghouse, and UNIPAC's (I106). It can perform on-line interactive computer searches of ERIC, *Psychological Abstracts, Social Sciences Citation Index,* National Technical Information Service, *Exceptional Child Education Abstracts, AIM/ARM,* and many scientific and commercial files.

A variety of services are offered to individuals and institutions on rather complex contractual terms: some services, with prices, are listed below.

RISE Bibliographies: $2.50 per bibliography.
Selective Response: Provides hard copy or microfiche of 10 citations from completed search packets for a service fee of $10 per search.

PASAR Search Request Guidelines

The **PASAR** Request Form has been designed to assist you in constructing a comprehensive statement of your requirements. However, it should not restrict your input. Provide whatever other information you feel will augment the information specialist's understanding of your requirements. These guidelines should help to clarify items on the Request Form.

ITEM 1. Narrative statement of search topic. Provide a detailed description of the subject matter you wish to be retrieved. Please avoid submitting multiple, discrete requests on a single **PASAR** Request Form, since such cannot be processed for a single fee. However, multiple aspects of a primary subject may be requested. The distinction is illustrated in the following examples:

> *Acceptable:* "the effects of socioeconomic status, education level, or birth order on career motivation in women."

"Career motivation" is the primary element of this request, while the other elements serve merely to qualify or narrow the scope of this rather broad subject area.

> *Unacceptable:* "the measurement of employee attitudes concerning wages and benefits. Also desire references dealing with the factors that influence management decision-making with respect to personnel policies and procedures."

Although these two topics are closely related to the design and administration of personnel policies and procedures, two separate search strategies would have to be executed to retrieve the specific information requested, and a separate charge for each would have to be made.

ITEM 2. Descriptor(s) relevant to dependent variable(s). Provide a list of words or phrases that indicate the subject matter of prime interest. Descriptors for the "acceptable" example (see Item #1) might include: career motivation, career preference, and career aspirations.

ITEM 3. Descriptor(s) relevant to independent variable(s). Provide a list of words or phrases that will qualify or narrow the scope of the dependent variable. Descriptors for the "acceptable" example (see Item #1) might include: socioeconomic status, social class, educational level, birth order, and women.

ITEM 4. Search qualifications. Once the subject matter of the search has been defined, you may wish to refine it with specific requirements such as population or time frame. These qualifications are often essential to the actual information need; however, they can unnecessarily limit the search, causing retrieval of few of the relevant records. Therefore, consider your requirements carefully.

ITEM 5. Sorting requirements. Please indicate whether you would prefer to have references sorted alphabetically by author or chronologically by year.

ITEM 6. Intended use of search results. Provide a description of how the references resulting from your search will be used (e.g., definition of a research project, preparation of an article, proposal preparation, dissertation, etc.).

Ordering information: When ordering a **PASAR** search, please read the above guidelines carefully before completing the request form. A purchase order must accompany all institutional requests for a **PASAR** search. For individuals requesting a **PASAR** search, the signature of the person responsible for payment must appear on the **PASAR** request form.

FIGURE 19   Guidelines prepared by American Psychological Association's information specialists result in well-structured, productive searches.

Duplicates of Existing Searches: $35 for out-of-state clients ($25 for Pennsylvanians) or $0.10 per page, whichever cost is greater.

Computer Searches: The basic fees are $25.00 per file (ERIC, *Psychological Abstracts,* etc.) for 10-descriptor searches. ERIC documents are available in microfiche format at $0.25 per fiche ($0.40 per fiche for out-of-state clients) or $0.15 per reader-printer page. Journal articles are available for $0.10 per Xerox page.

Comprehensive Searches: Include all of its data bases, and cost $300 per search or $15 per hour, plus duplication costs. Turnaround time is approximately three weeks.

P15 **SCHOOL RESEARCH INFORMATION SERVICE (SRIS)** Center on Evaluation, Development, and Research, Phi Delta Kappa, P.O. Box 789, Bloomington, Ind. 47401. (812) 339-1156

This research service, originally funded by a Kettering Foundation Research Grant, is now underwritten by Phi Delta Kappa. Its resources are magnetic tapes of *Resources in Education (RIE)* and *Current Index to Journals in Education (CIJE).* Computer searches of ERIC are run in response to written requests containing a clear statement of the problem, prepayment, and an indication of whether the searcher wants to use the *RIE* data bank, the *CIJE* data bank, or both ($15 for one data bank, $21 for both). A computer printout of abstracts for the first 100 citations, and citations only for subsequent items, is mailed within approximately three weeks. *CEDR Quarterly* ($3/year), a quarterly publication, provides current information on the nature of the processes of evaluation, development, and research, as well as techniques for their implementation.

P16 **SMITHSONIAN SCIENCE INFORMATION EXCHANGE (SSIE)** Suite 300, 1730 M St., N.W., Washington, D.C. 20036. (202) 381-5511

The purpose of SSIE is to provide research scientists and administrators with information on current federal and state agency research projects, as well as privately funded and commercial basic research. The computerized data bank consists of one-sheet summaries of research in progress: approximately 85,000 to 100,000 items are added per year. Project information includes project title, location, a 200-word summary of the work in progress, principal investigator, and duration, all updated annually. Although the basic areas cover science and technology, both behavioral and social sciences are included. Some relevant areas are cognitive processes, communication, developmental psychology, education and training, learning and retention, economics, manpower, governmental studies, and management science.

SSIE publishes an interesting *SSIE Science Newsletter* (10 issues at

$6/year), which provides current coverage of ongoing research and research agencies, and offers subscriber discounts for SSIE services. Both custom and package searches are offered. Custom individual searches (subject, administrative, and other) generally start at $50 for 50 documents, plus $10 for each additional 50 documents or fraction thereof. Package searches are somewhat cheaper. For example, $35 for 95 references, covering the effect of drugs on learning and cognition. The variety is wide and impressive. For a more extensive description on the scope of the agency and its searches, write for a brochure and a sample copy of the newsletter.

P17 **SYSTEM DEVELOPMENT CORPORATION (ORBIT)** 2500 Colorado Ave., Santa Monica, Calif. 90406. (213) 829-7511; 7929 Westpark Dr., McLean, Va. 22101. (703) 790-9850

The bibliographic search service of this experienced information retrieval group offers the SDC-developed ORBIT system for searching 16 data bases currently, including the ERIC tapes, as well as a variety of other data bases in the natural and social sciences. If the user has a terminal (most commercial terminals are compatible with this system) and an acoustic coupler for telephone hook-up, access to the system can be made on a time-sharing basis. The rates for use vary from data base to data base, but the user pays only for what is used, with the first two hours of computer time free. Since the system is congruent with standard library searching procedures, it is relatively easy to master for anyone who is familiar with a typewriter and research methods. SDC Search Service, available at both of the above locations, can provide additional information.

P18 **WESTERN RESEARCH APPLICATION CENTER (WES-RAC)** University of Southern California, 809 W. 34th St., Los Angeles, Calif. 90007. (213) 746-6132

Its data bank includes *RIE*, *CIJE*, and various government data banks from *Government Reports Announcements (GRA)*, the Department of Defense, and NASA, as well as from *Chemical Abstracts* and *Engineering Index*. Its DATRACON system provides on-line retrieval at $25 per hour for users with their own terminals and provides in-house, batch-mode services for others. If the user sets up his own search strategy, the cost is $40.00 for 200 references, plus $0.06 for each subsequent reference. For an additional $40.00, WESRAC will set up the search strategy. Services are available at a reduced rate to Los Angeles city and county school personnel, through the Los Angeles Center for Education Resource Services.

18 | *Gaining Access to Educational Information and Materials*

Although the bulk of this book is devoted to annotated listings intended to convey the usefulness and scope of selected reference materials in education, it would be overly optimistic to assume that these tools are necessarily available to all teachers, administrators, or individuals who could put them to use. Ideally, the relevant tools listed here should be part of a network of educational resources, open to those who need them. Actually, locating adequate libraries or other sources of educational materials can be difficult for many teachers, administrators, and citizens. There is no directory of education libraries per se, although Chapter 3 does include some directories which can lead to libraries, and Chapters 14, 15, 16, 17, and 19 provide some directory information.

ACCESS TO MATERIALS

While a good library is an ideal source for materials and services, these also can be obtained from other sources when an adequate library is not available. The balance of this chapter deals with library as well as alternative sources for some services and materials.

REQUIREMENTS	SOURCES
Reference Service	Large public libraries, school of education libraries, state libraries, and large school district libraries. If reference books or services are not available at a library, it may be part of a network which offers these services by mail, phone, or TWX. Try to specify your subject and the sources you have already checked. If the library cannot provide the desired information, it may be able to advise where or how it can be obtained.
Interlibrary Loans	Generally handled through public, university, and state libraries. Clearly describe the subject and sources checked thus far. For a particular book, include, at a minimum, its author, title, and date of publication.
Journal Articles	Best sources are libraries, interlibrary loan, photocopies, reprints, and single issues from publishers. For interlibrary loan, include complete citation—author, title, journal title, volume number, page numbers, month, and year. Publishers can supply single issues of recent journals and, occasionally, reprints or photocopies of articles. Publishers' addresses and journal prices can be found in *Educator's World* (B39), in the abstract journals and indexes listed in Chapter 7, and in the periodical directories listed in Chapter 4. Photocopies can be obtained from libraries and from some publishers. The *Directory of Library Reprographic Services,* edited by Joseph Nitecki (Weston, Conn., Microform Review, Inc., 1973), which is widely available at interlibrary loan desks, provides information sources and costs of various kinds of library photocopies. University Microfilms (Q2) offers photocopies of some journals, while tear sheets are offered through the OATS service of *Current Contents* (F4).
Pamphlets	Sources are usually included in the indexing source. Photocopies of materials from *P.A.I.S.* (F16) are available from the New York Public Library.
Microfiche	ERIC microfiche copies are available for reading and consultation in most of the sources indicated in B32. Check local school districts, state educational library services, and state RCU's to see if they provide microfiche copies or have microfiche readers. Microfiche or hard copies of ERIC microfiche can be purchased through the ERIC Document Reproduction Service, discussed in M12. Include ED numbers, name, return address, and postage with check, when ordering by mail.

ERIC microfiche on specified subjects, in Micro-Libraries form, are available from Microfiche Publications, 305 East 46th Street, New York, N.Y. 10017. NTIS microfiche are available from the National Technical Information Service, 5825 Port Royal Road, Springfield, Virginia 22151, at $0.95 per microfiche. For other sources of microfiche, see "microfiche" in the index.

State Government Documents

Usually available at state libraries and large public libraries. State documents dealing with education often are available through state departments of education, while single copies of other documents similarly are available from issuing agencies. Copies generally are free to libraries or professionals. Sale copies are available through the State Printer or its distribution agent. Send check with appropriate information if necessary to purchase. State directories listed in Chapter 3 provide names of some state sources to contact for documents.

Local Documents

Similar to state documents, in that copies are available in local libraries (municipal, school, or law); single copies can sometimes be obtained free, and if free copies are not available, a sales agency often exists which can be located through local telephone directories.

U.S. Government Documents

Federal documents are available in approximately 1,400 complete depository libraries and university libraries throughout the country; many libraries are partial depository libraries, while most libraries have some government documents.

Publications are announced in many ways—through the *Monthly Catalog* (F15), which should list everything published the previous month; and through a *Selected U.S. Government Publications List,* a free publication now issued monthly, with lists of new and popular titles (including most education titles). To get on the mailing list for the *Selected List,* send a postcard with name and address to Box 1821, Washington, D.C. 20013. Single copies of many government publications are available free on request from the issuing agency.

Copies can be purchased from a growing number of U.S. Government Printing Office bookstores—see lists in Q1 (current lists appear on the inside cover of the *Monthly Catalog*)—and from the U.S. Government Printing Office in Washington, D.C. For good service, include complete information (title, issuing agency, date, price, and stock or document number,

REQUIREMENTS | SOURCES

if available) and enclose check, money order, special documents coupons, or open a deposit account. If materials are not from the *Selected List* or not in stock at your local government bookstore, but are needed urgently, send request with complete information and date required (together with check) to the U.S. Government Printing Office, Superintendent of Documents, Customer Service Section, P.O. Box 1533, Washington, D.C. 20013.

Books

Available from local libraries, interlibrary loan, bookstores, and publishers. Addresses of publishers are available in library tools, including *Books in Print*. If not available from local bookstores or bookdealers, try the publisher; include check with purchase request for faster service.

Materials Listed in This Book

Sources and addresses are included for most nonstandard items. Send check with request for faster service. When requesting free materials, use letterhead stationery (of school, etc.) or clearly designate your role and interest. A self-addressed stamped envelope, or mailing label with postage, will expedite receipt.

MATERIALS SOURCES

Q1 U.S. GOVERNMENT PRINTING OFFICE BOOKSTORES

Following is a list of U.S. Government Printing Office Bookstores. A typical bookstore stocks approximately 1,500 different publications and provides access to the 200,000 publications available by mail order from the Superintendent of Documents, U.S. Government Printing Office, Washington, D.C. 20402.

Atlanta Bookstore
100 Federal Bldg.
275 Peachtree St., N.E.
Atlanta, Ga. 30303
(404) 526-6947

Birmingham Bookstore
Room 102A
2121 Bldg.
2121 8th Ave., N.
Birmingham, Ala. 35203
(205) 325-6056

Boston Bookstore
G25 John F. Kennedy Federal Bldg.
Sudbury St.
Boston, Mass. 02203
(617) 223-6071

Canton Bookstore
Federal Office Bldg.
201 Cleveland Ave.
Canton, Ohio 44702
(216) 455-8971

Chicago Bookstore
1463 Everett McKinley Dirksen
  Bldg., 14th Fl.
219 S. Dearborn St.
Chicago, Ill. 60604
(312) 353-5133

Cleveland Bookstore
Federal Office Bldg., 1st Fl.
1240 E. 9th St.
Cleveland, Ohio 44114
(216) 522-4922

Dallas Bookstore
1C46 Federal Bldg.
U.S. Courthouse
1100 Commerce St.
Dallas, Tex. 75202
(214) 749-1541

Denver Bookstore
1421 Federal Bldg.
U.S. Courthouse
1961 Stout St.
Denver, Colo. 80202
(303) 837-3965

Detroit Bookstore
229 Federal Office Bldg.
231 W. Lafayette Blvd.
Detroit, Mich. 48226
(313) 226-7816

Kansas City Bookstore
144 Federal Office Bldg.
601 E. 12th St.
Kansas City, Mo. 64106
(816) 374-2160

Los Angeles Bookstore
1015 Federal Office Bldg.
300 N. Los Angeles St.
Los Angeles, Calif. 90012
(213) 688-5841

New York Bookstore
Room 110
26 Federal Plz.
New York, N.Y. 10007
(212) 264-3826

Philadelphia Bookstore
U.S. Post Office and Courthouse,
  Main Lobby
9th and Chestnut Sts.
Philadelphia, Pa. 19107
(215) 264-3826

San Francisco Bookstore
1023 Federal Office Bldg.
450 Golden Gate Ave.
San Francisco, Calif. 94102
(415) 556-6657

Seattle Bookstore
1056 Federal Office Bldg.
909 First Ave.
Seattle, Wash. 98104
(206) 442-4270

Washington, D.C. Bookstore
710 N. Capitol St.
Washington, D.C. 20402
(202) 783-3238

Q2   **UNIVERSITY MICROFILMS**   300 N. Zeeb Rd., Ann Arbor,
      Mich. 48106. (313) 761-4700
Specialize in the microfilm format to produce materials likely to be of
value to universities and university scholarship. Collections include
approximately 3,000 microfilmed periodicals, dating back to 1669, a
substantial number of theses, and a collection of curriculum materials,
discussed in O10. Theses access tools are discussed in F2, F6, and P2.
    As a service to scholarship, University Microfilms provides on-demand
copies of back issues of periodicals for which publishers have granted
reprint permission. Standard fee (paid in advance and requiring complete bibliographic information) for copying articles is $2.00 for one

copy of a complete article and $0.50 for additional copies. A list of publications and information on current prices, quantity discounts, and deposit accounts will be sent on written request.

University Microfilms has microfilm files, in various stages of completeness, of 158 periodicals indexed in *Education Index* (F8), including a subject listing of the periodicals indexed. Another subject listing of education journals not indexed in *Education Index* also is available on request.

EDUCATION LIBRARIES

Q3 **BRADLEY UNIVERSITY** AIDE, 1501 W. Bradley Ave., Peoria, Ill. 61625. (309) 676-7611, Ext. 281
Offers computerized searching of ERIC data bases through the reference desk of the library. Free to graduate students and faculty; others, $10.00, plus $0.10 per item for more than 100 items. Also offers a computerized search of Bradley University's education book collection (BIRDS), which locates books by course numbers and subject headings.

Q4 **HARVARD UNIVERSITY** Graduate School of Education, Monroe C. Gutman Library, 6 Appian Way, Cambridge, Mass. 02183. (617) 495-3423
Subject areas of this collection are education and related social sciences. Collection includes 120,000 books, 10,000 pamphlets and journals, 550 current periodical titles (2,200 titles, including noncurrent), 93,000 microfiche, and 3,000 noncirculating tests. The library, primarily for Harvard faculty and students, is open to all users, although borrowing is restricted, except for individuals who purchase special user or special borrowing privileges. Publications are mostly in-house. Media and other services are limited to Harvard personnel. The Gutman Library publishes *Education Journals. A Union List* (edited by Malcolm C. Hamilton; 1974; $5, prepaid), which lists periodical holdings of the Monroe C. Gutman Library at the Harvard Graduate School of Education and of 34 other academic and special libraries in Massachusetts.

Q5 **INDIANA UNIVERSITY** School of Education, Education Library, Bloomington, Ind. 47401. (812) 337-1798
Deals with education and includes 10,000 books, 1,700 pamphlets, approximately 2,000 documents, 211 periodicals, 72,000 microfiche, and 827 microfilm. Performs ERIC/PROBE searches of *RIE* and *CIJE*

indexes through a computer program developed at Indiana University. Free to students, faculty, and educators from Indiana; $12 or $18 for out-of-state requesters. Approximately half of the requests are from out-of-state. Children's literature collection is available in the main library.

Q6   **LOUISIANA STATE UNIVERSITY** Library, Baton Rouge, La. 70803. (504) 388-2217

The education collection is incorporated in a general library which includes humanities, social sciences, and sciences; a total of 1,213,500 books, pamphlets, and documents, and 15,000 periodicals. ERIC computer searches are available through the North Carolina Science and Technology Research Center. Requests are written in the library and mailed to the Research Center.

Q7   **OHIO STATE UNIVERSITY** Education Library, 1945 N. High St., Columbus, Ohio 43212. (614) 422-6275

Deals with education and psychology and includes 150,000 volumes, 1,200 current periodical titles, and 100,000 microfiche. Performs both retrospective and current awareness searches of the ERIC data bases through profiles prepared by reference librarians. Searches are free to faculty and staff, with a fee for others.

Q8   **STANFORD UNIVERSITY** Cubberley Library, Stanford, Calif. 94305. (415) 497-2121

This library, which deals with education, includes 60,000 books, 3,000 pamphlets, 50,000 documents, 400 periodical titles, and 20,000 college catalogs. An ERIC microfiche collection is available elsewhere on campus (at the ERIC Clearinghouse on Information Resources, O17), while the School of Education performs computer searches for non-Stanford individuals.

Q9   **UNIVERSITY OF CALIFORNIA, LOS ANGELES (UCLA)** Education and Psychology Library, Powell Library Bldg., Los Angeles, Calif. 90024. (213) 825-4081 and 825-3652

Subject areas are education, psychology, kinesology, physical education, and teaching English as a second language. Collection includes more than 100,000 volumes, including 60,000 monographs, 40,000 bound periodicals, 16,140 pamphlets, and 190,000 microfiche. The library prepares information leaflets and performs computerized SDI searches on ERIC data bases. Reference service is available. Primarily for use by students and faculty of the University, but also open to members of the community. The Graduate School of Education at UCLA now houses the Data Bank Services and the Institutional Research File formerly available at the American Council on Education.

Q10 **UNIVERSITY OF ROCHESTER** Education Library, Rochester, N.Y. 14627. (716) 275-4481

Deals with education and includes 18,000 books in stacks (on another floor), 3,500 pamphlets, 300 documents, 500 periodical titles, all ERIC microfiche, 5,000 textbooks, 3,000 curriculum guides, 650 Master's papers from its College of Education, and 500 old Cooperative Research Project reports. Some of its curriculum guides and textbooks may be discarded as the collection is reviewed. ERIC computer searches are performed for education faculty and graduate students in education. Searches are structured through the library with Boolean algebra and forwarded to Albany, New York. Occasional bibliographies and selected acquisition lists are available to local users and individuals willing to pay postage and handling costs.

19 | *State Library Services to Educators*

This chapter contains state-by-state summaries of education-oriented library and information services of state (and District of Columbia) departments of education. The summaries are based on responses to letters of inquiry directed to all states in 1973 and 1974, supplemented by library research. Where adequate information was not received, the states were deleted from this compilation. Although inquiries were not addressed to state libraries per se, some voluntary information was received, which was incorporated when services in education seemed significant.

State libraries, in general, usually are depositories of U.S. and state documents, are the prime source of information on library services and facilities in their particular states, and often can be instrumental in arranging interlibrary loans or in locating copies of books and periodicals. They are listed in *Book of the States* (G2), the telephone directories of state capitols, and the *Guide to Federal Assistance for Education* (G46).

In addition to the sources listed in the library directories discussed in Chapter 3 (B41 and B46) and the services discussed in the previous five chapters, state Research Coordinating Units (RCU's) are statewide institutions which may provide specific services to educators. These agencies, which differ in scope from state to state, stimulate, coordinate, and disseminate research for vocational and technical educators. Each state has the option of broad or narrow interpretation of dissemination and of developing appropriate programs. (State plans, prepared state-by-state, describe the functions, organization, staff, training programs, pilot programs, and dissemination activities for each state.) RCU's often include complete ERIC (*RIE* and *CIJE*) collections, as well as ERIC's vocational materials, and may be the only source of access to ERIC in some states. They generally can be contacted through the Vocational-Technical Divisions of various state departments of education.

The Center for Vocational and Technical Education at Ohio State University recently completed a telephone survey from which information was compiled on state information resources—primarily RCU's, but including some other state information dissemination agencies—plus a listing of computer software installations and ERIC microfiche collections by state. According to the center, some form of computer-searching ERIC collections is available through the RCU's in Alabama, Arkansas, California, Colorado, Connecticut, Florida, Indiana, Kentucky, Maine, Massachusetts, Michigan, Minnesota, Missouri, New Hampshire, Oklahoma, Oregon, Pennsylvania, Rhode Island, South Carolina, Tennessee, Texas, Utah, Vermont (through the New England Resource Center for Occupational Education), Virginia, Washington, West Virginia, and Wyoming. The RCU's in Alaska, Arizona, Idaho, Mississippi, Nebraska, New Jersey, North Dakota, Ohio, and Puerto Rico perform manual searches for vocational educators. Some ERIC microfiche collections (either complete or limited to vocational materials) are available through the Delaware, Georgia, Illinois, Kansas, Louisiana, Maryland, Nevada, New Mexico, and North Carolina RCU's.

Other statewide sources are the media library sources listed in J23, which provide drug resources and similar materials for health education groups. Some of the sources listed, although not quite statewide, are, in effect, part of a statewide network or, occasionally, local substitutes for these missing services. In *Dissemination Policies Procedure Programs on Nine State Education Agencies* (Washington, D.C., Council of Chief State School Officers, 1974; ED 090 967; $7.80, plus postage; microfiche, $0.75), Virginia M. Cutter has provided a rather detailed theoretical analysis of dissemination roles, strategies, and policies of state education agencies in Colorado, Florida, Illinois, Iowa, Michigan, Montana, New York, North Carolina, and Pennsylvania without specifically referring to their individual collections and capacities.

STATE LIBRARY SERVICES FOR EDUCATORS

OFFICIAL AND
SUPPLEMENTARY
EDUCATION LIBRARIES   RESOURCES AND SERVICES

Alabama
Computerized Educa-
tional Resources In-
formation Unit
Occupational Research
and Development
Unit
115 Petrie Hall
Auburn University
Auburn 36803
(205) 826-5320

This RCU (intended primarily for vocational educators) has, on computer tape, the resumé files of *ERIC, CIJE* and *AIM/ARM*. Performs QUERY method of batch searches for a flat fee of $10. Searches are numbered and indexed so individuals can request copies of previously completed searches. Is acquiring a micro-fiche duplicating machine.

Alaska
Alaska State Library
Pouch G
Juneau 99801
(907) 586-5242

Subjects cover general education, government documents, and ERIC files. Collection as of June 1975 consisted of 80,000 books, 835 periodical titles, 6,200 microfilm reels, 140,000 microfiche, 2,300 phono-records, 1,200 art reproductions, and 2,000 films. ERIC computerized searches include *RIE* and *CIJE*. Provides all types of library services—statewide through other libraries—or direct services where libraries do not exist. Photocopies are free for the first 20 pages and $0.10 per page for additional pages.

Arizona
Department of
Education
Professional Library
1535 W. Jefferson St.
Phoenix 85007
(602) 271-5198

This professional library of approximately 3,500 volumes deals with various areas of education. It includes several thousand items in vertical files; receives approximately 125 periodicals; houses sample copies of Arizona state-adopted elementary textbooks; and contains a basic adult education collection; as well as extensive files of catalogs of educational publishers and producers. The library is part of the Library/Media Services Division, which places emphasis on its library collection for school libraries, and includes a small sample collection of recently published children's books.

Arkansas
State Department of
Education
State Education Bldg.
Little Rock 72201
(501) 371-1461

Its modest collection includes 300 books, 200 pamphlets, 175 documents, 2 periodical subscriptions, 350 microfiche, and 400 other items, available to department personnel only.

OFFICIAL AND SUPPLEMENTARY EDUCATION LIBRARIES	RESOURCES AND SERVICES
Computing Services University of Arkansas Administration Bldg. 125 Fayetteville 72701 (501) 575-2901	Provides free ERIC computer searches for Arkansas educators and citizens via mail, telephone, and walk-in.

California

| California State Library Courts Bldg. P.O. Box 2037 Sacramento 95809 (916) 445-4374 | Covers general research, government publications, science and technology, literature, and social sciences. Collection includes 837,500 books, 2,300,000 documents, 3,705 periodicals, 200,000 microfiche, and 42,000 films and microfilms. Although state government employees are its primary users, this library heads an integrated interlibrary loan system which eventually will deliver almost any book to public libraries making requests for users. Special bibliographies and consultant services also are available. Its quarterly *News Notes* (free to libraries) includes an annual directory of most California libraries. |
| San Mateo County Educational Resources Center (SMERC) 333 Main St. Redwood City 94063 (415) 364-5600, Ext. 4403 | Offers contractual services to 22 counties in California and to five special projects. Deals with all aspects of education, mostly kindergarten to grade 14, from a collection including 10,000 books, 2,000 pamphlets, 700 periodical titles, 100,000 microfiche, and 8,000 sample textbooks. Provides ERIC (and *CIJE*) computer searches from an on-line ERIC/ DIALOG terminal; produces monthly bibliographies and newsletters and an annual compilation called *FIDO* (*Fugitive Information Data Organizer*), which lists its own microfiche collection of local and state educational documents. Microfiche are available from this center. |

Like other California county education offices, it houses examination copies of textbooks adopted (that is, acceptable) in California, and has participated in activities describing and evaluating state-adopted textbooks. Since 1974, has served as the depository library for curriculum materials produced by California's school districts, county offices, and the state department of education. These documents are made available in microfiche for $0.50 per microcard (which holds approximately 45 to 70 frames); less to participating agencies and standing order customers. An annual catalog of documents, *California Curriculum Guides, 1974,* is available from SMERC for $3.50.

OFFICIAL AND
SUPPLEMENTARY
EDUCATION LIBRARIES   RESOURCES AND SERVICES

Standing orders are shipped quarterly and billed annually. Approximately 500 microfiche were available as of May 1975. SMERC also houses a microfiche collection of career-education materials, originally selected and compiled by the Career Education Task Force of the California State Department of Education. These microfiche also are available, at $0.50 per microcard, to nonparticipating agencies. The catalog, *Career Education Microfiche Collection*, is available for $0.50 from the Publication Office, California State Department of Education, Sacramento, California 95418.

ACCESS
Educational Media
 Center
2371 Stanwell Dr.
Concord 94526

With a base of 10,000 books, 5,000 pamphlets and documents, 200 periodicals, and a complete ERIC microfiche collection, this center offers ERIC/DIALOG computer searches; educational "Fastpaks" research, and publication announcement services to the educational community of Contra Costa County. Also duplicates microfiche.

Colorado
Colorado State Library
Colorado Department
 of Education
1362 Lincoln St.
Denver 80203
(303) 892-2212

Includes 20,000 volumes, more than 500,000 government documents, more than 100,000 Colorado state documents, and 20,000 documents from other states. It provides library services to the blind and physically handicapped, reference services on state issues to state employees and Colorado citizens, and is currently developing microfiche services. A film service provides free 16-mm sound films to Colorado citizens through local libraries from a collection of 600 titles (900 prints).

Northern Colorado
 Educational Board
 of Cooperative Ser-
 vices (NCEBOCS)
830 S. Lincoln St.
Longmont 80501
(303) 772-4420

This information retrieval center, although it has a small backup collection of books and periodicals, specializes in computerized searches of *RIE, CIJE*, and *AIM/ARM*, backed by manual searches of educational journals by reference librarians. The center houses the entire ERIC collection in microfiche, and duplicates microfiche for contracting states, which (in 1974) included Washington, Wyoming, and Montana. Performs computer searches for individuals on request. Computer searches cost $27.50 for the first data base and $10.00 for each additional data base; individual manual searches cost $27.50. Some additional products, developed to meet the assessed needs of educators, include *Journal Articles for Concerned Educators*, $10.50; *ERIC Materials for Concerned Educators*, $15.50; *Mini-Monographs* (problem-

OFFICIAL AND
SUPPLEMENTARY
EDUCATION LIBRARIES

RESOURCES AND SERVICES

solving or issue papers); and two *Idea Books* of supplementary activity ideas for teachers—kindergarten to grade 6, $3.50; grades 7 to 12, $7.50.

Connecticut
Charles D. Hine
 Library
Connecticut State
 Department of
 Education
350 State Office Bldg.
Hartford 06115
(203) 566-2676

Includes 21,000 books, 2,000 pamphlets, 302 periodicals, 10,000 microfiche, and 2,000 reels of microfilm. Offers services to administrators, teachers, and education students, as well as to state education department personnel.

Delaware
State Department of
 Public Instruction
 Library
Townsend Memorial
 Bldg.
Loockerman and
 Federal Sts.
Dover 19901
(302) 678-4692

Collection deals with education, Delaware history, and Delaware education, and includes 5,590 books, 289 boxes of pamphlets, 287 periodical subscriptions, 53 boxes of out-of-state educational materials, and the entire ERIC microfiche collection. Provides lending services to public schools, performs research, and reproduces ERIC materials on request. Primary users are state school personnel, state officials, and the general public. Also provides an updated monthly *Supplement to School Laws of Delaware.*

District of Columbia
Research Information
 Center
D.C. Public Schools
415 12th St., N.W.
Washington 20004
(202) 347-6727

Collection is comprised of 500 books, 60 periodicals on education, and the complete ERIC microfiche collection. Performs computer batch searching of ERIC and *CIJE*, and reproduces microfiche for District of Columbia school employees.

Florida
Florida Educational
 Resources Infor-
 mation Center
 (FERIC)
Department of
 Education
111 W. St. Augustine St.
Tallahassee 32304
(904) 488-2986

Dealing with public education, this collection includes 200 books, 310 periodical subscriptions, 95 newsletters, 5 file drawers of mostly newspaper clippings, and almost 5,000 pamphlets, documents, and bibliographies, as well as the ERIC microfiche. Services are for public educators in Florida—preschool through higher education—as well as for state employees, including legislators and special and state libraries. Performs ERIC computer searches on *RIE*, *CIJE*, and *AIM/ARM*, using the QUERY system.

Department of
 Education Library
111 W. St. Augustine St.

Primarily serves the staff of the Florida Department of Education, with an education library of 10,000 books, 20,000 pamphlets, 1,000 documents,

OFFICIAL AND
SUPPLEMENTARY
EDUCATION LIBRARIES

RESOURCES AND SERVICES

Tallahassee 32304
(904) 488-2918

300 periodical subscriptions, and the ERIC collection of microfiche relating to the disadvantaged. Cooperates with other state agency libraries in Florida.

Georgia
Department of
  Education
Education Information
  Center
312 Education Annex
156 Trinity Ave., S.W.
Atlanta 30303
(404) 656-2569

Holdings consist of 3,000 books and monographs with strengths in educational evaluation and planning; vertical subject files of articles, papers, and other fugitive materials; a collection of newsletters; the complete ERIC microfiche collection; curriculum materials microfiche; the ENTELEK file of materials on computer-assisted education; and on-line capacity for searching *RIE, CIJE, Psychological Abstracts, AIM/ ARM, Exceptional Child Education Abstracts, Social Sciences Citation Index,* National Technical Information Service, and others. Services include computer and manual searches, annotated bibliographies, document loan, microfiche duplications, and circulation of current awareness materials. Services are free to staff members of the Georgia Department of Education, local school systems superintendents, Georgia Learning Resources Centers, Cooperative Educational Services Agencies, and are available to walk-in users on a limited basis.

Georgia Association of
  Educators (GAE)
Research Division,
  Materials Center
3951 Snapfinger Pkwy.
Decatur 30032
(404) 289-5867

Maintains a basic reference collection of approximately 100 books; a vertical file of 200 to 300 subjects; and a collection related to instructional techniques, which includes 700 books, films, filmstrips, records, and cassettes. It subscribes to 30 periodicals and newsletters, including *RIE*. Prepares its own studies on topics such as salaries and fringe benefits. Answers information requests on classroom methods and materials. Its services are primarily for teachers who are GAE members, but its collection is also open on a drop-in basis to anyone interested in educational research.

Georgia Learning
  Resources System
Division of Early
  Childhood and
  Special Education
Georgia Department of
  Education
Atlanta 30303
(404) 656-2534

The Learning Resources System, administered through this office, currently includes nine centers (Albany, Atlanta, Cleveland, Columbus, Macon, Scottdale, Rome, Savannah, and Vidalia) which provide instructional materials and staff development for teachers of handicapped children. All are staffed by at least one professional person and one secretary.

Hawaii
State Department of
  Education

Hawaii is one state which has intelligently and almost completely integrated its public libraries and

OFFICIAL AND SUPPLEMENTARY EDUCATION LIBRARIES	RESOURCES AND SERVICES

P.O. Box 2360
Honolulu 96816
(808) 548-2811

school libraries. The headquarters office maintains a loan collection of 16-mm films for Hawaii public schools and serves as a central purchasing agent. Its previews and evaluations of audiovisual materials are distributed to schools in loose-leaf format.

Idaho
State Department of
 Education
Professional Library
Boise 83720
(202) 384-2186

This small library deals with education and contains 200 books, 500 pamphlets, 50 periodicals, and a complete file of ERIC microfiche for the benefit of Idaho educators, legislators, and trustees. Its computer searching of ERIC through NCEBOCS (see Colorado) apparently was discontinued as of July 1973. Publications include an occasional periodical, *News and Reports,* and a list of free state publications—with an order blank enclosed—listing administrative publications, curriculum guides, and subject matter.

Illinois
Instructional Materials
 Center(s)
1020 S. Spring St.
Springfield 62706
(217) 525-2436

10400 W. Diversey St.
Franklin Park 60131
(312) 455-4033

Swen Franklin Parson
 Library
DeKalb 60115
(815) 723-0254

907 W. Nevada St.
Urbana 61801
(217) 333-6770

227 Pulliam Hall
Carbondale 62901
(618) 457-7031

Illiinois has five Instructional Materials Centers located throughout the state—part of a special education network. Springfield, which may be typical, covers all areas of education. Its collection includes 5,000 books, 500 pamphlets, 2,000 documents, 80 periodical subscriptions, 20,000 items of curriculum and instructional materials and equipment, and a complete ERIC microfiche collection. No computer searches, but manual searches of ERIC are available. Also serves as a depository for braille, large-type books, and tangible aids for visually handicapped. Open to all educators in Illinois, as well as to parents of the handicapped, students in special education, and public and private agencies dealing with exceptional children and youths.

Indiana
State Department of
 Public Instruction
Professional Library
108 State Office Bldg.
Indianapolis 46204
(317) 633-4790

Services primarily the professional staff of the Department of Public Instruction, covering all areas of education. Collection includes 2,000 books, 214 periodical subscriptions, 300 sets of microfiche, and 239 pieces of audiovisual materials. It uses PROBE at Indiana University for ERIC computer searches,

and circulates audiovisual materials to educators and
educational organizations throughout the state.

Iowa
Department of Public
  Instruction
Educational Media
  Section
Grimes State Office
  Bldg.
Des Moines 50319
(515) 281-3475

This section includes a library, a complete ERIC
microfiche collection, and audiovisual equipment
and materials covering all areas of education. Its
library includes 14,000 books (professional text and
trade), 12,000 pamphlets, 300 periodical subscriptions, ERIC microfiche, and 1,000 media materials
(movies, filmstrips, transparencies, AV kits, etc.).
Serves local educators and the department of education, and performs computer searches of ERIC
through a batch searching method using "Alternative
to QUERY Program." Microfiche readers are available
at regional media centers.

Kansas
State Department of
  Education
Project Communicate
120 E. 10th St.
Topeka 66612
(913) 296-3136

Contains approximately 300 books, several hundred
pamphlets, 324 periodicals, and a complete ERIC
microfiche collection. Performs computer searches
of ERIC and *CIJE* for Kansas educators using the
RIC batch method.

Kentucky
Department of
  Education
Capitol Plz.
Frankfort 40601
(502) 564-5385

Education collection includes 10,000 books, 2,000
pamphlets, 1,000 state and U.S. documents, 60
periodicals, and a complete ERIC microfiche collection. Users are primarily Kentucky educators, for
whom it performs manual, but not computer,
ERIC searches. Publications include quarterly booklists, annual bibliographies, and film and tape lists.

Resource Service
  Center
Suite 427
College of Education
Western Kentucky
  University
Bowling Green 42101
(502) 745-2451

This center, part of an ESEA Title III project,
serves professional educators in 22 countries in
West Central Kentucky, as well as Western's faculty,
undergraduates, and graduates. Its resources include
3,150 books, 1,500 curriculum guides, reference and
bibliographic services, 60 professional periodicals,
Croft professional services, ERIC materials, and
free computerized searches to qualified patrons.

Louisiana
State Department of
  Education
Bureau of Research
  and Data Collection
P.O. Box 44064
Baton Rouge 70804
(504) 389-6244

Devoted to education and related areas, this library
contains approximately 1,000 books, 7,500 pamphlets, 54 periodicals, and the ERIC microfiche. It
plans to expand its resources to include nonprint
materials, and is organizing a special collection of
vocational rehabilitation materials. Also plans to
initiate an information system in cooperation with the

OFFICIAL AND SUPPLEMENTARY EDUCATION LIBRARIES	RESOURCES AND SERVICES

data processing department. Publications include a *Louisiana School Directory*, a list of department of education publications, and an annual report. Services are provided for Louisiana school systems (statewide) and for state departments of education.

Maine
State Department of
  Education
Augusta 04330
(207) 289-3561

According to information from other sources, this office has a computer installation that searches ERIC (*RIE* only) for the state department of education.

Maryland
State Department of
  Education
Division of Library
  Development and
  Services
P.O. Box 8717
Baltimore-Washington
  International Airport
Baltimore 21240
(301) 796-8300,
  Ext. 255

Deals with education, library science, and curriculum (guides). Collection includes 6,000 books, 12 file drawers of pamphlets, 500 documents, 300 periodical subscriptions, 2,000 microfiche, as well as films, filmstrips, slides, and cassettes. Clients are the department of education staff, Maryland teachers, and the general education community. Publications include an occasional free newsletter, *Keynotes*; film catalogs; and a *List of Curriculum Materials* developed in Maryland are distributed on request. Part of a statewide system of library services, public libraries, library services to the physically handicapped, and interlibrary loan. Brochures and directories on any or all of these services are available on request.

Massachusetts
Merrimack Education
  Center
101 Mill Rd.
Chelmsford 01824
(617) 256-3985

Subject content of this NIE-sponsored information center covers educational management, in-service education, individualized instruction, and information systems. Its library includes all media, but is largely an ERIC collection. Operates a local curriculum exchange bank (in microfiche) and provides problem-solving consultation. Performs ERIC computer searches for its users, primarily local educators, educational systems, and community residents. Its *Linker Newsletter* includes information on ERIC materials and some other current information sources.

Michigan
State Library
Department of
  Education
735 E. Michigan Ave.
Lansing 48913
(517) 373-1580

Contains 1,200,000 volumes, a complete ERIC collection, a complete Curriculum Materials Clearinghouse collection, a depository collection of all textbooks sold in the state, a library for the blind and physically handicapped, and a law library of 100,000 volumes. It is a depository for state and federal documents, subscribes to 2,000 periodicals, and has access offices at the University of Michigan and Michigan State University.

Materials Center
Science-Math Teaching
  Center
104 McDonel Hall
State University
East Lansing 48823
(517) 355-1725

Subject areas of this center cover science and mathematics education. Collection includes 7,000 books, 1,000 pamphlets, 50 periodical subscriptions, and 250 miscellaneous publications. Open to pre-service and in-service Michigan educators. Services include lending of both equipment and instructional materials.

Minnesota
State Department of
  Education
Library
401-A Capitol Square
  Bldg.
St. Paul 55101
(612) 296-6684

This library, a joint operation with the Higher Education Coordinating Commission, deals with education from preschool through higher education, including rehabilitation and vocational-technical education. Its collection includes 3,000 books, 3,000 pamphlets, 5,000 documents (including some state and federal documents), 350 periodical subscriptions, and a complete ERIC microfiche collection. Services, available to state government employees, include literature searches, preparation of bibliographies, and interlibrary loan. ERIC computer searches are contracted out, since the library does not have its own search capability. Publications include a weekly *Federal Register Alert* and a weekly list of *New Materials*, as well as a semiannual *KWIC Index*, all available to the staff without charge.

Mississippi
State Department of
  Education
Educational Media
  Services
P.O. Box 771
Jackson 39205
(601) 354-6864

Dealing with education, this library is available to educators. It contains 10,000 books, 230 periodical subscriptions (with back issues on microfilm), and 300 16-mm films. Services include school media consultation, administration of ESEA Title II funds, and administration of a Special Education Instructional Materials Center. A quarterly newsletter, *Media News*, is issued for school media specialists.

Missouri
State Department of
  Education
P.O. Box 480
Jefferson City 65101
(314) 751-4212

"The Missouri State Department of Education does not maintain a central library of professional books. Each section maintains its own library. We also make use of the Missouri State Library (Jefferson City)." Computer searches are performed through the ERIC Center for Research for professional educators in Missouri's public schools. Publications include a monthly newsletter and a monthly periodical, *Missouri Schools*, both free to Missouri schools.

Montana

Staff Library
Office of the State
  Superintendent of
  Public Instruction
Helena 59601
(416) 449-2511

Basically concerned with education. Includes a periodical library, a professional library, computerized information retrieval and dissemination services—carried out through NCEBOCS (see Colorado), and a vertical filing system. Its collection includes curriculum guides and state education agency publications, including the monthly *Montana Schools*. Access to ERIC microfiche is limited to staff.

Nebraska

State Department of
  Education
233 S. 10th St.
Lincoln 68508
(402) 471-2476

Collection is basically educational; contains 5,000 books, 3,000 pamphlets, 1,000 documents, 180 periodical subscriptions, and 3,000 microfiche. Its publications include curriculum guides, available without charge to state educators.

Nevada

Nevada State Library
Carson City 89701

"The State Library coordinates a statewide interlibrary loan and reference service. . . we do reference work for educators. . ." The documents section of the state library houses all Nevada documents, ERIC, and Office of Education publications. Other state education libraries are located at the University of Nevada (Reno and Las Vegas).

New Hampshire

Department of
  Education
Educational
  Information System
State House Annex
Concord 03301
(603) 271-3652

No inventory is available for this collection, whose subject areas cover statistical information on public elementary and secondary school education, including two-year vocational-technical colleges. Its users are local educators, legislators, state agencies, and the general public. Yearly compilations include an *Educational Directory, School Board Member Directory,* and single-topic statistical reports.

New Jersey

Department of
  Education
225 W. State St.
Trenton 08625
(609) 292-8135

"Provides planning, coordinating, monitoring, and development activities relating to the establishment and operation of a statewide network for the acquisition, dissemination, and utilization of research-based information."

New Mexico

State Department of
  Education
Capitol Bldg.
Santa Fe 87501
(515) 827-5364

This library's holdings include approximately 1,000 books, 1,800 pamphlets, 180 periodicals, and an ERIC microfiche collection. It performs library services for the staff of the state department of education. Computer searches are carried out through the state library or state university.

New York
State Department of
Education
Education Library
333 State Education
Bldg.
Albany 12224
(518) 474-5961

Subject areas cover all aspects of education. Some special collections include a historic collection of New York state documents in education, a publishers' display of current textbooks, curriculum guides, a historic collection of school and college catalogs, and a complete ERIC microfiche collection. Total collection contains 110,000 books, 89 file drawers of pamphlets, 600 periodical subscriptions, 50 drawers of microfiche, and 400 audiovisual items. Its users are state employees, state legislators, and all members of the educational community. Provides interlibrary loan services to all libraries, including out-of-state and foreign libraries, through the interlibrary loan unit of the New York State Library.

Educational Programs
and Studies
Information Service
(EPSIS)
330EB State Education
Bldg.
Albany 12224
(518) 474-3639

Collection deals with all aspects of education and contains 10,000 books, pamphlets, and documents, mostly curriculum materials from New York and out-of-state, plus the complete ERIC collection. Performs ERIC computer services for New York state educators through regional representatives. Other services include Selective Dissemination of Information (SDI), technical assistance training, and reproduction of microfiche and journal articles.

North Carolina
Department of Public
Instruction
Research and
Information Center
581 Education Bldg.
Raleigh 27611
(919) 829-7904

An education library containing 6,700 books, 9,000 pamphlets, 224 periodical subscriptions, and the ERIC microfiche collections. Its services, for local and North Carolina educators, include ready reference, compilation of bibliographies, research, and repackaging of materials to be disseminated. Runs ERIC computer searches for educators through the Science and Technology Research Center, and serves as a microfiche production center. Searches cost $15 to $20, with printing of up to 150 abstracts. Issues two free monthly publications, *ERIC Instant Research* and *Emphasis*.

North Dakota
State Department of
Public Instruction
State Capitol
Bismarck 58501
(701) 224-2281

The department library maintains for its professional staff a collection of 2,400 volumes, 85 periodical subscriptions, and many pamphlets and bulletins from other states. The department also contracts with the ERIC center at the University of North Dakota in Grand Forks to provide free computer searches for department personnel and elementary and secondary school educators in the state. Additional reference volumes and periodical services are available from the state library and the interlibrary loan network which serve all state residents.

OFFICIAL AND
SUPPLEMENTARY
EDUCATION LIBRARIES   RESOURCES AND SERVICES

Ohio
State Library of Ohio
65 S. Front St.
Columbus 43215
(614) 466-2693

Principal reference library for state officials and employees. It has an extensive collection of materials in the field of education, and issues a monthly list entitled *Education: Recent Acquisitions.*

Oklahoma
State Department of
    Education
329 State Capitol Bldg.
Oklahoma City 73105
(405) 521-3331

Maintains only limited materials in affected sections. It uses OTIS (Oklahoma Teletype Interlibrary System) to obtain needed books and documents. Publications include a monthly, *Oklahoma Educator,* published for state teachers and administrators, and curriculum guides, available to concerned educators.

State Department of
    Education
Library Resources
Oklahoma City 73105
(405) 478-2361

Provides consultative and referral services for school librarians from an education collection which includes books, pamphlets, and periodicals. It prepares occasional bibliographies on topics relating to elementary and secondary education, available to anyone on request.

University of Oklahoma
College of Education
820 Van Fleet St.
Norman 73069
(415) 325-6227

Free ERIC computer searches of *RIE* and *CIJE* are provided to faculty and graduate students. It appears to have a low workload and may possibly be able to provide some ERIC computer searches for state educators.

Oregon
Board of Education
942 Lancaster Dr., N.E.
Salem 97310
(503) 378-3968

Deals with all areas of education, and includes 1,800 books, 1,000 pamphlets, 3,000 documents, more than 125 periodical subscriptions, and a complete ERIC microfiche collection. Services to Oregon educators include information searches, consultant services, and free computer searches of an ERIC data base which includes *AIM/ARM, RIE,* and *CIJE.* The Oregon Board of Education issues many publications, including *EDU-GRAM,* a monthly aimed primarily at teachers.

Pennsylvania
Department of
    Education
Division of School
    Libraries
13 N. 4th St.
Harrisburg 17101
(717) 787-6704

3045 Babcock Blvd.
Pittsburgh 15237
(412) 931-1306

The Division of School Libraries has established three branches in the Harrisburg, Pittsburgh, and Philadelphia areas to provide examination copies of library books and instructional materials, as well as professional consultative services for teachers, librarians, media specialists, and administrators. Publications include *School Library Resources Booklists, School Library Standards,* and special bibliographies; all free on request. The Harrisburg Central Area Branch, which deals with all areas of elementary and secondary curriculum, includes 25,000

RESOURCES AND SERVICES

6801 Ludlow St.
Upper Darby 19082
(215) 352-1866

books 1,000 pamphlets, 20 periodical subscriptions, 1,000 microfiche, and 15,000 audiovisual materials. Other collections are similar in scope.

Research and
Information Services
for Education
(RISE)
198 Allendale Rd.
King of Prussia 19406
(215) 265-6056

An information service which is part of the Montgomery County Intermediate Unit, providing services to educators and education students in Montgomery County and to the Bureau of Planning in Pennsylvania's State Department of Education. Its library, which deals with administration, curriculum, and supportive services for education, includes 3,000 books, 18,000 documents, 225 periodical subscriptions, 800 miscellaneous items, and a complete ERIC collection. It performs computer searches on ERIC, *Psychological Abstracts,* National Technical Information Service, and Council for Exceptional Children abstracts, using an on-line interactive DIALOG. Its other services include in-depth search services, provision of duplicates of existing searches, and bibliographies. Publications include a newsletter and occasional papers.

State Library of
Pennsylvania
Harrisburg 17126
(717) 787-2646

This state library of 700,000 volumes and 3,200 periodical subscriptions has good collections in education, library science, government, public administration, and law. It is a full government depository library and has the complete ERIC microfiche collections. Serves both state employees and the general public.

Rhode Island
Department of
Education
Education Information
Center
22 Hayes St.
Providence 02908
(401) 277-2035

Education collection includes 3,000 documents often not available in libraries, plus education periodicals and ERIC microfiche. The center, part of the Bureau of Technical Assistance, serves all practicing educators (from kindergarten to graduate school) in Rhode Island. Services include literature searches; reproduction of educational documents, in microfiche or hard copy; resource guides; topical bibliographies; and technical assistance in utilizing research. Its computerized data sources include the Lockheed Information Retrieval System via DIALOG, through its own terminal.

South Carolina
State Department of
Education

This group, which updates its ERIC tapes every three months, searches the ERIC files by computer

OFFICIAL AND
SUPPLEMENTARY
EDUCATION LIBRARIES

RESOURCES AND SERVICES

Planning Resources
Section
Office of Planning
and Dissemination
1208 Rutledge Bldg.
Columbia 29201
(813) 758-3458

(modified QUERY program) twice a week. Free for key district and department staff. Computer searches also are available to college professors and students at $15/search. Publications include two quarterlies, *Targeted Communications* and *Awareness Bulletins*, both available without charge to teachers and adminis- trators.

South Dakota
Business Research
Bureau
University of
South Dakota
Vermillion 57069
(605) 677-5287

According to information from other sources, this group duplicates ERIC documents, provides micro- fiche readers, and facilitates computer searches of ERIC.

Tennessee
State Department of
Education
Professional Library
132-A Cordell Hull
Bldg.
Nashville 37219
(615) 741-3116

Services the department of education staff and con- tains 3,000 books, a variety of pamphlets, 70 periodical subscriptions, and is a depository for ERIC and PREP materials.

University of
Tennessee
College of Education
Bureau of Educational
Research and Service
212 Claxton Education
Bldg.
Knoxville 37916
(615) 974-2272

Under the general supervision of an RCU Library, this group has a collection of 70 pamphlets, 1,500 (hard cover) documents, 45 periodical subscriptions, 12 periodicals on film, and the ERIC microfiche. It performs computer searches of the ERIC data base for educators, administrators, state planners, boards of education, counselors, and vocational-technical specialists; free for the last group and $15 for others.

Texas
Texas Education
Agency
Resource Center
Library
201 E. 11th St.
Austin 78701
(512) 475-3468

The collection of this library covers education and related social sciences, with emphasis on public school education in Texas. Its collection includes 12,000 books, pamphlets and documents, 160 period- ical subscriptions, 500 reels of microfilm, and the complete ERIC microfiche. Performs library ser- vices for Education Agency staff and other Texas educators.

Texas Information
Service (TIS)
6504 Tracor Lane
Austin 78721
(512) 926-8080

Computerized information bank of TIS includes *RIE* and *CIJE* and is available on a subscription basis to agencies and institutions within and without the state at rates which decrease with the number of guaran- teed searches (for instance, 100 searches annually for

$2,000; 200 for $3,600), on a fixed-access schedule, with a slightly different rate for open-access schedules. Each search includes a computer-generated *RIE/CIJE* bibliography, plus a list of other relevant materials from the TIS library, and 10 ERIC documents on microfiche. TIS also searches local document resources, when appropriate, and routinely searches some of the standard reference compilations. These searches also are available, at $25 per search, to anyone who sends in a Student Search Request form with payment. Other search options include a Hot-Line Telephone Service and a written literature review or summary.

Utah
State Board of
  Education
Information Service
  Agency
1400 University Club
  Bldg.
136 E. South Temple
  St.
Salt Lake City 84111
(801) 328-5891

Collection includes a few books and periodicals, some fugitive files and innovative projects, and ERIC microfiche from 1968 to date. Performs ERIC computer searches on *RIE* and *CIJE* through the Utah State Board of Education. Services are available free to all state educators, administrators, and specialists; others are charged a fee for these services.

Vermont
Twin State Education
  Information System
State Department of
  Education
Montpelier 05602
(802) 828-3165

According to printed sources, the system maintains an ERIC collection and can provide computer searches of Lockheed's data bases for Vermont educators through DIALOG. Typical *RIE* and *CIJE* searches cost approximately $15 per search. Other services include the reproduction of documents in microfiche and hard copy. Journal articles are available through interlibrary loan and the State Department of Libraries.

Virginia
State Department of
  Education
P.O. Box 6-Q
Richmond 23216
(804) 770-2068

This collection, concerned with education, has 100 books, 1,000 pamphlets, 1,000 documents, 20 periodical subscriptions, and the ERIC microfiche collection from 1967 on. Performs free computer searches of ERIC (via QUERY). Its users include state employees and the public.

Washington
Superintendent of
  Public Instruction

Education collection, including 3,000 books, 15,000 pamphlets, 350 periodical subscriptions, and an

OFFICIAL AND SUPPLEMENTARY EDUCATION LIBRARIES	RESOURCES AND SERVICES
Professional Curriculum Library P.O. Box 527 Olympia 98501 (206) 753-6741	ERIC microfiche collection. Users are state office staff and educators. Performs computer searches of the ERIC data base by contract with NCEBOCS (see Colorado).

West Virginia

West Virginia Research Coordinating Unit Marshall University Huntington 25701 (304) 696-3170	This group, an RCU primarily established for vocational educators, has a library, an ERIC collection, microfiche readers available for loan, and access to computer searches of the ERIC data base.

Wisconsin

Department of Public Instruction Professional Library 126 Langdon St. Madison 53702 (618) 266-2529	Subject areas of this library include education, administration, handicapped children, and Wisconsin public school curriculum guides. The collection includes 2,800 books, 2,300 pamphlets, 300 periodical subscriptions, 3,000 curriculum guides, and the ERIC microfiche. Services are primarily for the professional staff of the Department of Public Instruction. Performs on-line computer searches of ERIC. Other services include reference, interlibrary loan, preparation of bibliographies, and a semiannual bibliography of *Classified Books in DPI Professional Library*.
Wisconsin Information Retrieval for Education (WIRE) Division for Planning Services Department of Public Instruction Madison 53702 (608) 266-2741 and 1999	This demonstration project of DPI provides computerized searches of the ERIC data base for Wisconsin educators, administrators, students, and laymen for a fee of $10, which includes question negotiation or clarification and a free follow-up search, if necessary. (See Figure 20)
Research Coordinating Unit HFSOB, 7th Fl. 4802 Sheboygan Ave. Madison 53702 (608) 266-3705	Collection is concerned mostly with vocational and technical education, and includes 50 books, 2,000 pamphlets, and the ERIC microfiche collection. It operates under the Wisconsin Board of Vocational Technical and Adult Education for vocational educators and education students. Provides manual ERIC searches and duplications of microfiche. Its publications include a newsletter, *Bits About Research*, and a semiannual *Research Activity Report*.

WISCONSIN DEPARTMENT OF PUBLIC INSTRUCTION
WISCONSIN INFORMATION RETRIEVAL FOR EDUCATION
INFORMATION RETRIEVAL REQUEST
PI-PS-2 (R. 7-73)

WIRE

INSTRUCTIONS: Return request to:
Information Services Section
Management & Planning Services Division
Department of Public Instruction
126 Langdon Street
Madison, Wisconsin 53702

NAME OF PERSON REQUESTING INFORMATION	POSITION OR TITLE	HOME TELEPHONE AREA	EXCH.	NUMBER	REQUEST DATE
ORGANIZATION NAME (SCHOOL DISTRICT)		BUSINESS TELEPHONE AREA	EXCH.	NUMBER	DATE NEEDED
STREET ADDRESS	CITY	STATE			ZIP CODE
REQUEST AUTHORIZED BY: (If Different from Above)	PURCHASE ORDER NO. (If Necessary)	Is this your first request ☐ Yes ☐ No			

NOTE: The most important factor in obtaining relevant information on your topic is effective communication of your need to the Information Retrieval Center. Please think your request through thoroughly and fill in this form completely. Care taken at this point will have considerable effect on the quality of the information you receive.

1. WHAT IS THE **TITLE OR MAJOR SUBJECT AREA** OF YOUR REQUEST? _____

2. WHICH OF THE FOLLOWING LEVELS (IF ANY) APPLY TO YOUR TOPIC? (CHECK ALL THAT APPLY)

☐ PRE-PRIMARY   ☐ INTERMEDIATE   ☐ SENIOR HIGH   ☐ COLLEGE   ☐ ADULT
☐ KINDERGARTEN ☐ ELEMENTARY   ☐ SECONDARY   ☐ GRADUATE ☐ PROFESSIONAL
☐ PRIMARY   ☐ JUNIOR HIGH   ☐ JUNIOR COLLEGE ☐ HIGHER EDUCATION ☐ NO LEVEL ☐ OTHER (Specify) _____

3. WHAT IS THE GENERAL PURPOSE OF YOUR INFORMATION SEARCH?

☐ PROPOSAL DEVELOPMENT   ☐ ADMINISTRATIVE MANAGEMENT   ☐ COURSE REVIEW OF LITERATURE
☐ PROJECT OPERATION   ☐ INSTRUCTIONAL IMPROVEMENT   ☐ INSERVICE TRAINING
☐ CURRICULUM DEVELOPMENT ☐ THESIS/DISSERTATION   ☐ SCHOOL/COMMUNITY RELATIONS (Communications)
                                                        ☐ OTHER (Specify) _____

4. WHAT TYPE OF SEARCH DO YOU NEED? ☐ OVERVIEW ☐ IN DEPTH ☐ PROGRAM ORIENTED ☐ RESEARCH ORIENTED

5. HOW MANY REFERENCES DO YOU EXPECT OR PREFER? ☐ UP TO 10 ☐ UP TO 25 ☐ UP TO 50 ☐ UP TO 75 ☐ OVER 75

6. PLEASE WRITE A **DETAILED STATEMENT** DESCRIBING YOUR SPECIFIC INFORMATION NEEDS IN YOUR OWN WORDS, CONSIDERING THE INFORMATION INDICATED BY YOUR CHOICES AS CHECKED. BE SPECIFIC AS POSSIBLE. USE ADDITIONAL SHEETS IF NECESSARY.

7. IF POSSIBLE, LIST AUTHORS' NAMES, PROJECT/PROGRAM TITLES, ERIC ABSTRACTS (ED NUMBERS), DESCRIPTIVE TERMS, AND ANY OTHER PERTINENT INFORMATION WHICH MAY BE HELPFUL SEARCH KEYS TO THE RETRIEVAL STAFF.

FOR OFFICE USE ONLY

RETRIEVAL NUMBER	CASE NUMBER	REQUEST TAKEN BY: Initial	Phone	Mail	Visit	SENDER INITIAL	CLIENT	ACTION TAKEN ON SEARCH
PROC. TIME IN MINUTES	CHARGES $	REQUEST RECEIVED DATE				REQUEST PROCESSING DATE		REQUEST COMPLETION DATE

5

FIGURE 20   WIRE Information Retrieval Request form used by the Wisconsin Department of Public Instruction.

Wyoming

State Department of
   Education
Instructional
   Resources
State Capitol Bldg.
Cheyenne 82001
(307) 777-7532

This library, which deals with educational research and public school needs, includes 250 books, 50 pamphlets, 5 documents, 25 periodicals, and the ERIC microfiche files. Its clients are Wyoming educators and graduate students in education. Provides consultative services for Wyoming schools and can arrange computer searches of the ERIC data base by contract with NCEBOCS of Colorado. Its monthly publication, *The Educator,* is free to Wyoming public schools.

Index

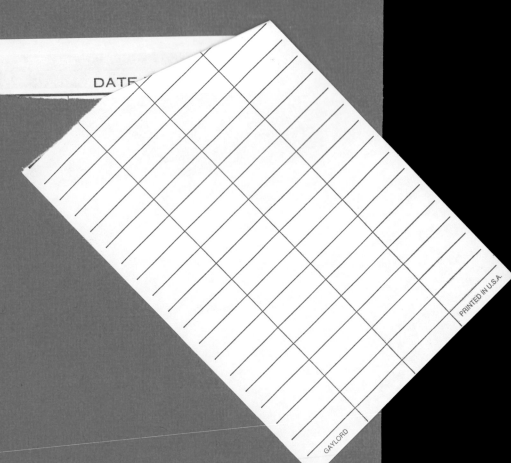

DATE

PRINTED IN U.S.A.

GAYLORD